Alexandros Ph. Lagopoulos and Karin Boklund-Lagopoulou
Theory and Methodology of Semiotics

Semiotics, Communication and Cognition

Edited by
Paul Cobley and Kalevi Kull

Volume 28

Alexandros Ph. Lagopoulos and
Karin Boklund-Lagopoulou

Theory and Methodology of Semiotics

The Tradition of Ferdinand de Saussure

DE GRUYTER
MOUTON

Originally published in the Greek language by Patakis Publishers, Athens, Greece (2016)

Title of the Greek edition: Θεωρία σημειωτικής: Η παράδοση του Ferdinand de Saussure

Translated into English, with revisions and additions, by Alexandros Ph. Lagopoulos and Karin Boklund-Lagopoulou

ISBN 978-3-11-099158-1
e-ISBN (PDF) 978-3-11-061880-8
e-ISBN (EPUB) 978-3-11-061630-9
ISSN 1867-0873

Library of Congress Control Number: 2020943704

Bibliographic information published by the Deutsche Nationalbibliothek
The Deutsche Nationalbibliothek lists this publication in the Deutsche Nationalbibliografie; detailed bibliographic data are available on the Internet at http://dnb.dnb.de.

© 2022 Walter de Gruyter GmbH, Berlin/Boston
This volume is text- and page-identical with the hardback published in 2021.
Typesetting: Integra Software Services Pvt. Ltd.
Printing and binding: CPI books GmbH, Leck

www.degruyter.com

Prologue

This book was originally meant as an introduction to semiotics for our students at Aristotle University of Thessaloniki. Over the years, we gradually became more and more deeply involved with the teaching of semiotics, a discipline which was in fact responsible for bringing us together in the first place, though we came to it from very different directions.

The male half of the present couple of authors, Alexandros, trained in Greece and in France as an architect-engineer, planner and social anthropologist before becoming professor of urban planning in the School of Architecture of Aristotle University. In the late 1970s he developed a course on the semiotics of space which he taught until his retirement in 2005. The female half, Karin, studied comparative and mediaeval literature in the United States and eventually became professor in the School of English of Aristotle University, where she taught literary theory with special emphasis on structuralism and semiotics from the early 1980s up to her retirement in 2015. Both of us were among the founding members of the Hellenic Semiotic Society in 1977. Together we developed and taught a series of postgraduate courses in semiotics, and eventually gave in to the repeated demands of our students for a written text to accompany the seminars.

About a year later, we were surprised to discover that there was enough interest in the topic to warrant an English-language edition. With the encouragement of Paul Cobley and Kalevi Kull, who mediated between us and De Gruyter, we have produced an English version which we hope will live up to their expectations.

The book was originally designed as an introductory textbook. However, there are many good introductions to semiotics available in English and little would be gained with the publication of one more. We have thus taken the opportunity to make corrections, amendments, extensions and some rather substantial additions to the English edition. Although it presents the basic concepts of the field, it is not meant as a general introduction. It is a critical presentation of the semiology of Ferdinand de Saussure and the canonical narrative model of Algirdas Julien Greimas, including the contributions of other scholars (notably Hjelmslev, Barthes and Eco) as we deemed them to be relevant and with some excursions to later developments. It is written for scholars and advanced students, not only in semiotics but also in the language sciences, communications, cultural and media studies, anthropology and sociology, as well as for interested researchers in related fields. Our goal has been to present a coherent theory and methodology, with special emphasis on applications for textual analysis.

A few words should be said about terminology. There are many excellent English-language sources on Saussure and his work; we have generally used the translation by Roy Harris (Saussure [1916] 1971), though we have occasionally preferred our own readings. Things are more difficult with Greimas. There are very good English translations of *Sémantique structurale* (Greimas 1966*)* and *Sémiotique: Dictionnaire raisonné de la théorie du langage* (Greimas and Courtés 1979); the *Dictionnaire* also suggests English terminology for all its entries. Still, translating Greimas into any language is a challenge.

We are, in fact, well aware that we are not ideally positioned to present Greimasian narrative theory to an English-speaking audience. There are many scholars – notably of course the original members of the Groupe de Recherche Sémio-linguistique at the École Pratique des Hautes Études – who could with greater justification undertake to do so, and many of them have indeed published extensively on Greimasian narratology, but in French. We, who both grew up in places where the local language was neither French nor English, feel that Greimasian narratology is both a powerful theory and a particularly valuable method of textual analysis, and that it needs to be made more easily accessible to non-Francophone scholars. We hope that our French-speaking semiotician friends will forgive us and find our version satisfactory.

Finally, we would like to thank the many people who have contributed to the making of this book, first and foremost our students and colleagues. Many thanks also to Dr. Dimitris Drakoulis, architect and planner, and our daughter Katerina, artist, for their essential help in preparing the visual material of the book. We also owe warm thanks to the publisher of the original Greek edition, Stefanos Patakis, for his generosity in changing our initial contract and transferring the rights of the English translation to us so as to allow its present publication by De Gruyter.

Contents

Prologue —— V

Part I: **The field of semiotics**

Chapter 1
Introduction: What is semiotics? —— 3

Chapter 2
A brief history of semiotics —— 8
1 The beginnings of modern semiotics —— 8
2 European semiotics —— 9
2.1 Russian formalism —— 9
2.2 Semiotic theory and Marxism —— 10
2.3 Vladimir Propp —— 11
2.4 The Prague Linguistic Circle —— 11
2.5 The Linguistic Circle of Copenhagen —— 12
2.6 The Tartu–Moscow School —— 12
2.7 French structuralism and semiotics —— 13
2.8 Cognitive semiotics —— 15
2.9 Poststructuralism and postmodernism —— 17
3 Semiotics in the USA —— 19

Part II: **The semiotics of *langue***

Chapter 3
The basic concepts of *langue* —— 25
1 The four linguistics —— 25
2 *Langue* and *parole* —— 28
3 The communication circuit and the definition of the sign —— 31
4 The principles of *langue* —— 32
4.1 The first principle: Conventionality —— 32
4.1.1 The conventional relation between signified and signifier —— 32
4.1.2 The conventional relation between the signifier and the external world —— 34
4.1.3 The conventional relation between the signified and the external world —— 37
4.2 The second principle: Linearity —— 38

5	The rules of *langue* —— 39	
6	*Langue* as a system of relations and elements —— 42	
6.1	The relation between the syntagmatic and paradigmatic axes —— 42	
6.2	Distinctive features and phonemes —— 42	
6.3	Morphemes —— 44	
6.4	Semes, sememes and lexemes —— 46	
7	The concepts of difference and value in *langue* —— 48	
8	Form and substance —— 53	
9	The non-semiotic triangle —— 59	
10	The signified as a cultural unit —— 68	
11	Denotation, connotation and metalanguage —— 72	
11.1	The theory —— 72	
11.2	Examples of connotation —— 77	
12	From *langue* to speech: Sociolinguistics and Greimasian semiotics —— 81	

Part III: **The semiotics of *parole* (textual semiotics)**

Chapter 4
Syntagmatic analysis: Narrative theory —— 93

1	Narratology —— 93
1.1	The generative trajectory —— 93
1.2	Fundamental syntax —— 97
1.3	Fundamental semantics —— 101
1.4	Surface narrative syntax —— 103
1.4.1	The narrative programme —— 103
1.4.2	The modalities —— 107
1.4.3	The narrative schema —— 108
1.5	Narrative semantics —— 113
1.6	Discursive syntax —— 115
1.7	Discursive semantics —— 118
2	An example of narrative analysis: *The life of Saint Alexius* —— 122
2.1	*The life of Saint Alexius*: Summary —— 123
2.2	Narrative syntax —— 125

Chapter 5
Paradigmatic analysis: Isotopies, qualitative approach —— 130
- 1   The theory of isotopies —— 130
- 1.1   The definition of isotopy —— 130
- 1.2   Nuclear semes and classemes —— 134
- 1.3   Operating with isotopies on the two semiotic planes —— 134
- 1.4   The hierarchical levels of analysis of isotopies —— 138
- 1.5   The relation between simple isotopies —— 142
- 1.6   The composite isotopies —— 147
- 1.7   Relations between composite isotopies —— 150
- 1.8   The empirical textual network and the hierarchy of isotopies —— 152
- 1.9   The extended concept of isotopy —— 160
- 2   Qualitative analysis of isotopies: Examples —— 163
- 2.1   Isotopies in prose: *The life of Saint Alexius* —— 163
- 2.1.1   Identifying the isotopies: Figurativisation —— 164
- 2.1.2   The internal structure of the isotopies: The codes —— 165
- 2.1.3   Relations between codes: Thematisation —— 169
- 2.1.4   The semiotic square —— 172
- 2.2   Isotopies in poetry —— 175
- 2.3   The use of isotopies for the analysis of ideology —— 183

Chapter 6
Paradigmatic analysis: Isotopies, quantitative approach —— 190
- 1   Theoretical background —— 190
- 1.1   The quantitative approach in semiotics —— 190
- 1.2   Techniques for the quantitative analysis of isotopies —— 192
- 1.3   The utility of graphs for other operations —— 197
- 2   Examples of quantitative analysis of isotopies —— 201
- 2.1   The discourse on space —— 201
- 2.2   The spatial discourses on the city of Thessaloniki —— 215
- 2.3   The semiotic square revisited —— 228

Chapter 7
Late and post-Greimasian theory —— 234
- 1   The second Dictionary —— 234
- 2   Greimas and the semiotics of passions —— 236
- 3   Fontanille and the semiotics of passions —— 240
- 4   Some critical thoughts —— 244

Part IV: The semiotics of communication

Chapter 8
A global model of communication —— 253
1   The field of communication —— 253
2   Fourteen models of communication —— 254
2.1   Model 1: Saussure's circuit of *parole* —— 254
2.2   Model 2: The positions of communication —— 256
2.3   Model 3: The active semiotic labour of the dialogists and their interaction —— 263
2.4   Model 4: Communication through objects —— 267
2.5   Model 5: The channel of communication and signification —— 270
2.6   Model 6: Jakobson's functions of language and the message —— 273
2.7   Model 7: The intra-textual contexts of the text —— 282
2.8   Model 8: The extra-textual contexts of the text: Intertextuality —— 285
2.9   Model 9: Simple, accompanying and complex semiotic systems —— 298
2.10   Model 10: Text and (micro-)situation —— 300
2.11   Model 11: A and B as competent cultural subjects —— 304
2.12   Model 12: Pragmatics: A and B as overtly acting subjects —— 307
2.13   Model 13: Communication micro-networks and their structures —— 313
2.14   Model 14: From sociosemiotics to social semiotics: A and B as material social subjects in a macro-situation —— 316

Chapter 9
Social semiotics —— 321
1   School of Paris vs sociology —— 321
2   Semiotics and sociology —— 323
3   Social semiotics as a legitimate field of semiotics —— 331

References —— 337

Index —— 345

Part I: **The field of semiotics**

Chapter 1
Introduction: What is semiotics?

Semiotics studies the processes of semiosis. This means that it studies meaning, and the specific perspective that defines and constitutes its domain is *meaning* – *sens* in French – but more strictly, in both languages, *signification*. All cultural systems – language, literature, art, cinema, music, architecture, dress, etc. – are vehicles of signification. But such phenomena are virtually omnipresent. Is it possible to bring all these separate phenomena under one and the same umbrella? And what is the relation of semiotics to sociology, social or cultural anthropology, philosophy or psychology?

All semiotic systems have a material vehicle, though this vehicle may be more or less obvious. Oral speech seems to be immaterial, but linguists know that its sounds are carried by sound waves. Literature seems to consist only of meaning, but it too needs a material vehicle, whether in the form of paper and ink or marks on a computer screen (or even traces carved in stone). Painting needs a canvas and colours. In all these cases, the material seems insignificant in comparison to the meaning, though it is always present. But in other cases, the material vehicle overshadows the meaning. An automobile, for example, is constructed with metal and a building with concrete and bricks or steel and glass, and these objects as such are not made by meaning, but they can still be vehicles of meaning.

The difference between the semiotic and the non-semiotic or extra-semiotic aspects of cultural objects and phenomena is clarified by Umberto Eco. He writes that it is possible to study all social phenomena *"sub specie communicationis"*, that is, from the viewpoint of semiotics, which is why he considers semiotics as a "general theory of culture" (Eco [1968] 1972: 28, 1976: 26–27). However, he adds that social phenomena cannot be *reduced* only to their semiotic aspect, and that studying them from the semiotic perspective does not imply the reduction of material life to the life of the mind (which would be philosophical idealism).

Consider, for example, the clothes that we wear. If you ask a tailor, he can give you an exact description of how to make a suit. The description presupposes an empirical descriptive geometry, most notably in respect to the tantalising area of the shoulder. A salesperson in a men's clothing store probably cannot tell you how to make a suit, but they will be able to inform you about the texture, the quality and the properties of the cloth, for example if it is wool or cotton, or if it is impermeable. The cloth has physical properties (texture, impermeability, endurance, thermal capability) and chemical properties (organic or chemical origin), and the suit itself has a price. All these are not objects for semiotics, no more than the construction of a car or a building. But clothes and cars and buildings are also vehicles of meaning and, from this point of view, they are objects for semiotics.

Clothes become an object for semiotics from the moment we approach them not as a material substance, but as a vehicle of meaning. This is not a revelation, given that we all have experience of the meaning of dress. For example, we dress more formally when going to the office and more casually on the weekends. We dress in sportswear in order to project an "athletic" style and maybe feel a bit like real athletes. For a night out we "dress up", conveying to ourselves and others that this is a special occasion. If we showed up at a formal reception wearing combat boots, it would *mean* either that we are ignorant of the "appropriate" dress for receptions or that we are being deliberately provocative, and the other guests would probably either feel insulted or dismiss us as ignorant and impolite. Traditional folk costume is a product of history and culture; each part of it had a meaning and marked the identity of the people who made it, and who in wearing it *experienced* this identity.

The semiotics of dress, and other empirical everyday semiotics (such as the semiotics of "good manners"), are inextricable parts of our culture, of ourselves and the image we want to present to others – and, of course, to ourselves. Literature and the visual arts take it for granted that we know how to interpret the meaning of dress. Below is a passage from a popular novel (Child [1999] 2011: 44–45), in which Chester Stone III, a businessman facing bankruptcy, is preparing for a humiliating visit to the office of Victor Truman "Hook" Hobie at nine o'clock in the morning to ask for a loan of 1.1 million dollars:

> He shaved and spent his shower time thinking about what to wear and how to act. Truth was he would be approaching this guy practically on his knees. . . . Not on his knees. . . .
>
> A white shirt, for sure, and a quiet tie. But which suit? The Italians were maybe too flashy. Not the Armani. He had to look like a serious man. Rich enough to buy a dozen Armanis, for sure, but somehow too serious to consider doing that. Too serious and too preoccupied with weighty affairs to spend time shopping on Madison Avenue. He decided heritage was the feature to promote. An unbroken three-generation heritage of business success, maybe reflected in a dynastic approach to dressing. Like his grandfather had taken his father to his tailor and introduced him, then his father had taken him in turn. Then he thought about his Brooks Brothers suit. Old, but nice, a quiet check, vented, slightly warm for June. Would Brooks Brothers be a clever double bluff? Like saying, I'm so rich and successful it really doesn't matter to me what I wear? Or would he look like a loser?
>
> He pulled it off the rack and held it against his body. Classic, but dowdy. He looked like a loser. He put it back. Tried the gray Savile Row from London. Perfect. It made him look like

a gentleman of substance. Wise, tasteful, infinitely trustworthy. He selected a tie with just a hint of pattern and a pair of solid black shoes. Put it all on and twisted left and right in front of the mirror. Couldn't be better. Looking like that, he might almost trust himself.

Lee Child's hero is here engaging in some intensive empirical semiotics. He knows that what he wears conveys meaning, and he is very concerned that it should be exactly the right meaning, the image of himself that he wants to project for this important meeting. Clearly there is, in our culture, an approach to dress for which dress has meaning, and when considered from this point of view dress becomes an object of semiotics, whether everyday empirical semiotics or theoretical study.

Child's hero is concerned not simply with his suit as a signifying object, but specifically with what it will communicate to the person he is meeting. As Eco explains, any act of communication presupposes the existence of a system of signification, and thus the semiotics of communication and the semiotics of signification are indissolubly connected in the framework of cultural processes (Eco 1972: 25–30 and 1976: 6–9, 26–27, 158).

We can now define more clearly what semiotics is. Our culture (any culture) is made up of a multitude of systems of signification and communication, which we use in a practical way as part of our *cultural competence*, the knowledge that we have as members of this culture. These are our empirical semiotic systems. The theoretical domain of semiotics studies the various empirical semiotics of a culture. Every meaningful whole to be analysed, every empirical semiotics, is an *object-semiotics*. We analyse this whole using general semiotic theory (Greimas and Courtés 1979: Sémiotique), which studies the structure of signification systems and their function and use in communication. Theoretical semiotics is in a position to advance much further in its understanding than empirical semiotics, because it has the tools and the ability to analyse its object in depth in ways that go beyond what everyday experience is able to do. Semiotics is an instrument of *revelation*, and for this reason it can be a powerful political tool for the study of ideology.

There is a general belief, repeated by our students during all our decades of teaching, that semiotics is difficult. In fact, as attractive as it has proved to be, it also inspires a kind of awe.

The understanding of semiotics does not demand more of Hercule Poirot's "little gray cells" than the understanding of any other specific scientific field. It is true that a certain amount of intellectual effort is required to familiarise oneself with it beyond the elementary level. It is an autonomous area of knowledge, which as all scientific fields has a systematic theory, and its concepts constitute a strongly coherent system: they are strictly defined (though there may be divergences in their definition), they explicitly fall under superior concepts and are also explicitly subdivided into more analytical concepts, and elements of the same level are connected with explicit relationships.

The present book is not intended as a general introduction or overview, and we do not have the ambition to cover the whole field. There are many introductions to semiotics available on the market, and several very helpful standard reference works that aim to cover the whole domain, such as Thomas A. Sebeok's ([1986] 1994) two-volume dictionary, the *Handbook* of semiotics edited by Roland Posner, Klaus Robering and Thomas A. Sebeok (1998) or the four-volume anthology of texts edited by Mark Gottdiener and ourselves (2003). There is also a large bibliography of specialised literature in English. A part of this bibliography deals with the general presentation of semiotic theory, sometimes with philosophical extensions. Another part is oriented towards the presentation of one or both of the main trends of semiotics, Saussurean and Peircean, with an orientation to theory rather than methodology. A third part discusses different semiotic systems and subfields or specific cultural codes. Finally, we also find works treating the relation of semiotics with adjacent fields, such as psychoanalysis.

Our own book, as is clear from its title, focuses specifically on the Saussurean tradition, and includes only some introductory references to other semiotic tendencies (chapter 2). It does not even cover every possible aspect of the Saussurean tradition, but focuses on systematic theory and methodology and techniques for textual analysis. Our aim is *operational*: to show the reader how we can apply semiotics in concrete analysis. We present examples from different semiotic systems in order to illustrate various ways the theory can be applied. The discussion of the semiotics of *langue* within a wider epistemological framework emphasises the radical conception of the system implicit in Ferdinand de Saussure. We also extend the theory of isotopies by bringing quantitative analysis into the qualitative paradigm commonly used in semiotics and showing how to articulate quantity with quality. The chapter on the semiotics of communication presents fourteen models of communication, starting from the simplest one described by Saussure and leading up to a discussion of both sociosemiotics and what we call social semiotics, the articulation of semiotics with social structure.

We referred above to Eco's view that semiotics is a theory of culture. This view is much older than Eco and is central to several semiotic trends. Semiotics is not the only theory of culture, but we believe that it is the most elaborated and sophisticated among cultural theories. Semiotics is far from a unified field and is crossed by a variety of trends, many comparable, some essentially incompatible. Even poststructuralism, and hence postmodernism, are clearly semiotic trends, but they do not present any interest for the present book, since they reject as a matter of principle that which is our main aim, the use of precise instruments for textual analysis. The main scientific approach we chose for narrative theory, the School of Paris, has separated into different directions and we shall refer to some of these developments, but they are still tentative and have not yet crystallised into a definitive theory accepted more widely. For this reason, we have elected to remain with the standard theory.

Semiotics is not fashionable nowadays, partially because of its astonishing success. Its logic has been diffused in all the social and cultural sciences and its concepts absorbed by them each in its own way, which in a sense has rendered semiotics invisible as an autonomous theory. Still, it surfaces systematically in all books on cultural studies. What is lost from these traces is its great power for the operational analysis of texts, a power that we shall try to bring back. We believe that anyone who is interested in cultural phenomena, not only the semiotician but the literary scholar, the linguist, the anthropologist, the sociologist, the archaeologist, the artist, will find in the following pages a valuable instrument for studying them. While it is addressed to a wide public of students, scholars, specialists and other interested persons, the book is not designed for casual reading. Our hope is that it will be an initiation into a world which, for us, remains magical.

Chapter 2
A brief history of semiotics

1 The beginnings of modern semiotics

It is a ritual in textbooks and introductory courses in semiotics to refer to two founders of the discipline, the francophone Swiss linguist Ferdinand de Saussure (1857–1913) and the North American philosopher (trained as a chemist) Charles Sanders Peirce (1839–1914), since they were contemporaries and both developed theories of the sign. However, this habit disguises fundamental differences between them. Saussure was a linguist and was interested in the study of natural language and, by extension, of cultural systems; hence, his concept of the sign refers exclusively to these systems. Peirce worked in the philosophy of knowledge and his "sign" is of a very general nature, appertaining to a theory of logic. The two approaches also had very different historical developments.

Saussure is generally acknowledged as the father of modern linguistics. His work became known through the book *Cours de linguistique générale* (published in English as *Course in general linguistics*), edited by two of his students on the basis of his lectures during the 1907–1911 period and first published in 1916. It is here that he introduced the idea of a "science which studies the life of signs as part of social life" and which he called "semiology" (1971: 33). His theory spread rapidly throughout Europe and had a very significant impact, not only on linguistics but also on the social sciences and the humanities. This material was completed much later, in the 1990s, when his lectures were published in three volumes, once more on the basis of the notes of his students. At the same time, a hitherto unknown manuscript by Saussure for a manual on general linguistics was discovered in the orangery of the Saussure family estate in Geneva; this unfinished manuscript was published in 2002 under the title *Écrits de linguistique générale* and offers an important complement to his linguistic theory.

In the case of Peirce, the publication of the *Collected papers of Charles Sanders Peirce* in 1931 was a landmark in making his views on what he calls "semiotic" more widely known. In 1938, the philosopher Charles W. Morris elaborated on Peirce's ideas with his *Foundations of the theory of signs* (included in Morris 1971: 17–71). Through the writings of Morris, Thomas A. Sebeok, a linguist who had immigrated to the US from Hungary, became acqainted with Peirce's philosophy, which deeply influenced his work from the end of the 1970s to his death in 2001. Sebeok's unique managerial capability and his uninterrupted and imposing presence in semiotic events of all kinds around the world greatly contributed to the diffusion of Peircean semiotics.

2 European semiotics

2.1 Russian formalism

A prominent figure in the long and continuous development of European semiotics (see Lagopoulos 2004: 114–115, 121–128, 134, 148–156) was the Russian Jewish linguist and literary theorist Roman Jakobson. Jakobson was influenced by the artistic avant-garde movements of Futurism and Cubism and very interested in the differences between the various forms of art and literature. In 1914, at the age of 22, he played a central role in the establishment of the Linguistic Circle of Moscow, and two years later he participated in the founding of the Society for the Study of Poetic Language (O.PO.JAZ), the nursery of the Russian Formalists, in Saint Petersburg. In 1915 one of Saussure's students, Sergei J. Karcevskij, brought Saussurean linguistics to Moscow, where they deeply influenced Jakobson and Nikolai S. Troubetzkoy, whose work in structural phonology was to become a landmark in the field (for this and the discussion below, see Sebeok 1994, 2: Russian Formalism).

We may distinguish three stages in Russian Formalism (1914–1934). The first focuses on the study of poetic language and takes a revolutionary position in respect to poetry. In opposition to the Romantics, who considered content as the essence both of poetry and prose, the Formalists performed a full inversion, arguing that it is form that produces content. Important names of this stage are the literary scholar Viktor B. Shklovsky and the historians of Russian literature Boris M. Eichenbaum and Boris V. Tomashevsky.

Shklovsky introduced the concept of "defamiliarisation", a key concept of the avant-garde still relevant for today's literary theory. Rejecting the received idea that poetry is written in a special "poetic" language, Shklovsky argued that the literary work depends for its aesthetic effect not on a particular language, but on a specific *use* of language that causes a deformation of the conventional and familiar, thus revealing new ways of seing things. For him, literature is marked by deviation from the conventional rules of language, whether literary or social. In this first stage, then, the Formalists focused on the basic mechanisms structuring the poetic work. In the second stage, the Formalists took a more global approach to literary texts, studying the function of linguistic elements according to their position within a text.

The third stage of Formalism, closely following Jakobson's ideas, presents a special interest, because it is ahead of its time by about half a century. Here, the Formalists go beyond the narrow study of the text and turn to its relation to its environment, which they study from two perspectives. The first is the integration of the text within continuously wider environments, starting from genre, which implies a typology of texts, and ending with culture as a whole, considered as a "system of systems". This development from a semiotics of texts to a semiotics of culture founded the semiotic theory of culture. The cultural system as conceived by the Formalists is a super-system including partial cultural systems and reserves a place for popular literature. They also introduced the idea of kinship between different texts that Julia Kristeva later borrowed from Mikhail Bakhtin and called "*intertextualité*" (chapter 8: 2.8).

The second, very important perspective introduced by the Formalists focused on the communication circuit of literature. They studied the communicative space between author and reader, and they saw this space as mediated by economic factors, institutions and public opinion. They also introduced an important new concept, that of the collective reader, who has a horizon of expectations and possibilities expressing the taste of a period – we encounter a similar concept, once more about half a century later, in reception theory. This study of the author-reader circuit resulted in an extension of semiotics to sociosemiotics and, with the idea of communicative space, pointed to the articulation of semiotics with sociological theory which we have called social semiotics (chapter 8: 2.14 and chapter 9).

2.2 Semiotic theory and Marxism

In 1919, in the early days of the Formalist school, there emerged a group of Marxist authors known as the Bakhtin Circle (1918–1929), who criticised the ideas of the Formalists arguing for an articulation of semiotics with Marxism. A central figure of this group was the philosopher and literary scholar Mikhail Bakhtin; we should also mention the literary scholar Pavel N. Medvedev and the linguist Valentin N. Vološinov. The synthesis they achieved integrates semiotics within society as a whole and thus surmounts a problem inherent even in today's semiotics, namely the tendency to study signification systems independently from social dynamics. With the work of the Bakhtin Circle, the step of the third stage of the Formalists towards sociosemiotics acquired its integral form as social semiotics.

For Bakhtin and Medvedev, the world of signs, which they consider as coextensive with ideology, is incorporated within a "semiotic material", such as words, dress, gestures, the organisation of people and objects – a perspective also including space as a semiotic object. Ideology is projected onto this material, which becomes a semiotic material composed of "object-signs" and produces material products such as art, religious rituals, even the sciences, all products that thus become vehicles of meaning. This meaning is social, as it is produced by social communication. The object-signs constitute the "ideological environment" of society, which is its materialised social consciousness (Medvedev and Bakhtin [1928] 1978: 7–15, 18).

Being Marxists, the authors understand that signs do not descend from heaven, but arise from the socio-economic existence of a collectivity. They thus offer a theory according to which signification systems are indissolubly related to the material processes of a society.

2.3 Vladimir Propp

The folklorist Vladimir Propp was not technically a member of the Russian Formalists, but his approach is closely related to theirs. In 1928 he published a seminal work entitled *The morphology of the Russian folktale*. By analysing hundreds of fairy tales, Propp concluded that it is not possible to define any of their regularities with the help of the traditional logic of "themes", such as the "wise maiden" or those "unjustly persecuted" (Propp [1928] 1968: 8). In place of these concepts, he proposes the fundamental concept of the *function*, that is, the result of the action of an episode on the development of the plot (for further discussion of this approach, see chapter 4: 1.1 and 1.4.4).

This is a truly structural analysis of fairy tales. It holds out the promise of a similarly structural analysis of narratives in general, something which took form with Greimas's narratology, the most powerful theory of its kind that we dispose of today (chapter 4: 1).

2.4 The Prague Linguistic Circle

In the early 1920s, the Formalists were effectively shut down by the Stalinist regime. Jakobson moved to Prague, where together with the Czech linguist and literary historian Vilém Mathesius he in 1926 founded the Prague Linguistic Circle (1926–1939/1952); it also included Karcevskij and the Czech literary scholar Jan Mukařovský. It is in this circle that Troubetzkoy developed his phonology, with the participation of Jakobson and other members. In 1929 the Circle published a set of Theses (English translation in Steiner 1982: 3–31), which broadened the Formalist views and laid the foundations of the structuralist movement by elaborating the concept of structure. However, its views are not simply structuralist; the Prague Circle worked with a functionalist-structuralist theory. In fact, Jakobson diverged from Saussure in that he paid special attention to communication. Thus, for example, the Circle focused on the poetic function, which later took its place among the six functions of Jakobson's communication model (chapter 8: 2.6). In the later development of the Prague Circle, structure was generalised as an all-encompassing epistemological principle relevant to any scientific domain (Winner 1998).

2.5 The Linguistic Circle of Copenhagen

The Linguistic Circle of Copenhagen (from 1931 to the mid-20th century) represents the most rigorous continuation of Saussure's theory. Its central figure was Louis Hjelmslev, who in 1936, together with Hans Jørgen Uldall, presented the general principles of a theory of language that they called "glossematics" (*glossematik*). Glossematics is an extremely abstract theory, one which according to Hjelmslev aims to produce "an immanent algebra of language", and systematises Saussurean theory while also developing it further. Hjelmslev's work had a strong international impact and, while not universally used, was respected for its rigorous proposal for a formalised linguistics (Johansen 1998: 2272–2273, 2286). It was used by Roland Barthes and decisevely influenced the theory of Greimas. We shall not discuss it here in detail, since we will be referring to it frequently in later chapters.

2.6 The Tartu–Moscow School

The School of Tartu–Moscow (also referred to as the Moscow–Tartu School) was active mainly between 1964 and the end of the 1980s, but its tradition still continues today at the University of Tartu in Estonia. It may be considered as a continuation of Formalism. It was obviously inspired by French structuralism and combined Formalism with this trend and with cybernetics, then an emerging scientific field.

The School evolved in four stages. Its third stage (1970–1979) opened with the manifesto Theses on the semiotic study of cultures (1973), written by the founder of the School, the literary scholar Juri Lotman, and other famous semioticians such as the poet Vjačeslav V. Ivanov, with a background in history, archaeology and philosophy, and the linguist and literary scholar Boris A. Uspenskij

(Uspenskij et al. 1973). The Theses, in the Formalist tradition, develop the position of semiotics as a theory of culture. The influence of cybernetics led to an approach to culture as a mechanism for storing, processing and communicating information. Culture is considered as a holistic, complex cybernetic system, composed of relatively autonomous, functionally correlated and hierarchically ordered semiotic sub-systems. Without eliminating the concept of sign, priority is given to the *text* as the unit of semiotic analysis. This choice is closely connected to the main focus of the School which is typological, the upper level of typology ending at culture itself. According to the Theses, language holds a central place among the systems of meaning; it is a "primary modelling system" while all other meaning systems, such as literature, music or painting, are built on language and are "secondary modelling systems".

About ten years later, Lotman formulated the influential concept of "semiosphere", which he identifies with culture. The ideas connected to it almost totally overlap with the Theses, but there is also a novel element. Lotman conceives the semiosphere by analogy with Vladimir I. Vernadsky's concept of "biosphere". Following Vernadsky, he considers as the foundation of communicative processes, thought and meaning the Vernadskian pair symmetry–asymmetry, mirror symmetry, which he calls "enantiomorphism" and which according to him combines structural similarity and structural difference. Lotman states that the right–left pair is the fundamental universal structure, which rules not only the bilateral asymmetry of the human brain, but also the whole spectrum from the genetic-molecular level to the general structure of the universe to semiotic systems (Lotman 2005: 219–225 and 1990: 3, 36, 124, 133). This is an overambitious and unfortunate attempt to ground culture in biology and ecology, by surpassing the opposition between the exact sciences and the humanities (on the Tartu–Moscow School and Lotman, see also Lagopoulos and Boklund-Lagopoulou 2014: 436–446).

2.7 French structuralism and semiotics

During World War II, a young French sociologist named Claude Lévi-Strauss, who had been doing field work with his anthropologist wife among the Indians of the Amazon Basin, found refuge at the École Libre des Hautes Études, a university-in-exile for French academics located at the New School for Social Research in New York. There, he followed a course given by Roman Jakobson, who initiated him into the theory of structuralism and more specifically of structural phonology as formed by Troubetzkoy and himself. After the war, in 1949, Lévi-Strauss submitted his work *Les structures élémentaires de la parenté*, founded on structural phonology, as part of the requirements for his PhD. This work inaugurates a radically new approach to anthropology, structural anthropology, and is the first landmark of French structuralism and semiotics, followed in 1958 by the second landmark, *Anthropologie structurale*, by the same author. In addition to semiotics, Lévi-Strauss was influenced by psychoanalysis and Marxism, which he however subordinated to a semiotic logic. The above two works had a huge effect on the social sciences, the humanities and the arts, and founded the French school of anthropological structuralism.

The next big step of structuralism, the step that turned it into "semiology", is due to Roland Barthes. Six years after *Anthrolopologie structurale*, and with the evident influence of Lévi-Strauss, Barthes went back to the roots, Saussure's linguistics and its more formal elaboration by Hjelmslev. These influences are apparent in his own landmark work, Éléments de sémiologie (1964a; published in English in 1967 as *Elements of semiology*). In this first, if abridged, textbook of semiotics, Barthes replaces the Formalist "structuralism" with the Saussurean *sémiologie*, a replacement that by no means implies a rejection of structuralism. In the same issue of the journal *Communications* Barthes also published Rhétorique de l'image (1964b), his analysis of an advertisement which laid the foundations of visual semiotics.

The above change of terminology is not fortuitous. Earlier, in 1957, Barthes in his *Mythologies* had studied a set of everyday semiotic phenomena in Western society from a semiological perspective, a work parallel in some ways to what Lévi-Strauss had done for the study of so-called primitive societies. However, these texts by Barthes reveal a divergence with Lévi-Strauss. Lévi-Strauss is more focused and technical than Barthes, because he uses semiotics as an instrument for applied analysis and aims specifically at building an anthropological theory. Barthes, on the other hand, elaborates a general theory of semiotics which converges with the holistic positions of Formalism. This move by Barthes is symptomatic of the shift from structuralism to semiotics as its direct successsor. The work of Barthes as a whole had a tremendous impact on the humanities and the arts, but no specific school, in the sense of an institutionalised group, emerged from it.

The mid-1960s is also the period of the early semiotic activity of Algirdas Julien Greimas, a Lithuanian linguist living in Paris. In 1965 he became director of studies in the prestigious 6th section of the École Pratique des Hautes Études en Sciences Économiques et Sociales, where he and a group of his students founded the Groupe de Recherche Sémio-linguistique, the Research Group in Semio-linguistics, which from 1982 became known as the Paris School of semiotics. His work has the mark and rigour of Hjelmslev, is deeply influenced by Lévi-Strauss and at several points touches on the ideas of Barthes, while also showing influence from the phenomenology of Husserl and Maurice Merleau-Ponty.

The first stage of Greimas's work opens with the landmark *Sémantique structrale* (1966; English translation *Structural semantics*, 1983) and closes with another landmark, the Dictionary *Sémiotique: Dictionnaire raisonné de la théorie du langage* (with Joseph Courtés, 1979; English translation as *Semiotics and language*, 1982), presenting a complete and mature semiotic theory. The landmark of the second stage, in the midst of a more general anti-systemic intellectual climate both inside and outside the School, followed about ten years later with the iconoclastic *Sémiotique des passions* (with Jacques Fontanille, 1991), which is epistemologically founded on affect, i.e., psychological states. The death of Greimas in 1992 essentially marks the end of the Paris School as a coherent group (Landowski 2017: 16–17, 27–28), though many of its members continue to produce work in the field, mainly in the form of further elaboration of the semiotics of passions in different variants (chapter 7).

Although he worked mainly in Italy, we would include Umberto Eco in the French schools of semiotics, as well as in the Hjelmslevian tradition.[1] In 1968 he published *La struttura assente* (French translation 1972), the second basic textbook of semiotics, much more extensive than Barthes's *Elements of semiology*. In addition to general semiotic theory, the book also covers visual semiotics, including advertising and cinema, and the semiotics of architecture. It was followed by another foundational text, *A Theory of Semiotics* (1976), written directly in English though translated and published a year earlier in Italian as *Trattato di semiotica generale*. With these works, semiotics had reached maturity.

2.8 Cognitive semiotics

This orientation of semiotics originated among the followers of Greimas and emerged very soon after his death. It represents a reaction against the static structural analysis of the Paris School and attempts to articulate it with what it considers as the dynamic processes leading to the emergence of meaning. It looks for the roots of semiosis specifically in the cognitive processes, rather than in the general biological processes of an organism, as does biosemiotics (see below), and it attempts to explain the foundation of cultural systems on this basis, thus searching for semiotic universals. Two authors representative of the domain are Jean Petitot and Per Aage Brandt.

---

[1] This observation is valid for the first stage of his work, informed by a philosophical background, and partly valid for his later work, in which Peirce comes to the foreground in an attempt to combine his philosophy with Hjelmslev's linguistics.

Petitot attempts to combine Greimasian semiotics with René Thom's catastrophe theory while also integrating cognitive neuroscience and the phenomenology of perception of Husserl, resulting in a very high level of abstraction. He considers that there are two basic levels of semiosis. The foundational level consists of interconnected elementary units that process information, thus constituting an underlying sub-symbolic process; this is the level of physical reality, natural semiotics, fundamental geno-physics and objective phenomenology, comprising universal topological syntactic-semantic infrastructures. From this level derives the deep cognitive level of macro-symbolic dynamic structures; this is the morphological level of the natural world, that of the physics of meaning, pheno-physics and the phenomenological structures of meaning in the sense of the phenomenology of perception. Petitot identifies it with Peirce's Firstness and Eco's primary iconism and considers that it is structured by qualitative discontinuities (Petitot 1990 and 2017: 19, 24–25, 26, 28).[2] At the deep cognitive level there is compatibility between syntactic logico-combinatory structures and semantic topologico-dynamic perceptual structures, the latter studied by morphodynamic models. This interrelation constitutes, for Petitot paraphrasing Greimas, the semiotics of the natural world.

Brandt's cognitive semiotics is based on a stratified three-level semiotic construction and in a first formulation starts from the "deepest" cognitive operations, performed exclusively by the mind itself. The operations of this level then pass through a dual filter of situational determination: a more general ("shallow") level, that of culture, and a more narrow ("surface") level depending each time on the specific situation (Brandt 2003: 12–13). We observe, as in the case of Petitot, a move towards processes, related to situation.

Brandt's further elaboration of this schema still retains three levels, to which he adds a metalinguistic level referring to forms of knowledge. He uses Greimas's generative trajectory as a model to formulate a "generative phenomenology" and specifies these levels as follows.

First, there is a "deep" structure covering the natural world as the cognitive organisation of lived experience in its corporeal aspect. Brandt asserts that this structure is not a biplanar semiotics, as argued by Greimas and Courtés, and includes in it four "semantic domains", the physical, the social, the mental and the symbolic, without reference to a theory that would integrate them into a structural whole.

---

[2] As we shall see (chapter 3: 9), for Eco primary iconism precedes the level of perception and is an unstructured *continuum*.

Out of this level grows the next, narrative cognitive, level, which seems to be subdivided into two sub-levels. The first sub-level includes three new semantic domains, slightly more abstract according to Brandt, following from the combination by pairs of three among the four first domains. These domains, work, cult and family,[3] which Brandt considers as fundamental cultural practices, are also juxtaposed without reference to a social theory integrating them, and their production from the previous level is not substantiated. Out of this sub-level grows the second sub-level, which includes three kinds of values, generated by the repetition of the pattern of generation from the deep structure to the first sub-level, namely by the combination by pairs of the domains of the first sub-level. Here again, we encounter the same theoretical problems as with the previous sub-level. Finally, there follows the manifesting surface, the surface of lived experience, which is even more abstract for Brandt, corresponding to the conceptual as immediately given in consciousness. The surface level also includes three domains, generated according to the pattern above, that is, from the combination by pairs of the sub-level of values (Brandt 2017: mainly 86–89). Brandt's proposal represents the cognitive variant of the semiotics of passions.

2.9 Poststructuralism and postmodernism

The trends briefly presented above constitute the European approach to semiotics, and the French variants of it especially may be considered as "classical" or "orthodox" semiotics. They were followed by poststructuralism. At this point, a clarification is necessary. Poststructuralism did in fact emerge after structuralism and thus the prefix post- could be considered a historical reference, but the use of the term implies a more ambitious interpretation, since it wants to stress that this is a radically new approach to meaning, more powerful than the previous tradition. In fact, structuralism and poststructuralism are strongly connected, both in respect to their representatives – for example, the structuralist Barthes gradually turns poststructuralist in the later 1960s, as shown in his *S/Z* (1970) – and in respect to geography, which is not even represented by France in general, but specifically by Paris.

Manfred Frank makes a similar point, arguing that although there may be no direct continuity, there is a close and internal relationship between neo-structuralism, as he calls it, and "classical" structuralism. According to Frank,

---

[3] The first and the third of these are strongly reminiscent of sociolinguistics.

the approach of these "new Parisians" comes from the joining together of classical structuralism (the continuity) and a reinterpretation of German philosophy (the discontinuity), which became an instrument for radicalising structuralism while also subverting it. Frank argues that neo-structuralism revives the old German anti-modernist and anti-Enlightenment Romanticism, adding as influences upon it psychoanalysis and Marxism, mainly through the Frankfurt School. The opposition between structuralism and neo-structuralism is, for him, an opposition between a scientific and positivist orientation and a philosophical and interpretative orientation. He concludes that neo-structuralism is more of a philosophical movement than an approach to the human sciences (for the above discussion, see Frank [1984] 1989: 7–30).

A strong, though generally neglected, influence on poststructuralism were the avant-garde movements of Dadaism and Surrealism, especially through the Situationist International led by Guy-Ernest Debord. The turning point for the impact of Surrealism was the rising of May '68; poststructuralism, which had emerged a few years before this event, took its final form based on it. Among the major figures of poststructuralism, we should mention Roland Barthes in literary criticism; Julia Kristeva, a linguist focused on feminism and psychoanalysis; Jacques Derrida and Jean-François Lyotard in philosophy; Michel Foucault, a philosopher working in the field of the history of ideas; Jean Baudrillard, with a background in literature and sociology, in cultural studies; and Jacques Lacan in psychoanalysis. It is noteworthy that all these intellectuals had strong bonds with the political Left, even with the extreme Left; the exception is Lacan, whom May '68, however, also added to the same list. Psychoanalysis, reinterpreted through a radical Left-wing perspective, thus also entered the agenda of poststructuralism.

Postmodernism as a cultural phenomenon had existed in the US since the beginning of the 1960s, initially as a reaction to the high modernist avant-garde; in the following decade it acquired a purely iconoclastic profile. While structuralism did not have a strong impact in the US, poststructuralism crossed the Atlantic early, shortly after the mid-1960s, starting with Derrida. Lyotard's book *La condition postmoderne* (1979), translated into English five years later, had a decisive impact, since in it Lyotard for the first time connects postmodernism and poststructuralism. This acted as a trigger for intense theoretical discussions in the US concerning the possible synthesis of the local postmodern tradition with the imported French tradition, which in the end resulted in a loose local reinterpretation of poststructuralism. Derrida's deconstruction lost its theoretical rigour and tended to take the form of "every reading is a misreading".

We encounter repeatedly in postmodernism the following key concepts (Hassan 1987: 167–173):
(a) concepts considered as deconstructionist, such as "indeterminacy", "fragmentation" (cf. montage and collage), "decanonisation" (for example of culture or authority), "selflessness" and "depthlessness", the "unpresentable" and the "unrepresentable" (that is, the negation of representation); and
(b) concepts considered as reconstructionist, such as "irony", "hybridisation" (that is, the mutation and mixing of genres, for example of high and low culture), "carnivalisation", which implies polyphony, the absurd and the comic, "performance" and "participation", "constructionism" (that is, the construction of reality on the basis of meaning), and "immanence", more specifically the conversion of nature into a semiotic system.

Like structuralism, poststructuralism and postmodernism are trapped within the sphere of signification, in spite of their frequent ritual invocations of the extra-semiotic phenomenon of capitalism. The enclosure within the semiotic, a danger for structuralism and semiotics which Eco avoids with his *sub specie communicationis* (making clear that the semiotic viewpoint is an epistemological choice, not a universal philosophical truth), leads postmodernism to an idealist philosophy. Extra-semiotic material society is banned as an epistemological object.

3 Semiotics in the USA

Before the American transformation of poststructuralism into postmodernism, there emerged in the US a semiotic current based on the work of Peirce, whose revival owes much, as we saw, to Thomas Sebeok. In 1965 Sebeok published his first article defining what he considers to be a new field of semiotics, zoosemiotics: its object would be the study of the use of signs by animals, thus pushing the limits of semiotics beyond human culture. In its early stages of development in the 1970s, this was generally accepted as a branch of semiotics, though with some reservations; even Eco, the proponent of semiotics as a theory of culture, accepts zoosemiotics as the lower threshold of semiotics (Eco 1976: 9) and the same holds for Greimas, who considers it as a very promising field (Greimas and Courtés 1979: Zoo-sémiotique).

In 1984, Sebeok together with a group of other researchers published a manifesto (Anderson et al. 1984) in which they combined Peircean semiotics with the theories of the early 20th-century Estonian-German biologist Jakob von Uexküll. Uexküll was interested in how living beings perceive their physical environment. He argued that an organism experiences living in terms of a species-specific spatio-temporal reference frame that he called *Umwelt* (environment). The *Umwelt* is not what a human observer would perceive as that organism's external physical surroundings, but is founded on the interaction of the organism with its environment and the information on the external world conveyed by its senses (its sensorium).

The *Umwelt* is constituted by a set of functional components, approximately corresponding to perceptual features and referring to the organism's relation to its environment in respect to crucial aspects of its survival, such as (positively) the search for food or shelter and (negatively) the detection of threats; simultaneously, the organism ignores what is irrelevant to its interests. This is where Peircean semiotics comes into the picture, because the organism "interprets" this sensory input, that is, in Peircean terms, perception at the level of *Umwelt* already implies a semiotic process.

This approach was presented as a new paradigm. It proposes a new general and holistic "ecumenical" or "global" semiotics founded on Peirce (se also Sebeok 1997). It has the once fashionable ambition of unifying social, human and cognitive sciences with the biological sciences, as well as overcoming the epistemological opposition between realism and idealism. With this paradigm, cultural semiotics becomes "anthroposemiotics", constituting one part only of a general semiotics, the other part of which is "biosemiotics", which would study the processes of semiosis in all living organisms. As a consequence, zoosemiotics was soon joined by phytosemiotics and mycosemiotics. Sebeok avoided the further step of "semiophysics", which would extend semiotics beyond the study of life to that of inorganic matter. Twenty-five years later, biosemiotics was proposed as a general biological theory (Kull et al. 2009). This approach has been cultivated especially at the University of Tartu in Estonia.

Biosemiotics is the second major new form of Peircean semiotics after zoosemiotics, and thus we observe the beginning of a development of the Peircean school comparable to, though still much poorer than, the succession of Saussurean schools. Epistemologically, it represents a generalisation of semiotic theory to fields alien to it – because semiotics is a cultural theory – and empirically it harms semiotics, because a scientific theory pretending to study everything is not in a position to deal with the specificities of each object of scientific investigation. Biosemiotics has so far given rather poor results. For example, the argument was advanced (Kull et al. 2009: 169) that the structure of haemoglobin is "a 'representation' [the quotation marks are in the original text] of both oxygen and its role in the cellular molecular process of metabolism", whence the authors conclude "that the primary unit of biosemiotic research is a *sign* – not merely a molecule or cell"; a claim based on the concept of indexical signs following from a cause-and-effect relation (chapter 3: 9). Still, a number of questions remain: which are the other "signs" of biology, how are they related to each other, which are their hierarchical levels and how are they articulated? In sum, the expected result of the biosemiotic enterprise would be a *complete* Peircean theory of biology.

A more serious criticism of the biosemiotic project has been well expressed by Eco ([1997] 2000: 107–108), who refers to the use by some biologists of terms such as "communication", "sign", "meaning", "interpretation", "choices" and "to recognise" for interactions between cells and argues that these terms are used metaphorically and the processes involved are not semiosic properly speaking. In fact, the major drawback of biosemiotics is its metaphorical nature.

In our opinion, biosemiotics is at its best when using and developing the concepts of von Uexküll to study animal behaviour, and perhaps to advance certain suggestions about the possible biological ancestry of some cultural phenomena, without, however, attempting to argue that these phenomena can be explained simply in biological terms (see, for example, Cobley 2016).

In the US, Peircean semiotics and postmodernism developed quite independently from one another from the mid-1980s. European semioticians have used Peirce occasionally or adopted certain Peircean concepts, absorbing them, however, within a different theoretical framework each time, as we can see with the cases of Jakobson, Eco and Derrida. As for the purist Peirceans, their attitude towards "classical" semiotics, poststructuralism and postmodernism is emphatically dismissive, as in the *opus magnum* of John Deely (2001), the theoretical successor of Sebeok.

Due to its long development, European semiotics have achieved not only a high level of conceptual sophistication, but also the creation of both general analytical methodologies and techniques and specific ones for individual fields. Peircean theorists generally limit themselves to the repetition of the master's ideas without any attempt at conceptual enrichment. At the same time, their research objects have been greatly extended; in addition to zoosemiotics and biosemiotics, there have been increasingly frequent attempts to apply Peircean semiotics to the domain of cultural studies. From Sebeok's times to our day, however, no systematic theory of ecumenical semiotics combining biological and cultural semiotics has been formulated.

Any attempt to apply Peirce's theory without mediation encounters a serious epistemological problem, because philosophy and science are two different domains of knowledge and each one of them follows its own, different logic. No transition is possible from any individual philosophy to a specific scientific analysis without first epistemologically establishing, on the basis of this philosophy, the scientific field in the framework of which this analysis takes place.

There is, for example, not *one* positivist science in general, but a positivist philosophy, on the basis of which were founded several comparable but parallel scientific fields, such as positivist psychology, positivist sociology or positivist history, all fields referring to the same paradigm but having their own formation. In a comparable way, European semiotics established literary semiotics, visual semiotics or the semiotics of space by specialising general semiotic theory to each particular epistemological object of research.

There are reasons why philosophers and scholars interested in animal behaviour tend to have recourse to Peircean semiotics, while researchers in culture prefer to use the tradition of Saussure. Peirce's theory is essentially a theory of the (individual) sign as *representation* (Daylight 2012), while Saussure is interested in sign *systems* as social systems of *signification*. If we wish to study how living organisms relate to their environment, the question of representation is clearly crucial (as, in the case of humans, it may be for a neurologist or a philosopher). If we are interested in the conventions governing narrativity in cinema or in the symbolism of space for the Aztecs, the Saussurean tradition is likely to be more useful to us.

Part II: **The semiotics of** *langue*

Chapter 3
The basic concepts of *langue*

1 The four linguistics

With its maturation, semiotics has freed itself from the mimetic transfer of concepts from linguistics by assimilating it within a full-grown *semiotic* theory. However, this in no way diminishes the importance of linguistic theory for semiotics, as will become clear below. With very few exceptions, the concepts discussed are valid for all semiotic systems, from "soft" systems such as literature to the "hardest" of all, built space.[4]

According to Saussure, all sciences should pay greater attention to the fact that their object exists on two different axes. The first is the "axis of simultaneity" (*axe des simultanéités*), which refers to the relationship between things that coexist in time and thus is time-independent, while the other is the "axis of succession" (*axe des successivités*), which refers to individual (as opposed to global) changes in these things over time. These two axes define the first two of the four fields of linguistics identified by Saussure.

The first field, of major importance, is the one defined by the axis of simultaneity. This is the field of synchronic (or static, as Saussure calls it) linguistics (*linguistique synchronique*), which studies the structuring of *langue* (the "language system", a concept we shall define below) as a static and synchronous phenomenon; it studies linguistic "states". This is a strategic decision, because the mechanism of the language system must be *"prise partout à UN MOMENT DONNÉ, ce qui est la seule manière d'en étudier le mécanisme"* [captured everywhere at A SPECIFIC MOMENT, which is the only way to study its mechanism] (Saussure 2002: 43). Saussure conceptualises the language system as *"la partie sociale du langage"* [the *social* part of language, our emphasis], as *"une institution sociale"* [a social institution] (Saussure 1971: 31, 33); the language system is the product of a "collective consciousness" (Joseph 2012: 586). It is comparable to other institutions such as the political system, forms of marriage and religious rites, but also radically different from them, because they are founded to varying degrees on natural relations between things; for example, fashion is

---

[4] The concepts analysed in this chapter are founded on Saussure's structural linguistics as defined in his *Cours* and their further elaboration by Hjelmslev and Greimas. We have also used additional bibliography and integrated our own experiences from half a century of research and teaching on semiotics.

subject to the constraints of the human body (Saussure 1971: 105–108, 110 and 2002: 178, 211–214, 219–220).

The second field is evolutionary or diachronic linguistics (*linguistique diachronique*), which is defined by the axis of succession and studies successive temporal forms of individual elements of the language system.

The third field of linguistics, of secondary importance according to Saussure, is the linguistics of speech (*parole*) – to which we shall return below – that is, of the *use* of the language system (for the difference between *langue* and *parole*, see also Barthes 1964a: 92–97; Greimas and Courtés 1979: Langue, Parole). *Langue* and *parole* both depend on the natural faculty of language.

These three fields of linguistics concern the internal aspects of language, in the sense that they focus on language as such. He then adds a fourth field, "external" linguistics (*linguistique externe*), which may be considered as a social linguistics since it links language to its external social, historical and geographical environment (cf. our social semiotics, chapter 8: 2.14 and chapter 9). Saussure offers as examples the relation of language to institutions, such as the church, the school system, the court or the Academies; to political history, both external (for example, the influence of Roman conquests on local languages) and internal (for example, the impact of cultural development on the creation of specialised languages, such as legal or scientific languages); and to geography as a consequence of the geographical diffusion of a language.

For reasons that will become clear below, Saussure's theory as a whole concerns synchronic linguistics. John E. Joseph argues that Saussure did not intend to demote the diachronic to a lower position and did not want to render the two domains autonomous; he posited their complete independence but simultaneously indicated that they were interdependent. Joseph considers that for Saussure this separation is purely an abstraction, comparable to that between the two aspects of the linguistic sign (Joseph 2012: 545, 634–635). This comparison clarifies the sense of the separation between synchrony and diachrony, because, in spite of their inseparability, the signifier and the signified as separate concepts are necessary operational tools for semiotic analysis. Saussure did not underestimate the diachronic, but he believed that the strategic way to analyse language was synchronically.

Saussure believed that a systemic approach to diachronic linguistics is impossible. He considered, in other words, that it is not possible for the relations between two different historical stages of a linguistic system to be of a comprehensive nature; for Saussure, these are always relations between isolated elements, the one of which replaces the other. This view is aligned with his emphatic opposition to the historical and etymological approaches to the study of language, approaches which conceive of language as a set of terms juxtaposed one next to the other, the subsequent meaning of each term being derived from its previous one. Saussure's position on this point is due to his radical thesis that the signification of a linguistic term is neither isolated nor historically defined, but follows from its synchronic relationship to the other terms of language as a whole.

The key role of synchrony is corroborated by modern linguistics, in the sense that the study of diachrony, phonological, syntactic[5] or semantic, is not possible without anchoring in the synchronic system of a language. However, contemporary research does not support the imperative to limit diachronic linguistics to the study of changes in isolated terms. It has been shown that linguistic changes result from micro-systems and are integrated again into such systems, or that they are transformations from one stage of a language to the next. Even further, there is evidence that it is possible to explain the whole of a subsequent stage of language from its previous one, if the two successive synchronic stages are analysed in depth. Due to these relationships of diachrony with synchrony, these two dimensions of language can no longer be considered as independent, as Saussure envisaged them on the structural level, but are seen as closely interrelated on the basis of systemic relationships (Ducrot and Schaeffer 1995: 334–346).

This relation between synchrony and diachrony had been announced as early as the Theses of the Prague Circle. The Theses state that language is a "functional system" and its essence is revealed by synchronic analysis, but also, and contrary to the "Geneva School" (i.e., Saussurean theory), that "There is no insurmountable distance between the synchronic and the diachronic methods". The "synchronic moment reflects the disappearing, present, and coming stages [of language]". This view invests synchrony with a macro-temporal dynamism, to which we should add a micro-temporal dimension, because we never have absolute synchrony; synchrony is an abstraction, though quite acceptable with reference to human time. And this synchrony, necessarily studied statically, is not static for Saussure and is never in equilibrium (Saussure 2002: 157–158); it is a *dynamic stability*. According to the Theses, linguistic changes are not "destructive, purposeless and heterogeneous from the viewpoint of the system" and "often reflect the needs of the system". Such changes "demand [. . .] an evaluation in terms of the system which is the subject of these changes". The comparative study of Slavic languages should turn to the study of "the structural regularity of systems of language and their evolution" (Steiner 1982: 5–6). This view, then, is in line with contemporary linguistics;

---

[5] Morris (1971: 28) called "syntactics" the study of the relations between signs in isolation from other concerns, such as their signification, the study of which he attributes to "semantics".

both offer a further insight into Saussure's findings that the language system is not a parthenogenesis and is not immobile but changes, that these changes are continuous transformations, leading each time to a state with its own existence in comparison to the previous and the following state, all of which are nevertheless linked by the principle of continuity (Saussure 2002: 157–158).

The structural relation between synchrony and diachrony was studied early and systematically in social anthropology by Lévi-Strauss. For Lévi-Strauss, there is in every society a group of individual structures, such as marriage rules, kinship systems, mythology, religion, art, even cooking, which constitutes a transformation group, that is, a group of structures related to each other on the basis of a set of rules of transformation. According to Lévi-Strauss, these structures change over time, that is, diachronically. The change is due to chance events that do not present any structural character, but is itself structural and regulated by rules of transformation. Exactly the same rules apply for synchronic change in geographical space – observed in the case of synchronic comparisons – and diachronic change in time, and Lévi-Strauss's thesis is that the rules of diachronic change reproduce those of synchronic change. In this way, he relates these two kinds of changes on the systemic level with the use of the concept of "structural transformation" (Lévi-Strauss 1958: 102–103, 240–241, 252–253, 306, 342).

2 *Langue* and *parole*

It goes without saying that it is imperative for linguistics, as for every other science, to define its object in order to be constituted as a science, and such a definition presupposes the epistemological delimitation of this object. This principle, the establishment of a *point de vue* [point of view], later called the "law of relevance" (*loi de la pertinence*), is the starting point of Saussure's theory of language. However, he detects a major obstacle for the application of this principle to linguistics. As he states, the other sciences operate on objects that are given *a priori*. To give an example, if we define society as an empirical object of research, this allows the creation of not only one but a constellation of sciences, each one of which defines a specific epistemological perspective on the object: sociology defines a sociological perspective, social anthropology its own perspective, economics a different perspective, demography a fourth one and so on. However, as Saussure states, this is not possible in the case of linguistics, because the object empirically present, speech, is multifaceted. In this case, it is not the object that precedes the point of view, but it is the point of view that constitutes the object, an abstract object which is not offered directly to experience.

The law of relevance implies Hjelmslev's principle ruling scientific description. He points out that a theory must be founded on the presuppositions that are necessary for its object and the results of its application must be in line with the empirical data. The requirement for empirical correspondence is satisfied by the "empirical principle", which includes three conditions ruling scientific description: in order of importance, coherence, i.e., description without contradictions; exhaustiveness; and the greatest possible simplicity of description (Hjelmslev [1943] 1961: 10–11). Greimas and Courtés also define their rule for scientific description on the basis of Hjelmslev: of the numerous possible features of an object, only those necessary and sufficient to exhaust its description are selected, that is, the object must be described from only one specific perspective (Greimas and Courtés 1979: Définition, Description, Opération, Pertinence, Procédure).

There are two different ways of understanding and applying the concept of relevance. The narrow one, traditionally used in semiotics, is to connect it solely to the immanent analysis of semiotic texts. A wider understanding of relevance, however, is that it concerns any approach, strictly textual or extra-textual, however broad, that is limited to the study of signification, without taking into account extra-semiotic factors. It is in this last sense that we use "relevance" in the present book.

The object of relevance for Saussure is *langue* as the language system,[6] as a social product belonging to all members of the same linguistic community. This is the reason why *langue* is a social language. The term *langue* can be used for all semiotic systems and every semiotic system is a *langue*. The term is equivalent to "Code", with a capital C (as differentiated from "code" with a lower-case c, which we shall discuss later, chapter 5: 1.1); thus, we can speak of the Code of painting or the Code of cinema.

The development of Saussurean linguistics by both Eco and Greimas, as well as by Lacanian psychoanalysis, has shown that the concept of *langue* may be used also at a lower level than the social, even at an individual one. Thus, for example, according to Eco (1972: 232–233), a modern work of art can install a new *langue*, and for Greimas and Courtés (1979: Génératif [parcours]) every text is produced by a process – the generative trajectory – regulated, at a deep and abstract level, by its own *langue*, which is then manifested through "discursive structures" (*structures discursives*) on the level of speech (chapter 4: 1.6 and 1.7).

---

6 Saussure, writing in French, uses the term *langue* when referring to the systemic nature of language, while *langage* covers both *langue* and *parole* (Saussure 1971: 36, 37, 112). English does not have such a useful terminological distinction. We have elected to use the "language system" to translate Saussure's *langue* and "language" when referring to natural languages. However, it is not always possible to be completely consistent in this respect.

The language system is the foundation of Saussure's linguistics. It is the object of his *Cours*, and he considers it as the necessary precondition for the study of any other aspect of linguistics. It is the foundational concept of structural synchronic linguistics. Its invention is the revolution brought by Saussure, not only in linguistics, as we saw from our historical review, but in the study of culture as a whole. It has been criticised, justly up to a point, for being a static conception, detached from society and historical becoming. However, the law of relevance shows us that this epistemological decision is necessary for the delimitation of a specific field of knowledge, and that it is pointless to try to stuff into this field every possible empirical aspect related to it. There may be, indeed there have been, different epistemological decisions concerning the object of language and, in this case, the power of each approach is proven by its results. For more than a century, however, the structuralist linguistic approach has remained a strong competitive paradigm.

That Saussure adopted this structuralist view on language, avoiding further empirical stuffing, does not imply that he had no conception of the historical and social background of language, quite the opposite. While speech presupposes *langue*, it precedes it historically and is the *cause* of its changes (Saussure 1971: 37, 138), and we have already referred to his unambiguous views of the language system as a social phenomenon and to his "external" linguistics.

There is, however, in our opinion a further step to take, which we shall discuss in the context of our presentation of social semiotics at the end of this book. The law of relevance is a fundamental epistemological necessity, but it should not lead to epistemological ring-fencing. No epistemological object in the social sciences is completely autonomous, and there is a hierarchy and a nesting of epistemological objects, according to which the articulation of a lower-level with a higher-level epistemological object allows a deeper comprehension of the former: the next more general epistemological object offers the framework completing the analysis of the lower-level object, thus allowing a more global analysis. In the case of *langue*, as well as of speech, the higher-level epistemological object is social dynamics and the completion of the linguistic, and semiotic, analysis is its articulation with this higher level of analysis, that of material society, leading to a social linguistics and a social semiotics. Such a view is entirely justified by Saussure's own writings, as we shall see (chapter 9: 3).

In spite of his socio-historical sensitivity, Saussure leaves no doubt about the theoretical primacy of *langue*. He considers it as essential and in fact as passively inscribed as a whole in individual minds, as opposed to speech, which is its by-product, a product due to individual initiative that obeys no specific rules. We have no doubt that Saussure's choice, partial as it is, was historically justified, but we should clarify that linguistics no longer conceives of speech as a purely individual act, as will become clear from Part Three of this book. There is a wealth of examples to the contrary, from the social conventions of turn-taking in conversation to the traditional literary genres.

3 The communication circuit and the definition of the sign

The crucial definition of the nature of the language system, which sets Saussure's epistemological paradigm, is that it is a *system of signs*. Saussure begins his presentation of the object of linguistics by discussing the "speech circuit", that is, spoken communication between two persons (Figure 1).

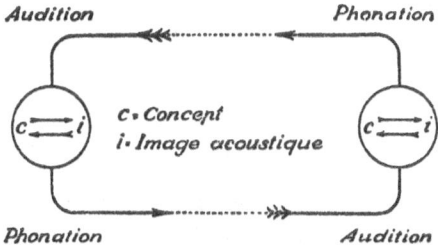

Figure 1: The communication circuit according to Saussure (1971: 28).

The starting point of the circuit is in the mind of person A, whose consciousness includes "concepts". These concepts are associated within the mind with elements expressing them, the "acoustic images". Later in the *Cours*, Saussure will call the concept "signified" (*signifié*) and the acoustic image "signifier" (*signifiant*). Both of them are in the mind, but, as Saussure explains, the signifier is more tangible, is in a sense "material"; we would add that it also has a material vehicle, physical sound. Of course, the linguistic signifier is not the vehicle itself but its mental imprint, its representation by our senses, as Saussure explains. Saussure considers that signifier and signified constitute an indissoluble unity (he says that they are comparable to the two sides of a piece of paper). This unity he calls "sign" (*signe*) (for these concepts, see, for example, Barthes 1964a: 103–109; Greimas and Courtés 1979: Signe, Signifiant, Signifié).

The sign is the fundamental unit of the language system. When A communicates with another person B, the acoustic image produced by A, activated by a concept in his or her mind, is transferred to B, and through it B recalls the concept referred to by A. The same process is repeated in the reverse direction from B to A (Saussure 1971: 27–30; a more extended description of this process is given in chapter 8: 2.1).

As we can see, Saussure uses the communication circuit in order to define theoretically the language system.[7] The result was the identification of the concept of sign as the foundation of the language system and the focus of its study. The language system is not a simple juxtaposition of signs, but a coherent whole; it is *"un système de signes"* [a system of signs], a synchronic system of signs (Saussure 1971: 26). This concept of "system" is equally radical with the concept of sign. We shall examine it carefully in section 6 below and we shall show that it is the epistemological paradigm founding the whole of the Saussurean linguistic edifice. As we shall see (section 7 below), it is firmly linked to the concepts of "value" and "difference".

4 The principles of *langue*

4.1 The first principle: Conventionality

4.1.1 The conventional relation between signified and signifier

We just saw that a signified is unthinkable without a signifier and vice versa; these two are indissolubly related. But what kind of relation connects them? The answer to this question is given by what Saussure's considers as the first principle ruling the language system: the relation between signified and signifier is arbitrary (*arbitraire*), or more exactly unmotivated (*immotivé*) or conventional,[8] and is not due to any physical or metaphysical relation between them. The linguistic sign, and generally any sign, is conventional. This first principle closely connects the two fundamental concepts of "sign" and "system", because, as we shall soon see, convention founds the abstract systemic character of the language system.

Let us follow the rationale according to which Saussure arrives at the conclusion that the relation between signified and signifier is conventional. Both signifier and signified are mental concepts, but a semiotic system cannot hover

---

[7] This circuit was developed by Saussure only in his third course (1910–1911), but we believe that its close relation to the definition of *langue* justifies the decision of the two editors of the *Cours* to present it in §1 of chapter III with the title *La langue; sa définition* [Langue; its definition]. That this is not a new problematic for Saussure, can be seen from his rudimentary sketch of the circuit, the "acoustico-psychological cycle" and relevant observations in his third notebook from the period 1883–1885 (Joseph 2012: 302).
[8] This is a more felicitous term, because it indicates a social background.

in the air, in a world of Platonic ideas; it must exist in the actual world and have a material vehicle, comparable to the one we encountered above for language, physical sound. We thus have three concepts: signified, signifier and the material vehicle of the latter.

Saussure poses the revolutionary idea that there can be no ideas without the constitution of the sign as a whole, that is, before the emergence of the language system. Without the sign, thought has no distinctions; it consists of "confused ideas" (*idées confuses*), is chaotic (*chaotique*), hazy (*nébuleuse*), an amorphous mass. The material vehicle of the signifier, the "phonic substance" (*substance phonique*) is equally amorphous and unspecified, a flexible material (*matière plastique* – Saussure 1971: 55–56). Thus, there are no pre-existing ideas, waiting to be manifested with the help of the phonic substance, nor is there any phonic substance offering itself to be spiritualised. There are two "substances", one of amorphous thought and the other of amorphous phonic substance, and the language system functions as a mediation between thought and sound, linking and subdividing them both into units, which become the signs (Figure 2: a and b). As Saussure writes, "*la langue élabore ses unités en se constituant entre deux masses amorphes*" [the language system constructs its units by establishing itself between two amorphous masses]. When the elements of the two different orders of units are brought together, "*cette combinaison produit une forme, non une substance*" [this combination produces a form, not a substance] (Saussure 1971: 156, 157). We thus understand that thought, as a form, only emerges *after* and *inside* the segmentation of the above two substances. This is the conceptual framework that led Saussure to his first principle, the conventionality of language.

The language system has the mediating function of bringing together these two orders, in performing the transition from substance to form. Actually there is something more that allows the transition, namely the very fact of the function of semiosis itself. For Saussure, due to its mediating function, the language system becomes the domain of "articulations", in the sense of defining units having the quality of the Latin *articulus*, a conjunction on a small scale. With this conjunction, a specific piece of each "amorphous" substance is linked to the production of a form. As we shall see (section 8 below), these are two fundamental concepts in Hjelmslev's glossematics. The process of segmentation producing form is not due to any conscious decision, but is "arbitrary". The reason is, for Saussure, that no individual person is in a position to define even one linguistic unit; only a collectivity can perform such a task, because the units can exist only as a result of their general acceptance by the linguistic community using them.

This rationale explains a phenomenon empirically observable. When, for example, we want to express the signified /dog/ and we use for this purpose the signifier "dog", the latter has absolutely no internal quality that makes it

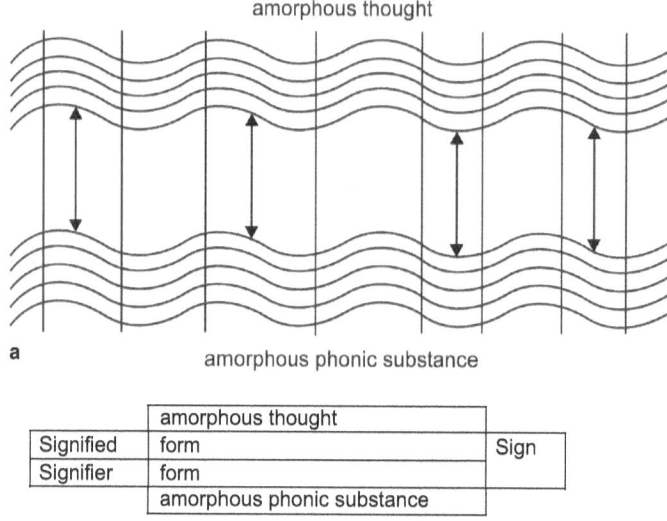

Figure 2: a. The segmentation of amorphous thought and amorphous phonic substance. b. Form and substance according to Saussure.

suitable to express this signified. This is evident from the obvious fact that the same signified is expressed by quite different signifiers in other languages, such as the French *chien* and the German *Hund* or the Swahili *mbwa*. It would be entirely possible to call the dog in English "blackberry", provided this signifier had been socially institutionalised for that signified.

The conventionality of the sign is a general and inviolable principle, but Saussure himself points out that there exist gradations of conventionality. To paraphrase one of his examples, "six" is purely conventional, but "thirty-six" is to a certain extent motivated, because it is constructed like "thirty-five" and "twenty-six". Saussure also sees a motivated relation, which he calls "natural", between signifier and signified in the case of symbols, such as the scales as a signifier of Justice. We shall refer to a more analytical definition of this concept later in this chapter (section 11).

4.1.2 The conventional relation between the signifier and the external world

Saussure's discussion of the conventionality of the sign mainly focuses on the above relation between signified and signifier (let us call it the first type of conventionality), but he also refers to a second type of conventionality, that of the relation between the signifier and the external world.[9] He detects the existence of a relative conventionality in the cases of onomatopoeia and exclamations, to which he hesitantly attributes a symbolic character, as in the case of the scales standing for Justice. He also finds relative conventionality in what we would call today "gestural semiotics". He gives as an example the signs of politeness, which he considers as "entirely natural" in the sense that, as in the cases of onomatopoeia and exclamation, they are signs with a physical vehicle. Nevertheless, he specifies that they are "fixed by rule" (Saussure 1971: 100, 101).

In spite of this, it is common even today to conceive of onomatopoeia as "realistic", that is, to see a direct connection between an onomatopoeic signifier and a natural phenomenon. In our times, this impression is exacerbated by the introduction of Anglo-Saxon expressions in non-Anglophone countries through popular culture and the Internet, which has led to the local adaptation of this foreign influence and a superficial levelling of the differences between languages. Borrowings of this kind have always been common between languages that are close culturally, geographically or economically, but it has become particularly widespread with globalisation.

However, Saussure is right, and onomatopoeia is in fact conventional. This is not easily perceived by people belonging to the culture in which the onomatopoeic words occur, but it becomes striking on the comparative level.

There are often more or less equivalent onomatopoeias within one and the same language. In English, for example, *bump*, *thump*, *thud*, *bam* and *bang* are more or less equivalent onomatopoeic words for a loud dull sound; an even closer relation exists between the essentially synonymous *ding*, *dong*, *ding-dong* and *ting-a-ling*, all referring to the ringing sound of a bell. The same is the case with the French *drelin*, *ding*, *dring* (the sound of a small church bell or a door bell) or *floc*, *plouf-plouf* and *flic-flac* for a splashing sound (see below).

However, onomatopoeic words with similar sounds from different languages do not seem as a rule to have an absolute coincidence of meaning, although there is usually some semantic overlapping. The English *crack*, the French *crac* and the Greek *krak* correspond closely as signifiers, but they are not semantically identical though they are closely related. The English *crack* is a sudden sharp or explosive noise. In French, the meaning is again a dry noise,

---

9 This is not the place to discuss the epistemological status of this external world.

such as an explosion, but *crac* also refers to the sound of a collision, even the closing of a lock, which in English would be rendered as *click*. The Greek *krak* has nothing to do with explosions, but is still a slight dry noise, referring to the breaking of an object or the sound of creaking bodily joints.

Semantic kinship, on the other hand, is regularly found in onomatopoeias with little or no correspondence of signifiers. *Splash* originates from the less common *plash* and is commonly found in the form *splish-splash* (or *splish-splosh*) – we recall Bobby Darin's rock song: "Splish, splash, I was takin' a bath . . . ". It refers to the noise produced by a liquid or semi-liquid when it splatters, is poured out or falls with a certain force, or by the loud mixing of water. On the other hand, *plop* indicates the sound of a small, solid object dropping into water without a splash. *Splash* corresponds in meaning to the French *plouf*, *plouf-plouf* and *flic-flac*, which has no phonetic affinity to *splash*. French also has *pschitt*, meaning the eruption of water from a container, such as when opening a champagne bottle, in which case the reference is to the noise of the liquid itself in the air; for this, English has no equivalent. In Swedish the onomatopoeic *plask* is semantically equivalent to splash, while the Greek *plats* only means the sound of something like a stone falling into water. The Greek expressions *plats-plouts*, *platsa-ploutsa* and *plits-plats* are similar in meaning to *splash*, but are used for a person (not a thing) splashing around in water.[10]

We also encounter cases in which two cultures may use the same onomatopoeic signifier, but in one of them no onomatopoeia is intended. The word *boom* in English means a loud hollow noise and is close to *bang*, meaning a sudden loud, but sharp, noise. There is a French equivalent, *boum* (and there are Swedish equivalents: *boom*, *bom*, *smäll* and *knall*). But *boom* has also been given a new metaphorical meaning in English: it refers to a sudden increase of something in amount, frequency or success, such as a boom in the stock market. In French, *boom* has only this metaphorical meaning; this is also the case with the Italian and Spanish *boom*.

The conventionality of onomatopoeia is also clear in the domain of natural sounds. The sound of sneezing, *atshoo* in English, is *atchoum* in French, *attjo* in Swedish, *apsoú* in Greek, and *eccì* (*etchî*) or *ecciù* (*etchoú*) in Italian. In English, dogs go *woof-woof*, *arf-arf*, *ruff-ruff* and *bow-wow*; in French, *wouaff-wouaff*, *vaf-vaf*, *ouah-ouah* and *whou-whou*; in Italian *arf-arf* and *bau-bau*, in Greek *ghav-ghav*, in Malayan *gong-gong* and in Japanese *wan-wan* and *kian-kian*. British cats

---

10 The equivalent of splash is *Plumps* in German and Polish, *molskis* in Finnish and *žbluňk* in Czech and Slovak.

say *meow*, French cats say *miaoú*, Danish cats *miav*, Greek ones *niáou* or *niárr* and Indonesian ones *ngéong*. The sound of British birds is *tweet-tweet*, of Norwegian birds *kvitt-kvitt*, of Greek ones *tsiou-tsiou*, and of Danish, Austrian and Polish birds *pip-pip*. Finally, there are the pigs. In English, a pig says *oink*, in Hungarian *röf* and in Polish *chrum*, while the cosmopolitan Swedish pigs apparently know how to count in French, since they say *nöff-nöff* (*neuf* means nine in French).[11]

4.1.3 The conventional relation between the signified and the external world

In addition to the conventional relation between signified and signifier and that between the signifier and the external world, a third type of conventionality is posed by Saussure, namely that between the signified and its referent in the external world (on the concept of referent, see section 9 below). This third type poses tantalising philosophical problems and leads to a radical epistemological rupture in the study of language as well as culture as a whole.

From the very manner in which the signified is constituted, it is defined as a function of the internal structure of the language system and not of some external given (i.e., a referent, though this term is not used by Saussure). On this point, Saussure breaks completely with the philosophical tradition which conceives of language as a nomenclature, i.e., a list of names, each one corresponding to an external phenomenon; such a conception of language implies that, from the linguistic viewpoint, ideas correspond directly to these phenomena and pre-exist their manifestation in words.[12]

---

[11] For this account of onomatopoeias, we have used a great number of sources from the Internet, including several dictionaries, and checked (again through the Internet) the pronunciation of words from foreign languages we do not know. We found great help in an excellent and charming little illustrated book by Pierre Gay and Agnes Rosenstiehl (1989). It is an empirical record of European onomatopoeias and includes onomatopoeias referring to animals, human activities, musical sounds and lots of noises (from the breaking of a match and the knocking on a door to collisions and explosions).

[12] As Saussure argues (2002: 230), the view of language as nomenclature postulates *"D'abord l'objet, puis le signe; donc (ce que nous nierons toujours) base extérieur donnée au signe"* [First the object, then the sign; which thus provides an external basis for the sign (something that we shall always deny)]. He continues: *"Si un objet pouvait, où que ce soit, être le terme sur lequel est fixé le signe, la linguistique cesserait instantanément d'être ce qu'elle est, depuis le sommet jusqu'à la base; du reste l'esprit humain du même coup"* [If an object, wherever it might be, could be the element on which the sign is fixed, linguistics would instantly stop being what it is, from top to toe; so would at the same time the human spirit].

If language were a nomenclature, the domain of ideas would consist of the juxtaposition and addition of individual, unconnected words (or signs). However, this is not the nature of the language system, precisely because it is a system. Its systemic nature renders impossible an onomatological approach, because the systemic constitution of *langue* excludes the notion of the union of an individual *a priori* defined signified with a corresponding individual signifier. On the contrary, the systemic nature of *langue* implies than an individual sign cannot be (theoretically) considered independently from the whole set of the other signs of the language system; to put it in another way, the segmentation leading to the constitution of signs is neither mechanistic nor individual, because it is *simultaneous* and fully founded on the interrelations between signs. The language system as a whole is not constructed by starting with individual signs and at the end adding them together, but in exactly the opposite way, and this is why each individual sign is defined as a function of the system as a whole.

According to Saussure, the interrelation between signs is founded on the concept of "value", a revolutionary concept that we shall examine later (section 7 below). The three types of conventionality we have discussed all follow from the systemic nature of *langue*, which in turn ensues from the self-organisation of language as *langue*. Such a detachment of the language system from reality seems to be dangerously idealistic; however Saussure is certainly not an idealist. His detachment does not follow from any all-embracing philosophical position, but from the particular need to epistemologically define a breakthrough in the study of language and a specific field for linguistics. It is related to the modern realisation that a direct and transparent knowledge of reality is impossible, because such knowledge is inevitably mediated by the process of semiosis.

4.2 The second principle: Linearity

The second principle ruling the language system is, according to Saussure, the linear deployment of the signs. He deduces this principle from oral language, as he also did when defining the nature of the sign from its use in linguistic communication. The signifiers of oral language are deployed in time in a manner that is one-dimensional: a line, a chain, which is converted into a spatial line in the case of writing. He considers the principle of linearity as equally important with the first principle, conventionality, because he believes that the structure of the language system depends on it.

This statement comes as a surprise, because the scientific power of the two principles is quite unequal. First, the epistemological importance and the philosophical impact of the first principle are much greater than those of the second. Second, the second principle is not generalisable to all semiotic systems, as is the case with the first principle. It seems that we have here a confusion between a *principle* of the language system and what we will call below a *rule* of the system: Saussure elevates to a principle the rule we shall discuss below for the construction of linguistic syntagms. Saussure does seem to understand the narrowness of linearity, because he contrasts it to iconic signs, which are for him multi-dimensional. We believe that his claim to found a *sémiologie* would be better served if he did not emphasise the one rule at the expense of the other and that it is better to demote linearity from "principle" to what we call "rule", though of a limited generality.

5 The rules of *langue*

Together with the principle of arbitrariness, there are two rules that for Saussure form part of the laws of the language system (Joseph 2012: 600). Saussure first posits these two rules on the occasion of his analysis of the speech circuit. As he explains, when we pass from the individual sign to a set of signs, two different mental capacities are activated: coordination and association. Much later in the *Cours*, he clarifies that these two capacities regulate two different types of relationship and difference between linguistic signs.

Saussure believes that it is because of the principle of linearity that words in language are ordered linearly. This linear relationship, which involves the mental capacity of coordination, follows the first rule of the language system, that of the "syntagmatic relations" (*rapports syntagmatiques*) between linguistic signs. The linear combination of two or more linguistic signs he calls a "syntagm" (*syntagme*).[13] He gives as examples "re-read", "against all", "the life of man", "God is good", "if the weather is fine, we shall go out". The relationship of linguistic signs on the syntagmatic axis is a relationship of conjunction following the form "both–and" (Greimas and Courtés 1979: Paradigmatique, Syntagme). This relationship is, according to Saussure, *in praesentia*, because all its terms are present, and presupposes a specific order of succession and a limited number of terms.

The second rule follows from the capacity of association and refers to "associative relations" (*rapports associatifs*), later found in Hjelmslev (1961: 52–54) as "paradigmatic". The mind, according to Saussure, is not limited to bringing together terms with an affinity, but also grasps the relations between them, thus

---

[13] Syntagmatic relations are not identical to syntax, although syntax falls within "syntagmatics" (Joseph 2012: 551).

creating a whole series of associative relations following from the different nature of these relations; each series is a virtual mnemonic series. He gives examples of classes of such relations starting from the word *enseignement* [teaching]:

(a) Relations due to a common stem: for example, *enseignement, enseigner, enseignons* [teaching, to teach, we teach], etc. have the common stem *enseign-*; these are relations between both signifiers and signifieds.
(b) Relations due to a similarity between signifieds: for example, *enseignement, instruction, apprentissage, education* [teaching, instruction, apprenticeship, education], etc.
(c) Relations due to a common suffix: for example, *enseigne*ment, *arma*ment, *change*ment [teaching, armament, change], etc.; or a common prefix, for example, *dé*faire, *dé*coller, *dé*placer, *dé*coudre [undo, come unstuck, displace, unpick]; these are relations essentially between signifiers.
(d) Rare relations due simply to a similarity in the perception of the sound of the signifiers: for example, between (the noun) *enseigne*ment [teaching], (the adverb) *juste*ment [precisely], (the adjective) *clé*ment [lenient], etc.

The associative relationship of signs on the paradigmatic axis is based on disjunction and follows the form "either–or" (Greimas and Courtés 1979: Paradigmatique, Syntagme). Both Barthes (1964a: 121–123) and Greimas and Courtés (1979: Paradigmatique, Paradigme) follow Hjelmslev in considering that the paradigmatic axis renders the language system as a set of relationships between paradigms. According to Saussure, the paradigm is an indeterminate and usually undefined order of words. Unlike the syntagmatic relationship, the associative relationship is a relationship *in absentia*, because a paradigm is represented in a syntagm by only one out of the set of words constituting it, while the other words are absent, but each one of them could occupy the same position on a realised syntagmatic axis (Greimas and Courtés 1979: Paradigme). For example, in the sentence "John kicks the ball" we can replace "John" with "George", "Harry", "Mary" or any other name, provided it refers to someone that can kick a ball. The same procedure can be repeated with any of the other words of the sentence; for example, we can use "strikes" instead of "kicks" and "bag" instead of "ball".[14] Saussure's examples of paradigms emphasise the relative arbitrariness of the paradigmatic classes (and in fact all classifications are relatively arbitrary). Arbitrariness increases as we broaden the semantic field of reference.

---

14 These substitutions are much more limited than Saussure's examples, because he reasons within the general and abstract limits of the language system, while our example belongs to speech and thus has to follow semantic constraints.

"John" could be grouped in a paradigmatic class of only male names, or in a class of all proper names, male or female. We chose in our example to consider "kick" as part of a paradigm of verbs applicable to ball games, but, on the level of the language system, the paradigm could extend to the whole class of physical action words: John could bite the ball, or sit on it, or break it.

Roman Jakobson in a famous article (1963: 61–67) associates the rhetorical figures of metonymy and metaphor with syntagm and paradigm, respectively. However, there are important divergences between these pairs which usually pass unnoticed. Jakobson argues that speech develops according to two processes: one theme relates to another through either similarity (or difference) or contiguity. The first case is a metaphorical process, the second a metonymic one. He then goes on to connect these discursive processes to Freud's theory of the interpretation of dreams.

If we say "John could have kicked himself" instead of "John kicks the ball", we are using the verb "to kick" metaphorically, implying strong self-criticism of some personal action or behaviour. This is the spirit of metaphor according to Jakobson. For metonymy, we shall borrow an example from Eco. He points out that it is a well-established habit to replace "the President of the United States" with "the White House", and that this replacement works because of the spatial contiguity of the President with the White House (Eco 1976: 280)

There are, however, three important differences between Jakobson's metonymy–metaphor couple and Saussure's syntagm and paradigm. First, Jakobson is referring to speech, while Saussure to the language system; however, such a transposition may be legitimate. Second, Jakobson deals only with the semantic level, while Saussure in the case of the syntagm focuses on the signifiers – though not, of course, independently from the signifieds – and his associative axis is based on both signifieds and signifiers. Third, for Jakobson, the metaphorical process presupposes the selection and replacement of comparable terms, while the metonymic process is based on the contiguity between terms, but in both cases only one term is present. On the other hand, for Saussure, while the paradigmatic relation presupposes the absence of all but the selected term, the syntagmatic relation demands the simultaneous presence of both terms. It is clear that Jakobson's metonymic relation is triggered by a contiguity, but in its actual form, with only one term of the couple realised and the other absent, the absent term is transformed into a connotative reference of the present term, i.e., the present term becomes a metaphor for the absent term; thus, Jakobson is essentially discussing two variants of metaphor (for the two axes of the language system and Jakobson's concepts, see also Barthes 1964a: mainly 114–118, 121–123). It is in any case risky to draw close parallels between discursive and psychological processes; both language and the mind are protean in their ability to find ways to generate meaning.

6 *Langue* as a system of relations and elements

6.1 The relation between the syntagmatic and paradigmatic axes

We have already several times encountered the concept of "system". We saw that *langue* is a system of signs and we observed that both the concept of "system" and that of "sign" are crucial to the understanding of *langue*. Saussure conceives of the system in exactly the same way as we define it today: a set of elements connected to each other by a set of relationships, forming a whole subject to a set of rules.

According to Saussure, the two mental capacities of coordination and association play a fundamental role in the organisation of the language system. We may understand that the two axes of syntagmatic and paradigmatic relations are in a position to build a coherent system if we think of them, not as parallel, but as intertwined. Each axis is constituted by a set of elements and their relations. The syntagmatic axis offers a sequence of nodes on which paradigmatic sets can develop in the form of classes of virtual mnemonic series. Multiple paradigms articulate with every node (for example word) of a syntagm.

Thus, the two fundamental axes of the organisation of the language system are structurally linked subsystems of the language system as a whole. The set of elements linked together according to the rules of a syntagm are in turn linked with all the possible associative sets of the paradigms to which each element can potentially belong, in a huge multi-dimensional network of elements and relations.

6.2 Distinctive features and phonemes

As we saw, the syntagm is a set of elements linked in a chain and, for Saussure, these elements are signs. However, the linear organisation of the language system starts from a level below the sign. Consecutive hierarchical levels of units are then structured according to the syntagmatic axis.

The minimal unit of this model is the "phoneme". Phonemes are abstract, clearly delimited, differentiated and few in number. The English alphabet includes 26 letters and a maximum of about 44 phonemes; in Modern Greek there are 24 letters and a maximum of 31 phonemes, and in Albanian 36 letters and 30 phonemes. Phonemes play an enormous role in the economy of language, because they allow the construction of thousands of words with a minimal number of basic units. Saussure observes that phonemes are aggregations of auditory impressions and articulatory movements (mainly in the oral cavity); that is, they are a composite of the unit which is heard and that which is spoken.

On the basis of the articulatory movements required to produce it, the phoneme is defined by a set of "distinctive features" or *phèmes* [phemes] in French.[15] N. S. Troubetzkoy ([1939] 1964: 36, 38) calls them "distinctive (phonological) units" or "distinctive marks". These features are the minimal, and abstract, units of the language system and are constructed on the basis of empirically recognisable elements. They are a metalinguistic scientific device, not to be confused with the empirical perception of language. A specific, simultaneous combination of distinctive features is unique for each phoneme.

The constitutive elements of this chain, the distinctive features, are not juxtaposed the one next to the other, but are combined according to the possible movements of the human articulatory mechanism.[16] The phoneme is defined by the simultaneous presence of a bundle of such movements, which presupposes the absence of the other distinctive features (Eco 1976: 84). The connection of two distinctive features is founded on such an internal relationship that it acquires the status of a rule. This conception of the phoneme is the cornerstone for the field of phonology. Saussure states that the relationships between phonemes may be considered as algebraic equations.

Linguistics has formulated a classification of distinctive features. For consonants, for example, it involves three major dimensions: place of articulation, manner of articulation and voicing (voiced or unvoiced). A larger or smaller set of distinctive features is defined in each dimension and the form of these sets is not linear but organised in a tree-structure.

The *place* of articulation covers distinctive features such as the bilabial (for the formation, for example, of the phonemes [b], [p] or [m]), the dental (as, for example, in the phonemes [θ] or [ð]) or the velar (involved in the production of phonemes such as [k] or [g] and due to the contact of the body of the tongue with the soft palate, i.e., the roof of the mouth, separating the mouth from the nasal cavity). The *manner* of articulation includes distinctive features such as the oral stops ("plosives", for example the phonemes [d], [p], [t]), the nasal stops (for example the phoneme [n]), or the fricatives (as in [f], [s], [ð]). Finally the dimension of voicing has two classes: voiced (as in [b], [g], [ð]) when there is a vibration of the vocal chords, and unvoiced (as in [p], [t], [k]) when there is not. It is the combination

---

15 Both terms are posterior to Saussure.
16 This would imply that language is not structurally linear at all levels.

of distinctive features that produces a specific phoneme; thus, [p] is an unvoiced bilabial plosive, while [ð] is a voiced dental fricative. The maximum number of distinctive features constituting a phoneme is six.

Greimas and Courtés point out that the distinctive features take their meaning inside a "phemic category" (*catégorie phémique*), which is an elementary binary structure of opposition (Greimas and Courtés 1979: Phème). This is once more indicative of the metalinguistic nature of the distinctive features: they do not represent any concrete phenomenon or essence, although the description of the process of their production corresponds to existing physiological processes. The concept of phoneme is a relative abstraction, because it does not represent any actual realisation in speech. The actual realisation of sounds in speech is not studied by phonology but by phonetics.

Troubetzkoy was the first to distinguish phonology from phonetics, which deepened Saussure's insights. Phonetics studies the physical, not the functional, qualities of linguistic sounds through three perspectives: (a) their production by the human speech organs, articulatory phonetics; (b) their acoustic qualities as sound waves emitted from speaker to listener, acoustic phonetics; and (c) their physical effects on the human ear, auditory phonetics (Lyons 1968: 101–111). As in the case of phonemes, the phonetic identity of a unit (a phone) is not unambiguous, but is deduced from a field of similar sounds. Its phonological identity, on the other hand, is exact, because it is determined by a stable classification of distinctive features (for example dental or velar, plosive or fricative, voiced or unvoiced).

Phonemes are not vehicles of meaning; their syntagmatic combination leads to the next-level linguistic unit, the morpheme, which is the smallest unit to be a vehicle of signification and hence a sign. However, while the phoneme has no signification inside the language system, it may be invested with meaning in speech, thus acquiring an expressive function (Martinet 1970: 62). In other words, a particular use of a phoneme in speech may endow it with expressive meaning, as, for example, in the case of "I'm c**rrrr**azy for you, babe", in which "r" is prolonged and enhanced.

The implied signified of this prolonged "r" is something like "beyond any limit" and belongs to a second level of meaning, that of connotation (section 11 below).

6.3 Morphemes

In order, then, to reach signification in the language system, we have to pass to a higher level of organisation than the phoneme. The relation between units at this level, where the units are vehicles of signification (signs), is called "first articulation" (*première articulation*), while on the previous level the relation between phonemes is called "second articulation" (*deuxième articulation*, Martinet 1970: 13–15). This double articulation is a major characteristic of the organisation of natural language. Because linguistics was for many years a pilot science for semiotics, semiotics initially tried to artificially impose the principle of double articulation on all semiotic systems. It was soon demonstrated that this principle is not generalisable, because there are semiotic systems with only one articulation, such as the "monoplanar" semiotics of Greimas and Courtés (1979: Sémiotique), which can be either scientific semiotic systems such as algebra or non-scientific ones such as games; indeed, Eco has at one point argued that cinema is unique in having three articulations (he later withdrew his assertion, but it is an intriguing possibility; Eco 1972: 225–230).

Our first impression is that the signs of the first articulation are words. This is, however, an oversimplification, because the first signs we encounter are not necessarily words. The verb "jump", for example, is found in forms that are a combination of two signs: *jump* + *s*, which as a whole signifies "this-act-in-the-third-person-of-the-present-simple", or *jump* + *ed*, signifying "this-act-in-the-past-simple", or *jump* + *ing*, signifying "this-act-in-the-present-participle". Saussure (1971: 146–147) demonstrates that the correct decomposition of a word into meaningful units is not syllabification, but a division that displays the units to which signification is attached.

Although there is some disagreement over the naming of the lexicographical first part and the grammatical second part of a word, we follow the usage of Greimas and Courtés (1979: Lexème, Monème, Morphème) and call them both "morphemes" (*morphèmes*); "lexical morphemes" in the first case, and "grammatical morphemes" in the second). The morpheme is the simplest, hierarchically lowest sign. It is a vehicle of signification, but it has no independent existence and always appears in conjunction with another morpheme. With the mediation of these elementary signs, we pass to the independent units of signification, the words.

According to Troubetzkoy (1964: 36–39), the phonemes as "distinctive marks" compose a word as a "phonic whole", with its own silhouette, and this whole is a separate individuality and something more than the sum of its parts. Following the Saussurean rationale, phonemes and morphemes are the first successive levels of elements and relations that build the syntagmatic axis of the linguistic system. Then follows the word, and beyond the word the limited combination of words that Saussure recognized as a syntagm; from there, we pass to the sentence and finally the text.

6.4 Semes, sememes and lexemes

Elements and relations, however, form not only the field of syntactics, but also that of semantics, a field not studied analytically by Saussure. In semantics, the term "sememe" (in French, *sémème*) indicates the unit of signification corresponding to a morpheme. Just as the phoneme is derived from distinctive features, each sememe is metalinguistically described with the help of its own set of distinctive features, the "semes" (*sèmes*); Eco (1976: 84–85) uses instead the term "semantic markers". Semes, like phemes, are not isolated elements, but are the two terms of binary structures of opposition, the "semantic categories" (*catégories sémantiques*). The resulting sememe is not a simple sum of semes, but a structured whole following rules of transformation (Greimas and Courtés 1979: Sème, Carré sémiotique).

One more concept is important in order to round out our idea of the basic semantic concepts, that of "lexeme" (*lexème*). The lexeme refers to the signification of a word, but is not identical to the sememe. Greimas explains the difference by using the word "*tête*" [head]. In French dictionaries, *tête* is defined as the upper part of the human body, connected with the trunk through the neck or, in the case of animals, as the frontal body part where the brain is located (the same definition is given in English). This word, however, also has other significations both in French and in English, different from its initial sense. According to English dictionaries, it may signify a person as a whole (as in *per capita* income) or a person's position (head of state, head of the family). "Head" is also the summit (head of the class, head of a list) or the protruding edge of an object (headlights); it is the part that is most important (head of the table) or that precedes (head of a procession), as well as the climax of a situation (the situation came to a head), or something that looks or is in some respect like a head (head of a nail, head of the phalanx of the hand or the foot), or simply pressure (head of steam). *Head* as a lexeme covers the whole set of these signifieds and also other possible signifieds for which *head* could be used, and this whole represents all the sememes corresponding to the initial lexeme. These sememes are variants of the initial meaning of the word and the exact sememe referred to in each case is activated by the context into which the word is inserted, being thus a phenomenon of speech, a subject we shall deal with later (chapter 5: 1.1).

The seme is an abstract construct, not found as such in a dictionary. Semes are metalinguistic entities of meaning, rendered with the endings -*ity* (French -*ité*) or "ness". Greimas (1966: 32–36), as a first approach to the semic system (*système sémique*), gives as an example an analysis of three pairs of opposed lexemes related to six semes and composing a hierarchical tree structure. Starting from "spatiality", the system is analysed into "dimensionality" (and "non-dimensionality", which can be further analysed), "dimensionality" into "verticality" (*high* vs *low*) and "horizontality" and "horizontality" into "perspectivity" (*long* vs *short*) and "laterality" (*wide* vs *narrow*).[17] The first column of Table 1 shows the lexemes (in italics); the first line of the table shows the semes, and the symbols + and – refer to the presence or absence of a seme, respectively.

Table 1: Semic analysis of opposed pairs of lexemes according to Greimas (1966: 35).

Seme Lexeme	spatiality	dimensionality	verticality	horizontality	perspectivity	laterality
high vs	+	+	+	–	–	–
low	+	+	+	–	–	–
long vs	+	+	–	+	+	–
short	+	+	–	+	+	–
wide vs	+	+	–	+	–	+
narrow	+	+	–	+	–	+

We observe that, while all the pairs have in common the two semes of spatiality and dimensionality, each pair of lexemes refers to the presence of a set of semes and the absence of another set, in such a manner that it is opposed to the two other pairs. Note that this matrix is not in a position to secure the distinction between the two terms of each pair; one more seme is needed to achieve that. The distinction, for example, between "high" and "low" presupposes the semantic category *summitness* vs *baseness*; "high" is characterised by a + in respect to the first term of this opposition and a – in respect to the second term, while the opposite is the case with "low". As in the case of the phonological distinctive features, the coexistence of semes does not presuppose any particular order, but is manifested as a whole.

The units of the semantic field are thus also the result of elements and their relations. This fact allows the grouping of sememes on the basis of semes in speech, a matter which will concern us in chapter 5 (section 1.1).

---

[17] We believe that a more exact decomposition of horizontality would be to start with "directionality" (opposed to non-directionality) and proceed with the typical differentiation between the two opposed terms *axiality* vs *laterality*, the first pair leading to the opposition *frontality* vs *rearness* and the second to *rightness* vs *leftness*. In this case, the pairs of opposed lexemes to be analysed would be *high* vs *low*, *front* vs *back* and *right* vs *left*.

7 The concepts of difference and value in *langue*

We saw above that each phoneme corresponds to a different combination of distinctive features, with the result that each phoneme is different from all other phonemes; we also saw that each signified corresponds to a unique combination of semes, different from all other combinations. We shall see later in this chapter (section 10 below) that different cultures segment their semantic units differently to constitute their conception of the world, but they do not do so by isolating one unit from the other (for example, a colour is not called "blue" independently of the colour called "green"); on the contrary, the segmentation is done in a holistic and relativistic manner, based on the mechanism of *difference* (blue is defined as blue due to its difference with green). This phenomenon is absolutely generalisable: every level of the language system is founded upon difference, is *differential* in nature.

This fundamental fact is fully displayed with the commutation test. This test was devised for the level of signifiers, and in a purely linguistic context the test operates by replacing one of the elements of a signifier with another. If this replacement changes the signification of the signifier, we may deduce that the two elements, the replacement and that which it replaces, are phonemes (Troubetzkoy 1964: 49–50), and that signification is produced through difference. Consider the following words and their phonetic transcription:

bite /baɪt/	kite /kaɪt/
white /waɪt/	write /raɪt/
fight /faɪt/	height /haɪt/
light /laɪt/	night /naɪt/
sight /saɪt/	tight /taɪt/

Knowledge of the English language leads to the semantic identification of each word and suggests that they all have a different signification, i.e., that each word is different from all of the other words. The phonemic analysis allows us to identify the cause of the difference, since the last two phonemes [aɪ] and [t] remain unchanged in all words and the only position in which change occurs is the first one. Thus, not only can we define [b], [k], [w], [r], [f], [h], [l], [n], [s] and [t] as phonemes, but we also see that their alteration, leading to the realisation of one of them in each case, causes signification to change by producing difference.

7 The concepts of difference and value in *langue*

The dynamics of difference in the language system is interwoven, for Saussure, with the principle of conventionality (Saussure 1971: 163). As he states (1971: 166), "*dans la langue il n'y a que des différences [...] sans termes positifs*" [in the language system there are only differences [...] with no positive terms]. That the language system should have "no positive terms" seems incomprehensible, if not preposterous. Still, this is the quintessence of Saussure's linguistic theory, which brings the concepts of "system" and "difference" to the highest possible level of abstraction.

As we saw, Saussure defined his two main linguistics with reference to the axes of simultaneity and succession. His fundamental linguistics, synchronic linguistics, corresponds to the first axis and is founded on the language system. We also saw that this system becomes such due to the relation between the syntagmatic and the paradigmatic axes, to the structuring of each axis separately and to the structuring of the semantic field. In each case, the language system is built by elements and relations, but we also found that these relations are based on difference. And we now come to what we meant by the most abstract level in respect to differences. Saussure writes (1971: 116; see also Barthes 1964a: 113–114): "*la langue est un système de pures valeurs que rien ne détermine en dehors de l'état momentané de ses termes*" [the language system is a system of pure values, determined by nothing but the momentary state of its elements]. Thus, the pattern ruling the relations, in the form of differences, is "value" (*valeur*).

Let us follow the way Saussure defines value and see why it leads to the highly abstract level mentioned above.

Saussure invites us to pass from his initial suggestion of the connection (let us consider it as "perpendicular") between a signified and a signifier to a conception of another kind of connection (let us call it "horizontal"), that between a sign and other simultaneously existing signs of the system. In the first case, a specific signification is assigned to a sign, while in the second we are dealing with a *value*, which cannot be considered as identical to this signification.

Saussure gives many examples to demonstrate the existence of value. He takes three French synonyms: *redouter* [to dread], *craindre* [to fear] and *avoir peur* [to be afraid] and states that they have value only due to their opposition, because, if *redouter* was missing from the language system, its signification would be diffused in the other words. That is, the lack of one word would enrich the others and so there would be a systemic redistribution of signification, with the result that each of the remaining words would acquire a new semantic attribute. The same phenomenon is observed without such a re-distribution. Saussure refers to the expression "*un vieillard décrépit*" [a decrepit old man], to which a new attribute is added due to the signification attached to "*un mur décrépi*" [a crumbling or dilapidated wall].

On this occasion Saussure also repeats his criticism of the conception of language as a nomenclature, consisting of preformed concepts defined individually *a priori*, and argues that signification conceived as a signified is neither stable nor primary. Instead, he proposes the conception of value as *relational* signification. It is the value of a word which is compared with similar, but not identical, values of other words related to it, and thus its content is really determined in function of something outside it. The word, *"faisant partie d'un système [. . .] est revêtu, non seulement d'une signification, mais aussi et surtout d'une valeur, et c'est tout autre chose"* [being part of a system [. . .] it is invested, not only with signification, but also and mainly with a value, and this is an entirely different matter] – Saussure 1971: 160.

Value is *not* positively defined by its content – as is the case with the signified – but its meaning is purely differential and defined *negatively* by its relationship to the other values of the system; that is, in each position of the system, a value is what the other values are not. The relation between signified and signifier may be to some extent precise and give an idea of the reality of the language system, but under no circumstances does it deliver the essence of the language system, which is value (on value, see Saussure 1971: 158–162).

We can attempt to explain the concept of value by constructing an example from science fiction. Let us postulate a vast spatial field having the extension of a language system X. A great number of trips (relations) take place within its different subfields, the trajectories of which cross but are not inscribed in space. Each crossing of trajectories creates a place – a node – in space, but no node is a starting point or final destination and all places are transit places. No place is determined by its identity, but according to an abstract system of Cartesian coordinates having the form x_m, y_n, and therefore each one of them has a relative value-signification, recognisable only in relation to all the other place-values of the subfield. Each couple of coordinates is the value of one place. Imagine, now, that a society projects a hologram in each of these places; the holograms are selected from a coherent system of holograms and shaped like buildings, a different building in each place. In this way it attributes to each abstract and relational coordinate – each place-value – a specific signified attached to a signifier. While the holograms give the impression of reality, they are not actually present, but just optical illusions located on the background field of a system of differences (for example the place $x_m y_n$ differs from $x_{m+1} y_{n+1}$). This is the mechanism supporting value. The system of holograms implies the existence of the whole of the language system of the society, historically created by it. While the "real" system is abstract, the holograms, which give the impression of reality when compared to the "real" system, are the actual means allowing the society to communicate and continue existing.

Value creates both the signified and the signifier, and this is also true, according to Saussure, for all grammatical entities, even for the letters of the alphabet. As he observes:
(a) The letters are conventional, because there is no *a priori* relation between a letter and the sound to which it corresponds.
(b) Their value is purely differential and negative, because a letter may appear in different variants (for example b, *b*, **b**, ***b***, B) and must not be confused with any other letter.
(c) Their values operate only on the basis of oppositions within a fixed system with a determinate number of letters. This feature is, for Saussure, closely related to the previous one, while both features derive from the first.
(d) Their appearance (white or black, incised or relief) is irrelevant to the system, a feature also deriving from the first one.

The concept of value, then, founds a tangible system, which includes tangible linguistic elements and is a multi-level system of elements and relations, on an abstract theoretical system dominated by relations, in which the elements are a *by-product* of the relations.[18] We may now fully understand why Saussure considers that the pattern of differences of the language system is inseparable from the principle of conventionality. He deduces value from the conventionality of the language system, which is triggered by his first principle, the conventional relation between signified and signifier. The conceptual twins of conventionality and the differential nature of value is clearly expressed: "*[la langue] se meut à l'aide de la formidable machine de ses categories négatives, véritablement degagées de tout fait concret*" [the language system evolves with the help of the formidable machine of its negative categories, entirely detached from any concrete fact] – Saussure 2002: 76; see also 64–66.

The conceptual twins of conventionality and the differentiality of value is the cornerstone of Jacques Derrida's deconstruction, with the profound difference, however, that Derrida inverses the hierarchy between these concepts. Saussure starts from the incompatibility between concepts and the external world, taking the external world as given, and his concern is to detach the language system from this world (whence the extension of conventionality to include the relation between signified and reality), ending with the systemic constitution of *langue*. Derrida, on the other hand, considers as given this constitution and, from this starting point, deduces the detachment of *langue* from

---

[18] This is also the principal idea of Lévi-Strauss's structural anthropology.

the external world, i.e., its conventionality, to argue on this basis that we cannot have any access to knowledge of the external world.

Criticising structuralism, Derrida observes that the concept of structure presupposes a present centre, a stable origin (a "transcendental signified"). This centre, which keeps the centred structure stable, has in the history of Western metaphysics received a variety of definitions (such as God, consciousness, substance, matter, history, class struggle, political economy, truth), all of which without exception define being as presence. Derrida concedes that the centre is a necessary function, resulting in the organisation of the structure and limiting the free play of signification, but he argues that it neutralises the "structurality of structure" (*structuralité de la structure*). Any "central" signified, which could be considered as primary, positive, transcendental, is simply part of the system of differences and any process of signification is just a play of differences. Because of this play, every linguistic element is constituted by the "traces" in it of the other elements of the system, with as a result than no element is actually present – this, we saw, is how Saussure defined value. Derrida applies exactly the same logic to the macro-level of texts (Derrida 1967a: 42, 409–411, 423, 427, 1967b: 78, 239–240 and 1972b: 16–18, 37–38, 45–46, 78–80, 87–88, 125–126). In other words, there is no element external to the semiotic system that can anchor the system.[19]

In a general sense, the omnipresence of semiotics is unquestionable, because there is no possibility of any direct knowledge of the world, given that any cultural knowledge is mediated by the semiotic apparatus. However, Derrida does differentiate between semiotically relevant and non-relevant phenomena. He points out that the word "*communication*" is not limited to a semantic or conceptual content, or to a semiotic operation, even less to a linguistic exchange. A shift of force may be communicated, in the sense of being transmitted, and two distant sites may communicate through a passage or an opening. In this case, Derrida concludes that "*ce qui est transmis, communiqué, ce ne sont pas des*

---

19 Compare this to Saussure (2002: 65), for whom the specificity of the science of language is that its objects "*n'ont jamais de réalité* en soi *ou* à part *des autres objets à considérer; n'ont absolument aucun substratum à leur existence hors de* leur différence *ou en DES* différences *de toute espèce que l'esprit trouve moyen d'attacher à LA différence fondamentale (mais que leur différence fait toute leur existence à chacun): mais sans que l'on sorte nulle part de cette donnée fondamentalement et à tout jamais négative de la DIFFÉRENCE de deux termes, et non des propriétés d'un terme*" [never possess an existence *of their own* or *apart* from other objects to be considered; they have absolutely no substratum for their existence outside *their difference* or in *DIFFERENCES* of all kinds that the mind contrives to attach to THE fundamental difference (but it is their difference that gives each of them their whole existence): but on the condition that we never depart from this fundamentally and forever negative given of the DIFFERENCE of two terms and not of the qualities of one term].

phénomènes de sens ou de signification" [what is transmitted, communicated, are not phenomena of meaning or signification] – Derrida 1972a: 367–368.

What Derrida implies here is that although every statement has meaning, not every statement is about meaning. We stress this point because it allows us to clarify what we meant with the articulation of the semiotic with material society. We do not conceive of material society as an objectively knowable essence, but as a cultural construct, as is also the semiotic dimension. Up to here, then, we would agree with Derrida. But we differ from him because his theory leads him to consider all texts as equivalent, while we consider the material social construct as explanatory (chapter 9).[20]

8 Form and substance

The two concepts of form and substance were, as we saw, postulated by Saussure, but the concept of substance was subsequently elaborated in depth by Hjelmslev. The discussion below is based mainly on Hjelmslev's essay (first published in 1954) La stratification du langage (1971: 44–76). He calls "plane of expression" the plane (or stratum) of the vehicles of ideas, the signifiers, and "plane of content" the plane of the ideas themselves, the signifieds, and he believes that the two planes may be studied separately. On this basis, the signifier becomes the "form of the expression" and the signified the "form of the content". The linking of these two forms constitutes the sign. The expression-form is connected to a "substance of the expression" and the content-form to a "substance of the content".

Hjelmslev extends this form/substance division, explicitly of Saussurean origin but modified by Hjelmslev (1961: 54, 74, 76, 77, 102, 123), to a concept that has been translated in English as "purport" (*matière* in French, *mening* in Danish). He starts by distancing himself from Saussure, considering that the Saussurean substance, because it does not exist independently from the form, has no temporal or hierarchical priority over it. Hjelmslev's purport is wider than Saussure's substance and is of two sorts: there is a content-purport and an expression-purport. For the content-purport, Hjelmslev generally uses terms very close to Saussure's terms for the thought-substance ("*nébuleuse*", "*chaotique*"), such as "thought itself", "amorphous thought-mass", "unanalyzed entity", "amorphous continuum" (50–52, 54–55, 74, 77). However, he clarifies that, for both expression and content,

---

[20] This is not the place to develop this argument, which goes back to the discussion and criticism of Derrida's narrow axiomatic point of departure (see Lagopoulos 2012a).

> ... the description of the purport ... may in all essentials be thought of as belonging partly to the sphere of *physics* and partly to that of (social) *anthropology*. [. . .] The substance of both planes can be viewed both as physical entities (sounds in the expression plane, things in the content plane) and as the conception of these entities held by the users of the language. Consequently for both planes both a physical and a phenomenological description of the purport should be required. (77–78)

Thus, unlike Saussure's substance, Hjelmslev's purport has a double nature: it covers both Saussure's linguistic – and by extension semiotic – substance and an ontological dimension "out there".

An example from the semiotics of urban space may be helpful to understand the difference between the ontological and semiotic substance for the expression plane. Imagine that you bring to mind the mental image of the street where you live. This mental image is not, in fact, an accurate image of the street as it would be depicted by a photograph or by surveying data. First, your mental image distorts the geometry of the environment as known from surveying data (your image and the data diverge on distances and on relations of scale between spatial volumes). Second, your image does not include all the details of the environment (it includes the bakery and your neighbour's blue door, but the balconies of the fourth – or fifth, you are not sure – small apartment building after your house, and the building on the other side of the street, are missing from your image). Our mental image is never actually a complete record of our whole environment; as a result of our interaction with the environment as socially, culturally and even psychologically constituted persons with individual characteristics, we conceive only certain selected parts of it. The urban environment rendered in the surveying data is for semiotics the ontological matter "out there"; it remains an inactive extra-semiotic material. However, a part of this material is activated, assumed by semiosis, "semioticised" and becomes the material vehicle of the urban signifier, its substance of expression (on the physical level, which we shall discuss below).

Hjelmslev deepens Saussure's position on the concept of substance, because he does not see the two substances of expression and content as uniform, but considers that both the substance of the expression and the substance of the content are subdivided into three hierarchical levels. These hierarchically ordered levels are, from the higher to the lower: the level of social ("collective") appreciation, apperception or evaluation; the socio-biological level; and the physical level; all three precede the two planes of the form.

A closer scrutiny of these levels reveals their direct debt to Saussure. More specifically, Saussure's circuit of *parole* starts with a mental concept, a fact of consciousness, a *signifié*, to which an acoustic image or *signifiant* is associated;

both are of a psychic nature in the mind of person A. The circuit then goes on to a process that Saussure calls physiological, focused on the organs of phonation, and continues with the physical process of the sound waves reaching the ear of person B and the acoustic image being transmitted to the mind, where it is associated with the corresponding concept (Saussure 1971: 27–29).

This is the point of departure for the three levels of Hjelmslev's substance (though he indicates that all levels need not be present in all cases). He uses the same term as Saussure for the physical process (and specifies it as "acoustic"); Saussure's physiological process Hjelmslev calls "socio-biological"; and Saussure's auditory process is located on Hjelmslev's level of social appreciation or apperception. The plane of the form is identical in its semiotic nature for both Saussure's model and Hjelmslev's model. It seems that Hjelmslev was inspired by Saussure's presentation of the processes of expression and adopted them to define the levels of content in a *symmetrical* manner (which is not *a priori* necessary).

Hjelmslev sees the relation between levels as syntagmatic: the lower level "selects" or "manifests", in the sense of *determines*, the higher level, and the latter "specifies" the former; the relation between the level of social appreciation and the plane of the form is also one of selection. The hierarchy for both substance strata is, from the higher to the lower, the level of social appreciation, the socio-biological level and the physical level. According to Hjelmslev, there is a unilateral function between the substance as a whole as variable and the form as constant.

When Hjelmslev (1971: 59) refers for the first time analytically to the levels of the phonic substance, he presents them in a particular order, starting with the description of the "physiological" (socio-biological) level, continuing with the description of the physical level and ending with the auditory description of the level of social appreciation. This order of description faithfully follows the Saussurean communication circuit, but he alters the order of the hierarchical levels in his final position (Hjelmslev 1971: 62 – 63).

These final hierarchical levels and their relationships, for both the expression substance and the content substance, are shown in Figure 3. Comparison of this to Figure 2b, illustrating the process according to Saussure, shows the far more complex construction proposed by Hjelmslev.

Figure 3 allows us to present in greater detail the nature of the substance levels according to Hjelmslev. We start with the substance levels of the expression stratum:

(1) *Level of social appreciation* or apperception. For both the stratum of content and the stratum of expression, this is the primary level and the immediate substance linked to form, directly relevant to semiotics. In linguistics it

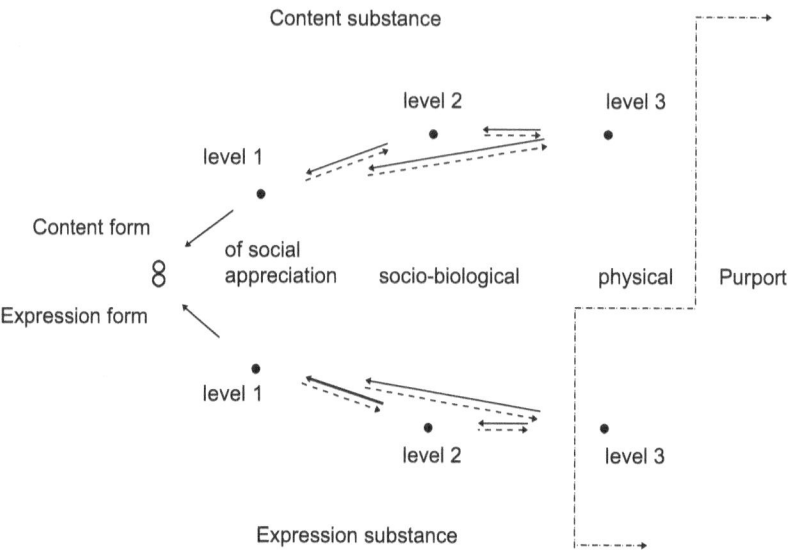

Figure 3: The three hierarchical levels of the substance strata and their relationships in Hjelmslev. ← : selection. --→ : specification. → : purport.

corresponds to the apperception of sounds and their auditory description. Hjelmslev gives as examples the description of sounds as *light* vs *dark*, *strong* vs *weak*, *long* vs *short*, etc.

(2) *Socio-biological level.* This level, which is not always present according to Hjelmslev, is physiological and in linguistics corresponds to the myokinetic and articulatory phonological description, in other words the description of distinctive features. The examples given by Hjelmslev concern pronunciation and oppositions such as *voiced* vs *unvoiced*, *nasal* vs *oral*, *rounded* vs *unrounded*, etc.

(3) *Physical level.* This is the acoustic level, implying the description of *physical* "things". It corresponds to the Saussurean description of sound waves and is studied, according to Hjelmslev (1961: 125), by the metasemiology of denotative semiotics. Since this is philosophically an ontological description and in linguistics belongs to phonetics, we infer that the physical level of the substance of the expression *does not* concern signification. To come back to our example from the semiotics of space, the sound waves are comparable to the materials from which space is constructed. Semiotics is concerned with the fact that a particular part of this material continuum is activated from the point of view of signification, not with the physical

description of geographical space as such, which belongs to the ontological level, "the sphere of physics" (1961: 77–78).

We observe that all three levels of the expression are of *metalinguistic* nature, whether they have a semiotic object or not.

The substance levels of the content stratum are:

(1) *Level of social appreciation*. Hjelmslev considers this level as the immediate substance of the content and the first duty of the semiotician. It is concerned with the description of public opinion and collective evaluations, related to tradition and uses. He clarifies that this level, like the corresponding level of expression, concerns relatively naive appreciations, in other words, spontaneous valorisations. He gives as linguistic examples the adjectives "big", "small", "good", "bad". At this level, for Hjelmslev, we find the contact between linguistics (and manifestly other semiotic fields) and anthropology.

(2) *Socio-biological level*. This level concerns the description of the factors that act on the elements of appreciation. It seems to us that it can be identified with *situation* and thus directly associated with sociolinguistics.

(3) *Physical level*. Concerning this level, Hjelmslev (1971: 60) states that *"une 'chose' physique peut recevoir des descriptions sémantiques bien différentes selon la civilisation envisagée"* [a physical "thing" may be the object of very different semantic descriptions depending on the culture being considered]. These "things" can be products of culture, such as "house" or "king", or belong to nature, as is the case with "mountain" or "firtree". They are, according to Hjelmslev, differently defined in a society which knows and *"recognises"* them (his italics) than in another society for which they are foreign. He points out that "elephant" means something different for a Hindu or African, who uses it and has certain feelings towards it, and for a European society in which it is an object of curiosity, exposed in zoological gardens, circuses or menageries and described in zoology textbooks. With the exception of the textbooks, where the word is used in a metalinguistic sense, all the other examples concern spontaneous cultural semiotics, which we believe is the centre of gravity of Hjelmslev's argument: he is referring to cultural semantic micro-sets, which would seem to contradict his position that the purport on this level refers to "physical entities" or "things".

Hjelmslev considers that the substances of level 3 of both the expression and the content are physical entities and subject to a physical description, while those of the other levels correspond to the "conception of these entities held by the users of the language" and are subject to a phenomenological description. He states that the ontological purport (level 3) is studied by non-linguistic sciences, a study leading "to a recognition of a 'form' essentially of the same sort as the linguistic 'form', although of non-linguistic nature". However, he considers all the substance levels as semiotic, because they are ruled by the form (Hjelmslev 1961: 77–80). This seems to be contradictory, and we prefer to opt for a third solution. Figure 3, in agreement with Hjelmslev's first position, excludes from semiotics the third level of the expression substance, but not the third level of the content substance, which as we saw still involves cultural meaning.

These five substance levels, then, are *cultural* levels. In the case of natural language, the socio-biological level for both Saussure and Hjelmslev refers to the myokinetic and articulatory movements of speech; that is, it has as starting point a physiological process. Perhaps the term "socio-*biological*" was used by Hjelmslev because of the physiological nature of this process, but it cannot be generalised, because this is not the case for other semiotic systems; the semiotics of space, for example, is to a large extent anchored in physical space and has nothing to do with biology. The second component of "socio-biological" must originate from the physical level of expression and the obvious term is "socio-*physical*".

Hjelmslev's complex stratification is the clue to understanding the ambition of his glossematics. He wants to install linguistics, and semiotics in general, as the cornerstone of all non-linguistic sciences, believing that "we are thus led to regard all science as centred around linguistics" (Hjelmslev 1961: 78, 108–109).

Helmslev (1961: 106, 132, 133) defines in very general terms the concepts of "selection"/"manifestation"/"determination" and "specification" and does not give concrete examples of their application. Let us take some examples. Referring to the content stratum, Hjelmslev argues that the level of social appreciation "selects" the content form. For Saussure, on the contrary, his *nébuleuse* is a passive substratum that comes to life only due to its segmentation by semiosis, whence the conclusion that it is the form that "selects" the substance. We can imagine a more complex situation, in which the *nébuleuse* is not passive but corresponds to the world of experience, which is a dynamic world virtually open to semiotisation. In such a case, the substance exerts *pressure* on the form and the latter "selects" within the context of this limitation.

Things are not symmetrical in the case of the expression stratum. As we saw, the physical sound continuum of level 3 does not concern meaningful units, as is the case with the corresponding content substance, but belongs to the physical world: the physical expression substance does not "select" the phonemic level, but inversely culture makes *cultural* selections from the physical sound continuum, as happens *mutatis mutandis* with the content substance.

Finally, there is an uncomfortable mixing of criteria in respect to the definition of the levels of each plane and between planes. The physical level of the substance of the expression plane is not, as we saw, of a semiotic nature and all three levels of this plane are metalinguistic. On the other hand, the first and the third level of the substance of the content concern spontaneous semiosis – and are thus not metalinguistic – and the situational factor is intercalated between them.

However, Hjelmslev's elaboration of the two concepts of form and substance bring to the foreground a major semiotic fact, namely that a form may be incorporated into more than one substance. To give an obvious example, the same linguistic form can use sound as the expression substance in speech and the letters of the alphabet in a written text. There are, however, many other cases in which things are not so obvious, which is why it is important to bear in mind that a semiotic text, either as a conceptual entity or in natural language, can use as vehicle a two-dimensional painting or a three-dimensional architectural substance. In other words, the concept of substance allows us to study the circulation of the same text between different cultural systems, a fact which confirms semiotics as a theory of culture. This is the case with transmedia translation and in part with intertextuality (chapter 8: 2.8). If a form can have as vehicle different substances, the opposite is also true, i.e., different forms can have as vehicle the same substance, as happens, for example, with different literary genres, all expressed in writing.

9 The non-semiotic triangle

As we saw earlier, if we leave aside the most abstract level of value, the sign and the domain of semiotics are defined, for Saussure, with the two terms of signifier and signified. Peirce does not use this dyadic conception, because for him the sign implies a relational triadic structure. In order to understand its origin, we must start from Peirce's initial philosophical premises. His starting point is Immanuel Kant's concept of categories, universal forms of understanding which are presupposed for the formation of logical judgements.

In Peirce's hierarchy of sciences, the top position is occupied by mathematics. Mathematics is followed by philosophy, the first part of which is phenomenology, followed hierarchically by "semiotic", also part of philosophy and equated with logic. Phenomenology is by Peirce given the task of defining the universal elements of experience, that is, the categories, and takes the form of a mathematical logic of relations, a use of mathematics prescribed by his hierarchy. On this basis, Peirce defines three universal categories, which correspond to three different modes of approaching phenomenal entities: "Firstness", the mode of considering them in their property of having "monadic", non-relational, qualities; "Secondness", the mode of approaching them as involving a "dyadic" (two-term) relationship, in which case each term of the relation has monadic properties; and "Thirdness", the mode of seeing them as terms of a "triadic" (three-term) relationship, such that dyadic relationships exist between each couple of terms. Peirce believes that a greater complexity of relationship is only apparent and can be reduced to combinations of these three modes. These categories as phenomenological principles allow semiotic, according to Peirce, to formulate all classes of signs, thus accounting for any kind of experience, knowledge and representation. In other words, these categories would lead to the fundamental classification of signs.

For Peirce, the sign (in the wide sense) – that is, anything that conveys meaning – implies a triadic relational structure, which for him is the only relationship that incorporates all three of the above categories. The first term of this relationship is the *representamen* ("sign" in the narrow sense), which stands in some manner for something (anything) else, its (immediate) "object" (the second term of the relationship) in such a way that it brings about a response to it, which is the idea it provokes, the interpretation of its meaning by an interpreter; this idea is its "interpretant", the third term of the relationship, which stands in the same relationship to the object as the *representamen*. This triadic relationship, the sign, is according to Peirce a "representation". His *representamen* is identical to Saussure's signified, but his interpretant is broader than Saussure's signified, though it overlaps with it. According to Peirce, the very definition of the *representamen* implies its naming by another *representamen*, which attracts its own interpretant and so on, opening a chain of a theoretically "unlimited semiosis" (Figure 4).

The Peircean categories and triadic structure are used by Eco to construct an interesting approach to the emergence of semiosis. Eco argues that Peirce's concept of "ground" can be identified with Firstness (as Eco writes, a "singularity", a "pure quality"). The ground "seems to constitute the initial moment of the cognitive process" (Eco 2000: 60; see also 62), an unsegmented continuum[21] which may be considered as the *terminus a quo* of semiosis and offers the "presemiotic" possibility of segmentation, thus installing a "natural primary iconism" that Eco calls "protosemiotics" or "natural semiotics" (Eco 2000: 3, 14, 62–64, 100, 102, 103, 107–109, 112, 114–117, 119).[22]

---

[21] Parallel to Hjelmslev's ontological substance of the expression and Saussure's *matière plastique*.
[22] Eco (2000: 109) specifies that this is a "presemiotic" domain.

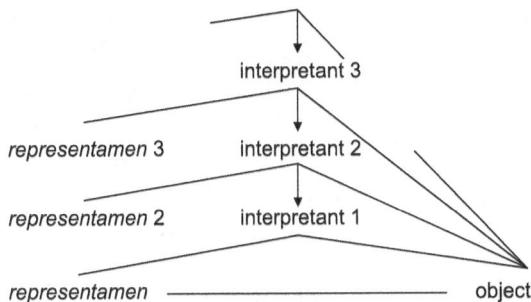

Figure 4: The process of unlimited semiosis according to Peirce.

Peirce distinguishes between the concepts of the "dynamical object" and the "immediate object". As Eco writes, the dynamical object or set of stimuli, Firstness, is the driving force for the production of semiosis. Eco considers that the ground, when consciously inserted into the process of interpretation, may be considered as a "selector", determining the perceptual signal (see below) by filtering the properties of the dynamical object that will be made relevant by the immediate object – which is, for Peirce and Eco, the object as represented in the sign, its meaning. Through this passage, primary iconism is transformed into meaning (Eco 2000: 14, 65, 112, 117, 358, 383, 402 n. 4).

Eco's focus for the discussion of Hjelmslev's form is Thirdness, Peirce's domain of the sign. This is, for Eco, the domain of conceptual understanding and perceptual judgement, identified with the immediate object. The latter maintains traces of primary iconism, but it transforms the dynamical object as token into a generic quality as type, through the mediation of the *representamen*. In Thirdness, the level of the "Nuclear Content", a content is associated to an expression coming from Secondness, and thus this content, an interpretation on a higher cognitive level, has as its basis perception (see below); these are collective interpretations. Once the immediate object emerges, it becomes subject to the process of unlimited semiosis; the Nuclear Content is identified with a set of interpretants (Eco 2000: 13, 60–65, 113, 115, 119, 136–137, 143, 145).

On the expression plane, Saussure passes directly from substance to form. Hjelmslev, on the other hand, as we saw inserts two semiotic substance levels between the two. Eco proposes one level, the nature of which is Secondness. The passage from Firstness to Secondness is achieved through individual sensation, "a reaction of the senses" (64). In Secondness, a stage of greater concreteness, two qualities may be opposed (Eco mentions a yellow chair with a green cushion). Something coming from Firstness enters perception, a stimulus, acting as an index that there is something to perceive, individualising the chair, which is then incorporated into the perceptual judgement. Secondness is the level of the Peircean percept, a "dumb", "stupid and inane" percept (114–115), a perceptual signal (117) standing for itself, not for something else (109, 114, 125), a perceptual iconism (340) and not a sign (107). Nevertheless, the percept is a "Cognitive Type" attached to naming and implying recognition and reference. It is meaning of a pre-linguistic, pre-categorical, pre-classificatory nature. The perceptual process establishes the identity between the perceptual judgement and the immediate object and between the latter and the *representamen*. The percept is not represented by the perceptual judgement, but the latter warrants the former (Eco 2000: 103, 110, 119, 130–131, 136, 138–139, 144–145, 340, 377). At this level, "we must perceive substances as forms of expression" (383).

It is this level, an "unclear blend" (64), that Eco wishes to integrate within semiotics, i.e., to see "perception as a semiosic process" (125; see also 138, 382–383).[23]

Eco's argument stems, as he himself writes, from the question whether the limits of interpretation "are only cultural and textual or something that lies concealed at greater depths" (3–4). His concern seems to be that Saussure's insistence on the complete arbitrariness of the sign risks leading to an idealist conception of meaning, in which semiotic systems (and thus culture) are seen as entirely independent of the real world. However, in his praiseworthy effort to root semiosis in a materialist conception, against mentalism (Eco 2000: 107, 401, n.4), Eco risks ending up with universals. As he puts it, the unsegmented continuum of experience, "while it is *propositionally amorphous*, it is not entirely *perceptually chaotic*" and "provides directives for intersubjectively homogeneous perception, even between subjects that refer to different systems of propositions" (256). The recognition of "likeness" functions on the perceptual level as an "innate experience of likeness" (347–348).

In order to support his argument, Eco has to present "the equivalences established by a code" as "a scleroticized form of semiosis", so that he can conclude that the perceptual process is one of primary semiosis, a perceptual semiotics (254). The continuum is not perceptually chaotic, because it has been

---

23 There is a marked convergence between Eco and Deely, though there are also important divergences. One of the major differences is that Deely combines Peirce with the ideas of Uexküll; he is one of the co-writers of the semiotic manifesto referred to in chapter 2 (section 3). Like Eco, Deely operates with a direct passage from the physical world to sensation and a continuous development of the cognitive activity of semiosis from sensation – thus pushing the threshold of semiosis even lower than Eco – to perception, the domain of the human *Umwelt*, and, finally, to the world of signs, the *Innenwelt*, through the mediation of culture (Deely 2001: 119, 338, 379–380, 649–650, 660, 683, 695–697, 721).

subject to "a 'wild' and as yet nonsystematic semiosis" (256).²⁴ Of course, Eco is well aware that he is opening a can of worms, this is why he states that "it might be decided that the question is wholly nominalistic" and that, if we identify semiosis with institutionalised signs, then primary semiosis "would be purely metaphorical", "only a precondition of semiosis", and he has "no problem in speaking of perceptual presemiosis" (127). His way out of this dilemma is that there is "no evident fracture" between these two phases (127). But this argument would make pointless his use of the three Peircean categories and does not provide a satisfactory resolution of the conflict between culture and universals.

In sum, Eco's position is doubly disturbing: it involves the individual emergence of a kind of pre-signifier determined by the referent (see below), a view analogous to the additive logic of nomenclature instead of Saussure's relational definition of the sign system, as well as the priority of a pre-signifier *leading* somehow to a full signified, as opposed to the Saussurean conventional link between the two.

Peirce's triadic definition allows us to understand his fundamental epistemological attitude in respect to the sign. He conceives of the sign as an individual representation and, as we shall see immediately below, the different theoretical classes of signs that follow from operations with the main concepts of the above framework lead him to a quest for their classification. Saussure also advances a theory of the sign, but focuses not on the individual sign but on the relations between signs and the rules governing these relations. Structural linguistics and Saussurean semiotics operate epistemologically with a structural framework of a network of signs. Sociolinguistics (section 12 below) shifts from structure to function, from the language system to speech/discourse and to the environment of speech and communication, and thus operates epistemologically with a functional framework of the sign. Peirce, however, operates epistemologically with the individual sign in isolation and a classificatory framework for different signs, which is why it is not possible epistemologically to pass from this philosophical stance to any syntagmatic textual analysis or to relate the paradigmatic analysis to the syntagmatic.

On the basis of his threefold definition of the sign and the three categories, Peirce proposes two groups of interrelated classifications of signs. The first group follows from the application of his three universal categories to each term of the triadic sign structure and thus leads to three consecutive trichotomies. The first, considered as the simplest trichotomy, follows from the application of the categories to the *representamen* and defines three possible classes of signs: "quali-sign", "sin-sign" and "legi-sign". The application of the categories to the object leads to

---

24 We note the metaphorical nature of the pair of opposites – *scleroticized* vs *wild* – that Eco uses to support his position.

a second trichotomy, establishing three kinds of relationship of the *representamen* to the object, the well-known classification of "icon", "index" and "symbol". A third trichotomy, which is the most complex, follows from the application of the categories to the interpretant and leads to three possible types of interpretants, "rheme" (concept), "dicent sign" (sentence) and "argument".

For the second of Peirce's groups, which follows from the relation between the above trichotomies, we can imagine that the classes of each trichotomy are arranged according to three lines, the one following the other from top to bottom according to the sequence above and forming a tree structure. Specific possibilities of relations between the classes of each level and those of their inferior level are established and, in this manner, the ten sign classes formulated by Peirce in 1903 are generated.

Thinking that the logic through which this classification was constructed was not unquestionable, Peirce – but generally not the semioticians following him today – passed in 1904 to a different logical scheme and classification. This classification is far more extensive and in theory results in the generation of sign classes up to the tenth power of ten, although in practice they are much fewer. Peirce never stabilised his sign classification and his later estimates range from 66 classes up to ten billion (on the above, see Peirce 1932, 1: § 300–353 and 2: § 228, 233–264, 303–308; also Pape 1998; Sebeok 1994, 2: Peirce, Charles Sanders (1839–1914); Eco 1976: 68–69).

While Saussure's position, rejecting nomenclature and opting for value, excludes the relation of the sign to the external world, this is not the case with Peirce's semiotic. His second trichotomy distinguishes, as we saw, three types of signs which result from the way in which a sign indicates its object. The first is the icon, which resembles or imitates its object; thus, Peirce considers as icons not only images, but also diagrams based on analogy and metaphors. The second is the index: he states that "psychologically, the action of indices depends upon association of contiguity". The index refers to a "dynamical (including spatial) connection", between two physical objects, and this is the usual understanding of it in the bibliography, with examples such as the footprint of an animal indicating its passage or the presence of smoke indicating fire. However, Peirce's definition of the index should be understood in a wider sense, because it includes, for example, certain grammatical categories, the letters used as symbols in algebra, the letters A, B, C, etc. accompanying a geometrical figure, or a label accompanying a diagram.[25] The third type of sign is

---

[25] As he writes,"No matter of fact can be stated without the use of some sign serving as an index. If A says to B, 'There is fire', B will ask, 'Where?' Thereupon A is forced to use an index [. . .]. If A

the symbol, which Peirce defines as ruled by habit, that is, a set of associations, and as denoting by virtue of its interpretant (Peirce 1932, 2: § 305). The symbol no longer has any resemblance or real connection to the object, i.e., it is arbitrarily linked to it, and it is the set of associations that ensures its interpretation. Thus, Peirce's symbol is identical to Saussure's conventional sign.

The two concepts of icon and index clash with Saussurean theory, because they bring into the relevance of semiotics the extra-semiotic "referent". This term was introduced by Charles K. Ogden and Ivor A. Richards. Apparently based on Peirce, they formulated a theoretical diagram in the form of a triangle, which they argue is central to the "science of symbolism" or "theory of signs", the aim of which is the study of language and other kinds of symbols and their relation to thought. This science, for Ogden and Richards, is the essential presupposition for any other science.

With their triangle they intend to illustrate the three factors involved in any proposition formulated or understood during communication. These factors are: the "symbol" (left vertex at the base of the triangle), which is a sign used as an instrument of thought and for communicational purposes; the "reference" or "thought" (upper vertex) and the "referent" (right vertex at the base of the triangle), which is that which is represented by the symbol. The symbol symbolises the reference and the latter refers to the referent. When we speak, the symbol is caused by the reference (cf. Saussure's direction from *concept* to *image acoustique*), but also by the associated non-verbal, emotional factors connected to the "feeling-signs" (these connotative factors are not illustrated in the diagram, but their place would be to the left of the reference). When we hear a spoken word, the symbol causes the appearance of the reference (once more, cf. Saussure), as well as of the feeling-signs.

Ogden and Richards also explain the relations between the vertices of their triangle. On the right side, referent and reference are related either by a (to a greater or lesser degree) direct relation or by an indirect relation of cause-and-effect (we recognise here the concept of language as nomenclature rejected by Saussure). At the base of the triangle, the symbol and the referent are not directly connected, except in cases where the symbol resembles the referent to a greater or lesser degree, i.e., is a representation of the referent (Ogden and Richards [1923] 1985: xiv–xv, 6–15, 23, 203, 205, 223, 243, 249–250). Such a triadic relation was formulated almost two and a half millennia ago by the Stoic philosophers.

---

points his finger to the fire, his finger is dynamically connected with the fire [. . .]. If A's reply is, 'Within a thousand yards from here', the word 'here' is an index; for it has precisely the same force as if he had pointed energetically to the ground between him and B".

For them, Ogden and Richards's symbol is the "*simaínon*" [signifier], identified with the voice; what Odgen and Richards call reference is the "*simainómenon*", the situation denoted by the voice and conceived by the mind, and their referent is the "*tynchánon*" [the thing referred to], the external thing.

Ogden and Richard's referent, the external thing referred to, is clearly not part of semiotics. Greimas and Courtés (1979: Culture, Monde naturel, Référent) replace the referent with their "semiotics of the natural world". In this manner, they argue, the problematics of the referent turns into a correlation between any semiotics (for example linguistic or visual) and this semiotics of the natural world. The "objective" world is replaced by this discursive structure of multiple semiotics, covering the vast domain of the semiotics of culture, that is, the semantic universe of a culture.[26]

The icon and the index of Peirce are not throughout extra-semiotic, but are so in their aspect of resemblance (in the first case) and causal connection (in the second) between two physical objects. Thus, from the Saussurean viewpoint, only their other aspects, together with the Peircean symbol, appertain to the domain of semiotics; as Eco writes, "Objects are not considered within Saussure's linguistics and are considered within Peirce's theoretical framework only when discussing particular types of signs such as icons and indices" (Eco 1976: 60). For Eco, the icon and the index imply "the presence of the referent as a discriminant parameter, a situation which is not permitted by the theory of codes proposed in this book" (178; see also 115–116 and the discussion in the chapters The referential fallacy, 58–66, and Critique of iconism, 191–216).

In his later work, however, Eco revised his view of the visual image, bringing it much closer to Peirce (as is evident from his use of Peirce discussed above). He argues that "there are semiosic phenomena in which, even if we know that we are dealing with a sign, before perceiving it as a sign of something else we must first perceive it as a set of stimuli that creates the effect of our being in the presence of the object" (Eco 2000: 377). He nevertheless insists that this Peircean approach is compatible with the structuralist and anthropological framework of his earlier work. In any case, while his new views may present a philosophical interest, they do not lead to any useful methodological and technical semiotic operations.

To do justice to Peirce, he is a philosopher, not a linguist. We referred at the end of the previous chapter to the difference between science and philosophy as two distinct domains of knowledge. Science is constituted exclusively

---

[26] They also state that the semiotics of the natural world consists of perceptible qualities, affecting an individual without any linguistic mediation.

on the basis of the law of relevance, while philosophy meditates on just about everything, without concern for the principle establishing science. Thus, Peirce is fully legitimate within his own domain, and his views are a subject of discussion among philosophers, but they encounter science only on a high level of abstraction, as for example on the matter of the emergence of semiosis. The scientific point of view will adopt the more operational theory, which is what Eco does in his structuralist vein.

In Figure 5, we present the vertices of the theoretical triangle according to the five approaches presented above. The very structure of this triangle makes it a non-semiotic triangle, since it involves the referent.

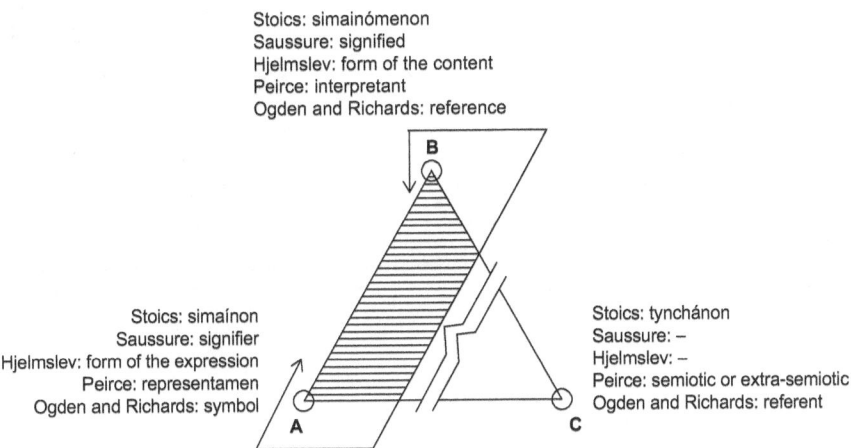

Figure 5: The theoretical triangle according to different approaches. Hatching: the domain of semiotics.

This triangle becomes non-semiotic in the cases of the Stoics, Peirce (with reference to the aspects of the icon and index discussed above) and Ogden and Richards. It remains semiotic in the cases of Saussure, Hjelmslev and Peirce (with reference to the semiotic aspects of the icon and index, as well as the symbol). Peirce's referential fallacy follows from his epistemology of the sign as representation. When the triangle is limited to the couple A and B – when, that is, A, B and C are no longer in a triadic relation, not vertices of a triangle but a dyadic couple of terms – only then do we enter the semiotic domain. There is a world of difference between the two models.

10 The signified as a cultural unit

The banishing of the referent from semiotics is in alignment with the rejection of the concept of language as a nomenclature and the adoption of the principle of conventionality. It is also in alignment with Eco's position that meaning "from a semiotic point of view [. . .] can only be a *cultural unit*"; he also states that this "cultural unit can be defined semiotically as a semantic unit inserted into a system" (Eco 1976: 67). We shall try to illustrate this position with some examples, starting with two examples from Hjelmslev.

Hjelmslev (1961: 54) constructs a table comparing the "semantic zone" covered by the words for wood, tree and forest. He uses three languages, Danish, German and French, to which Eco (1972: 73–74 and 1976: 73) added Italian and we add Greek and English (Table 2). To simplify things, we have omitted words for "small groups of trees" (*copse* and *grove* in English, *Gehölz* in German, *alsos* and *alsyllio* in Greek).

Table 2: The signified as a cultural unit.

Danish	German	French	Italian	Greek	English
trae	Baum	arbre	albero	déndro	tree
skov	Holz	bois	legno	xýlo	wood
			bosco	dásos	
	Wald	forêt	foresta		forest

Table 2 shows how these six different languages, and thus six different cultures, segment a zone of the content purport into different sets of signifieds, and the correspondences and non-correspondences between these signifieds (the signifieds have as vehicles the corresponding words shown in the table). We observe that:
(a) In no case is there a general correspondence between the six languages. The greatest degree of correspondence appears in the case of the concept of "tree", in respect to which coincide five languages, but not Danish.
(b) There may be coincidence of signification when we compare languages in pairs, as in the case of the French set *arbre, bois, forêt* which is comparable univocally to the English set *tree, wood, forest* (*forest* is borrowed from the French) or the Italian micro-set *albero* and *legno* (wood as material) compared to the Greek *déndro* and *xýlo*.

(c) However, the general rule is a lack of coincidence of signification. For example, as Eco also observes, the French *bois* compared to German covers both *Holz* and part of *Wald*. We also see that, for example, in Italian the two different significations of *legno* and *bosco* are both covered by the French *bois*.

(d) This lack of coincidence of signification, without excluding partial coincidence, is striking if we navigate through the whole table. Take, for example, the Greek *dásos* (forest, irrespective of size[27]). It has the same semantic zone as the Danish *skov*, but a wider semantic zone than the German *Wald*, the French *forêt* and the English *forest*, because it also covers part of *bois* and *wood* respectively; and it is also wider than the Italian *foresta*, because it also covers *bosco*.

In each language, the semantic zone extracted from the content purport is divided in a specific way and the cultural units acquire their own value through their systemic opposition. And we must take into account that we are dealing with cultures in close historical contact, whence we can infer that the differences are even greater between remote cultures. On the basis of the concept of cultural unit, Eco (1972: 73) criticises Peirce: *"Une unité culturelle ne se caractérise pas seulement par la fuite des interprétants; elle est définie en tant que 'lieu' du système des autres unités culturelles qui s'opposent à elle et la délimitent"* [A cultural unit is not only characterised by the flight of interpretants; it is defined as a "place" in the system of the other cultural units which are opposed to it and delimit it].

Another example given by Hjelmslev (1961: 52–53) is the cultural colour spectrum. As he writes, this spectrum is an "amorphous continuum" analogous to the phonic substance of natural language. In terms of physics, the spectrum is electromagnetic in nature and the frequencies of its wavelengths that the typical human eye can see range from 430 to 770 10^{12} Hz. All cultures divide this spectrum in their own way, resulting in the definition of a set of cultural units. As in the case of the signs of natural language, the units of the cultural spectrum are conventional. Hjelmslev observes that, though there are

---

[27] In Greek, as in other languages, a difference in size may be expressed by using an adjective together with the noun, for example in Greek *megálo dásos* [great forest], but the semantic space does not change, it only acquires gradations. However, since the Danish *trae* covers both the Greek *déndro* and *xýlo*, which refer to clearly different signifieds, it is a lexeme signifying two different sememes.

cultural similarities in the division of the colour spectrum, there are also differences. He gives the following example from English and Welsh (Table 3):

Table 3: The cultural division of the colour spectrum in English and Welsh according to Hjelmslev.

English	Welsh
green	gwyrdd
blue	glas
gray	llwyd
brown	

Hjelmslev observes that the Welsh *glas* covers a part (semantic zone) of the spectrum referred to in English as *green*, but that it also covers all of what English calls "*blue*", and so the English boundary between *green* and *blue* does not exist in Welsh; Welsh does not discriminate between *blue* and part of *grey* (they are both *glas*) or between the rest of *gray* and *brown* (they are both *llwyd*); and the area covered by English *gray* is not unified in Welsh, since part of it is grouped as *glas* together with *blue* (and some of *green*) and another part as *llwyd* with the English *brown*.

Examples of this kind may be multiplied. A prominent school of painting in ancient Greece was the austere four-colour school, attributed by some scholars to Polygnotus (second half of the fifth century BCE). Polygnotus's painting was based, according to the sources, on four basic colours, white, yellow, red and black. Some scholars argue that the four-colour system was due to the pre-Socratic philosopher Empedocles (roughly contemporary with Polygnotus), who starts from the four cosmic elements and seems to associate the four colours to them as follows: fire–white, air–yellow, earth–red and water–*mélas* [black].

There is, however, an insurmountable artistic problem with this set of colours, because without blue it is not possible to produce all the colours of the spectrum, for instance green. An answer to this problem was proposed by V. J. Bruno (1977: 56–58, 63–64, 83, 96), who argues that the colour referred to as black was in reality dark blue. In fact, in ancient Greece, there was a word for black, *mélas*, meaning black or dark, but there was also another word for dark, *kýanos* (in modern Greek *kyanós*, the colour of the clear sky), which corresponded to a shade of dark blue, while there was no word for either dark blue or blue.[28] Certain Homeric heroes, when in an intense emotional state, are said to have hair or eyebrows of the colour *kýanos* and Minoan frescoes show blue pates and monkeys. In other words, black is rendered as *kýanos* and the word for black, *mélas*, is used instead of *kýanos*; the two terms were interchangeable, even if they refer to two different colours. We thus find in ancient Greece the phenomenon of a lexeme, *mélas*, with two sememes, "black" and "dark blue", as well as a peculiar non-naturalistic conception of colours.

The borrowing of colour words from a chromatically richer culture by a poorer one is a frequent phenomenon. In the nineteenth century, the traditional Greek spectrum was greatly enriched with borrowings from French, importing among other terms *bleu turquoise*, blue-green (from the word "*turc*", Turkish, which shows that there was a gap in this place in French); *chakí*, khaki, light brown to green; *beige*, the colour of natural wool; *écru*, the colour of unbleached white cloth; *rose*, from the Latin *rosa* [rose]; *saumon*, the colour of salmon, between pink and light orange; *tabac*, the colour of tobacco, a mixture of yellow, red and brown; *lilas*, purple, red to blue; *mauve* from the Latin *malva*, the mallow plant, blue to red; *bordeaux*, the dark red colour of Bordeaux wine.

The divergence of words between cultures poses the crucial problem of the very perception of colours. There is no correspondence in Greek to the English syntagms *blueish green* (bluish shade of green) and *greenish blue* (greenish shade of blue) and we believe that, if someone does not draw attention to their difference, it is not perceived by a native Greek speaker, who will identify them as the *same* colour under the imported concept of *galazoprasino* (blue-green). The Greek shades of blue are, in addition to blue-green, light blue and dark blue. This spectrum is extremely poor when compared to the French spectrum, where we find: *bleu acier* (darker blue), *bleu d'azur*, *bleu barbeau* (blue approaching grey), *bleu ciel* (light blue), *bleu de roi* or *bleu de France* (greenish blue, a colour traditionally used to represent France), *bleu électrique*, *bleu-gris*, *bleu horizon* (the colour of the French military uniform during WWI), *bleu indigo*, *bleu jade*, *bleu lavande*, *bleu lin* (the blue of the flax flower), *bleu marine* (dark blue), *bleu Nattier* (between bleu marine and bleu roi), *bleu paôn* or *bleu canard* (greenish blue), *bleu pastel*, *bleu pervenche* (the colour of the periwinkle flower, light blue tending toward violet), *bleu pétrole* (teal), *bleu roi* (the colour of the uniforms of the French royal guard constituted in 1563), *bleu sarcelle* (teal), *bleu turquoise* (lighter greenish blue), etc. If Greeks had to cope with this remarkably rich

---

[28] The sky was "brass-coloured", not in the literal sense, but meaning dazzlingly shiny like a well-polished shield, and the sea and sheep were *porfyroún* [purple].

variety of words for blue, they would be culturally constrained to compress it within an extremely narrow set of terms. We would suggest that in such a situation, the individuals of the chromatically poorer culture *do not* perceive the slight nuances of the richer one and will in most cases level them out.

Eco (2000: 415, n. 16) reminds us of the objections raised against Hjelmslev's approach. He argues that a French speaker can have two different percepts (a stage that precedes the level of content), one for trees and another for wood, even if they are both covered by only one term. Do such arguments cancel Hjelmslev's argumentation? We do not think so. Even in cases of equivalences of the kind Eco poses, the differences between segmentations reveal for each case *different connections* between concepts, which explain the peculiarity of each culture in reference to each semantic zone, that is, the unitary semantic zone must not be considered in isolation, but as specification of the nature of a particular culture. We hope that the examples of colours above show that, if we admit percepts of this kind, though there are cases which support the argument of equivalences, they are not necessarily the rule, because there may be no equivalences. The detailed scale of analysis, allowing us to raise certain very specific questions and possibly partial objections, should not act as the *træ* (tree) that hides the *skov* (forest), because it is indicative of the larger scale, that is, the semiotic/cultural system and the evident structural variation of these systems.

11 Denotation, connotation and metalanguage

11.1 The theory

Up to now, we have referred to the signified of signs in the sense of their standard signification as presented in a dictionary. We have also referred to signifiers such as lexemes which can have two or more significations (as, for example, the lexeme "crane", which may signify a bird or a machine moving objects vertically and horizontally or a verb for "to stretch", all present in the dictionaries). These are the first and direct significations of a sign. Saussure also recognised another kind of signification, a non-direct one, that of the symbol: it emerges when a signified surpasses the direct signification of a signifier and refers to another, indirect signification which however has a certain analogical – that is, paradigmatic – semantic relation to the direct one, as in the case of the scales that can symbolise Justice. We owe to Hjelmslev (1961: 114–125) the theorising of symbolism by means of the semiotic concept of connotation, part of the triad of denotation, connotation and metalanguage (see also Greimas and Courtés 1979: Connotation, Dénotation, Métalangage).

11 Denotation, connotation and metalanguage — 73

Hjelmslev observes that not only natural language, but any structure analogous to it, is a semiotic; language is just a special case of a semiotic structure. He uses the term "denotative semiotic" for a sign system consisting of two non-isomorphic planes, an expression plane of signifiers (Sr in Figure 6 below) and a content plane of signifieds (Sd in Figure 6), and where none of the planes is itself a semiotic. Hjelmslev's denotative semiotic is called "biplanar" by Greimas and Courtés, who use this term for their semiotics of the natural world. Hjelmslev then broadens his view by posing two other types of semiotic.

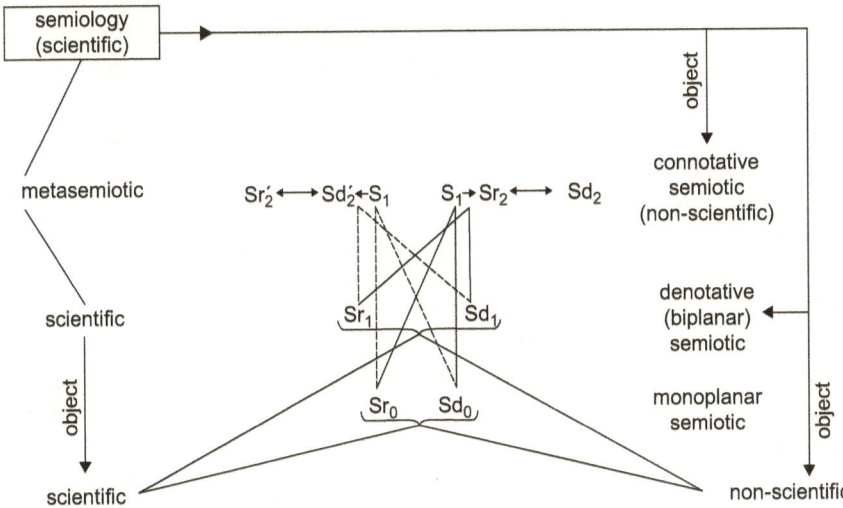

Figure 6: Types of semiotics according to Hjelmslev and Greimas and Courtés. Sr: signifier. Sd: signified.

For the first type, the expression plane is already a denotative semiotic; Hjelmslev calls this type a "connotative semiotic". The transition from the level of the denotative sign S_1 and its first and direct signification Sd_1 to a second and indirect signification Sd_2 is not achieved, for Hjelmslev, only by the signifier or the signified of denotation, but by the two of them as a whole (the whole sign S_1), which is transformed into a connotative signifier Sr_2 with a connotative signified Sd_2 (see, in Figure 6, the right side of the central part of the diagram with continuous lines: the sign S_1 leads to Sr_2 associated to Sd_2; see also Barthes 1964a: 130–132). Connotation and denotation constitute a paradigmatic group. It should be emphasised that there is no connotative sign without articulation with a denotative sign.[29]

Hjelmslev calls the signifieds of connotation (Sd_2) "connotators", while Barthes uses this term for the signifiers of connotation (Sr_2). Hjelmslev (1961: 116) gives as an example of connotation that all the signs of any textual class of a language refer to the connotative signified "this language": in the case of the Danish language, the connotator is "Danish" ("Danish-ness" or "Dani-city"). We note that "Danish-ness" is a symbol, this is why the connotative layer is symbolic. The same idea is expressed by Barthes, when he writes that French messages refer to the connotative signified "French" ("French-ness") and that a literary work can refer to "literature" ("literari-ness"). Barthes points out that many denotative signs may be grouped to refer to one and the same connotation. For Barthes, the signifiers of connotation are discontinuous, "*erratiques*". According to him, the set of these signifiers constitutes a form – in Hjelmslev's sense – which is a "rhetoric" and the set of the corresponding signifieds of connotation another form, that of "ideology". This leads him to make a radical connection of semiotics with culture and society, arguing that the connotative signifieds "*communiquent étroitement avec la culture, le savoir, l'histoire, c'est par eux, si l'on peut dire, que le monde pénètre le système*" [are in direct communication with culture, knowledge, history and it is through them, so to speak, that the world invades the system] (Barthes 1964a: 131–132). Connotation is an inescapable dimension in any text, but it is also part of both the language system, where it usually appears as metaphor, and cultural conventions attached to isolated signs.

For Hjelmslev's second type of semiotic, not the expression plane but the content plane is a denotative semiotic; he calls this type "metasemiotic". A metasemiotic is, for Hjelmslev, a "metalanguage", that is, a semiotic that has as its object another semiotic. As in the first type, the starting point is the denotative sign S_1, which is transformed as a whole, not into a signifier this time, but into a signified Sd'_2, which is associated to the metalinguistic signifier Sr'_2, of greater precision than the initial signifier Sr_1 (see the left side of the central part of the diagram of Figure 6 with dotted lines: the sign S_1 leading to Sd'_2 is expressed by Sr'_2). If, for example, the denotative sign is "salt", the metalinguistic signifier (Sr'_2) could be "sodium chloride", more analytically explaining what salt is.

---

[29] Catherine Kerbrat-Orecchioni (1977: 83, 85) considers this articulation with the denotative sign as possible but not necessary. She believes that the connotative signifier is not necessarily a "complete" denotative semiotics and there are cases in which the signifier of connotation is derived (only) from the signified of denotation. Bur a signified without signifier belongs to the realm of Platonic ideas and not to Saussurean linguistics, because the existence of a signified is unthinkable without a sign and hence a signifier.

A metalanguage is not stabilised once and forever, since in the sphere of science every innovative approach functions as a new metalanguage on the previous one.[30] Helmslev points out that the last two types of semiotics are of a relative and insecure nature, something that we should remember, but we do not agree with him when he expresses doubts about their utility, because they are of prime importance for semiotics.

According to Hjelmslev, in these two types of semiotic, at least one plane (the more usual case) and possibly both are related to a semiotic; Greimas and Courtés consider these types as biplanar, but due to the second possibility above, they call them "pluriplanar". Hjelmslev discusses systems with essentially only one plane, such as algebra and games like chess, but does not consider a monoplanar system as a semiotic. Greimas and Courtés object on this point, because they consider that both categories of the monoplanar semiotics they define (formal languages or systems of "symbols", as they call them following Hjelmslev, and "molar" or semi-symbolic semiotics, such as prosodic or gestural semiotics) involve signification.

We see that the terms denotation, connotation and metalanguage indicate three different types of semiotic systems, the denotative, the connotative and the metalinguistic. As shown in Figure 6, Hjelmslev superimposes a second classificatory grid on the one just discussed, by differentiating two classes of semiotics, namely scientific and non-scientific semiotics. Greimas and Courtés define as scientific semiotics the systems of symbols of monoplanar semiotics, and, among the pluriplanar semiotics, the scientific part of denotative biplanar semiotics and meta-semiotics. For Greimas and Courtés, non-scientific semiotics include semi-symbolic (or spontaneous) monoplanar semiotics, non-scientific denotative biplanar semiotics and the (spontaneous) connotative semiotics among the pluriplanar semiotics.

Figure 6 also clarifies the Saussurean, Greimasian and in general European conception of semiotics as a cultural enterprise in the line of Saussure's *sémiologie*. More specifically, Greimas and Courtés, rigorously following Hjelmslev, divide metasemiotics (on the extreme left side of Figure 6) into "scientific metasemiotics", the semiotic object of which is a scientific semiotic, and "semiology", which has as object a non-scientific, connotative semiotic (on the extreme right side of the figure). Hjelmslev specifies that he uses the term "semiology" in the same sense as it is used by Saussure. Semiology studies non-scientific semiotics (for the above, see Hjelmslev 1961: 106–120; Greimas and Courtés 1979: Sémiotique).

This view, which differentiates between non-scientific and scientific semiotics, is in direct collision with Derrida's view that all texts are equivalent, a view

---

[30] In Peirce's terminology, we pass from a first interpretant to a second one.

that levels out the difference between, among others, metalanguage and connotative semiotics. On the one hand, there is a remarkable convergence between Derrida, Peirce and the group of Hjelmslev, Greimas and Courtés, because for all of them anything conceived by the human mind participates in signification (irrespectively of their different definitions of the sign) and semiotics. On the other hand, however, there is a major divergence on the definition of semiotics, because, while for Derrida and Peirce semiotics is coextensive with all the approaches presented in Figure 6, for Greimas and Courtés semiology is just one of the approaches included in the domain of metalanguages.

We point out – and this is a concession to Derrida – that in respect to texts the oppositions *denotation* vs *connotation* and *metalanguage* vs *connotation* are not absolute but relative. It is possible in the first case to have an overlapping, an intermediate area which blurs the distinction between the two. To give an example, the windows of the architect Charles Jencks's studio are arranged in a form which was designed to remind us of a human face. The design is not naturalistic and only offers some abstract morphological clues, which may cause a direct denotative recognition by people with a trained eye, but may also lead a lay individual indirectly to the connotation through a vague perception of the clues. There may also be an alternation between denotation and connotation when we compare different texts: for example, in one text the creation of the world may be its ultimate connotation, while in the Bible it is presented as a factual description.

Denotation may be more or less delimited with the definition offered by Kerbrat-Orecchioni (1977: 15, 226), i.e., the main meaning attached to the referential mechanism, which she considers as assertion (though we would not accept her observation that a linguistic unit establishes a relation with an extralinguistic object). On the other hand, her idea of connotation is semiotically problematic, because she considers it from a narrow linguistic point of view as a secondary, additional, subsidiary suggested meaning (15, 18, 107, 113), although connotation on the textual level is often the vehicle of the main meaning of a text. While Kerbrat-Orecchioni makes this differentiation, she clarifies that connotation may also play a denotative role and reinforce or enrich denotation, concluding that their difference is not one of content but of status (226, 227). She gives meticulous examples of connotation based either on signifiers (23–87) or signifieds (89–164). Below, we give examples of connotation based on denotative signs, but we shall also present in this book examples of connotation starting from signifiers (chapter 5: 1.3).[31]

---

31 We cannot agree with Kerbrat-Orecchioni that there are cases where the signifier of connotation is not a denotative sign, as with rhythmic repetition (81). If something is considered as a

To understand the flexibility of the differentiation between metalanguage and connotation, we have only to think of the ultimate epistemological foundation of any metalanguage. Foucault offers us an important approach to this issue with his concept of "*épistémè*". Writing about Western societies, he indicates with this concept an epistemological field, historically determined, which poses the fundamental preconditions of knowledge for a particular historical period. He argues that these preconditions delimit for experience a possible domain of knowledge, define the mode of being of the objects constituting this domain, set the context in which a discourse recognised as true can evolve and determine its possible theoretical approaches (Foucault 1966: 12–13, 170–171). This view reminds us that there is no such thing as an "objective" discourse and that all discourse is ultimately founded in the last instance on ideology.

It is also historically possible that a metalanguage has through time developed from a connotative discourse, as, for example, chemistry developed from alchemy. This was also the case with Kepler's cosmology. Kepler was engaged with astrology and the musical views of the Pythagoreans, and opted for the heliocentric system because it was, according to him, more satisfactory geometrically and had at its centre the symbol of God. He built his universe initially on the basis of the sphere, the symbol for him of God and the Holy Trinity, and the five Platonic solids intercalated between the planetary orbits. Kepler's three classical laws, crucial for celestial mechanics, emerged from this magico-religious background. Kepler was quite uneasy with his first law, the elliptical orbit of the planets, because it ran counter to the circle as the ideal geometrical form (Koestler [1959] 1960: 234–381, 506–509). It is also possible to find, for example, metalinguistic elements integrated within a non-metalinguistic text, something common in postmodern literature.

11.2 Examples of connotation

Metalanguages can thus develop historically by stages. Something similar can happen with connotation, though synchronically and in a much more limited manner; connotation may develop through superimposed layers.

We have already discussed the phenomenon of the subdivision of the colour spectrum by different cultures, so that each culture creates its own set of

---

signifier, then *by definition* there must be a signified, since they are the two sides of a single piece of paper, to recall Saussure's metaphor. Before becoming a poetic connotation, rhythmic repetition means "rhythmic repetition" and a sudden noise, before being interpreted as alarming, means a sudden noise.

chromatic signs. The connotations of colours are also culturally defined – for example, in the West, the colour of mourning is black, in Japan it is white. But even within a single culture, colours can have multiple connotations. Let us take the colour red. Whether we find the word "red" in a text, hear it in a conversation or see a red cloth, in all these cases there is a signifier Sr_1 (red colour) referring to a signified Sd_1 ("red colour") – Figure 7. But red also has many connotations and a specific text or context selects one of them. Probably its most common connotations are "passion" (desire, love, sexuality) and "danger" (warning). However, it can also connote blood (the red flag of international Communism represents the blood of the workers who died in the struggle against capitalism**)**, strength and courage, heat, immorality, anger. In creating a connotative meaning, to follow Hjelmslev, the sign S_1 as a whole becomes a new signifier Sr_2, associated to a connotative signified Sd_2, which – depending on what semes are activated by the context – may signify "passion" (as connoted, for example, in the context of a red dress) or "danger" (as connoted in the context of a traffic light).

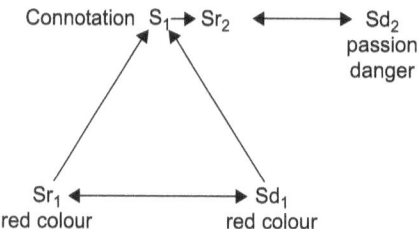

Figure 7: The different connotations of "red colour" on the same connotative layer.

In most contexts, the colour red has a single connotation (though it is possible to think of a context in which a red dress could connote both "passion" and "danger"). However, there are plenty of cases of signs with two layers of connotation. We all know the Western custom of hanging ornaments on fir trees during the Christmas period, or using branches of evergreens or holly to decorate the house. The Christmas tree, whether standing in our house or represented on a postcard, has the connotation of an enjoyable and festive holiday season. Actually, this well-known and deeply felt connotation has been grafted onto an older one. Fir and holly are evergreen trees and as such symbolise the continuation of life through the harsh winter. This latter symbolism is probably lost today, but it is the indispensable step to reach the modern connotation of the Christmas tree. We can follow this course in Figure 8. We pass from the initial

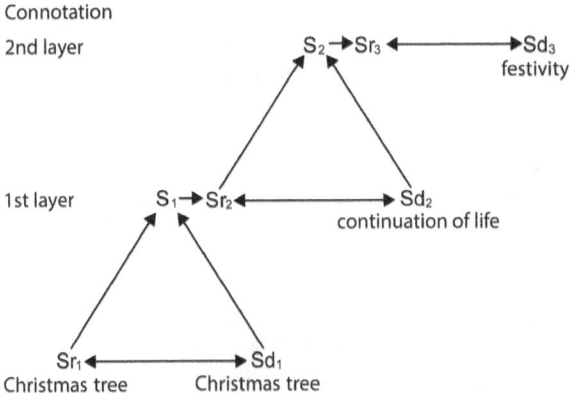

Figure 8: The two-layered connotation of "Christmas tree".

denotative sign S_1 "Christmas tree" to its first-layer connotation which is "continuation of life" (Sd_2) and, through a second-layer connotative sign S_2, we end up with today's connotation of "festivity" (Sd_3).

Our last example is borrowed from the semiotics of space and includes three layers of connotation. In the mid-fifties, the Brazilian government took the bold decision to build a new capital, Brasilia, in the centre of the country, deep inside the jungle far from the coastal area where all the main cities were located. An international competition was proclaimed for the plan of the city and the first prize was won by the Brazilian architect Lúcio Costa. Unlike the red colour and the Christmas tree, the symbolic content of this plan is not a matter of cultural convention, but a textual device due to deliberate individual choice.

The diagrammatic representation of the general form of the city, given in Figure 9, follows from the specific rationale used by Costa, namely a process of semiotic urban production.[32] The plan was conceived starting from the connotative layer of the sign S_3 (Sr_4/Sd_4) and working down to the morphological signifier of denotation Sr_1, which is the urban form of the city. To simplify the discussion, we shall not follow the actual process of production of the city plan but start our description from the denotation layer, as in the previous cases. This course implies not the production, but the reading of the city plan, and presupposes an ideal well-informed reader who starts the

---

[32] Of course many other non-semiotic, material factors intervene in the production of an urban plan, such as traffic and ecological factors. Our discussion here concerns only the semiotic aspect of the production, i.e., only the symbolism of the plan.

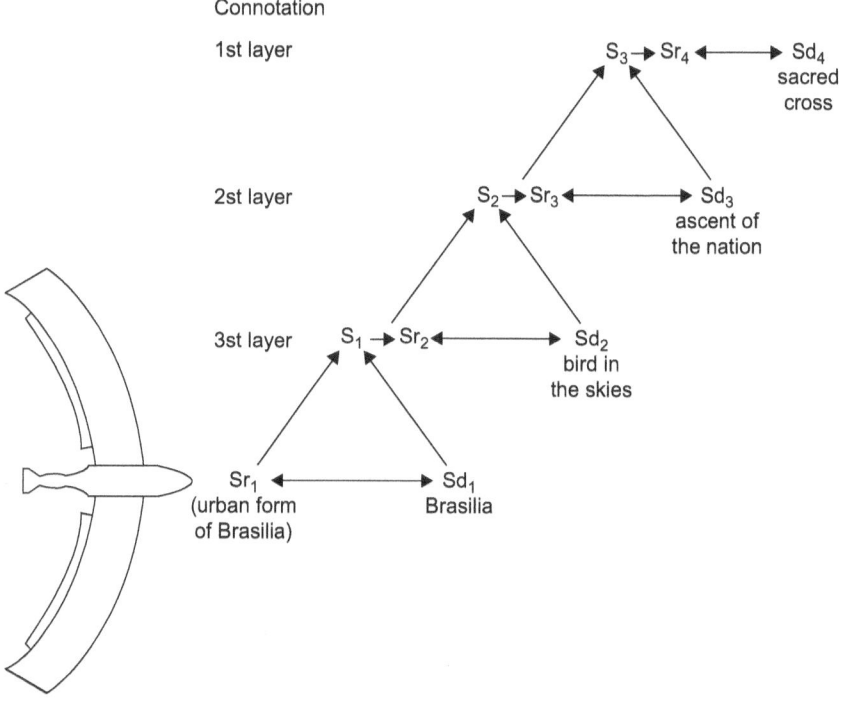

Figure 9: The semiotic process of the symbolic production of the plan of Brasilia.

reading from the perception of the design of the city and from there moves step by step to successively deeper layers of connotation.

Starting from the bottom up, the plan of the city Sr_1 signifies "urban form of Brasilia". The new signifier Sr_2, following from the denotative sign S_1, is linked to a new signified, the connotative signified "bird in the skies" (Sd_2), and in fact the city has a body-like axis (which is the official axis of the city with all public buildings) and two "wings" (including the housing areas). This is, then, the first connotation in reading the city (the third during the production process). Costa wanted his bird to fly in the skies and thus we pass to a second connotative layer, emerging from the connotative sign S_2 and defining the signification "ascent of the Brazilian nation" (Sd_3). The last movement of connotation starts with the topmost sign S_3 creating the signifier Sr_4, which is linked to the ultimate connotation of the city.

The above description of the first two connotative layers indicates the expected reading of the city. In testing this reading with students of architecture, we found that the legibility of the city as bird is far from assured, but a great deal of publicity was associated with the plan in Brazil and both this connotation and the second connotation of "ascent of the Brazilian nation" were widely publicised through the mass media. This was not the case with the final connotation, which remained secret for about twenty years. The reason was political. Costa was a socialist, as were the other main players in this huge undertaking, President Juscelino Kubitschek de Oliveira, affiliated to the Partido Social Democrático, and the socialist architect Oscar Niemeyer, one of the key figures of modern architecture, who designed all the civic buildings of the new capital. Brasilia was intended to be a socialist experiment.

This political framework did not allow Costa to reveal his deeper motive for the design of the city. The ultimate signified behind the plan of the city is "sacred cross" (Sd_4) and copies the practice of the Spanish *conquistadores* of planting a cross in the ground when they were founding a new colony.[33] The symbol of the sacred cross traverses the layers of connotation, which start from a religious *isotopy* (see on this concept chapters 5 and 6), pass through a national isotopy and conclude with a zoological-and-celestial isotopy, to end with the form of the cross-like morphology of Brasilia. This design condenses a religious and national narrative extending from the colonial past of Brazil to its expected brilliant future. Though this symbolic secret was well hidden, the cross appears in a marked manner in Costa's very first diagrammatic sketches of the city.

12 From *langue* to speech: Sociolinguistics and Greimasian semiotics

For Saussure, the syntagm represents the largest possible unit of the language system. He observes that the type *par excellence* of the syntagm is the sentence, but that the sentence no longer belongs to the language system but to speech, in other words is no longer governed by structural laws. For Saussure, the linguistics of the language system cannot be extended to the freedom of the domain of speech; its upper limit consists of linguistic forms bequeathed from the past and stored in the language system. Thus, a sentence such as, for example, "John kicks the ball" falls outside the limits of Saussure's linguistics.

---

[33] Brasilia was founded in 1960. During this and the following year, one of the present authors was finishing his studies of architecture and working on his final research project with two classmates (Loudovikos Wassenhoven and Patroklos Apostolidis) on the critical analysis of the urban plan and architecture of Brasilia. At the end of 1960, the Brazilian Embassy in Athens informed the students that Costa was visiting Athens incognito and they could arrange a meeting with him. During their long discussion, he revealed his secret and asked his interlocutors not to make it public.

This is not the case with Noam Chomsky's linguistics. While Chomsky founds his linguistics on Saussure, he criticises him both for limiting linguistics to words and stereotyped formulas, and for abandoning the sentence to the liberty and creativity of speech. For Chomsky's "generative grammar", the language system is not a system of signs, but a system of "generative rules", successive rules of transformation describing the process of sentence formation, a process of transition from deep structures to surface structures. His linguistic theory went through different stages of development, restructuring its structural components and increasing the complexity of its analysis, with the ambition to achieve a holistic interpretation of the syntactic, semantic and phonological components of this process (see, for example, Chomsky 1964: 10–11, 23–24).

Chomsky's initial – but decisive – approach, phrase structure grammar, allows us to understand the foundation of his linguistics. His constituent analysis has the form of a dynamic tree structure, developing through decomposition from one level to the next, with the help of generative rules with the form X→Y. The decomposition starts from the "initial string", which represents the basic structure of a sentence: NP (Noun Phrase) + VP (Verb Phrase). Chomsky takes the example "The man hits the ball", which we paraphrased above, and demonstrates its structural "derivation". More specifically, NP is decomposed into T + N, T (definite article) leading to "the" and N (Noun) leading to "man". VP is decomposed into V (Verb) + (a new) NP, V leading to "hit" and the new NP to "the ball" (see, for example, Chomsky [1957] 1971: 26–30).

Mainstream linguistics after Chomsky includes in its objects a sentence like "The man hits the ball", but it still fails to go beyond the sentence to connect two simple sentences and to explain our understanding of such connections. In the example "The man kicks the ball. It goes into the net", we understand that the "it" that goes into the net is the ball that the man kicks in the previous sentence and not a new grammatical subject, although this is not explicitly stated. We are dealing here with an elementary text, and neither Saussure's nor Chomsky's theories extend to this level. The pronoun "it" in this example is one of the forms of referencing, anaphoric reference, which is one of the devices creating textual cohesion, that is, the connection of ideas at the syntactic level, as distinguished from coherence, the connection of ideas at the semantic level. The complexity of this kind of analysis increases with the complexity of a text, even with that of an elementary text of the kind "The man kicks the ball. At that very moment, the wind suddenly changed. While previously it was blowing at low speed from the northwest [. . .]".

The extension of mainstream linguistics beyond the sentence was undertaken by sociolinguistics and discourse analysis starting in the 1960s. This kind of analysis is oriented towards speech as the use of language and generally revolves

12 From *langue* to speech: Sociolinguistics and Greimasian semiotics — 83

around the concepts of "speech act" and "speech situation", the second concept indicating the intention to relate speech to the specific situation of its uttering.

The relation between the terms "speech", "text", and "discourse" is rather confusing. A usual differentiation in Anglophone bibliography is that text refers to written material, does not specify the agent of information and is not inserted into an interactive process, while discourse or speech is the use of language in situation (the sociolinguistic approach), specifying the agents of information and thus interactive. In sociolinguistics, the term "text" is used to indicate the final product of a wider discursive process, "discourse"; different types of discourse are identified, such as business discourse, media discourse or entrepreneurial discourse. This is also Fontanille's approach, which clearly differentiates discourse from text: discourse is a process of signification (Fontanille expresses this in terms of the act and product of enunciation), while a text is the organisation – in one or more dimensions – of the concrete elements which express the signification of discourse (Fontanille 1999: 16).

In general, however, the French use of the terms is much more diverse. Saussure uses *parole* to cover any use of the language system, oral or written (without differentiating process from product), and Greimas and Courtés observe that this equivalence is explicit in discursive linguistics, but that in other cases we find a differentiation between *written* (text) vs *oral* (discourse, speech). Greimas and Courtés also mention several other significations of "text", one of which is "corpus". Discourse, they indicate, can refer to the whole of the generative trajectory (chapter 4: 1.1) or to a typology of texts, as in literary, political or religious discourse (Greimas and Courtés 1979: Discours, Text). In this last case, "discourse" refers to different types of texts, as it does in sociolinguistics. In the work of Foucault, implicitly text and discourse are fully identified; though the material he uses are historical texts, his key term is "discourse", appearing continuously in this form, or as "discursive event" or "discursive formation".

As we can see, text and discourse are overlapping terms, and the decision to differentiate them is linked to the viewpoint chosen. However, these viewpoints are multiple and the choice of one of them excludes other equally legitimate viewpoints. We use the two terms interchangeably in this book.

This issue has already taken us into the field of sociolinguistics. We shall make a small detour from the tradition of Saussurean linguistics in order to briefly discuss some major theoretical approaches to this field.

Dell Hymes's "ethnography of speaking" has precisely the aim that we mentioned above, to investigate "the use of language in contexts of situation", an aim that he approaches with the help of Jakobson's model of communication (for this model, see chapter 8: 2.6). Hymes criticises Chomsky on the grounds that his linguistic theory is a theory of grammar, not of language, and that linguistics of the Chomskian type reduces the concept of speech community (see below) to that of language. He does not dismiss this kind of linguistics and states that socially constituted linguistics does not replace it, but also that this different approach reconstructs linguistics as sociolinguistics, giving priority to the "system of speech (*la parole*)". For Hymes, there is a primacy of speech over code, of function over structure and of context over message; the sphere of speech is conditioned by the linguistic codes, but is not under their control (Hymes 1974: viii–ix, 3–4, 9, 47, 79, 196, 206).

According to Hymes, the "speech act", his central concept, is attached to the "speech event", a concept belonging to a hierarchy of speech circumstances ("social contexts"). He argues that the overall framework for the organisation of linguistic means is the "speech community" and in each community there are many "speech situations", such as hunting, meals, or parties; speech situations are not governed by rules determining their composition. The speech event is a unit of the speech situation, for example one conversation taking place during a party; it is governed directly by formal rules for the use of speech. Finally, a speech event normally comprises more than one speech act, for example a joke within a conversation during a party. The speech act, which should not be confused with a sentence or any other grammatical unit, is the minimal term of the above hierarchy and is also governed by formal rules (Hymes 1974: 35, 47–53).

A comparable approach is that of M. A. K. Halliday. Halliday's founding concept is the "context of situation", which he defines strictly semiotically as only those features of the environment of speech that are relevant to it. Halliday believes that there is a rather limited number of types of situations, founded on three semiotic components of the speech situation, the "situational determinants" (the field of social action, the tenor of role relationships and the mode of symbolic organisation), strongly related to three major "functional components" (the ideational function, the interpersonal function and the textual function); the functional components are connected to the situational determinants through univocal relationships of derivation. He concludes that, from the lexicogrammatical viewpoint, there is a systematic relationship between functional components and specific grammatical structures, called by Halliday "structural configurations".

According to Halliday, access to particular areas of language is a meaning potential, what he calls a "code". There are configurations of potential meaning, which, together with the structural configurations, constitute the "register", the structure supporting the actual text; thus, the movement from situation to register is based on the code (Halliday 1978: see, for example, 29–33, 45–49, 62–63, 68, 70, 111–113, 116–117, 185–189).

While Hymes frequently uses the term "social" (social structure, social context, social function, social action, social relationships), he does not use it in the sense of material society, but as a substitute for "semiotic" (for example, he refers to the "'semantics' of social relationships"). His sociolinguistics is, as he himself states, an ethnography of communication (Hymes 1974: vii, 3–5, 8, 60, 112, 196). We observe with Halliday a similar limitation within the semiotic. He includes in his sociolinguistic theory extra-semiotic concepts of society, but the material social system is identified solely with culture and considered as a semiotic system. His concepts of situational and functional components, as well as those of code and register, are strictly semiotic in nature.

What is absent from this tendency of sociolinguistics is an articulation with material society, a task comparable to our earlier reference to the articulation of the language system with society, what we called "social semiotics" (which also includes the articulation of a text with society). This issue escapes from the interests of today's semioticians, who seem reluctant to take this next step. However, one of the tendencies of sociolinguistics has this orientation and aims at the articulation of speech with society in the material sense. The standard references on this issue are the works of Basil Bernstein and William Labov.

Central to Bernstein's approach is the concept of "code". A code is, for him, the principles regulating speech events: it is a speech model. He argues that there is a verbal planning process during which, when confronted with a message, a person scans it to detect the pattern of its dominant elements (process of "orientation"), chooses to respond to this pattern of verbal and non-verbal elements (on the basis of "associations") and organises the selected elements with the aim of producing a sequential reply (process of "organisation"). The principles regulating these three processes compose the code. Bernstein's definition of code thus is not limited to the linguistic response to a message, but also takes into consideration the meaning processes and the structuring of meaning. Bernstein's concept of code covers both the syntactic level, his "surface structure" of language, and the semantic level, the "deep structure", which guides the former level.

Beyond this causal link, Bernstein takes a step towards the speech situation. The new link in his causal chain are social roles in their interactional situation, which he sees as the locus of the social structuring of meaning. Turning to the socialisation of children, Bernstein distinguishes four major agencies or situations involved in this process: the family, the child's peer group, the school and the workplace. With this final step, Bernstein locates the foundation of his causal chain in social structure (the macro-sociological level) and emphasises the social division of labour. He thus ends up with a relation – a flexible one – between code and social class (Bernstein 1971: see, for example, 12–16, 24–25, 42, 61–62, 76–79, 128–129, 148–150, 171, 181–186, 194–196, 241, 244–247).

We detect a very similar orientation in the work of William Labov. His sociolinguistics starts from the phonetic level. He demonstrates, for example, the existence of a correlation between the pronunciation of the [θ] index and a composite variable, namely the combination of socio-economic class with "contextual style", referring to the degree of formality of speech. As he states: "We may define a *sociolinguistic variable* as one which is correlated with some non-linguistic variable of the social context: of the speaker, the addressee, the audience, the setting, etc.". For Labov, such a correlation displays "exterior, sociolinguistic controls" (Labov 1972: 283–285, 287, 305). As early as the 1970s, Labov extended his research to the study of oral narratives, elicited and non-elicited, and formulated a model for their structure. In general, the major difference from the semiotic approach is that sociolinguistics is interested not only in the structure of narratives, but also in their production according to their environment (Thornborrow and Coates 2005: 1, 3, 7).

Critical discourse analysis (CDA) is closely connected to this sociologically oriented sociolinguistics, more specifically to its Marxist aspect. According to Norman Fairclough, a prominent figure in this field, discourse as the use of language, hence as a social practice, contributes to the construction of social relationships, including power relationships, identities and knowledge. There is a bidirectional influence between discourse and other social practices. Fairclough uses as key concepts the "communicative event" and the "order of discourse", referring in the second case to sets of "discourse types" present in a society, such as the media or the recruitment campaigns of universities. A communicative event consists of a "text" as such (linguistic or visual), its aspect as a "discursive practice", which incorporates it within a communicative circuit of production and consumption, and a third aspect of it as "social practice", connecting it to the existing order of discourse and more broadly to the partly non-discursive social conditions, such as economic or institutional, which influence discursive practice. Thus, discourse analysis is supplemented with the analysis of wider social practices (Phillips and Jørgensen: 2002: 64–71, 81–89).

The recent development of sociolinguistics has revolved within the spectrum defined above, with as foundational principle the study of language "in context". Its interests overlap with semiotics, but also extend to more contemporary issues, such as identity, power relationships and gender. Sociolinguistics has also turned to the study of cultural models (value systems or belief structures) supporting language use, language learning and language variation (Thornborrow and Coates 2005: 7–8; Kristiansen and Dirven 2008: 9–11; Meyerhoff 2006: 4, 212–248; McGroarty 2010: 17; Mayr 2008: 3).

12 From *langue* to speech: Sociolinguistics and Greimasian semiotics — 87

In the tendency of sociolinguistics that studies discourse in its relation to material society, there is a pronounced Marxist orientation. Marxism is considered as especially fruitful by Rajend Mesthrie, who points out that any "coherent theory of language in society can only unfold within a particular theory of society" and concludes that "many of the insights emanating from sociolinguistics do fit the Marxist critique of social systems quite well". Mesthrie does not elide the reverse influence; he states that language not only reflects social organisation, but as a practice also impacts on the nucleus of this organisation, being imbricated in power relationships (Mesthrie 2009: 6, 27, 32).

There are overlappings and differences between sociolinguistics and Greimasian semiotics. The background of Greimasian semiotics is structuralist, while sociolinguistics is functionalist. Greimasian semiotics include an extension to sociosemiotics, which is *mutatis mutandis* comparable to the purely semiotic tendency of sociolinguistics, but there has not been much work in this field by semioticians, nor do Greimasian sociosemiotics advance to the articulation of semiotics with material society.

For sociosemiotics, Greimas and Courtés present the following research programme. Sociosemiotics has two objects of study: the dynamics of communication and the classification of semiotic systems. They study the dynamics of communication in its purely textual dimension, and they see it as activated at both extremities not by neutral instances but by integral semiotic subjects (their specific approach to this issue will be discussed in Part Four below). They also briefly present a classification of semiotic systems (which also delivers a typology of cultures), identifying three different types which they generally approach from the viewpoint of their social connotations.

The first type is "mythical epistemologies", a society's discourse on signs, including philosophies of language. The second are "cultural ontologies", which support the above discourses, establishing truth criteria. The third type are the taxonomies of social languages; these they see as strictly defined in archaic or traditional societies (according to categories such as *sacred* vs *profane* or *superior* vs *inferior*), but greatly increased in complex societies (for example, sacred language was subdivided into religious, philosophical, poetic, etc. discourses).[34] They relate this third type to ethnosemiotics, a planned extension of ethnolinguistics, which they see as studying ethnotaxonomies, extending from grammatical taxonomies (for example, the study of the conception of time on the

---

[34] Greimas and Courtés observe that today new literary genres have developed (such as detective stories, westerns, romances and horoscopes) and outside literature there are new forms of spectacle (such as athletic events and tourism).

basis of verb tenses) to lexical taxonomies (such as kinship terminology or botanical and zoological classifications) to connotative taxonomies (such as a typology of social languages according to different social groups). All the above semiotic objects, including the study of mass media, constitute for Greimas and Courtés a vast area of research for sociosemiotics, but we once more stress that there is not yet any notable corpus of research in this field.

According to Greimas and Courtés, the main axes of sociosemiotics (and of semiotics, we would add) are "axiologies" and "ideologies", which they consider as the two fundamental aspects of the organisation of the universe of values. By axiologies they mean that values are paradigmatically organised into micro-systems and take the form of taxonomies; axiologies belong to the deep semiotic structures (chapter 4: 1.1 and 1.2). Their definition of ideology is semiotically oriented and indicates the syntactic (textual) organisation of these values, through which axiologies are invested in an ideological model and actualised in the surface structures of texts by actants, individual or collective (Greimas and Courtés 1979: Axiologie, Éthnosémiotique, Idéologie, Sociolecte, Sociosémiotique).[35]

A major epistemological difference divides semiotics and sociosemiotics from sociolinguistics. Sociolinguistics attempts to directly elaborate a linguistics of speech, in the widest possible sense, independently from any linguistics of the language system. Greimasian textual analysis, on the other hand, relies fundamentally on the premises of the structuralist Saussurean language system, as becomes clear from the axes above. The Saussurean syntagm is, as we saw, extremely limited and his concept of the paradigmatic dimension, though suggestive, is only of very general assistance in respect to the analysis of the language system. However, the Greimasian universe of textual values is founded on axiologies, structured according to the paradigmatic level, and ideologies, structured according to the syntagmatic level. The Greimasian approach demonstrates how to capitalise on the concept of syntagm in textual analysis and offers the possibility of full development of the paradigmatic dimension leading to the key concept of isotopy, a decisive instrument for textual analysis (chapters 5 and 6). These two dimensions, in combination with Lévi-Strauss's structural anthropology, Chomsky's generative model and Propp's

---

[35] We note that our definition of ideology does not coincide with the definition of Greimas and Courtés, but follows (as does Barthes) the non-evaluative concept of ideology as worldview (contrary to the pejorative view of ideology adopted by Marx and its use for political belief systems). This conception is akin to the axiologies of Greimas and Courtés, though not necessarily with the strict formal character they attribute to them, although in precapitalist societies, for example, they are of a formal nature as classification systems (chapter 5: 2.3).

structural narrative analysis, form the foundation of Greimasian narratology, which achieves what Saussure considered to be impossible and Chomsky did not elaborate, namely a systematic structural theory of *parole*. It is our conviction that the general model of narratology, as that of *langue*, is applicable to all semiotic systems.

Part III: **The semiotics of *parole* (textual semiotics)**

Chapter 4
Syntagmatic analysis: Narrative theory

1 Narratology

1.1 The generative trajectory

As we saw, Saussure's linguistics focused on the language system, and we have pointed out the epistemological weight of this decision. Saussure was not concerned with speech, and a theory of the language system cannot be used without appropriate adaptation for the analysis of speech, i.e., of a text or discourse.

We have already mentioned the work on speech by sociolinguistics, as well as the focus on texts by critical discourse analysis and the Tartu–Moscow School. However, the most systematic and coherent theory of the text is the narratology developed by Algirdas Julien Greimas and his School of Paris, and this is the theory we shall discuss in detail. Greimas achieved what sociolinguistics did not: the anchoring of a complete theory of speech in a full-fledged theory of the language system.

There is a traditional view, revived with the advent of the North American deconstructionists, that comments on a text take the form of a critique, that is, the subjective interpretation of a critic. Semiotics is fundamentally opposed to this approach. Already in the work of Lévi-Strauss, structuralism and semiotics take the position that the structural–semiotic approach is not axiological but analytical. The semiotician possesses an analytical tool with which to approach a text and attempts to understand its construction, not to judge it. Semiotics is a scientific, not a subjective or phenomenological approach, and its aim is to arrive at an analysis that is as objective as possible. Of course, complete objectivity is an illusion, since no analysis can be completely free from value judgements, but the view that texts are by nature completely opaque is equally illusionary, since it ignores their anchoring in culture.

The semiotic approach is applied without any axiological judgements to texts of both "high" and "low" cultural provenance, a democratic lack of differentiation and movement of unification inherited from Jakobson and the Formalists. However, the persistence of the tradition is such that even today the term "literary criticism", for example, is still more common than "literary analysis".

The logic behind the narratology of Greimas can be understood by his comment (Greimas 1966: 173) that he was impressed by an observation made by the French linguist Lucien Tesnière that a sentence is like a drama, because words play different roles in a sentence: subject, object, verb, etc. There are thousands of words in a language, but their syntactic roles are limited. Greimas's narratology starts from the hypothesis that a narrative is "like" a sentence: someone does something. This hypothesis leads him to two sources: Vladimir Propp's morphology of the folktale and Noam Chomsky's generative grammar.

The decisive step taken by Propp in the study of the folktale was that, instead of trying to classify stories in terms of their motifs, he focused on what he called the "morphology" and we today would call the "structure" of the narrative. Morphology, for Propp (1968: 19), is "a description of the tale according to its component parts and the relationship of these components to each other and to the whole" (this is the strict definition of structure as given by structuralism, mathematics and even by the Pythagoreans).

The basic components of a tale are for Propp its "functions". A function is the significance, for the course of the plot, of an action by some character; in other words, a function is an action that alters the course of the narrative. While the number of characters is extremely large, the number of roles or *dramatis personae* is limited to just seven (Propp 1968: 79–80): the "villain", the "donor", the "helper", the "princess and her father", the "sender", the "hero" and the "false hero".

Propp (1968: 26–64) identifies 31 functions distributed among these seven roles. Each role concentrates certain functions, which make up its "sphere of action". Action takes precedence, and thus the functions define the roles (see also Hénault 1992: 92–98). A function is a constant, while the means of its realisation are variables. The meaning of a function is not intrinsic to the action it describes, but derives from its effect on the course of the plot. All folktales are founded on the same functions. Not all functions are present in every folktale, but all the functions that are activated by the tale always appear in the same order.

Below are some examples of the functions that Propp identified in the folktale:
- (function I) one of the members of a family absents himself from home;
- (function II) an interdiction is addressed to the hero;
- (function III) the interdiction is violated;
- (function VIII) the villain causes harm or injury to a member of a family;
- (function IX) the hero is approached with a request or command;
- (function XII) the hero is tested, interrogated, attacked, etc., which prepares the way for his receiving either a magical agent or a helper;
- (function XVI) the hero and the villain join in direct combat;
- (function XXIII) the hero, unrecognised, arrives home or in another country;
- (function XXIV) a false hero presents unfounded claims;
- (function XXX) the villain is punished;
- (function XXXI) the hero is married and ascends the throne.

The characters of a tale are not primary elements, but are defined by their functions. The same function may be performed by different characters, and the same character may perform more than one function. Propp (1968: 19–20) gives a set of examples of this:
- A tsar gives an eagle to a hero. The eagle carries the hero away to another kingdom.
- An old man gives Súčenko a horse. The horse carries Súčenko away to another kingdom.
- A sorcerer gives Iván a little boat. The boat takes Iván to another kingdom.
- A princess gives Iván a ring. Young men appearing from out the ring carry Iván away into another kingdom.

We can formalise all these examples as: A gives S to B and S carries B to another kingdom K. This pattern is independent of what characters play the part of A or B, or of what is the S that passes between them. The characters that can appear in the folktale are nearly infinite, but the roles they play in the plot – the *dramatis personae* – are very limited in number. The radical discovery of Propp was that the action defines the roles of the characters.

This is the idea of a fundamental narrative grammar regulating folktales that Greimas borrowed from Propp and generalised to any kind of narrative, in fact to any kind of discourse. He combined it with Chomsky's generative grammar, which led him to the concept of the "generative trajectory" (*parcours génératif*). The generative trajectory is a model of the process governing the internal production of whole texts (not only sentences and not only in natural language, as with Chomsky's model) according to a process of transition from the abstract to the concrete and from the simple to the complex. Both syntactic and semantic components develop in parallel throughout the whole trajectory. In contrast to Chomsky's generative grammar, the generative trajectory of Greimas is not aligned with Saussure's principle of linearity, which as we saw is not generalisable to all semiotic systems.

Our presentation of Greimasian narrative theory relies mainly on the Dictionary published by Greimas and Courtés in 1979. According to the 1979 account, the generative trajectory consists of three levels: two levels of deep structures (or grammars) and a final one of discursive structures (Table 4), though the possibility of additional levels is not excluded. The first two levels of the trajectory are the "deep level" (*niveau profond*) and the "surface level" (*niveau de surface*). The deep level includes a "fundamental syntax" (*syntaxe fondamentale*) and a "fundamental semantics" (*sémantique fondamentale*), to which correspond on the next level a "surface narrative syntax" (*syntaxe narrative de surface*) and a "narrative semantics" (*sémantique narrative*). The structures of

Table 4: The syntactic and semantic levels of the generative trajectory.

Structures	Components / Levels	Generative trajectory	
		Syntactic	Semantic
Semio-narrative	deep	fundamental syntax	fundamental semantics
	surface	surface narrative syntax	narrative semantics
Discursive	level of discourse, less deep	discursive syntax = discursivisation: – actorialisation – temporalisation – spatialisation	discursive semantics: – thematisation – figurativisation

these levels are "semio-narrative structures" (*structures sémio-narratives*). The term "surface level" is an oxymoron, given that these two levels are both deep levels, as is explicitly clarified by Greimas and Courtés, who state that they correspond to Saussure's language system and Chomsky's competence, extended to cover the sphere of discourse.[36] The "least deep" level, as the two authors put it, is the level of "discursive syntax" (*syntaxe discursive*) and "discursive semantics" (*sémantique discursive*; for the above, see Greimas and Courtés 1979: Génératif [parcours], Procès, Structure).[37]

In the sections below we shall present analytically the six "classic" components, three syntactic and three semantic, of the generative trajectory.

---

[36] This is a major extension of Saussure's theory. For Saussure, the language system is social, while here the concept is transferred to the individual text.

[37] François Rastier criticises Greimas for the isolation of content at the expense of the full process of semiosis and for the conception of expression as a surface phenomenon. He considers Greimas's approach as legitimate, but as missing the specificity of each semiotic system. With this choice, according to Rastier, Greimas abandons expression for generativity, which is absent in Saussure (Rastier 2017: 7–8). His counterproposal, interpretative semantics, starts with the abolition of the dichotomy between deep logical structures and surface linguistic phenomena, and with the idea that the global determines the local, implying the existence of continuous determinations from the corpus to the meaning of texts and from them to the meaning of smaller units, down to the elementary linguistic units, the morphemes (2017: 9–10).

1.2 Fundamental syntax

The fundamental syntax is anchored in the semiotic square. This square is the regulatory factor of the whole generative trajectory and thus needs careful examination. We shall start, following Greimas and Courtés, with the analysis of its categorical terms, which are interrelated.

It starts from a basic opposition *A* vs *non-A*, which constitutes a "semantic axis" (*axe sémantique*). The opposition should be of a "categorical" (*catégoriel*) nature, that is, it should refer to a semantic pair of opposites (for example, *life* vs *death*) characterised by the presence of the same trait in both terms, but in a different aspect each time, and by a relation of mutual presupposition between the terms. In other words, in the case of *life* vs *death*, the common trait is "lifeness" and the two terms of the pair belong to the two extremities of the axis life–death. It belongs to the class of "binary relations" and it is the one we shall encounter below as "relation of contrariety" (*relation de contrariété*).

There is also another type of binary relation, characterised by the opposition that follows from the presence and the absence of a specific trait. For example, the opposition *voiced* vs *unvoiced* is of a privative nature and indicates the presence (marked term) and the absence (unmarked term), respectively, of the same trait.[38]

Greimas and Courtés state that on the basis of the initial pair *A* vs *non-A* it is possible to perform two operations (Figure 10):

(a) The first operation is *negation*, which, when applied to each term of this relation, produces terms which, in reference to the initial term from which each one was generated, follow the logic of contradiction: the two new pairs are A–Ā (where Ā = negation of A) and non-A–$\overline{\text{non-A}}$ (where $\overline{\text{non-A}}$ = negation of non-A). Contradiction, that is, follows as a static comparison

---

38 Petitot (2017: 12) believes that the Greimasian negations should be replaced by these privative oppositions, in which case the diagonals of the square take the form X/Ø and Y/Ø, where Ø is identical in the two pairs. He reminds us that Greimas insisted that the relations of contrariety and contradiction are linguistic and not logical. Greimas and Courtés, as we saw, state that contradiction implies that the two terms cannot coexist. They thus define contradiction as a logical incompatibility *between* terms, while according to Aristotelian logic, contradiction implies that one of the two terms must be true and the other false, thus introducing the extra-semiotic referent.

We should also mention a third type of opposition, not used in the construction of the square: the gradual one, constituted by successive oppositions in the course of which a signified acquires a continuously increasing or decreasing quality, as happens, for example, in the case of the temperature of water: *hot* vs *warm* vs *lukewarm* vs *room temperature* vs *cool* vs *cold* vs *freezing* (Courtés 1991: 181–182).

produced by the dynamic operation of negation, having as a result that the derivative from each initial term cannot logically coexist with it: the first term becomes absent if the second is present.

(b) The second dynamic operation is *assertion*, which is applied on each of the contradictory terms. It implies the recognition of the existence of a relation between Ā and non-A, as well as between non-Ā and A. In both cases, the second term is a *presupposition* for the first term and, as a consequence, the first term *implies* the second. The operation of implication creates a relation of *complementarity* between the two terms. The relation between non-Ā and Ā is one of assertion (Figure 10).

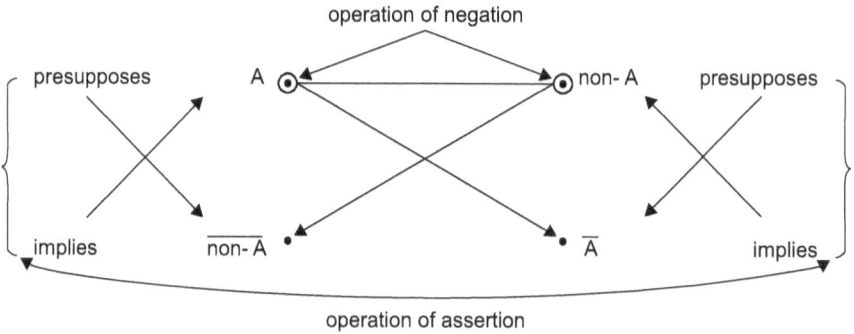

Figure 10: The operations leading to the semiotic square.

Only if this double assertion leads to parallel implications do the two initial terms constitute a semantic category, otherwise the initial terms and their contradictory terms belong to different semantic categories. This issue needs special attention, because the initial semantic axis which is selected may present an unclear logical relation between the two terms and thus be unsuitable for the construction of the semiotic square. Assertion, leading to implication and complementarity, is the necessary test to check the accuracy of the initial opposition. The vertices of the semiotic square are not semes, which depend on natural languages, but noemes, units formulated by the semantic metalanguage prior to any investment with content (Rastier 2009: 32–33).

According to the above premises, the semiotic square takes shape as in Figure 11. The pair $\bar{s}_1$ vs $\bar{s}_2$ is neutral from an axiological point of view, but this is not the case with either the contradictions or the indicators. The concepts of positive and negative schema follow from the dependence of the relations of contradiction on the first positive term or its opposite term respectively. The opposition *positive* vs *negative* indicator is due to a positive or negative assessment respectively, based on the "thymic" (*thymique*, from the ancient Greek θυμός, meaning affect) category constituted by the semes *euphoria* vs *dysphoria* (an opposition having as neutral term "a-phoria"). That is, the relationship $\bar{s}_2 - s_1$ is euphoric (it has a positive connotation), while the relationship $\bar{s}_1 - s_2$ is dysphoric.

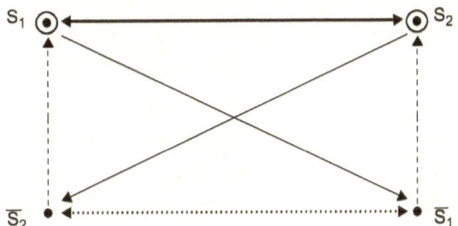

Figure 11: The structure of the semiotic square.
⟷ axis of contraries: $s_1 - s_2$
⟶ relations of contradiction:
 $s_1 - \bar{s}_1$, positive schema
 $s_2 - \bar{s}_2$, negative schema
--⟶ relations of complementarity:
 $\bar{s}_2 - s_1$, "positive indicator" (*deixis positive*)
 $\bar{s}_1 - s_2$, "negative indicator" (*deixis négative*)
⋯⟶ axis of sub-contraries: $\bar{s}_2 - \bar{s}_1$

The initial semantic category on which the whole semiotic square is founded is considered by Greimas and Courtés as an "elementary structure of signification" (*structure élémentaire de la signification*). Contrariety, contradiction and complementarity are the logical types ruling the relations of the square. The authors point out that the four terms of the square are not defined substantially, but only as by-products of relations, and refer to Saussure's position that we mentioned earlier (chapter 3: 7) "*dans la langue il n'y a que des différences*" [in the language system there are only differences]. Logico-semantically, the passage from one term to the other is defined as a *transformation*, due to the operations of negation and assertion.[39]

---

39 There have been criticisms of the semiotic square. One proposal is to replace the square with the more complex logical hexagon, which however does not take into account that its logic is

The semiotic square establishes a first hierarchy, because the logical types governing the relations between terms are hierarchically superior to the terms themselves. There is a superior hierarchical level, which represents a second generation of categorical terms. The terms of the new semiotic square follow from the relations between the terms of the initial square and these relations are hierarchically superior to the previous relations. This square, then, belongs to a second hierarchical level and its terms, which surround the first square, are meta-terms and follow from the combination in pairs of the terms of the initial square, a combination of the logical type "both–and".

Now, two new syntactic meta-axes emerge: the first is created by the linking of the pairs of the meta-terms $s_1 + s_2$ and $\bar{s}_2 + \bar{s}_1$ (the perpendicular meta-axis of the external square), which are contradictory, and the second from the linking of $\bar{s}_2 + s_1$ and $\bar{s}_1 + s_2$ (the horizontal meta-axis of the external square), which are contraries. It is obvious that the combination of the terms which are connected to the two diagonals of the initial square is impossible, because they are contradictory and so cannot coexist (for the semiotic square, see Greimas and Courtés 1979: Carré sémiotique, Contradiction, Contrariété, Deixis, Hiérarchie, Sémantique fondamentale, Structure, Syntaxe fondamentale, Thymique (Catégorie), Transformation, Valeur). In the case of the first semiotic square, we saw that we can test the accuracy of its initial opposition through the relations of complementarity. We now have a second test of accuracy, which is to confirm, when a second-level square is constructed, that its two axes in fact deliver the logical oppositions of contradiction and contrariety.

---

totally alien to semiotics, since it is structured by the truth values of six statements. Operating abstractly, it is possible to go as far as the Hasse diagram of mathematical order theory and its application to Boolean algebra, ending with an n-dimensional hypercube. Greimas and Courtés (1979: Carré sémiotique) mention the logical hexagon (with reference to Robert Blanché), as well as Jean Piaget and Felix Klein's (four-)group theory. However, they emphasise that the semiotic square is a semantic structure and follows from the epistemological problematics concerning signification and the methodological presuppositions of this field; they warn us that, due to this, it is different from logical or mathematical constructions. They conclude that "*Toute identification hâtive des modèles sémiotiques et logico-mathématiques ne peut être dans ces conditions, que dangereuse*" [Under these conditions, any hasty identification of the semiotic with the logico-mathematical models can only be hazardous]. Rastier, who together with Greimas developed the semiotic square, at a later stage criticised it as unable to cover simultaneously Saussure's duality of content and expression (Rastier 2017: 2–4). This argument is in line with Rastier's abandonment of the generative trajectory.

1.3 Fundamental semantics

Fundamental semantics is the semantic investment of the semiotic square. It is produced by projecting on the semiotic square a set of signifieds which transform it into a structured semantic field establishing the fundamental semantics of a text. The fundamental semantics of a text need not derive from a single semiotic square only, but may be based on two interrelated squares. The fundamental semantics are subject to successive semantic investments throughout the other levels of the generative trajectory, resulting in the construction of a discursive micro-universe (chapter 5: 1.1).

The axiology of a text is grounded in the semiotic square of its fundamental semantics. The semantic category composed by the square corresponds to a neutral state of the values invested in it; however, its indicators are structurally axiological, because of their connotative investment by the affective category *euphoria* vs *dysphoria*. These are "virtual" values, which become actualised on the next level of the generative trajectory. Such axiological pairs, constituting elementary axiological structures, are of a paradigmatic nature, logical, ethical or aesthetic in character; they represent micro-systems of values and may be considered as universal, but on the metalinguistic level (Greimas and Courtés 1979: Sémantique fondamentale, Valeur).

We mentioned above the concept of a second-level semiotic square. Greimas and Courtés offer an example of such a construction (Figure 12). They start by investing the opposition s_1 vs s_2 with a precise semantic form, *being* vs *seeming*, which generates the sub-contraries *non-seeming* vs *non-being*. The terms of the second level, surrounding the first-level square, follow from the combination of the pairs of the initial square based on a "both–and" relation.

The four new terms are now meta-terms, of which the pair *truth* vs *falseness* (the perpendicular axis) is constituted by the contradictory meta-terms, while the pair *secret* vs *lie* (the horizontal axis) by the contrary meta-terms (Greimas and Courtés 1979: Carré sémiotique).

In order to better understand the way the second-level square works, we shall select another semantic category, *life* vs *death* (Figure 13). Rather than repeat the details of the construction of the square, we shall concentrate on the semantics of the meta-terms and the relations between them (perpendicularly and horizontally).

First, we generate the sub-contraries *non-death* vs *non-life* and check if the two indicators of the first-level square give us terms related through implication.

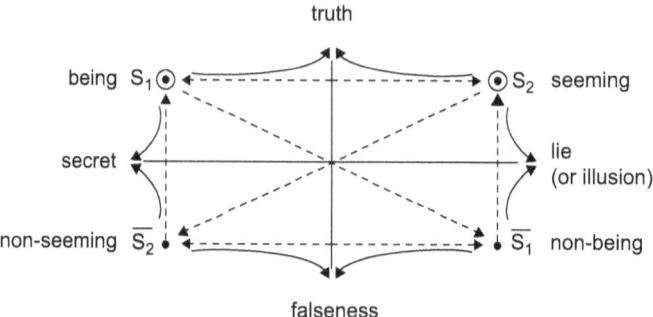

Figure 12: The second-level semiotic square of the semantic category *being* vs *seeming*. Horizontal axis: meta-axis of contraries. Perpendicular axis: meta-axis of contradiction.
⊙ ←--→ ⊙ the initial relation of contrariety: s_1 vs s_2 = *being* vs *seeming*
- - - the relations of the initial semiotic square:
   s_1 vs s_2 = *being* vs *seeming*
   $\bar{s}_2$ vs $\bar{s}_1$ = *non-seeming* vs *non-being*
⎯⎯⎯ the relations of the second-level semiotic square
⤤ The second-level semiotic square:
   s_1 (being) + s_2 (seeming) = truth
   $\bar{s}_2$ (non-seeming) + $\bar{s}_1$ (non-being) = falseness
   $\bar{s}_2$ (non-seeming) + s_1 (being) = secret
   $\bar{s}_1$ (non-being) + s_2 (seeming) = lie (or illusion)

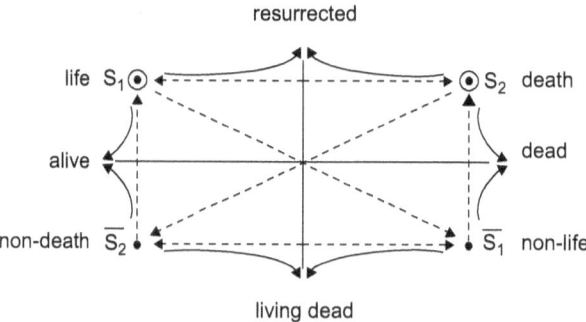

Figure 13: Second-level semiotic square of the semantic category *life* vs *death*.

The positive indicator $\bar{s}_2$–s_1 is non-death–life, and in fact non-death implies life, while the negative indicator $\bar{s}_1$–s_2 is non-life–death, and non-life implies death. Thus, the pair *life* vs *death* really constitutes a semantic category.

Having ensured that the first-level square is well-built, we proceed with the second-level square. Life and death refer to states of being, but we shall render the terms in a more concrete manner by using adjectives. Bringing together the two terms of the positive indicator, life + non-death, leads us to "alive"; the two terms of the negative indicator, death + non-life, lead to "dead"; linking together the two terms of the axis of contraries, life + death (i.e., both life and death), leads to "resurrected"[40]; the two terms of the axis of subcontraries, non death + non-life (i.e., neither life nor death), lead to "living dead".[41] If we check the relations between the meta-terms, we see that the meta-axis of contraries is: s_1 (life) + $\bar{s}_2$ (non-death) = alive (euphoria) vs $\bar{s}_1$ (non-life) + s_2 (death) = dead (dysphoria), and in fact alive is the opposite of dead. The meta-axis of contradiction is composed of s_1 (life) + s_2 (death) = resurrected vs $\bar{s}_2$ (non-death) + $\bar{s}_1$ (non-life) = living dead, and resurrected and living dead are contradictory.

Oppositions such as *being* vs *seeming*, *life* vs *death* or *nature* vs *culture* used in Greimasian theory are metalinguistic conceptions that serve the requirements for the building of a coherent theory, and as such they constitute universals, as is the case with any theory. They should not be confused with actual textual oppositions, since each text creates its own semiotic world. In a post-human robotic world, for example, where all of humanity has been extinguished, the main opposition could well be *nature* vs *roboworld*. And, if some humans have survived, we could have three pairs of opposition: *nature* vs *roboworld*, *nature* vs *culture* and *culture* vs *roboworld*, in which case the opposition *nature* vs *culture* would only be one of the significant oppositions and not necessary the prevalent one.

1.4 Surface narrative syntax

1.4.1 The narrative programme

The surface narrative syntax is the literal syntax of a narrative, which is produced according to rules of conversion from the fundamental syntax. This is of great importance theoretically, because it achieves the conversion from the paradigmatic structure of the fundamental syntax to the syntagmatic structure of the narrative. While the operations on the level of the fundamental syntax

---

[40] Like Lazarus, Osiris and a number of other deities that appeared with the development of agricultural societies and repeat perpetual cycles of death and resurrection in imitation of the annual cycles of nature.
[41] Like vampires and zombies.

concern terms, the narrative syntax can be expressed as "utterances" (*énoncés*), i.e., in the sphere of discourse. In other words, we have here the beginning of the passage from the system, *langue*, to the text, *parole*, although at this level it is still part of *langue*.

The elementary syntagm of the surface narrative syntax is the "narrative programme" (*programme narratif*, PN), constituted by the association of an "utterance of doing" (*énoncé de faire*) to an "utterance of state" (*énoncé d'état*). Each one of these two types of enunciates is an elementary utterance, an elementary narrative syntagm, with a dual structure. Taking as model the structure of natural language, Greimas and Courtés conceive the utterance of state as a "relation-function" between a Subject (*Sujet*) and an Object (*Objet*), which is a relation of "junction" (*jonction*):

$$F \text{ junction } (S - O),$$

in which junction may take two different forms, "conjunction" or "disjunction". Thus, two different forms of utterances of state can result, conjunctive utterances of state:

$$(S \cap O), \text{ where } \cap = \text{conjunction}$$

and disjunctive utterances of state:

$$(S \cup O), \text{ where } \cup = \text{disjunction}.$$

On the level of the surface narrative syntax there are as yet no specific characters, only syntactic roles (S, O). However, to clarify the presentation, we shall borrow some characters from the next level, that of discursive syntax. If we postulate that S is "John" and O is "the ball", "John has the ball" would be an example of a conjunctive utterance of state, and "John does not have the ball" an example of a disjunctive utterance of state.

Utterances of doing formulate the transition from one state to another. Doing is ruled by transformation, which is incorporated in the narrative programme according to the canonical schema:

$$PN = \text{transformation } (S - O)$$

or, in more analytical form,

$$PN = F\,[S_1 \rightarrow (S_2 - O)],$$

where F and $\rightarrow$ = function (of doing), i.e., function of transformation; S_1 = subject of doing; S_2 = subject of state; O = object of state; [ ] = utterance of doing and ( ) = utterance of state. $F\,[S_1 \rightarrow (S_2 - O)]$ is an "act".

Using as before a simplified example, we can construct the utterance of doing "Mary takes the ball from John", where S_1 is represented by Mary and S_2 by John who has the ball O. We see that, due to the utterance of doing, the initial situation has changed: John no longer has a ball and the ball is no longer John's. We have constructed an elementary narrative, which corresponds to the narrative programme of S_1, in our case Mary's. It would also be possible to make S_1 and S_2 coincide in one and the same person, for example John, giving the canonical schema the form:

$$PN = F\ [S_2 \rightarrow (S_2 - O)],$$

in which case the signification would be "John makes John (himself) to be without a ball", whence a new narrative, according to which John either loses the ball or renounces it voluntarily (he gives it as a present or throws it away); in this case the act is reflexive.

The subjects of the relation–function, which is present in both utterances of state and of doing, are called by Greimas and Courtés "(syntactic) actants" – *actants* (*syntaxiques*). These are the subjects S_1 and S_2, as well as the object O. They are formal syntagmatic units, prior to any semantic investment. In our examples, we anticipated on this process by giving the formal units the semantic contents "John", "Mary" and "ball" to facilitate the reader.

The narrative programme is the representation of an *act*, the act of "making-to-be" (*faire-être*) by a Subject (in our example, "Mary makes John to be without a ball"). Making-to-be is a "modal" structure (section 1.4.2 below), and the act is the act of someone or something that creates or changes a situation, an act of transformation. Here, the utterance of doing ("Mary makes John to be without a ball") rules the utterance of state ("John is without a ball"); the transformation of the utterance of state, due to disjunction (in another case, it could be conjunction), is the result of the utterance of doing. In these cases, the utterance of doing is called "modal utterance" (*énoncé modal*) and the utterance of state "descriptive utterance" (*énoncé descriptif*). In this particular case, the utterance of doing rules the utterance of state, but the modal utterance is not necessarily one of doing nor is the descriptive utterance necessarily one of state, because the utterance of state can take the place of the modal utterance and either one of them can rule an utterance of doing or state.

Making-to-be can partly be compared to a performance, which presupposes a modal competence, the modality of "knowing-how-to-do" (*savoir-faire*), and in this case the act is the result of the transition from competence to performance (in order for Mary to perform her act, she must find out where John is so that she can take the ball from him). The semiotics of doing is a semiotics attached to action, and performance as a whole is a syntagmatic arrangement of acts, which form the narrative programme of a Subject possessing competence.

The complete (micro-)programme, which starts from a modal utterance and ends with a complete programme of doing, is the "narrative trajectory" (*parcours narratif*) of the Subject, during which it acquires the necessary modal competence (in the case of Mary, the narrative trajectory could include the fact that she learned from John's mother when John goes to the stadium).

We can now grasp the nature of the conversion from the fundamental syntax to the surface narrative syntax: it is a transition from an abstract paradigmatic level, structured according to logical operations, to the syntagmatic structure of the narrative, based on utterances of doing and utterances of state, both presupposing the existence of subjects. The same transition activates the concepts of competence and performance. For Greimas and Courtés, the surface narrative syntax is of an anthropomorphic nature – though this does not imply that all narrative Subjects must be human.

Any single utterance may be replaced by a series of utterances, resulting in the extension of the narrative. The trajectory of the narrative discourse is a sequence of states followed and/or preceded by transformations. This trajectory leads from an initial to a final state, its narrative syntax structuring an "algorithm of transformations". The structure of narrative discourse is rendered by an actantial grammar, in the framework of which actants, i.e., roles associated with action, assume the values of the semiotic square of the fundamental syntax and semantics.[42]

In our example, the Subject S_1, Mary, learns where John is, acquiring a "knowing-how-to-do" (*savoir-faire*). This example shows that narrative doing may be of two types: it may be "pragmatic" (*faire pragmatique*), in which case the act involves a concrete objects (such as John's ball), or "cognitive" (*faire cognitif*), referring to cognitive abilities (such as the information about John's habits that Mary acquired). Narrative programmes may evolve along both of these dimensions. But knowledge is not the only factor that affects doing. Both utterances of state and utterances of doing can be modified in various ways in order to produce modal utterances (Greimas and Courtés 1979: Cognitif, Faire, Pragmatique).

---

[42] Greimas and Courtés 1979: Actant, Acte, Algorithme, Anthropomorphe, Compétence, Conversion, Énoncé, État, Modalité, Narratif (parcours), Parcours, Performance, Programme narratif, Syntaxe narrative de surface, Transformation; Greimas 1983: 49–66.

1.4.2 The modalities

The possible modalities of utterances are a rather complex matter, extending beyond purely narrative discourse. Greimas and Courtés suggest that the categories of modality are those presented in Table 5.

Table 5: Typology of modalities.

Modality	Ternary articulation		
	virtualising	actualising	realising
Exotaxic	ought-to	being-able	doing/making
Endotaxic	wanting	knowing (how)	being

Exotaxic modalities are those that relate two utterances with different Subjects, for example "*Mary* has the strength – ("being-able-to-do") – to make *John* lose the ball", while endotaxic modalities relate utterances with the same Subject, for example "*Mary* wants – ("wanting-to-do") – to take the ball".

Modalities can modify not only utterances of doing or state, but can also modify other modal utterances: we can say that "Mary wants to take the ball", but also "Mary wants to know how to take the ball" ("wanting-to-know-how-to-do"). Modalities can be projected on the semiotic square, producing their contrary and contradictory terms, as can combinations of modalities. An example of a semiotic square based on modalities is given below with the square of the modal utterance wanting-to-do (Figure 14).

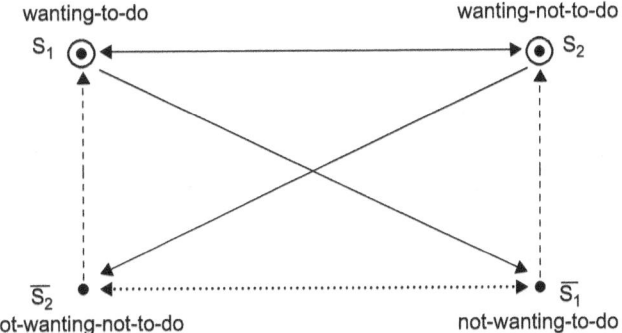

Figure 14: The semiotic square of the modal utterance wanting-to-do.

The same holds for the modalisations of the utterances of state. Starting from "wanting to be", with the help of the square we can produce "wanting-not-to-be", "not-wanting-to-be" and "not-wanting-not-to-be".

The modalities of doing ("ought-to-do", "wanting-to-do", "being-able-to-do" and "knowing-how-to-do") together constitute the modal competence of doing. The acquisition of modal competence by the Subject–hero is a major mechanism for the development of a narrative (Greimas and Courtés 1979: Actantiel, Actualisation, Compétence, Modalité, Structure, Syntaxe narrative de surface; Greimas 1983: 67–91).

In order for Mary to take the ball from John, she first has to acquire the will ("wanting") or the duty ("ought") to take the ball. Let us suppose that this incentive goes back to her childhood, when her father refused to give her a ball, and since then she passionately wants to have her own ball; or perhaps she has an obligation to become a football player because it is a family tradition. Then, she must learn John's habits ("knowing-how") to find out when he will have a game at the stadium. Finally, she must acquire the skill ("being-able") to take the ball from John – for example, by training for years in order to acquire the competence to play football. Her encounter with John in the stadium, which will take the form of a confrontation, presupposes that Mary has acquired the modal competence to perform the crowning act of taking the ball from John.

In a similar way we can construct a narrative on the basis of the modalities of being: Mary wants ("wanting-to") to be a football player, because it is a family tradition ("ought-to-be"); she finds out ("knowing") how she can be accepted in a football academy; she acquires the competence ("being-able") to play good football; and, finally, she triumphs in the stadium (or, possibly, she fails, with all the dysphoric narrative consequences such a version could have).

1.4.3 The narrative schema

We have already mentioned that the surface narrative syntax is assumed by actants and is of an anthropomorphic nature. Actants are not characters (characters appear on the next level of the generative trajectory), but formal roles comparable to the grammatical positions in a sentence. They are empty structural narrative positions, which are filled on the next level by characters or "actors" (*acteurs*) – section 1.6 below. Actors are not necessarily human; they can also be animals, objects, internalised values or feelings.

We saw above that Propp recognised seven roles in the folktale: the villain, the donor, the helper, the princess and her father, the sender, the hero and the false hero. Greimas and Courtés organise Propp's seven roles according to a higher level of abstraction into three pairs of actants: the Subject of the action

(*Sujet*, Propp's hero) – the Object of value (*Objet*, for example the princess); the Sender (*Destinateur*, Addresser, for example the princess's father); the Recipient (*Destinataire*, Addressee, usually the hero)[43]; the Helper (*Adjuvant*, positive auxiliary role, the donor and the helper); and the Opponent (*Opposant*, negative auxiliary role, the villain and the false hero). Each actant constitutes a semantic category, which can be developed into a semiotic square with its contrary and contradictory terms, potentially producing additional actantial positions; the most common of these are the Anti-Subject and the Anti-Sender (Greimas and Courtés 1979: Adjuvant, Anti-Destinateur, Destinateur/Destinataire, Narratif [parcours], Narratif [schema], Objet, Opposant, Sujet; Hénault 1983: 72).

We see that the Subject corresponds to the role Propp named "hero" and the Object is the role invested by the narrative with positive value, which in the case of the folktale is frequently the princess, although it can be any person or object the acquisition of which is the aim of the action. The pair Sender–Recipient is associated to two communicative roles *inside* the text: Propp's sender and the princess's father correspond to the first term of the pair, while the Recipient is usually the hero who undertakes the mission leading to action. The Helper, a positive role, corresponds to Propp's two roles of donor and helper, while the Opponent corresponds to the villain and the false hero. Later, Greimas observed that these two roles are personified forms of the modality of "being-able-to-do" and its contradictory "not-being-able-to-do", respectively, with the result that the three pairs of actants were reduced to two. We believe, however, that, while this view is theoretically legitimate, it is operationally less efficient and does not seem to be equally helpful for the analysis.

In the same manner as they redefine Propp's roles as the more abstract actants, Greimas and Courtés also redefine Propp's functions in a more abstract manner to form the "canonical narrative schema" (*schéma narratif canonique*,

---

43 Greimas and Courtés use a capital first letter for the pair *Destinateur-Destinataire* to avoid confusion with the same terms used by Jakobson, which they render with a lower-case letter. The difference lies in the fact that the pair of Greimas and Courtés is textual, while Jakobson refers to extra-textual entities (chapter 8: 2.6). *Destinateur-Destinataire* in French are used as purely linguistic terms or with reference to the postal service, but may also refer to the sending of an emissary, a generalisation aligned with Greimas's views on the communication of objects (chapter 8: 2.4). In their Dictionary, the two authors render this pair as "Addresser-Addressee", which in English refers only to purely linguistic concepts or to the postal service. The translators of the Dictionary (Greimas and Courtés 1979) opted for "Sender-Receiver", which has the handicap of bringing into semiotics the technocratic terminology of information theory (chapter 8: 2.1). To avoid this problem, and given that we could not find any exact term to replace "Sender", we chose to translate the terms as Sender and Recipient.

Greimas and Courtés 1979: Narratif [schema]). For example, Propp's first eight functions enumerate different ways in which, starting from an initial situation, a "lack" (*manque*) is discovered or provoked: one of the members of a family absents himself from home (function I); an interdiction is addressed to the hero (function II); the interdiction is violated (function III); the villain seeks for information (function IV); he receives it (function V); he attempts to deceive the victim (function VI); the victim is deceived (function VII); the villain causes harm or injury to a member of the family (function VIII) or a member of a family lacks or desires to have something (function VIIIa). In all these cases, an initial situation is disturbed because a lack is caused or a desire is expressed: a desired Object (someone or something) is missing or lost or sought for.

In the folktale, someone assigns the quest for this Object to the hero–Subject: the princess's father announces that whoever brings back the lost princess (or finds the water of life or kills the dragon) will receive his daughter in marriage and inherit half the kingdom, as a result of which the hero–Subject assumes the mission (functions IX and X). An agreement or "contract" is concluded between a Sender and a Recipient, who in the above example coincides with the Subject of the narrative. Greimas and Courtés use the term "manipulation" for this step. Manipulation is based on some form of persuasion, but it is not always explicit (the hero may undertake the quest because his conscience dictates it), and it may be the result of trickery (temptation or deception) or coercion (intimidation or blackmail). Manipulation transforms the Recipient into a competent Subject (Greimas and Courtés 1979: Manipulation, Narratif, schema): the Recipient–Subject is persuaded to assume the mission, he has acquired an "ought-to-do" and/or a "wanting-to-do", and sets out on his quest, which frequently involves a displacement to another space (function XI).

Greimas and Courtés observe that the structure of the canonical narrative schema tends to be essentially "polemical", in the sense that it is organised as a conflict between the Subject and the Opponent, who both want possession of the Object of value: the schema can be seen as the detachment and acquisition of this Object, first by the Opponent and then by the Subject. In the polemical structure, the action takes the form of a confrontation, which is a test for the Subject; the test is frequently doubled or tripled. Greimas and Courtés contrast this polemical structure to the "contractual" structure, establishing a circuit of communication, a system of exchange between Sender and Recipient (Greimas and Courtés 1979: Communication, Manipulation) which is peaceful in nature and constitutes a framework for the polemical narrative in the traditional folktale.

In the narrative trajectory, as we saw, the Subject must first acquire the modal competence to perform the narrative programme. In the folktale, once the hero has assumed the quest, there follows the function of the first test, the "qualifying (preliminary) test" (*épreuve qualifiante*). Someone (the donor, in Propp) tests the hero by, for example, attacking him or asking him for a gift or a service (function XII). The hero reacts correctly, offering the service or vanquishing the adversary (function XIII) and as a result acquires a magical agent (function XIV). Propp's donor is one of the two forms of Greimas's Helper and what the hero–Subject acquires is the ability to fulfil his quest successfully, the modality of knowing-how-to or being-able-to defeat his adversary. The function does not depend on the good will or intentions of the Helper (the Subject may take what it desires by force) but, like all functions, only refers to the effect of the act on the development of the narrative: the effect is that the Subject is equipped with the modal competences of ability and knowledge.

Propp's next function (function XV) is the spatial displacement of the hero to "another" place; this function may take the form of the hero's "knowing-how-to-do".

Having acquired the necessary competence, the hero is in a position to confront the villain in battle (function XVI in Propp). This is the performance, the "decisive test" (*épreuve décisive*) of the hero in the canonical narrative schema; the villain is defeated (Propp's function XVIII) and the initial lack is eliminated (function XIX). In some tales there then follows a set of three episodes which constitute a kind of sub-narrative in the form of a test. The hero sets out for home (function XX), is pursued by the villain (function XXI) and escapes (function XXII).

The narrative could stop here, but in many tales there is also a third test of the hero. In this case, the battle against the villain leaves the hero with a mark, or the hero is given a significant gift (function XVII).

If a third test – the "glorifying test" (*épreuve glorifiante*) – is included, the hero returns to his country unrecognised or disguised (function XXIII). A new Opponent (Propp's false hero) claims that he was actually the one who defeated the villain (for example, another knight claims that he was the one who killed the dragon) which imposes a last test on the hero (functions XXIV and XXV); the hero responds with success (function XXVI). In Greimasian terms, this is a repetition of the narrative structure of test.

The final step of the narrative trajectory is the "sanction". The hero is recognised and glorified (functions XXVII and XXIX), while the villain is revealed and punished (functions XXVIII and XXX); finally, the hero marries the princess and takes the throne (function XXXI). In Greimasian terms, the reward of the hero implies the recognition on the part of the Sender as adjudicator that the contract has been fulfilled, that the lack has been eliminated and the initial situation restored.[44]

Once more Greimas and Courtés have moved on a more abstract level than Propp, reducing his 31 functions to only two, the function of the contract (manipulation and sanction, Propps's functions IX–X and XXVII–XXXI) and the function of the test (competence and performance, Propp's functions XII–XIV, XVI–XIX, XX–XXII, XII–XXVI). Within the contractual framework of manipulation and sanction, the polemical narrative of competence and performance unfurls.

We can integrate the story of Mary into this pattern. Mary's initial situation is either a lack resulting from a childhood experience or an obligation to the family tradition, which until its fulfilment contributes to the conservation of the lack. Mary's qualifying test is her acceptance in the football academy and the acquisition of competence. Then follows the decisive test, the confrontation with the Opponent in the "other" space of the stadium, during which she succeeds in taking the ball from John. If, after this success, she manages to score an unexpected goal, she feels personally absolutely triumphant and the exuberant fans express their enthusiasm with applause and cries and slogans: she has completed the stage of the glorifying test and the initial lack has been eliminated.

The parallelism between the reward of the hero and the punishment of the villain shows, for Greimas and Courtés, that the lack with which the narrative starts may be seen as the result of a breach of an implicit collective contract: an initial positive situation is disturbed and a lack is produced, because someone or something causes a negative change. The Sender thus may represent a collectivity, a "final Sender", who will benefit from the execution of the contract (Greimas and Courtés 1979: Sanction). Reward and punishment demonstrate the restoration of the initial positive state.

Every step of a narrative may have a different outcome, which will correspond to another axis of a semiotic square: the Recipient may refuse the mission or fail in his quest. Every step of the narrative may be further developed: there may be many tests of the hero, many searches for Helpers, many displacements,

---

[44] Franco Moretti proposes a "literary geography" on the premise that there is an indissoluble link between narrative and geographical space. He believes that Propp's 31 functions can only be realised within specific spaces and classifies the functions into four groups on this basis: the "initial world" (functions I–XI and XIII–XXXI), the space of the donor (XII–XIV), the "other kingdom" (XV–XIX) and the "border" (XX–XXII). Moretti overemphasises space in believing that the major events of the narrative are produced by the opposition between the initial and the other world. If we compare his geography with Greimasian theory, Moretti's space of the donor coincides with the qualifying test, his other kingdom more or less with the decisive test and his final initial world with the glorifying test (Moretti [1997] 1998: 3, 8, 70–72).

many battles with secondary Opponents before the final confrontation. A typical trait of the folktale is the doubling, even tripling, of the same function. For example, three brothers set out to save a princess and encounter on their way an old beggar woman who asks them to give her some of their bread. First the elder and then the second-born brother refuse, resulting in the failure of their quest, but the third and youngest brother responds positively to the request and is given in return a magic ring that makes him invisible, and it is this ring that functions as the necessary Helper to defeat the Opponent.

Every narrative is the narrative of a specific Subject, which has its own narrative trajectory. Another Subject would have a different trajectory: the same tale would be very different if narrated from the viewpoint of the dragon rather than the princess. Many texts include the intertwined narrative trajectories of two or more Subjects. The Greimasian narrative model can analyse narratives that focus on only a part of the whole canonical schema, such as coming-of-age narratives, in which the Subject through tests acquires a general "being-able-to-do" and thus becomes able to face the future. It can also deal with narratives that do not have the happy ending of the typical folktale: stories of failure, in which the Subject cannot acquire the Object desired (*Tristan and Isolde*: the Subject desires an Object which he can gain only in death) or the Object proves to be a false Object, without value (*Macbeth*: the Subject gains the throne desired, but at the price of losing everything he values, his honour, his wife and finally his life); with narratives of uncertainty (*Hamlet*: the Subject wavers between accepting and refusing the mission assigned to him by the ghost of his father); or with narratives marked by tragic irony (*Oedipus Rex*: the Subject seeks for an Opponent, the murderer of the old king, only to discover that it is himself).

The Greimasian model of the canonical narrative schema can be used for the analysis, not only of folktales, but of any narrative form. A great number of narrative forms – mainly the traditional genres – follow Propp's functions, but the Greimasian model can analyse much more complex narratives, such as the epic, the drama or the novel (Greimas and Courtés 1979: Actant, Contrat, Énoncé, Épreuve, Narratif (schema), Polémique, Syntaxe narrative de surface; Greimas 1983: 19–66).

1.5 Narrative semantics

If into the representation of a narrative programme which records the effect of doing we introduce not only conjunction and disjunction, but also the semantic investment of the Object in the form of value (v), we end up with the following two possible forms:

$$PN = F\,[S_1 \rightarrow (S_2 \cap O_v)]$$

and

$$PN = F\,[S_1 \rightarrow (S_2 \cup O_v)].$$

Given that the utterance of state occupies the position of the Object of doing, the representation above is reformulated as follows:

$$PN = F\,[S_1 \rightarrow O_1(S_2 \cap O_{2v})]$$

and

$$PN = F\,[S_1 \rightarrow O_1(S_2 \cup O_{2v})].$$

The affective investment is transferred from the semiotic square of fundamental semantics to the next level of the generative trajectory, narrative semantics, and on that level values that were "virtual" become "actualised", being invested in the actant–Objects of the utterances of state. This transition from fundamental semantics to narrative semantics consists in the manipulation of the available values articulated on the semiotic square. The available values constitute a combinatorial axiological stock that forms the basis for the production of a predictable set of possible types of discourse, while on the level of narrative semantics constraints are placed on this combinatorial, partly specifying the kind of discourse that will be produced. Values belong to two classes. There are "modal values" (*valeurs modales*) – see the modalities of Table 5 – and "descriptive values" (*valeurs descriptives*). The latter may be subjective – for example "states of mind" (*états d'âme*), "essential" in the sense that in natural languages they are frequently associated to the subject by the copula – or they may be objective or "accidental" (for example, objects that can be consumed or stored), frequently attributed to the subject through the verb to "have" or its parasynonyms.

On the level of fundamental semantics, values like Subjects and Objects are in a virtual state, but they acquire substance (are actualised) in the semio-narrative surface syntax through the relation–function of junction. On this level, values, Subjects and Objects are actualised if Subjects and Objects are in disjunction, but when conjunction is achieved, they become "realised". Thus, the typology of values, Subjects and Objects follows the triadic articulation "virtualising–actualising–

realising", the same articulation ruling the typology of modalities (Table 5).[45] As in the transition from the fundamental to the surface narrative syntax, so the transition from fundamental to narrative semantics causes a transformation of the structure of values from paradigmatic (*euphoria* vs *dysphoria*) to syntagmatic (Greimas and Courtés 1979: Acte, Actualisation, Conversion, Descriptif, Objectif, Programme narratif, Réalisation, Sémantique fondamentale, Sémantique narrative, Subjective (valeur), Valeur; Greimas 1983: 19–48).

1.6 Discursive syntax

The discursive syntax is the surface level of the generative trajectory. To define it, Greimas and Courtés have recourse to the field of "enunciation" (*énonciation*), an act of communication which they do not locate outside the text but consider as the logical presupposition of an utterance incorporated *within* the text. Enunciation is the mediation between the language system and speech, between the virtual structures and the discursive structures, and belongs to the moment of the production of speech, being integral to the speech act. Enunciation, according to Greimas and Courtés, activates three processes which are sub-components of "discursivisation": "actorialisation", "temporalisation" and "spatialisation" (Table 6), which structure the discursive syntax by constituting its units and relationships. In other words, through these processes, the actants are invested by the actors of the discursive level and the logical narrative structures are inscribed in spatiotemporal coordinates (Greimas and Courtés 1979: Débrayage, Énonciation, Syntaxe discursive).

These three processes involved in enunciation perform a triple conversion. Enunciation unites three factors, "I", "now" and "here", but the utterance produced by it creates a field of actorial, temporal and spatial *representation*. Representation implies detachment from enunciation. In actorialisation, the disjunction from the "I" of enunciation projects into the utterance a "not–I", that is, a textual character, which however realistic it is, however much it seems to be none other than the "enunciator", the implied sender of the text, is nonetheless only an illusion of him or her. In temporalisation, the "now", the time zero of the utterance, is converted into a "not-now" which is the "objective" zero time of the narrative. In spatialisation, an "objective" space of "not–here", of elsewhere, is opposed to "here".

---

[45] An additional type of modality, potentialising, was added with the late Greimasian semiotics of passions (chapter 7: 2).

Table 6: The processes of discursivisation in syntax and semantics.

Discursive syntax	actorialisation	
	temporalisation	aspectualisation
		temporal localisation
		temporal programming
	spatialisation	spatial localisation
		spatial programming
Discursive semantics	thematisation ↓ figurativisation	figuration
		iconisation
		onomastics

The actor, just like the actant, replaces Propp's *dramatis persona*. The actor may be an individual (for example, Vladimir) or a collectivity (the voters), figurative (such as a man or an animal) or non-figurative (such as justice).

These three sub-components have specific effects on discursive syntax. Actorialisation leads not only to the investment of actants with actors discussed above, but is also related to "thematisation", which is technically part of discursive semantics (section 1.7 below). More specifically, an actor is constituted by the combination of at least one actantial role (investment from discursive syntax) and at least one thematic role (investment from discursive semantics): for example, our actor "Mary" assumes the actantial role of Subject and is invested with the thematic role of football player. Thus, an actorial typology has two poles, one of which consists of simple actors, combining a single actant and a single theme in one actor, and the other combining more than one actant and more than one theme in a complex actor. One actantial role may be invested in more than one actor: the role of Helper in the folktale is often invested in two or more actors. An actor can also change actantial role in the course of the narrative: the Opponent may be converted to Helper or vice versa. The conversion from narrative to discursive syntax is not static, because the actors also become recipients of the narrative transformations. The result of these processes is to create an actorial structure in the surface of the text (Greimas and Courtés 1979: Actant, Acteur, Actorialisation; Greimas 1983: 61–65).

Temporalisation produces in a text the impression of time, as a result of which the narrative organisation becomes a "story". It includes a number of sub-processes or sub-components. The first is "aspectualisation", which is the installation by the enunciator of an implicit observer within the text; this process also accompanies actorialisation and spatialisation. The second sub-process, pragmatic in nature, is "temporal localisation", which by segmenting and organising temporal sequences creates on the discursive level a temporal frame of reference for the inscription of the narrative programmes, which acquire a temporal dimension when converted. This inscription is static, because the positions defined represent utterances of state. Localisation follows from the conversion of the logical relationships between narrative programmes into temporal relations, that is, a programme presupposing another programme is considered on the discursive level as chronologically posterior to it. The third sub-process, also pragmatic, is "temporal programming", according to which the whole axis of the logical relationships between narrative programmes, an axis of logical presuppositions, is converted into an axis of temporal and pseudo-causal successions inside the narrative.

As we can see, temporal localisation sets the prerequisites for temporal programming. Temporal programming represents the utterances of doing, which involve a transition from one time period to another and establish on the discursive level the concept of *movement*, accompanied by *directionality* (origin to destination). Temporal programming is not limited to a simple linear arrangement based on the semic pair of contraries *anteriority* vs *posteriority* of the narrative programmes; it is also associated with temporal duration, and it also allows for the possibility of temporal concomitance. In this case, two or more parallel narrative programmes coincide temporally and, if they are of different duration, we encounter the phenomenon of temporal "nesting" (*emboîtement*), according to which a shorter duration is inscribed within a longer (Greimas and Courtés 1979: Aspectualisation, Concomitance, Localisation spatio-temporelle, Observateur, Programmation spatio-temporelle, Temporalisation).

The sub-processes of spatialisation are similar to those of temporalisation. "Spatial localisation" offers a spatial frame of reference for the static inscription of the utterances of state of the narrative programmes, so that they are located in space; the arrangement of spaces is organised around a reference "place zero". Greimas and Courtés propose as a very simplified organisational schema of spatial location a three-dimensional set of topological semes based on the axes horizontality–verticality–perspectivity (chapter 3: 6.4); their intersection point is the above place zero.

"Spatial programming", of a functional nature, is the process by which a syntagmatic connection and linear pattern is achieved between the individual spaces that resulted from localisation (though we point out that the patterns may be more complex than linear). In addition to the simple linear pattern, Greimas and Courtés mention spatial nesting, of surfaces within surfaces, for example, and volumes within volumes. The pattern of spaces is in accordance with the temporal programming of the narrative (Greimas and Courtés 1979: Acteur, Localisation spatio-temporelle, Programmation spatio-temporelle, Spatialisation).

We note that localisation and programming follow the Saussurean epistemology of the system: localisation defines elements and programming formulates the syntagmatic relationships between elements.

Such an approach may create the impression that space (as well as time) is a static container of action: spatial localisation and programming are directly determined by the narrative trajectories and space (like time) seems unable to have any feedback on action. We may think of an inexhaustible number of possibilities for space (as well as time) to affect action: for example, a certain place on a river would allow the hero to arrive safely at his destination, but the lack of a boat obliges him to look for a bridge, which happens to be guarded by a malevolent creature that he has to face; or the hero is within a labyrinth (a complex, non-linear pattern) which strongly constrains action, and his way out depends on a mix of spatial trial-and-error, spatial reasoning and maybe chance. However, the Greimasian approach does not in fact consider space and time as static. The impression created by the theoretical framework is the product of a reverse order, given that the impacts of space and time are already absorbed in the narrative trajectories, leading to the impression of space and time being static.

1.7 Discursive semantics

Just like discursive syntax, discursive semantics represents the surface level of the generative trajectory. It is subject to new semantic investments, which accompany the syntagmatic restructuring of the discursive level. It includes two processes, "thematisation" and "figurativisation" (Table 6).

Thematisation is the process which, assuming the values of fundamental semantics that have been actualised in junction with the Subjects on the level of narrative semantics, gives them the form of abstract "themes" (*thèmes*). It can be applied to Subjects, Objects or functions and is involved in all three processes of discursivisation; we already mentioned the thematisation of actors, but time and space are also subject to thematisation. It is a process of conversion of the original value, to which it gives various abstract forms.

Greimas and Courtés give an example of this process. They postulate that the initial value of a text in fundamental semantics is "liberty" and that this value is invested in an Object–actant of the narrative programmes. If the Object is in disjunction with the Subject, the aim of its narrative trajectory will be freedom. The inscription of this trajectory in discursive semantics may be related to the process of temporalisation and take the form of "temporal escape", or it may be related to the process of spatialisation and take the form of "spatial escape". In both cases "escape" is an abstract theme. A theme appears in a story in different forms, which together constitute a thematic trajectory following the narrative trajectory. If the thematic trajectory is condensed as qualities of a subject, it leads to the installation of a thematic role – for example, "escape" condensed installs a "fugitive" – which is a thematisation of the subject of doing.

The thematisation of space is closely connected to the function of displacement of the hero in the folktale. In folktale and myth, the hero in order to confront his opponent is transported or travels "elsewhere", far from the familiar space of family or community. This "other" space is thematised as the space of testing and frequently, if the aim of the hero is the restoration of an initial situation, as the space of anti-culture and chaos. The thematisation of space is also very important in literary texts, from medieval narrative poetry – for example, the knights of king Arthur must put their life in danger in the chaotic space of adventure in order to defeat their opponent and be permitted to return to the court – to the classical European novel, as shown particularly in the work of Franco Moretti (1998).

Analysing the historical novel, Moretti observes that it takes place away from the centre and near borders, either the internal borders between regions of a state or the external borders between states. External borders are a space of adventure and danger, of encounters with the unknown – frequently the enemy – and according to Moretti's bold assertion, this is what produces the narrative.[46] Internal borders, on the other hand, function differently and produce treason. Moretti believes that certain characters are closely connected to borders. For him, the semantic tension increases and metaphors become denser at the borders, and this can be generalised to other types of novels as well. Moretti concludes that in the classic European novel, the internal semiotic logic of the narrative depends to a large extent on space. He refers to Propp and Lotman, because for both of them the crossing of borders is usually decisive for the narrative.

The concept of the spatial boundary is central in Lotman's theory of the semiosphere, and he also uses it for the analysis of geographical space in

---

46 It seems to us that Moretti is misled by the fashion of the so-called "spatial turn" when he claims in general that it is space that produces narrative. In comparison, in Greimasian theory, spatialisation belongs to the lowest level of the generative trajectory and we cannot see how it could replace the foundation of narrative on the deep level of this trajectory.

literary texts. According to him, the border "both separates and unites" and "the hottest spots for semioticising processes are the boundaries of the semiosphere" (Lotman 1990: 136). The border separates the representation of the internal world from that of the external, which always appears as unstructured chaos. The movement that crosses the borders – as, for example, during the struggle of the hero against the forces of darkness – is one of the most common forms for the construction of the plot (Lotman 1975 and 1990: 131–142).

Figurativisation includes three components: figuration, iconisation and onomastics. The nucleus of figuration is the "figure". The figure is composed of a combination of semes linked as content (signifieds) to elements of expression (signifiers), the specific characteristic of which are that they belong to a semiotics of the natural world, that is, a semiotics referring to entities such as objects, natural phenomena and behaviours. Figuration originates in the conversion of the abstract thematisation, that is, it represents a possible though not necessary further development of thematisation with a new investment through a "metaphorical connector". It consists of a set of figures which are further specified during iconisation and thus functions as a genotype of iconisation. A theme may be taken up by different figures, for example the theme "university" can be expressed by "professor" or "student". Like the theme, the figure appears in different variants in a story, constituting a figurative trajectory that runs through the whole of the text.

To borrow once more an example from Greimas and Courtés (1979: Figurativisation), let us suppose that on the level of narrative semantics a Subject is disjoined from the Object it desires: $S \cup O$. Let us also suppose that the narrative programme aims at an Object of value (v), whence $S \cup O_v$, and that this value is "power", one of the forms (making-to-be) of the modality of being-able-to: $S \cup O_{v(power)}$. The Subject will attempt conjunction with this value so as to achieve a state $S \cap O_v$. There are innumerable ways of narrating a story of this kind and each one of them represents a different figuration. In each variant, the Object receives a specific semantic investment, which renders it recognisable as a specific figure, for example "automobile", whence $S \cup O_{(automobile)v(power)}$. In this case, one of the possible figurative discourses would be the quest for an automobile and the acknowledgement by others of the power it bestows, as well as the exercise of this power in the case of conjunction $S \cap O_{(automobile)v(power)}$.

The installation of the figure "automobile" transforms the processes into specific actions, invests the actor with a set of figures and establishes a set of spatio-temporal indices for him or her. Figurativisation as a whole creates figurative trajectories and, if they are coextensive with the totality of discourse, figurative isotopies emerge.

If, for example, the temporal escape referred to above takes the form of escape into "childhood memories", or the spatial escape takes the form of "sailing to distant seas", a transition from thematisation to figuration takes place. The parables of the Bible, which as a whole express the same religious idea, each in a different way, constitute a whole figurative trajectory, the central idea of which belongs to the higher level of thematisation. Signifieds such as "automobile", "forest", "winter", "king" belong to the lower level of figuration.

Iconisation, the next step in the full development of figurativisation, results in the creation of the illusion of the referent, of reality. It is related to onomastics, which introduces anthroponyms (the naming of the actors), chrononyms (designating precise durations such as "day" or "spring") and toponyms (precise designations of places), corresponding to and completing the processes of actorialisation, temporalisation and spatialisation of the discursive syntax, respectively. Thus, iconisation and onomastics specify figuration; onomastics contribute to the referential illusion, the sense of reality created by a text (Greimas and Courtés 1979: Acteur, Ancrage, Anthroponyme, Chrononyme, Connecteur, Figurativisation, Iconicité, Monde naturel, Onomastique, Référent, Sémantique discursive, Thématisation, Thème, Toponyme).

We can take as an example the first two sentences of the first chapter of Dorothy L. Sayers's *Gaudy night* (1936: 3): "Harriet Vane sat at her writing-table and stared out into Mecklenburg Square. The late tulips made a brave show in the Square garden [. . .]". The anthroponym "Harriet Vane" opens the novel by naming the principal Subject, the heroine. "The late tulips" is an iconisation contributing to the reality effect of the narrative and also a chrononym indicating late spring, the end of the tulip season. "Her writing-table" is an iconisation contributing to the reality effect and at the same time indicating the profession of the heroine. It is also an indication of place, which acquires a more precise character due to its proximity to Mecklenburg Square, a toponym. The figurativisation of the first two sentences tells us that the story begins in late spring and is about a woman who is a writer by profession and lives in an area of London known at the time for its fashionable intellectual and artistic life.

If we want to follow the process in the other direction, from thematisation to figuration to iconisation and onomastics, we can look at another example:
Level of thematisation: the sacred.
Sub-level of figuration: the priest (for example the deacon, not the church warden).
Sub-levels of iconisation and onomastics: "On the seventh day (chrononym), Father Alfonso (anthroponym) of the church of St. Sulpicius (toponym) in Paris (toponym) [. . .]".

We saw that for Greimas and Courtés the generative trajectory ends definitely with the discursive level. In the discursive syntax, the most detailed articulation of signification, we located the precise actors of the narrative, we acquired the impression of time through the temporal framework and the temporal causal succession offered, and we understood the syntagmatic organisation of space. The discursive semantics, the most concrete articulation of signification, invested actors, time and space with figurativisation, which gave us the illusion of reality by offering us precise names of persons, temporal durations and designations of places. The model thus leads us up to the full set of "realistic" data, but not to any precise and recognisable text. Why was the generative trajectory not completed with the next level, which manifestly would be the concrete appearance of a text?

Greimas and Courtés have a concept, "textualisation", which may give the impression that this is the missing link. However, this is not the case. This concept is part of a constellation of kindred concepts (Greimas and Courtés 1979: Linéarité, Manifestation, Représentation, Textualisation) which is totally unrelated to any final level of analysis. Textualisation is identified with representation, precedes manifestation and is restricted by linearisation (in a wider sense than the strictly linear), but these terms are intended as metalinguistic and are applicable to any level of the generative trajectory.

This void could leave us disappointed, since we miss the contact with the final semiotic project, the concrete text. But, if empirically we could ask for more, epistemologically the choice of the authors is unquestionable. The reason is simple. With the discursive level, we dispose of all the structural elements of a text, but the next step, the text itself, follows from the filtering of these elements through the preconditions for the production of a text, which are the specific requirements of the chosen substance of the expression. The substances of expression of the various semiotic systems (verbal, pictorial, cinematic, musical, etc.) are quite different. The same set of structural elements will take a different final form according to the substance used. The process of relating the generative trajectory to the form of expression depends on the semiotic system chosen for the text (Hénault 1983: 134–135). This process is thus of an entirely different nature than the generative trajectory, and we shall not be concerned with it here.

2 An example of narrative analysis: *The life of Saint Alexius*

The generative trajectory that we have analysed in this chapter is a model of the process of production of a text, more specifically of the logic of this process. It does not correspond to the intentions of the author during its composition, but to the logical levels of structuring that we need to assume in order to give a complete description of the structure of the text (just as the syntax of a natural language does not describe the conscious process followed by a speaker producing an utterance, but the logical structure of the phrase produced). However, when we want to interpret a text that already exists, we need to follow a different process: we might say that we follow the generative trajectory "backwards", starting with the discursive level and gradually penetrating to deeper levels of textual syntax and semantics.

We will use as our example a simple traditional narrative, because the narrative structure is more easily recognisable in such texts. It is the legend of Saint Alexius, which narrates the life of an exceptionally ascetic holy man who may have lived in Edessa in Syria around the end of the 4th and the beginning of the 5th centuries CE. The earliest written text of the legend of Alexius, *The life and times of the man of God*, exists in both Greek and Latin and dates from the 10th century (*Acta sanctorum*, vol 31 (July, part 4): 251–254). The story became very popular in medieval Europe and can be found in many vernacular versions (Boklund-Lagopoulou 1984).

2.1 *The life of Saint Alexius*: Summary

A Roman nobleman, Eufemianus, and his wife, both good Christians, have no heir. They pray for a child and God sends them a son who is baptised Alexius. In gratitude, they vow to abstain from sexual relations for the rest of their lives.

When Alexius has grown to adulthood, his father arranges for him to marry a young Roman girl of noble birth. When the marriage ceremony is completed, his father urges him to enter the bridal chamber. Alexius obeys, but instead of consummating the marriage, he "teaches" his wife about Christ (in the Latin text) or "speaks to her of mysteries" (in the Greek). He gives her a ring, a veil and his belt. He then leaves his father's house in secret, goes to the harbour and boards a ship going to Syria.

From Laodicea Alexius goes by foot to Edessa, where there is a church with a wonder-working icon. He gives all his possessions to the poor and settles among the beggars who live in the porch of the church. He wakes and prays all night, eats only two ounces of bread and drinks one ounce of water, except on Sundays, when he takes communion. His austere ascetic life renders him unrecognisable.

His family sends servants to search for Alexius. They arrive at the church and see him among the beggars, but they do not recognise him. Instead, they give him alms, which Alexius considers as an especial sign of grace. When the search fails, his mother moves into a small room of the house and vows not to leave it until her son is found.

After seventeen years, the icon in the church speaks and commands the caretaker of the church to seek for "the man of God". The caretaker searches but cannot find him. The icon speaks again and explains that he sits next to the door of the church. This time Alexius is found and brought into the church.

When Alexius sees that the people have "recognised" him, he leaves Edessa secretly and boards a boat for Tarsus. However, the wind takes the ship to Rome. Alexius understands that it is God's will that he should not be a "burden" to anyone, but should live in his father's house. He meets his father in the street and asks for shelter. His father remembers his lost son, invites the beggar into his house, assigns a servant to see to his needs, gives him a bed by the entrance to the house and feeds him from his own table.

For another seventeen years, Alexius lives as a beggar in his father's house. He has daily contact with his parents and his wife, who lives enclosed with her mother-in-law. He watches them mourn for their lost son and husband, without ever revealing his identity. The servants mock him and empty the slops on his head, but he bears everything with humility and patience.

Towards the end of the seventeen years, Alexius asks for paper and ink and writes down the story of his life. One Sunday, a voice is heard in the church telling the people of Rome[47] (together with the "archbishop" and two emperors) to search for "the man of God". They search all of Rome but do not find him. The voice speaks again and tells them that he is in the house of Eufemianus. The two emperors, the archbishop and all the people gather at the house of Eufemianus. Then the servant assigned to Alexius announces that the beggar has died and they all understand that he is the one they are looking for.

In the hands of the corpse is a papyrus with the story of his life, which he surrenders only to the archbishop. It is read publicly. The family of Alexius discovers the identity of the beggar who has been living in their house and mourn his death. The corpse gives off a sweet odour, and all who touch it are cured of their ailments. As it is carried to the church of Saint Bonifatius, miracles occur. To open a route for the bier, the emperors throw coins to the people, but the people ignore the money to follow the saint, who is buried in a monumental tomb.

---

47 Judging from the geographical descriptions in the text, "Rome" is probably the "New Rome", that is, Constantinople.

2.2 Narrative syntax

This little narrative, though not exactly realistic, has a rather full investment on the discursive level. It is rich in actors and spaces, which are endowed with names (Eufemianus, Alexius, Rome, Syria, Laodicea, Edessa, Tarsus) and specific characteristics (Roman, nobleman, beggar, caretaker of the church, servants, archbishop, emperors). The temporal dimension is less developed, but both the succession of events and the duration of situations are given in a realistic fashion.

As we are following the generative trajectory in reverse in order to analyse the text, we need to look "behind" the actors for the actantial roles of the narrative. We realise at once that the main Subject of the narrative is Alexius. The Object of value, that which the Subject desires, is apparently "sainthood". The Subject undertakes the quest for sainthood in consequence of a silent contract with a Sender, God, who also acts as Helper; thus, the roles of Recipient and Subject coincide in the same actor, Alexius, just as the roles of Sender and Helper coincide in the same actor, God. The role of Opponent, however, is shared among many actors, primarily the members of the family of Alexius, but also among more abstract concepts such as "sin", "the flesh" and "the world", so the action in this narrative is in part cognitive. The correspondence between actantial roles and actors is as follows:

Actants	Actors
Subject	Alexius
Object	sainthood
Sender	God
Recipient	Alexius, humanity
Helper	God
Opponent	family, sin, flesh, worldliness

Having matched actors and actants, we continue with the analysis of the narrative syntax.

Episode 1: Prologue. The birth of the hero

> A Roman nobleman, Eufemianus, and his wife, both good Christians, have no heir. They pray for a child and God sends them a son who is baptised Alexius. In gratitude, they vow to abstain from sexual relations for the rest of their lives.

The birth of the hero is a small independent narrative that functions as a prologue to the main narrative and has its own distribution of actantial roles. The Subject is Eufemianus and his wife. The text declares from the beginning that there is a "lack": they have no heir. The child is thus the Object of value and the Subject is already provided with a wanting-to-do (they want an heir), but does not have the modal competence of being-able-to-do (they cannot have a child). The couple prays for a child, and this creates a "contract" with the Sender, God. God responds by giving them a son, eliminating the lack. In return, the parents agree to live without further sexual relations, which in the context of this text must be interpreted as abstention from sin, as a virtuous life. Their promise seems to be the obligation – the "test" – that they have undertaken in return for the gift of the child (though in this case the fulfilment of the contract – the birth of the child – precedes the test).

We note that from the beginning the child Alexius functions as an intermediary, since his birth causes his parents to abstain from sin. This mediation between God and humanity is the basic function of a saint. In the narrative, this creates the "final Recipient" (*Destinataire final*, Hénault 1983: 66–72), namely humanity, whose salvation is assured by the successful completion of the mission of the original Subject–Recipient.

Episode 2: Discovery of a lack and qualifying test

> When Alexius has grown to adulthood, his father arranges for him to marry a young Roman girl of noble birth. When the marriage ceremony is completed, his father urges him to enter the bridal chamber. Alexius obeys, but instead of consummating the marriage, he "teaches" his wife about Christ (in the Latin text) or "speaks to her of mysteries" (in the Greek). He gives her a ring, a veil (?) and his belt. He then leaves his father's house in secret, goes to the harbor and boards a ship going to Syria.

This is the beginning of the main narrative, and the actantial roles are redistributed. The Subject is now Alexius, the primary Subject throughout the main narrative. His wedding is presented as a choice between two Objects: marriage or sainthood, or in other words, the life of a married Roman nobleman and *pater familias* or the life of an ascetic. The father of Alexius functions as anti-Sender and proposes the first Object, which is a false or anti-Object. Alexius chooses the second Object, that which will satisfy his lack. This is the "qualifying test".

It is obvious that the two Objects represent different values. On the one hand, the marriage is the decision of Alexius's father, who also urges him to enter the bridal chamber in order to consummate it. On the other, Alexius's decision to leave his father's house implies the choice of sexual purity rather than the pleasures of "the flesh". But the reason for the consummation of the marriage through sexual relations with the bride is to beget heirs, ensuring the continuation of a noble Roman family. Thus, the flight of Alexius implies the rejection of the values of such a family: honour, wealth, political power – "the world". His flight involves the rejection of the false Object, the pleasures of the flesh and the world, as well as a desire for the true Object of the ascetic life: purity, humility, poverty and obscurity, that is, the exact opposite of the life of a Roman nobleman.

Alexius thus expresses a wanting-to-do: through an ascetic life to acquire sainthood, which seems to be the fundamental value of the narrative semantics. This modality implies a contract with the true Sender, the one who wants humanity to aspire to sainthood, i.e., God. The acceptance of this contract is not made explicit in the text, perhaps because Alexius is already someone who was sent by God in response to his parents' prayers. However, the successful conclusion of the test is marked by the acquisition of a Helper, which takes the form of the modalities of knowing-how-to-do (Alexius knows what he must do) and being-able-to-do (he has the ability to endure the ascetic life).

At this point, we find a secondary narrative nested in the main narrative. Before he leaves, Alexius "teaches" his new wife. The teaching seems to have the goal of persuading her to also lead a "pure" life. Alexius thus continues his role as intermediary, that is, he takes on a role of subsidiary Sender in a secondary mini-narrative, the Subject of which is his bride. We could perhaps speculate that the objects that he leaves with her are symbolic of the contract between them (the ring), sexual purity (the veil?) and the abandonment of his worldly life (his sword-belt), though in the absence of more information about the meaning of these objects at the time of the composition of the story, this can only be a hypothesis.

Episode 3: Decisive test

> From Laodicea Alexius goes by foot to Edessa, where there is a church with a wonder-working icon. He gives all his possessions to the poor and settles among the beggars who live in the porch of the church. He wakes and prays all night, eats only two ounces of bread and drinks one ounce of water, except on Sundays, when he takes communion. His austere ascetic life renders him unrecognizable.
> His family sends servants to search for Alexius. They arrive at the church and see him among the beggars, but they do not recognize him. Instead, they give him alms, which Alexius considers as an especial sign of grace. When the search fails, his mother moves into a small room of the house and vows not to leave it until her son is found.
> After seventeen years, the icon in the church speaks and commands the caretaker of the church to seek for "the man of God". The caretaker searches but cannot find him. The

icon speaks again and explains that he sits next to the door of the church. This time Alexius is found and brought into the church.

It is gradually becoming clear that a basic theme of the text is the "hidden" life of the hero. The importance of the theme of the "hidden" life is demonstrated in the repeated episodes where people search for Alexius and do not recognise him. That he accepts alms from his own servants is a sign of his humility, but also proof that he is truly "hidden": the harsh ascetic life has rendered him unrecognisable even to persons who know him well.

His recognition by the icon as "the man of God" is a sign of the victorious outcome of the decisive test, but at the same time it endangers his decision to remain "hidden" and unknown, and for that reason he decides once more to flee.

Each time that Alexius wins a battle against the flesh and the world, he takes on the role of subsidiary Sender, functioning as intermediary in another contract in a subsidiary narrative in which another Subject follows his example and takes up an ascetic life. This time, it is his mother who vows to live enclosed in a small room. The enclosed life is a mirror image of Alexius's own flight away from his father's house. These two forms of the "hidden" life seem to correspond to a new distinction: the "hidden" life implies enclosure (inside) for women, flight (outside) for men.

Episode 4a: Glorifying test

When Alexius sees that the people have "recognized" him, he leaves Edessa secretly and boards a boat for Tarsus. However, the wind takes the ship to Rome. Alexius understands that it is God's will that he should not be a "burden" to anyone, but should live in his father's house. He meets his father in the street and asks for shelter. His father remembers his lost son, invites the beggar into his house, assigns a servant to see to his needs, gives him a bed by the entrance to the house and feeds him from his own table.

For seventeen years, Alexius lives as a beggar in his father's house. He has daily contact with his parents and his wife, who lives enclosed with her mother-in-law. He watches them mourn for their lost son and husband, without ever revealing his identity. The servants mock him and empty the slops on his head, but he bears everything with humility and patience.

The arrival of the ship in Rome rather than Tarsus is explicitly interpreted, both by Alexius and by the text, as an act of the Sender, God. It is a reaffirmation of the original contract: Alexius must continue his "hidden" life, but in the house of his father. This "hidden" life in his father's house is the final test of the hero. The servants mock him instead of serving him, but he shows humility instead of exercising power. His basic test, however, is to endure the mourning of his family without revealing himself. The natural bonds of family are a part of "the flesh", which the saint must resist. The text is completely uninterested in the feelings of the family; it focuses entirely on the patience of the hero.

Episode 4b. Recognition and glorification

> Towards the end of the seventeen years, Alexius asks for paper and ink and writes down the story of his life. One Sunday, a voice is heard in the church telling the people of Rome (together with the "archbishop" and two emperors) to search for "the man of God". They search all of Rome but do not find him. The voice speaks again and tells them that he is in the house of Eufemianus. The two emperors, the archbishop and all the people gather at the house of Eufemianus. Then the servant assigned to Alexius announces that the beggar has died and they all understand that he is the one they are looking for.
>
> In the hands of the corpse is a papyrus with the story of his life, which he surrenders only to the archbishop. It is read publicly. The family of Alexius discovers the identity of the beggar who has been living in their house and mourns his death. The corpse gives off a sweet odour, and all who touch it are cured of their ailments. As it is carried to the church of Saint Bonifatius, miracles occur. To open a route for the bier, the emperors throw coins to the people, but the people ignore the money to follow the saint, who is buried in a monumental tomb.

Alexius continues his "hidden" life to the end. His identity is revealed only after his death, when the archbishop, two emperors and all the people of Rome (representing humanity in general) have been commanded by God to find him. He now acts as general intermediary and subsidiary Sender, since the touch of his dead body cures illness and makes the people disdain worldly riches. The miracles that he works are proof that he has gained the true Object of value in the text, sainthood.

Chapter 5
Paradigmatic analysis: Isotopies, qualitative approach

1 The theory of isotopies

1.1 The definition of isotopy

The core of paradigmatic analysis is the concept of "isotopy" (*isotopie*),[48] and to understand this concept we need to return to the triad of concepts "seme", "sememe" and "lexeme". We recall that the lexeme covers a field of significations constituted by a set of sememes. The selection of a particular sememe from this pool depends on the textual context, that is, its actualisation takes place on the level of discourse. A sememe consists of a set of semes. It is the recurrence of a particular seme in the textual context that determines which sememe – which signification of a word – will be selected.

Greimas's concept of isotopy is founded on the seme. An isotopy is a paradigm built on the basis of sememes that share the same seme and develop along a syntagmatic chain. Isotopy is, for Greimas, the textual mechanism that links the text together.

We can identify paradigms on the level of the language system, for example the paradigms formed by the parts of speech – nouns ("noun-ness"), verbs ("verb-ness") or sub-classes of verbs, for example transitive verbs ("transitive-ness"). However, the paradigm as conceived by Saussure remains too general, because the classes that may be defined are too open and flexible, and overlap in many directions. On the contrary, when Greimas applies the concept of the paradigm, in the form of isotopy, to specific texts, it is revealed to be of strategic importance, because the text itself provides the framework for the closure of the paradigms.

As we saw (chapter 3: 6.4), a lexeme is structured around a stable structural nucleus composed of a set of semes, the "nuclear semes" (*sèmes nucléaires*). Attached to this there is usually another set of semes, the "contextual semes"

---

[48] The discussion of the linguistic and semiotic theory of isotopies is based on Greimas 1966 and Greimas and Courtés 1979, mainly on the entries Axiologie, Catégorie, Catégorisation, Classème, Code, Connecteur d'isotopies, Contexte, Hypotaxique/Hypérotaxique, Isomorphisme, Isotopie, Lexème, Micro-univers, Noyau, Phème, Pluri-isotopie, Polysémémie (Polysémie), Prosodie, Segmentation, Sème, Sémème, Suprasegmentation, Thymique). For an in-depth analysis of isotopies and their relations, see also Rastier 2009.

(*sèmes contextuels*), which are variable and conjunctural, that is, text-dependent; these are called "classemes" (*classèmes*)[49] and constitute a "classematic base" (*base classématique*) – Greimas 1966: 50–53. It is this second set which is sensitive to discourse, because it is context-dependent, and a transformation of the context may cause the emergence of a different sememe. The activation of semes belonging to the same classematic base creates a "semic trajectory" in the text, an iterative series expressed in semantic linearity. For Greimas, the iteration of classemes in discourse, i.e., their integration within semic trajectories, gives the text its homogeneity and coherence. Each trajectory creates its own isotopy. Greimas originally considered that isotopies are created exclusively through the iterative appearance of classemes. In later texts (see, for example, Greimas 1970), he accepts a more general definition of isotopy as the result of the iteration of any semantic category (Greimas and Courtés 1979: Isotopie; Hénault [1979] 1993: 91). As is clear from the above, these repetitions appear on the syntagmatic axis, but they operate according to the paradigmatic mechanism of the isotopy.

Iteration and trajectory are undeniably essential for the definition of isotopy, but we would like to make some supplementary observations concerning limit-cases which emerge with extremely short texts, texts which are not extensive enough to allow for repetition. The utterance "This is a flower" leaves no doubt that we are dealing with "plant-ness". However, in an utterance such as "This is a leg", we cannot know whether "leg" refers to a part of the human body or of a piece of furniture, in other words, which classeme would be realised if the text were more extensive. We could flip a coin and play with the probabilities: if there are x (for example 5) possible classemes of "leg", the probability of our guessing the right classeme and thus the correct meaning of the word on the basis of this textual fragment alone is 1: x (= 20% in this case). However, if we do not want to proceed by guesswork, we must be satisfied with the identification of an ambiguous lexeme. The same ambiguity exists, for example, in the utterance "Down to earth" or "Yesterday I caught sight of Venus". What does the word mean, earth = soil or the planet earth? Venus, a woman's name or Venus the evening star? If our text does not provide any further iteration, we should see this as a simple nuclear seme, not an isotopy.[50]

However, even in very brief texts, it may be possible to define an isotopy. In the phrase "The relation between earth and Venus", the meaning "soil" for earth is excluded, since soil cannot have a relation to Venus, and the interpretation of

---

[49] In some cases, it is possible not to have any classemes.
[50] In some of our examples below we use the concept of isotopy even though the brevity of the quoted discourse could make the lexemes seem ambiguous. In all these cases the examples are extracts from longer texts, legitimating the identification of isotopies.

Venus as a woman's name is highly unlikely, so we deduce on firm grounds that the reference is to the corresponding planets. "Earth-ness" and "Venus-ness" are now brought together through and under the classeme "planet-ness", resulting in a minimal isotopy.[51]

Minimal isotopies can also be created by other means. Take the example "George made a statement". We note the personal name of a certain George unknown to us and an act by him, a statement, which in itself only means that he pronounced a declarative sentence. But if we find "Churchill made a statement", we immediately recognise the classeme of "politics-ness" in the lexeme "statement": this phrase activates our cultural knowledge, which invests "Churchill" with "politics-ness", a contextual seme that can also be activated by "statement". This time, the iteration comes not from the text itself, but from the cultural context. We conclude, then, that isotopies can also be created by contextual or situational factors (on these two concepts, see chapter 8: 2.7, 2.8 and 2.10).

It is interesting to compare Greimas's two types of semes, i.e., the nuclear semes and classemes, to Eco's views. Eco considers that the sememe is constituted by "semantic markers" (the equivalent, as we saw, of Greimas's semes). He distinguishes between denotative and connotative markers and, among the former, between markers that are not altered by their integration within a context – Greimas's nuclear semes – and variable markers sensitive to the specificity of contexts – Greimas's classemes. Connotative markers have their point of departure in denotative markers. According to Eco, denotation is straightforwardly recognisable culturally, while connotation is less well defined.

On this basis, Eco proposes a semantic model inspired by the model of compositional analysis proposed by Jerrold J. Katz, Jerry A. Fodor and Paul M. Postal. He notes that their model is of a narrow lexicological character and neglects the enrichment of sememes by their semiotic environment, but nevertheless considers it a satisfactory point of departure for the formulation of his own Revised Model. This model starts from a sememe with stable denotative markers and then constructs a semantic tree diagram, unfolding different trajectories of signification resulting either as direct connotations (connotative markers) of the stable denotative markers, or as a function of different possible contexts and micro-

---

[51] François Rastier also defines minimal isotopies, but for him the minimal isotopy is established within a word, at the morphemic level. He gives as an example the Spanish word "chiquito" (little one), pointing out that it includes two morphemes, "chiqu-" and "-it", which both include the seme "smallness", whence a minimal isotopy (Rastier 2009: 129). Such an understanding of the minimal isotopy would render the concept useless as a mechanism of textual coherence, since the minimal isotopy would operate only on the level of the word, and the "coherence" of a word could not be created by iterative isotopies.

situations, or from the variable markers connected to them, from which there are further extensions to their connotations. Eco points out that his model is in a position to record only culturally conventional significations on the basis of statistical probabilities (Eco 1976: 84–86, 105–110). In spite of this limitation, the model is exceptionally rich, helps to predict the depth of the possible set of significations of a sememe and integrates signification with the dynamics of communication (chapter 8: 2.10).

An isotopy thus appears empirically as the presence of a common seme (or set of semes) occurring repeatedly in a series of lexemes and expressions in a text. But as we saw above (chapter 3: 6.4), semes form elementary binary structures, the semantic categories, consisting of an axis with two poles (and possibly intermediary positions), very often with evaluations attached (*positive* vs *negative*, or as Greimas puts it, *euphoric* vs *dysphoric*). An isotopy is always structured, though the structure may not always be explicitly realised in the text. Although it is often possible to locate lexemes in the text that correspond to the poles of an isotopy (i.e., for an isotopy of gender, we may find the words "man" and "woman" explicitly used in the text), the semantic categories structuring the isotopy are metalinguistic (in this case, *maleness* vs *femaleness*) and thus abstract elements.

We have already encountered the term "Code" with a capital C, which we equated with language as system. Greimas and Courtés also use the term "code" with a lower-case c in the expression "*code partiel*" [partial code] to indicate a sub-code of language which they describe with the traits of a semantic system. Here, we will use the term "code" with a lower-case c to refer to a structured isotopy. An isotopy may be empirically identified in a text without having acquired the full form of a semantic category; we have found that it is methodologically convenient to be able to distinguish between such an empirical isotopy, and the same isotopy as (simple) code when its internal structure has been established.

Greimas and Courtés also use a term related to partial code, namely *micro-univers* [micro-universe]. Since it is not possible to describe the general semantic universe of a whole culture, due to its scope and complexity, the term (semantic) micro-universe offers an operational instrument for the analysis of a part of this cultural semantic universe. The micro-universe is a semantic category (for example, *life* vs *death*), an isotopy, which is articulated into a limited set of hierarchically lower semantic categories (see also Greimas 1966: 127–128); thus the micro-universe is a systematic, composite and hierarchical isotopy (section 1.7 below).

Below, we discuss a series of issues related to the concept of isotopy, the relationships between isotopies and the manner of their manifestation in texts.

1.2 Nuclear semes and classemes

In a previous chapter (3: 6.4), we presented Greimas's analysis of the lexeme "head". After examining the different significations of the word, Greimas concludes that its nucleus is structured by the seme "extreme-ness", leading to a second seme, "spheroid-ness", and a third seme, "upper-ness", referring to an uppermost or anterior part. He also concludes that spheroidness is part of the semantic category *point* vs *spheroid* (Greimas 1966: 45–49), which implies that the semic nucleus is composed of semantic categories, but does not actually incorporate both their terms. As we noted above, Greimas's view is that nuclear semes are never independent, but any seme is always integrated within a semantic category, i.e., an elementary binary structure with the form *a* vs *b*, but, as the above example shows us, these structures are not necessarily present as a whole in any particular text.

Greimas observes that one of the semes attached to "head" corresponds to the idea of the summit of a person and thus to verticality. Verticality is related to a standing person, while another typical position of the body is reclining, whence his observation (here we paraphrase) that the head of a nail incorporates the seme "verticality", while the head of a procession incorporates the seme "horizontality". He thus concludes that, since these two semes, when realised, exclude one another, they are not nuclear semes, but classemes.

The existence of the classeme "verticality" allows "head" to be integrated within an isotopy which also includes the sememes of other lexemes incorporating the same classeme. This quality widens the field of possible connections between sememes and greatly enriches a textual isotopy.

We just saw that the semic nucleus is composed of semic units. The same is manifestly the case with classemes. During the first stage of the analysis of a text, what we find are usually single classemes, that is, not semantic categories but simple semes, identified through their repetitive occurrence along the text. Only in the next stage of analysis is a stricter grasp of the text achieved, allowing us to identify semantic categories, though we may find that only one term of certain categories is realised concretely in the text.

1.3 Operating with isotopies on the two semiotic planes

So far, we have discussed the concept of isotopy only with reference to the plane of content, and in fact this is the sense in which the term is generally used. However, the concept may have a wider application than the analysis of content. We already presented Hjelmslev's example of connotation, namely that the Danish language refers to the connotative isotopy "Danish-ness". For him, this very general reference results from the signs of Danish as a whole, that is, from both the content and the expression planes. In this case, then, the emphasis is not placed on the signifieds but on the expression plane.

This is not only the case for the native speaker, who, when reading a Danish text or speaking with a compatriot, has access effortlessly and subconsciously to the connotation "Danish-ness". When foreigners who visit Copenhagen and do not know Danish hear the locals speaking, they do not understand the words, but the speech sounds still have the same connotation as for a native speaker, "Danish-ness"; since there is no connotation without denotation, the denotation for the foreigner is repetitively and monotonously "incomprehensible Danish-sounding word".

We observe the same phenomenon in a wide range of cases. If, for example, we compare British and American English, the word "laboratory" is pronounced "lab'oratry" or "labor'atry" in British, but "lab'orato.ry" in American, hence the isotopy "English-ness" in the first cases and "American-ness" in the second. In Southern American English, the standard English expression "I have told him" takes the form "I done told him" and "you" becomes "y'all" (as in the expression "y'all come back now"). This quality of the expression plane may be closely connected to the content plane: if, for example, in a novel written in standard English, certain characters express themselves in a particular dialect, let us say Irish English, "Irish-ness" becomes an important part of the isotopy of the characters, attributing to them an ethnic identity.

The expression plane may give rise to particularly interesting isotopies. Greimas and Courtés give the example of music and poetry and observe that poetry may be approached through the angle of expression as a cluster of phemes which create symmetries, alternations, consonances and dissonances, as well as significant transformations of acoustic sets (Greimas and Courtés 1979: Isotopie). We can probably go further than that. Phemes refer to the phonology of phonemes and phonemes are discrete linguistic units, "segments", resulting from a detailed linguistic segmentation. They are studied by segmental phonology, but phonology also has another branch, that of supra-segmental phonology[52] (see also Greimas and Courtés 1979: Segmentation). The supra-segmental elements are prosodic units which go beyond the level of phonemes.

There are several supra-segmental or prosodic features. Stress is the emphasis on individual syllables of single polysyllabic words (lexical stress, for example "trústy", as opposed to "trustée"). Beyond the primary lexical stress,

---

[52] The same two branches are found in phonetics.

there may be a secondary stress (as in our example above "lab'orato.ry"), rarely a tertiary one, leaving the rest of the syllables of a word unstressed. This phenomenon may be extended to individual words in a sentence (sentential stress, for example "the train is **leaving**").[53] We recognise in stress a typical device of traditional poetry, which, used beyond the individual word and sentence level, creates an acoustic pattern of stressed and unstressed sounds (isotopy *stressed* vs *unstressed*), giving poetry its rhythm through metre. The effect of this pattern on the connotative level is the emergence in certain cultures of an aesthetic isotopy of "poeticity".

Another supra-segmental feature is the length of a phoneme (*long* vs *short* vowels or consonants) which is defined by the language system. Length can also appear on the discourse level, leading to effects comparable to intonation (see below). The language system also defines monosyllabic and polysyllabic words, which have a different duration. This kind of effect can be due to other factors, for example, to the repetition of a vowel or consonant, as in our example in chapter 3 (6.2) "I'm crrrrazy for you, babe", resulting in the connotation "beyond any limit", which stresses the isotopy of feeling.

A very important supra-segmental feature is pitch, a phenomenon related to the frequency scale. Pitch differentiates the voices of adults and children. High-pitch registers are used, for example, when we speak to a child or a cat, activating an isotopy of "other-ness". The voice of a *basso profondo* opera singer has the lowest possible pitch.[54]

The supra-segmental feature of intonation is also based on pitch and may refer to individual words or extend to all or part of an utterance. The simplest form of intonation is the emphasis on single words. In English, intonation is used to differentiate between declarative, interrogative and exclamatory utterances and between statements, questions and commands. Frequently intonation delivers just denotative information, but the interrogative and exclamatory modes may also be used as rhetorical devices loaded with connotative implications and the attached isotopies. The connotative level comes to the foreground when intonation is used, for example, to reflect the emotional state of the addresser or display irony. Variations in pitch create different patterns which

---

[53] In writing, stress is conventionally indicated by underlining, or, in print, by the use of bold or italic fonts.

[54] As we saw, word stress is also, and mainly, used to emphasise individual syllables of words. The comparable use of pitch instead of stress is tone, which consists in the use of a different pitch for the same syllable of a lexeme to differentiate between different sememes corresponding to the lexeme.

1 The theory of isotopies — 137

characterise discourse as a whole, giving it melody. Just as Hjelmslev observed that all the signs of Danish refer to the connotation "Danish-ness", the characteristic intonation of Italian may be recognised even by a non-Italian speaker as having the connotation "Italian-ness".

Several other features of the expression plane are traditionally used to create aesthetic isotopies. A conventional trait of poetry is rhyme, i.e., the repetition of one or more phonemes, always including a vowel, at the end of a line, following a particular pattern or rhyme scheme. We can take as example a stanza from the poem *The lake isle of Innisfree* by William Butler Yeats:

> I will arise and go now, and go to Innisfr**ee**,
> And a small cabin build there, of clay and wattles m**ade**:
> Nine bean-rows will I have there, a hive for the honey-b**ee**,
> And live alone in the bee-loud gl**ade**.

The last syllables of the first and third lines of the stanza form a phonetic isotopy with /i:/ as its common element, and the last syllables of the second and fourth lines form another isotopy with the common element /eɪd/. These two isotopies alternate. The rest of the poem follows a similar, though not identical, rhyme scheme, developing a series of new isotopies. Rhyme schemes recall Saussure's associative classes, since the isotopies are constituted on the basis of the common sound of a part of the signifier. The resulting connotative isotopy is "poeticity".

Metre is another feature traditionally used to create an aesthetic isotopy on the expression plane. Below are some lines (ll. 1179–1181) from *Sir Gawain and the Green Knight*, a Middle English metrical romance of the late 14th century (in the 1967 translation by Marie Borroff):

> ˘ ′ ˘ ˘ ′ ˘ ˘ ′ ′ ′
> And **G**awain the **g**ood knight // in **g**ay bed lies,
> ′ ˘ ′ ˘ ′ ˘ ′ ˘ ′
> **L**ingered **l**ate a**l**one, // till day**l**ight gleamed
> ˘ ˘ ′ ˘ ˘ ′ ˘ ′ ˘ ˘ ′
> Under **c**overlet **c**ostly, // **c**urtained about

Each line of this poem consists of two half-lines divided by a caesura; each half-line includes at least two stressed syllables in roughly the same places; the relation between stressed and unstressed syllables creates a rhythmic acoustic isotopy. But these lines also show another isotopy, resulting from the repetition of the phoneme [g] as the first sound in three of the stressed syllable in the first line, of the phoneme [l] in the second line, and of the phoneme [k] in the third line. The poem as a whole follows the same pattern: at least three syllables in each line, usually stressed, begin with the same sound.⁵⁵ The repeated sounds, distributed as two repetitions in the first half-line and one (occasionally two) in the second half-line, create a second acoustic isotopy of alliteration. This rhythmic repetition of stressed sounds, a combination of metre and alliteration, leads to the connotative isotopy of "poeticity".

Alliteration is a frequent rhetorical feature in many texts. Thus, we read in the Bible: "A **s**ower went out to **s**ow his **s**eed" (Luke 8:3); and, in Sophocles's *Oedipus Rex*, Oedipus gives an insolent reply to the respected blind seer Teiresias during a violent argument: "τυφλὸς τά τ' ὦτα τόν τε νοῦν τά τ' ὄμματ' εἶ" [you're blind in your ears and mind and eyes], investing all his rage in the repetitive spitting of [t] sounds.

1.4 The hierarchical levels of analysis of isotopies

Greimas is right when he observes that it is difficult to define the isotopies to which particular classemes belong. Ultimately, Greimas and Courtés conclude that the identification of individual semes depends on the text being examined, and hence that these semes are relative. However, their aim is much more ambitious, because they consider the possibility of the definition of a minimum number of primitive semantic categories – about twenty – analogous to Jakobson's twelve primitive binary phemic categories and of the same metalinguistic nature. These would be the universals of every language from which the sememes of any semiotic would be produced. They propose as a first approach two universal semantic categories: *life* vs *death* and *culture* vs *nature* (cf. 2.3 below).

Greimas and Courtés argue that the definition of classemes must be of great generality. They observe that these are the basis for the categories that each language uses to classify the world and state that they constitute classes of being (for example, *animate* vs *inanimate*) or things (for example, *animal* vs *vegetal*), adding that the specific semantic organisation depends on each culture. This organisation, for Greimas and Courtés, corresponds to the worldview of a culture (Greimas and Courtés 1979: Classème, Universaux); we would consider it the backbone of its ideology. With these concepts, semantic analysis encounters cultural studies and the social sciences in general.

We can infer from the position of Greimas and Courtés that they conceive of a hierarchy of semantic categories, which starts from the theoretical (and

---

55 In Middle English alliterative metre, a vowel alliterates with any other vowel, so a word that begins with a vowel will alliterate with any other word beginning with a vowel.

still unknown) primitive and universal semantic categories and then is expressed in lower-level isotopies with classemes of great generality which animate cultural categories structuring specific cultural ideologies. At such a high semantic level we still find rather abstract concepts, but the hierarchy continues, manifestly without any break of semantic continuity, to lower levels, depending on the requirements of each text; in other words, it is the text that dictates its isotopies. Below, we examine three cases of the hierarchical ordering of isotopies.

Greimas analyses the sentence "After a day of work, I feel tired" and observes that the subject "I" and "work" refer to the classeme *animate* (vs *inanimate*), and the ending of the adjective "-ed" and the adverb "after" refer to the classeme *caused* (vs *causing*). He also proposes that the verbal form used, "-ed", shows a dynamic quality which he defines as "process" (Greimas 1966: 80–81).

If the hypothetical primitive semantic categories constitute the highest hierarchical level of categories, the semantic categories in this example would probably belong to the next classificatory level. This level is still very general, given that Greimas is interested in theory-making, but it does not deliver the finer nuances of a text. An operational semantic analysis would move on the next – third – level, closer to the empirical meaning of the text. More specifically, "I feel tired" could belong to an experiential isotopy, "work" to an economic isotopy, and "After a day" to a temporal isotopy; and "tired" is a negative evaluation. Following such a rationale, we believe that, in an analysis of a poem, the lyric "I" expressing feelings is better understood as "experiential-ness" rather than "animate-ness".

Greimas is not unaware of this third level. We use as our second example his move from individual and "formal" texts to a collective corpus of everyday texts by studying the answers of students to a test. In two questions concerning the students' future, Greimas identifies two classemic categories which do not necessarily appear together in each individual case: *determined* vs *undetermined*, with a middle term *neither determined nor undetermined*, and *good* vs *bad* as a sub-category of "determined"; these categories are part of the wider triadic classemic framework *positive* vs *neutral* vs *negative* (Greimas 1966: 93–96). We note two characteristics of this analysis, first, that the corpus is constituted by fragments of discourse and, second, that the classemic categories are this time cultural and correspond to our third level of analysis above. If we wanted to define more specifically the kind of future envisaged by the students, we would have to pass to the next lower level of analysis.

Our third example comes from the semiotic analysis of a corpus of answers to a standardised questionnaire designed to collect material for a semiotic analysis of regional space in Greece. This study was situated on the third level of analysis, according to which isotopies were defined as "economi-city", "social-ness", "functional-ness", "aesthetic-ness", etc. The corpus quickly showed that these isotopies were quite general in nature and could be subdivided into finer isotopies, leading to a fourth level of analysis: for example, "social-ness" was subdivided into "social groups", "social origin", "ways of life", etc., all fourth-level isotopies. It is of special interest that the statistical operations revealed that the lower-level analysis does not cancel the need for the more general level, given that each level offers equally useful and complementary conclusions (Lagopoulos and Boklund-Lagopoulou 1992: see, for example, 211–217).

These examples show, then, the existence of a third and fourth hierarchical level of the analysis of isotopies, and further analysis is not to be excluded, depending on the nature of the text to be interpreted. While the second level reveals the structuring of general ideology, that is, the basic semantic categories through which the world is apprehended, the next level clearly deploys the strategic isotopies of a text and the following levels offer continuously finer grids of analysis. As we go from the top down, there is a movement from the more general, abstract and simple to the specific, concrete and complex, and ideology becomes continuously more tangible.

We find a comparable approach to the hierarchy of isotopies in François Rastier. Rastier divides isotopies into two categories, generic and specific isotopies. Generic isotopies are generally related to codified paradigms of the language system and are divided, as are the semes corresponding to them, into three classes. The first class, micro-generic isotopies, is defined by the recurrence of one seme characterising sememes belonging to a "minimal class" of sememes (the example the author gives is steak, rare, medium rare, well done, characterised by "degree of doneness"); the second class, meso-generic isotopies, is also defined by the recurrence of one seme which here characterises sememes belonging to the same "domain" (a man and a lion belong to different domains); and the third class, macro-generic isotopies, still defined by the recurrence of one seme, characterises sememes belonging to the same "dimension", such as *animal* vs *human* or *animate* vs *inanimate* (Rastier 2009: 180). Specific isotopies do not belong to codified paradigms and display the singularities of their sememes (Rastier 2009: 112–113). He does not include in this classification the primitive semantic categories of Greimas and Courtés.

There is a close correspondence between Rastier's categories and ours, though we envisage an extra level between meso- and micro-generic isotopies. On the other hand, we are sceptical about the extrapolation of the concept of isotopy, which is a textual concept, to the associative dimension of the language system, its paradigms. Although both isotopy and paradigm may be based on the same semantic phenomenon (the recurrence of shared semes), we feel it is preferable to retain the concept of isotopy specifically to describe the mechanism that creates textual coherence. "Steak, rare, medium rare, well done" is a paradigm, not an isotopy.

Rastier's classes of isotopies, which imply a course from more detailed to more general and abstract semes, are related by him to the successively expanding semantic fields offered by a text, but this does not seem to us to be the case. Let us take the example the author gives for a meso-generic isotopy, "Admiral Nelson commanded that the sails be furled", in which he identifies the isotopy of "navigation". A first observation is that there is also another isotopy of the same level, "military hierarchy" (admiral, commanded). But our main point is that, if this sentence was not isolated from its context, the previous sentence could be "A sleepy Nelson came on deck", in which case we would also have an isotopy of "Nelson-ness" (admiral, sleepy), which would be of a lower level. And even within the initial sentence, we could define a higher-level, macro-generic isotopy based on the semantic category *animate* (admiral, Nelson) vs *inanimate* (sails, furled), depending on the decision of the researcher concerning the level of analysis selected.

Rastier is aware of the possibility that two isotopies of different classes may coexist, as his example "Achilles is a lion" shows (Rastier 2009: 112). He states that "courage" constitutes their common specific isotopy, but also points out that they have in common the macro-generic isotopy "animate". However, he believes that these cases are due only to metaphoric or symbolic connections, while for us they are a matter of the level of analysis.

We can draw certain conclusion from the preceding discussion, which seem to us to be of capital importance for textual analysis. An inviolable principle in semiotic analysis is that it must be guided by the text. On the other hand, the selection of the level or levels of analysis depends on the aims of the researcher. However, semiotics is not a positive science and any kind of textual analysis is approximate, even with the use of the most refined theoretical tools. A second issue, parallel to the hierarchical levels discussed above, concerns the purpose of the analysis. The linguist will analyse a text with the help of text linguistics, which is focused on the linguistic aspects of the text, while the semiotician and the sociolinguist are interested in wider semiotic phenomena. However, in semiotics there is not only one point of view on the text, because the point of view is defined by what the researcher is looking for. It is possible that the personal interests of the researcher – for example, theoretical, historical, political or feminist – may focus on isotopies that are peripheral to the central isotopies of the text.⁵⁶ Two analyses of this kind with different points of view will deliver two different results, without implying that the one analysis is better than the other. Of course, if the aim is to identify the general structuring of a text, analysis by different researchers should arrive at more or less comparable results.

1.5 The relation between simple isotopies

It is possible to find an isotopy in a text, such as the one formed by the lexemes "garden", "trees", "forest", "clearing", which does not seem to show any specific structural relations between its constituents. We could, of course, use certain logical relations to form semantic categories, such as *high* (trees, forest) vs *low* (garden, clearing) or *open* (forest) vs *closed* (garden, clearing), but these would represent a forced choice for the text, imposing on it a semantic world foreign to it. We shall call such an unstructured (at least empirically) and linear sequence a "simple juxtaposed" isotopy. The same phenomenon may appear in respect to the relations between isotopies, for example in a text "sentimentalness" and "agriculture-ness" may well remain unconnected.

Greimas and Courtés identify a relation between isotopies which they call "pluri-isotopy". It presupposes the existence of more than one sememe in a lexeme, each sememe characterised by a different classeme, which creates a case of polysemy.⁵⁷ Puns are frequently based on this kind of polysemy (Greimas 1966: 70–71; see also Greimas and Courtés: 1979: Pluri-isotopie). An English example would be "Did you hear about the optometrist who fell into a lens grinder and made a spectacle of himself?" What creates the pun is the coexistence of two sememes in one and the same lexeme: "spectacle = glasses" and "spectacle = shocking sight". The common lexeme is the connector of two different and incompatible isotopies ("optic-ness" and "embarrassing-public-appearance-ness", both part of the isotopy "visuality").

Greimas and Courtés also give an example of compatibility between two different sememes, namely "This man is a lion". They point out that in this utterance we find the classemic category "both human and animal". They generalise the relation man–lion to the domain of culture, arguing that there are three possibilities: the two oppositional terms *man* vs *animal* may be in equilibrium (this corresponds to the middle term, *man* + *animal*, of this semantic category, for example in an

---

56 In such a case, we need to be careful not to bypass the articulation of these specific interests with the general semiotic orientation of the text, because if this is not taken into account, there is a risk of misrepresenting the structure of the text.
57 Mono-semic lexemes are characteristic of scientific and technical terms.

archaic society of lion-men); the first term prevails over the second (for example in our own society, in which the lion has the metaphorical signification "courage"); or vice versa (Greimas and Courtés 1979: Isotopie). They call this phenomenon "bi-isotopy" or "complex" isotopy. Coexistence of isotopies may also occur without explicit oppositional terms, as in the case of "forest", which may refer in a text both to "phytomorphic-ness" and "ecological-ness". Generalising the concept of Greimas and Courtés, we shall call the harmonic coexistence of two or more isotopies in a single unit a "complex" isotopy.[58]

Relations between isotopies may also be created by other means. One such case is the relation *determining* vs *determined*. Greimas offers as example the relation between the nuclear semes of *head*, "extreme-ness" and "upper-ness", the former leading to the latter by logical implication.

An especially interesting case of relation is isomorphism, a term closely related to the two terms analogy and homology. Analogy *stricto sensu* follows, according to Greimas and Courtés, from an identical relation between the terms of two or more different pairs. However, Greimas and Courtés prefer to replace the reasoning by analogy with the operation of homology, or in other words to replace analogy with homology, believing that analogy has lost its preciseness due to over-generalisation. They state that, given the structure A : B :: C : D (A is to B as C is to D), A and C are homologous to B and D if, from the semantic point of view, A, B, C and D are sememes structured by semes, if the terms A and C on the one hand, and B and D on the other have at least one common seme, and if the relation between A and B is identical to the relation between C and D and is one of the elementary logical relations (the ones operating in the semiotic square: contrariety, contradiction and complementarity).

Greimas and Courtés propose the comparable concept of isomorphism for relations between structures of different semiotic planes or levels, recognisable because they can be considered as homologies. They give as an example the isomorphism between the articulations of the plane of expression and those of the plane of content: pheme : seme :: phoneme : sememe :: syllable : semantic utterance (Greimas and Courtés 1979: Analogie, Homologation, Isomorphisme).

We believe that the above definitions are too narrow, and that both concepts can be applied advantageously to semantic categories in general. In our own analysis, we use the term "isomorphism" for the specific case of analogy

---

[58] Eco proposes a seven-fold typology of the interplay of two isotopies as a function of their position on the levels of the generative trajectory, but limits it to the two cases of pluri-isotopy and bi-isotopy. He considers that the concept of isotopy covers a great number of various semiotic phenomena, but is nonetheless useful in analysing textual coherence (Eco [1984] 1986: 189–201).

stricto sensu where the logical relation between the terms of the pairs of a set of pairs is contrariety (see below, 2.3).

We shall also retain the term "homology", but for the following case. Let us suppose that we have two pairs of categories that are isomorphic (in our sense):

a vs *b* :: *c* vs *d*, implying an isomorphism between a : b and c : d.

But this means that, beyond the relation between the pairs, a relation between their terms by two is also established:

a : b :: c : d,

which we shall call a relation by "homology" (akin to Greimas and Courtés's definition in the wide sense), in which the first and second terms in each pair are related by a relation of implication).

To give an example from cinema, in early Westerns, the heroes wore white hats and the villains wore black hats, making it easy for the audience to keep them apart, but also symbolising the opposition of good and evil. This leads to the isomorphic relations between semes

white-ness vs *black-ness* :: *good-ness* vs *evil-ness*,

and to the relations

white-ness – good-ness and black-ness – evil-ness,

resulting in the derived homology

white-ness : good-ness :: black-ness : evil-ness.

In a similar manner, we find in many precapitalist societies the isomorphic relation

male vs *female* :: *sacred* vs *profane*,

whence

male : sacred :: female : profane.

Also, in many precapitalist cosmologies,

navel vs *body* :: *centre of the cosmos* vs *the cosmos as a whole*,

whence

navel : centre of the cosmos :: body : the cosmos as a whole.

In these societies, homology takes the form of identity. In Greimas and Courtés's first scenario of "This man is a lion" discussed above, *man* is identified with *lion* in an archaic society of lion-men. This identification is quite generalisable to precapitalist cultures; that is, in the examples above:

    male = sacred and female = profane,

and

    navel = centre of the cosmos and body = the cosmos as a whole.[59]

A certain form of analogy is formulated by Lévi-Strauss to define his elementary structure of kinship, the "atom of kinship". He starts with four persons, the husband (a), the wife (b), and the wife's brother (c), who is the maternal uncle of the couple's son, his nephew (d). He then operates with *sui generis* analogies, the terms of which are not simple elements but relations. Thus, he uses four relations: between the uncle and his nephew (c–d, which we will indicate with A), the uncle/brother and his sister/wife (c–b, B), the father and his son (a–d, C) and the wife and her husband (a–b, D). The relations between these couples are evaluated in a simplified manner as either positive (+) or negative (–), for example c : d = + or – . In a following step, Lévi-Straus compares by two the relations A to B and C to D, still according to the evaluation +/–, for example A(–) : B(+), C(+) : D(–). With these two couples, the comparison already refers to relations between relations. More analytically, since A = c : d and B = c : b, A : B originates from the form c : d :: c : b. The analogy between the two pairs is due to the same characterisation, + or –, of the relation between their terms.

In a final step, Lévi-Strauss compares the relation between A–B and C–D, thus reaching the level of the relation between relations based on relations. He concludes that this last formula, that is, the relation between the uncle/brother and the son/nephew compared to the relation between the uncle/brother and the wife/sister is always analogous to the relation between the father/husband and the son/nephew compared to that between the father/husband and the wife/sister. Here, the term "analogy" has the logical meaning that, when A and B have similar evaluations (either + or –), C and D also present similar evaluations (either – or +); if A and B have dissimilar evaluations, C and D also have dissimilar evaluations (Lévi-Strauss 1958: 49–60). The analogy between couples of pairs follows when the pairs of each couple either

---

[59] Quite comparable operations are formulated by Rastier (2009: 188–190) in his discussion of the concept of analogy. While our pair of reference has the form *a* vs *b*, Rastier's pair is a : b; on the other hand we both relate with :: our two pairs. He considers that the relations we characterised as homology are symbolic or metaphorical connections (according to his own criteria of differentiation between the two) and concludes that the concept of analogy is not useful.

have a similar characterisation, even if this is different between the couples (for example, the pairs of one couple can be characterised as +/+ and the pairs of the other as −/−, as with A+/B+ and C−/D−); or have a different characterisation, even when they are not the same for the corresponding pairs (for example, +/− and −/+, as with A+/B− and C−/D+). As we can see, these kinds of analogies are abstract in the extreme.

There are also other types of relation between isotopies, based on less formal criteria, but frequent in texts. They are created through:

(a) A systematic association of different isotopies with a particular element, such as a place, an object or a character in the narrative. For example, if a character named George is described as having brown eyes, a dark complexion and a hearty manner, these elements (which in themselves belong to different isotopies) become part of an embracing isotopy of "George-ness" in this text.

(b) The appearance of a systematic sequence of groups including the same isotopies. Given two isotopies X and Y, a sequence such as: X–Y, X–Y–X, Y–a–X, Y–b–c–X (where a, b, c are any other isotopies) is indicative of an association between X and Y even if it is not explicitly stated. Let us say that in a text we find the description "near the river there was a cabin", and that we identify three isotopies: "near (topological isotopy, "topologi-city") the river ("water-ness"), there was a cabin" ("building-ness"). If these isotopies continue to occur together in different combinations in the text (i.e., if buildings are frequently found beside bodies of water), we can infer that they are significantly related (through spatial proximity in this example).

(c) An explicit cause-and-effect association between isotopies, though not a connection foreseen by logic. For example, "I ("individual-ness") stopped speaking ("behaviour-ness") to him ("individual-ness"), because he ("individual-ness") insulted ("behaviour-ness") me" ("individual-ness"). As in the above case, the relation between "individual-ness" and "behaviour-ness" becomes significant only if there is a systematic iteration of their relation throughout a text.

(d) A specific connotation, if it is all-pervasive. For example, the permanent darkness of Gotham city refers to the corruption among the city's civil authorities, a case in which the connotation is created by a metaphor.

(e) The similar relative weight of isotopies (chapter 6: 1.1).[60]

(f) Opposition between isotopies. An opposition between isotopies is not created by a direct opposition, such as the one between the members of a semantic category, but by an opposition between the values attributed to

---

[60] There is a partial overlapping of the types of relation between simple isotopies discussed above and Rastier's (2009: 115–116) criteria of the relations between them.

them. To give an example, let us postulate two interrelated isotopies, one urban: *dense fabric* vs *sparse fabric*, the other ecological: *stressed environment* vs *balanced environment*. The two first terms of these two pairs (*dense urban fabric, stressed environment*) are related to each other, as are the two second terms (*sparse urban fabric, balanced environment*), but the terms of the first pair (*dense fabric* vs *sparse fabric*) are valorised by planners today as euphoric (+) and dysphoric (−) respectively, while the terms of the second (*stressed* vs *balanced* environment) are valorised by ecologists as dysphoric (−) and euphoric (+) respectively. Thus, the opposition between the two isotopies follows from the simultaneous opposition between the values ascribed to their terms holding similar positions on the semantic axis.

These are relations between isotopies at the micro-scale, but we note that there is a close correspondence with the comparable relations formulated by Fontanille at the macro-scale of a text (see 1.9 below).

1.6 The composite isotopies

A common relation between isotopies is that of the more general to the more specific, which is a hierarchical relation; we shall call this kind of isotopy a "composite" isotopy or elaborated code. Each lower level of a composite isotopy is due to an analytical decomposition of the higher level. Let us take the following description:

> Then, I saw a marvellous night world, full of shining stars, and look, there was a planet, another world different from our own earth, bright Venus.

This text is ruled by an overarching composite isotopy, "cosmic-ness". There are at least five semes involved: in addition to "cosmic-ness", we have "star-ness", "planet-ness", "earth-ness" and "Venus-ness", with the last four subsumed under the first without losing their own (relative) autonomy. The articulation of this composite hierarchical isotopy, which we shall call "empirical" because it is not the result of any developed systematic logic but follows empirically from the text itself, is shown in Figure 15.

This isotopy is multi-level, more specifically a three-level hierarchical isotopy in the form of a tree structure. It starts from "cosmic-ness"; the following level subdivides "cosmic-ness" according to the semantic category *star-ness* vs *planet-ness* and the third level subdivides the planets according to the semantic category *earth-ness* vs *Venus-ness*.

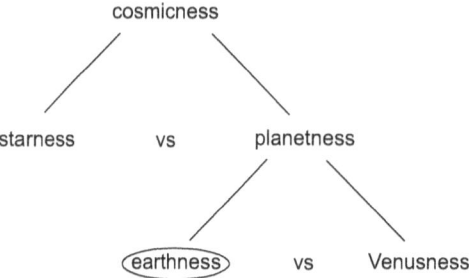

Figure 15: Empirical composite hierarchical isotopy.

There are more fully structured hierarchically organised isotopies. In pre-capitalist societies we find many cosmogonic and cosmological myths in which the place where this society lives is the centre of the earth and the cosmos, the point of cosmic equilibrium; there is a benevolent sky where the gods dwell, below that, there is the disc of the earth and below that the dangerous underworld; in the east where the sun rises there are mythical friendly beings as opposed to the hostile beings in the west, the axis east–west being of primary importance; and the friendly beings of the south are opposed to the hostile beings of the north. Texts of this kind include a large set of composite isotopies, such as the organisation of the divine pantheon ("divine-ness"), social hierarchies ("social-ness"), or the classification of animals ("animal-ness") and plants ("plant-ness"); in Figure 16 below, we focus on the spatial isotopy, which on the basis of the description above, takes the following form:

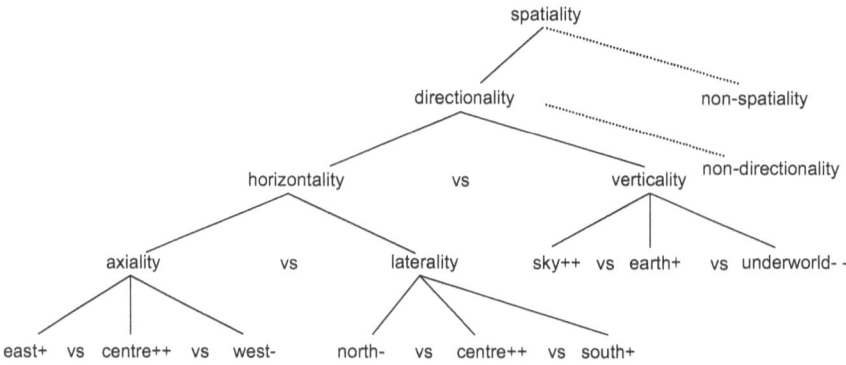

Figure 16: Systematic composite hierarchical isotopy. – – : very negative evaluation. – : negative evaluation. +: positive evaluation. + +: very positive evaluation.

Figure 16 shows a composite hierarchical isotopy developed according to a systematic logic with tightly connected semantic categories. We recognise here a variant of the semantic system of spatiality proposed by Greimas that we discussed earlier (chapter 3: 6.4), though here it is not an abstract system but the product of an artificial cosmogonic text created by us that closely resembles a great number of actual cultural cosmogonies. In Figure 16, the lower level of the hierarchy no longer includes the abstract pairs of semes *high* vs *low*, *front* vs *back* and *right* vs *left*, but the triads of the cultural concepts corresponding to them: *sky* vs *earth* vs *underworld*, *east* vs *centre* vs *west*, and *south* vs *centre* vs *north*. Figure 16 also enriches both Greimas's and our previous proposal in two ways. First, the semantic categories are no longer binary but tertiary, including a middle term, and thus taking the form *pole a* vs *middle term* vs *pole b*. Second, almost all terms are accompanied by an evaluation, which is of a connotative nature based on the semantic category *euphoria* vs *dysphoria*. Figure 16 renders this as two positive types of evaluation and two negative: the first two are gradations of euphoria, the other two of dysphoria.

These evaluations play a very important role in the cultural understanding of the concepts evaluated. The first interpretation of the concepts is of course denotative, and on this level there is only a conceptual differentiation, for example between east and west. But through the cultural evaluations attached to them, the differentiation becomes experiential, with the result that the east is felt as favourable and the west as ominous. If, in another cosmological myth, west has an equally positive connotation with east, the feelings for these two extremities of the horizon are the same. What is important in a text is not the dictionary definition of the terms, but the manner in which the text manipulates them. The text imposes its own logic, creating its own semiotic world.

When we analyse a text, the identification of composite isotopies, such as the ones described, comes at a later stage of analysis. During the first stage, which is more or less empirical and approximate, advancing by trial and error and subject to revision, we must record all the sememes or larger textual units that may be grouped together on the basis of a common classeme, in order to construct the major isotopies of the text. Then, the above units, initially juxtaposed one after the other, must be rewritten in a more orderly manner, following, of course, not an abstract logic, but the orientations given by the text.

It is possible that at the end of this process no general semantic category will emerge, but only certain partial lower-level semantic categories, probably scattered among the whole set of isotopies. In other words, we may find that the discursive surface of the text actualises only partial, unstructured isotopies, and many times textual analysis will have to be satisfied with them. Of course, semantic categories are always structured along an axis between two poles, and if one pole is actualised in a text, it may seem that we can infer the second, implied pole; that is, if we find an unstructured isotopy, for example "animal-ness", there must be an unrealised term "human-ness". This is, however, a risky procedure. Sometimes the text may allow such an assumption, but other times it would be a mechanistic intervention and addition to the text, which should not be undertaken. Thus, in our previous example referring to the two sememes of "spectacle", namely "glasses" and "shocking sight", it would not be advisable or useful to impose on the text some forced and abstract semantic category, such as *polite* vs *tasteless*. Only if we had a longer text, in which there was a systematic recurrence of this category, would we be entitled to have recourse to it. In empirical textual analysis, it is therefore useful to differentiate, as we suggested above (section 1.1) between simple isotopies, which we call "isotopies", and semantic categories, or structured composite isotopies, which we call "codes".

1.7 Relations between composite isotopies

The composite isotopy is by definition the product of a hierarchical relation between isotopies. As we just saw, the partial isotopies of cosmos-ness in our example are not developed. Every seme of this emotional description of the cosmos could be the object of a further textual elaboration, full of descriptions and emotional expressions about the vastness of the cosmos, the magic of the polar star and the constellations, the orbits and beauty of the planets, the presumed topography of Venus and the features of earth. In such a case, the hierarchy of semantic categories would be much richer. It is possible that, due to this development, the continuity of the hierarchical organisation would at some point be subject to a break, so that what was a continuous composite isotopy splits into separate isotopies.

Let us say that we extend the description of earth to a set of positive evaluations of earthly features, such as "mountains", "hills", "valleys", which would deliver an isotopy of "land-ness". Also, the text could continue describing the virtues of earth with references to "seas", "rivers" and "lakes", all referring to the seme "water-ness". We observe that landness and waterness constitute a semantic category, *landness* vs *waterness*. As long as references to valleys and rivers remain features of our original earthness, as long, that is, as landness and waterness are represented concisely as just simple descriptive enrichments of the character of earth, earthness can remain a simple seme of planetness – which is part of cosmicness – and a part of the initial composite isotopy.

If, on the other hand, the two terms of *landness* vs *waterness* were to become significant in the development of the text, they would acquire a certain autonomy and impose themselves as an integral code. In this case, earthness would be converted and promoted into a composite isotopy of its own. The text would then be articulated according to two composite isotopies and the articulation between them would be achieved through the seme of earthness, which is situated at the lower level of cosmicness and the summit of the new composite isotopy of earthness. In other words, the development of the hierarchical structure of isotopies depends on the degree of semantic complexity of the text.[61]

This new structure corresponds to a more fully developed text, which could be something like the following:

> Then, I saw a marvellous night world, full of shining stars, and look, there was a planet, another world different from our own earth, bright Venus. And I thought how beautiful our earth is, with its tall mountains, green hills and fertile valleys, and with its blue lakes, impetuous rivers and endless seas.

Still in reference to earth, the text could elaborate on other isotopies, for example one of personal relations, "interpersonal-ness", and one of social hierarchy, "(social) stratification-ness", as in the further development of the example above:

> Then, I saw a marvellous night world, full of shining stars, and look, there was a planet, another world different from our own earth, bright Venus. And I thought how beautiful our earth is, with its tall mountains, green hills and fertile valleys, and with its blue lakes, impetuous rivers and endless seas. There in the valley, beside the lake, was our garden and the little red brick cottage where my dear mother raised me, before I knew the loneliness of life in the city, the misery of the poor and the heartlessness of the rich. Here under the stars, my darling, we can make a new and better life.

Here, earthness becomes the umbrella for the pair of landness and waterness, as well as for two new semes, "interpersonalness" and "(social) stratificationness", which also constitute a semantic category, abstractly formulated as *individual* vs *collectivity*. Some isotopies, simple or composite, may remain unconnected to the structural organisation of this isotopy. For example, the "green" valleys and the "red" bricks belong to a chromatic isotopy, but it is probable that this isotopy is not central to the meaning of the text. The same could be the case for other isotopies used in the text (garden, house, bricks). If we compare *landness* vs *waterness* and *interpersonalness* vs *stratificationness*, we observe that the first is subsumed under the seme "natureness" and the second under the seme "socialness", in which case this new semantic category *natureness* vs *socialness* acquires a higher hierarchical position than these. The opposition *natureness* vs

---

[61] A parallel criterion that can be used to judge if an isotopy has an autonomous existence in a text is to assess its location and role within the complete structure of isotopies of the text.

socialness is the same isotopy as Greimas and Courtés's foundational opposition *nature* vs *culture*. "Earthness", then, in this text is a composite isotopy with three hierarchical levels, starting with earthness, continuing with the semantic category *nature* vs *culture* and ending with the two other semantic categories, each one corresponding to one of the two terms of this semantic category. The development of our brief initial text has enriched the original empirical isotopy and converted it into a rich systematic isotopy (Figure 17).

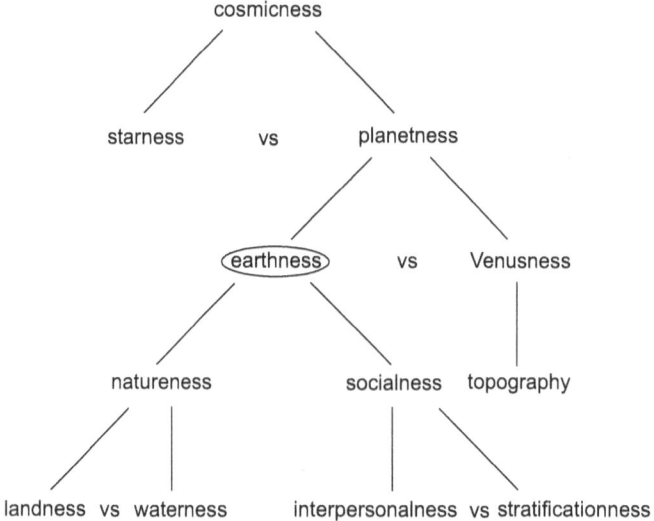

Figure 17: Further elaboration of the initial empirical isotopy.

As was the case with the spatial isotopy, our text is full of evaluations. It is apparently a very personal and sentimental text. All the isotopies, at all levels, are strongly evaluated, almost all very positively, with the exception of the dimension of social stratification, which is evaluated at the other extremity of the value scale.

1.8 The empirical textual network and the hierarchy of isotopies

The relations between isotopies that we have examined up to now are relations of juxtaposition, opposition or articulation. The relations of opposition and articulation are of a logical and classificatory nature, and these were examined and ordered in a hierarchical framework. There is also another type of relations, independent of this framework, which are empirically created by the text itself. For example, in the previous text, landness could be connected to stratification-ness, but waterness could remain unconnected to interpersonalness. A text not only constructs its own isotopies, but also defines the actual textual relations between them, which spread out in multiple directions, thus creating a complex semantic network. However, the text is not transparent, and it is the researcher who interprets it by using the metalinguistic tool of isotopy (see also Rastier 2009: 11–12).

The isotopies of this network do not all have the same qualitative importance. Some of them are displayed by the text as more important than others, and one isotopy may even dominate it. A text creates its own textual hierarchy of isotopies, through their qualitative importance, and this hierarchy does not coincide with the classificatory hierarchy examined up to now. It is expected that the nucleus of dominant isotopies, which reflects the actual structure of a text, will be directly connected to the semiotic square reflecting its deep level.

How to define the structure of this network has not been systematically studied by semiotic theory. However, we shall attempt below to present some techniques by which it can be identified. There are, in our opinion, two ways to approach this structure, one qualitative, presented in this section, and another quantitative, which will be presented in the first section of chapter 6.

The qualitative approach starts with the empirical identification of the major isotopies of a text and their internal structure.[62] As we have already remarked, the empirical grouping of words and phrases that at first sight appear to share some semantic component (seme) needs to be followed by a more careful analysis, in the course of which the relevant semantic categories are identified. Many simple isotopies that first appeared independent will at this stage reveal themselves to be part of composite hierarchical isotopies or codes. Although an isotopy may appear in a text in very many specific sememes, composite isotopies are in practice rarely very elaborate hierarchically; in other words, the text may refer to many sememes containing the seme "natureness" without developing its code of nature into a full-fledged hierarchy of plant species.

When we have identified the major codes of a text, we need to discover how they are related. Again, the relations between codes are determined by the

---

[62] What constitutes a major isotopy depends mainly on the relevance adopted by the researcher. A linguistic analysis would be interested in specifying all the semantic elements at work in all the sememes: the sememe *student* would be analysed as containing the semes /animate/ human/ male (or female)/ young/ education/ recipient of/, etc. A narrative analysis would probably assume the presence of the first two semes and look for isotopies of gender, age, and/or university-ness.

text itself. In the example we gave above, the code of natureness is clearly related to the code of interpersonalness by explicit statements: the speaker has fond memories of growing up by the lake and wants to live with her beloved there by the lake, under the stars. Similarly, the negative pole of natureness, socialness (represented in the text by life in the city), is identified with the negative aspects of social stratification, so the code of natureness is related to both interpersonalness and stratificationness. The marginal chromatic isotopy also seems to be related to natureness, though not to stratificationness or interpersonalness (unless the text were to specify that some colour has particular significance for the speaker and her beloved, for example because it was the colour of the dress she wore when they first met).

Analysing the two last verses of a poem by George Herbert, Rastier offers an especially interesting example of the relations between semantic elements in the form of a diagram (Rastier 2009: 198–200). In this diagram, the nodes are occupied by the lexemes of the poem and the relations are indicated with lines connecting the lexemes, resulting in the creation of a semantic network. What Rastier wants to show are the relations between the sememes of the lexemes, which he considers as metaphorically related, and the semes common to the sememes marking these relations and creating the isotopies of the poem. As a result, he defines two sememic and semic focuses, i.e., dominant nodes, resulting from the above double network of relations. In addition, he proceeds to a quantification of the relations, observing that each focus is the point of convergence of the maximum number of relations between sememes (and lexemes) and the relation between the two focuses is dense (actually, the densest in the whole diagram).

We believe that we can simplify a diagram of this kind by avoiding mixing three different levels of analysis (lexemes, implied sememes and semes).[63] We also think it is possible to go beyond this particular diagram, which is empirically adjusted to a specific case, and seek a general technique for studying the relations between isotopies.

As a first step, then, we choose the deeper level of analysis in comparison to sememes, that of isotopies. Once we have established the codes and determined how they are related, we can create a double-entry matrix based on this analysis. In both the rows and the columns of our matrix, all the major isotopies of the text are written in the same order (from left to right and from up down); for practical reasons, if there is a very large number of isotopies, marginal ones may be

---

[63] Rastier seems to have chosen this rather complex form because he is interested in the multiplicity, in this poem, of the relations he considers as metaphorical.

omitted. We can use either simple or composite isotopies in the matrix; ideally, the isotopies should be simple, but it is possible to also use composite isotopies, still for practical reasons and based on the judgement of the researcher. In the boxes of the matrix, we mark the relation between the isotopy at the head of each column and the isotopy at the left of each row: + if the two isotopies are related and – if they are not. Since the relation of an isotopy with itself is nonsensical, these boxes are left blank.

The blank boxes will create a diagonal running from the upper left to the lower right corner of the matrix. The matrix is symmetrical on the two sides of this diagonal (i.e., the marks in the two triangles created by the diagonal are mirror images of each other) and there is technically no need to fill in the boxes below the diagonal. The matrix may be square or rectangular in shape.[64]

Table 7 below presents an abstract and simplified form of this matrix. Let us suppose that, after the analysis of a text, we have identified twelve isotopies,

Table 7: Matrix of the relations between isotopies.

Isotopy	1	2	3	4	5	6	7	8	9	10	11	12
1		+	–	–	+	+	–	+	–	–	+	+
2			–	–	–	–	–	–	–	–	+	–
3				–	–	–	–	+	–	–	–	–
4					–	–	–	+	–	+	–	–
5						–	–	–	–	–	+	–
6							–	–	+	–	–	–
7								+	–	–	–	–
8									–	+	–	–
9										–	–	–
10											–	–
11												–
12												

---

64 Though it is not constructed for this reason, the matrix also provides information of a quantitative nature, namely the number of relations of each isotopy with all the other isotopies. These numbers are seen more directly if the matrix is also completed below the diagonal.

which we number here from 1 to 12. Let us also suppose that the relations between these isotopies are as shown in the matrix.

The matrix reveals the structure of the network of isotopies of the text, but it is not easily visualised in this form; to make the network visually accessible, we need to transform the matrix into a graph. This is done in two steps. The first is preparatory and sets the condition for the final visualisation. It is the mechanical construction of a graph which we shall call the *basic graph*, consisting of a circle on the circumference of which we create twelve points for the twelve isotopies. The sequence of isotopies may be totally fortuitous and the points can have any distance between them, but for reasons of order and balance we have used the arithmetical sequence of isotopies in the matrix and placed the points at equal distance from each other. Then, relations (+) between any two isotopies, detected on the basis of the criteria formulated in section 1.5 of the present chapter, are transferred from the matrix to the graph in the form of a line linking these two isotopies (Figure 18).

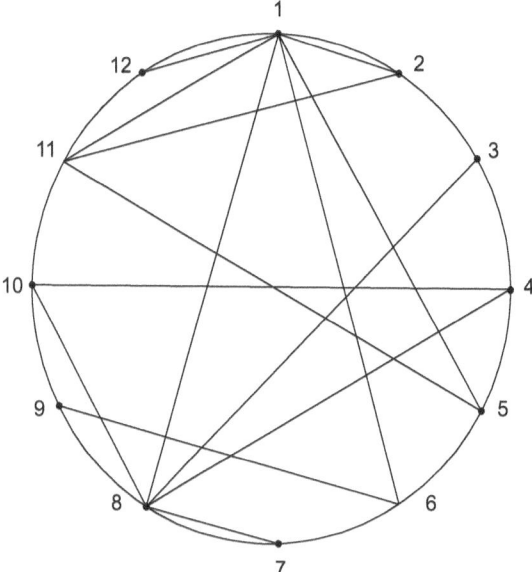

Figure 18: Basic graph of the relations between isotopies.

On the basis of the number of relations converging on each isotopy, we recognise in the graph of Figure 18 the existence of two sub-networks of isotopies, one with its common node in isotopy 1 and the other linked to isotopy 8, something that indicates that these are the dominant isotopies of the text. To make this relationship clearer visually, we proceed to a final transformation by constructing a new graph, this time not mechanically but according to the findings of our basic graph. This *final graph* is constructed by placing at its centre the dominant isotopies and grouping the other isotopies around these dominant nodes according to their relations to these and to each other (Figure 19).

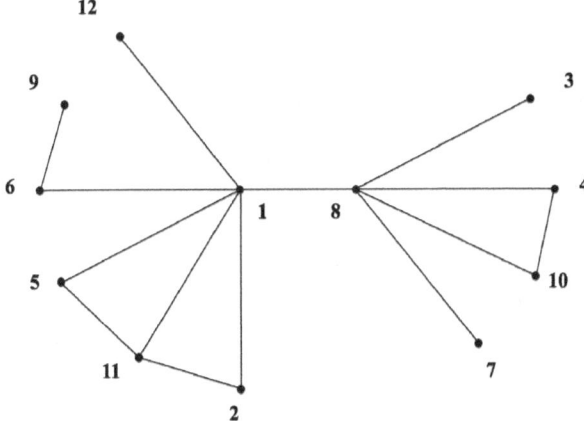

Figure 19: Final graph of the relations between isotopies.

If a relation of opposition exists between a pair of isotopies, and to the extent that this is judged as useful, we may add a minus sign (–) on the line relating the pair. The structure of the network of isotopies in the text is now displayed in the final graph. It shows a hierarchical relation between isotopies, which differs from the hierarchy ruling the internal structure of composite isotopies, although they both obey the textual imperatives. The hierarchical relations are "vertical" and imply a series of levels of continuously more specific semantic categories, while the relations shown in the graph are "horizontal" and follow from the principle of connectedness. The final graph in Figure 19 is a fairly tight graph, but not fully so, given the lack of many possible connections. It is organised, as expected, around the two dominant isotopies 1 and 8, which constitute a double textual nucleus, as opposed to mono-isotopic or multi-isotopic nuclei.

The remaining isotopies are arranged circumferentially around this double nucleus. Almost all the isotopies of the graph are directly connected to one of the two dominant isotopies, acquiring from the dominant isotopy a certain character and offering in turn a certain ambiance to it. More specifically, five of the isotopies (4 and 10, as well as 2, 11 and 5 – together 41% of the isotopies) are directly connected both to one of the dominant isotopies and to at least one of the other isotopies in their sub-network, which shows that they form two groups in the text and reinforces their presence. Three isotopies (3, 7, 12 – 25% of the isotopies) are relatively isolated and solely connected to one of the dominant isotopies, which renders them of secondary importance for the text. Finally, one isotopy (9) is indirectly connected to the nucleus (specifically to isotopy 1) through the mediation of isotopy 6, a trajectory that makes it marginal.

This account gives a statistical image of the qualitative structure of the final graph, but it only describes this specific structure. There is also a different statistical approach, complementary to the above, which identifies the general pattern of the graph and is thus useful for comparisons between graphs. It presupposes what we could call a "connectivity index".[65] This index starts from the calculation, based either on the matrix or the final graph, of the number of relations of each isotopy with all the other isotopies and then transforms this number into a percentage of the total number of relations in the matrix or graph.

This total number in our case amounts to 28 and the index for each isotopy in order of importance is as follows: isotopy 1, 6 individual relations : 28 total relations = 21%; isotopy 2, 18%; isotopy 11, 10%; isotopies 4, 10, 2, 5 and 6, 7% each; isotopies 3, 7, 12 and 9, 4% each (the position of isotopy 9 is weaker, because it is the only one not connected to the nucleus of the graph). As we can see, just two isotopies of the double nucleus, which amount to only 17% of the number of isotopies, account for almost 40% of the connectivity of the graph.

The graph examined above represents a simple form of graph. In the case of an actual text with a double nucleus, the sub-networks organised around each nucleus would probably not be as independent as in our example, but some isotopies of the one sub-network would be related to isotopies of the other.

The graph itself tells us nothing about the contents of the isotopies, and the same type of graph may correspond to the isotopic structure of quite different texts. In a text with a mono-isotopic nucleus, the central code could be, for example, *democracy* vs *authoritarianism*; in another text, it could be *freedom of speech* vs *censorship*. In a third text, we could have a double nucleus composed

---

[65] This index is not to be identified with the concept of connectivity in graph theory. Its starting point, our matrix above, is similar to the first matrix prepared by transportation studies for the formulation of their complex connectivity index.

of both these isotopies and possibly an isomorphism between the two, so that *democracy* vs *authoritarianism* :: *freedom of speech* vs *censorship*, whence the derived homology democracy : freedom of speech :: authoritarianism : censorship, from which we deduce that democracy implies freedom of speech and authoritarianism leads to censorship.

The relations between isotopies can take many forms, leading to different types of graphs. The two examples below come from the work of students in our 2018–19 postgraduate seminar on narratology.

Figure 20 shows a final graph with a mono-isotopic nucleus. The graph, from a seminar paper by Konstantinos Karagiannis (2019) on the film *Black panther* (2018), directed by Ryan Coogler, shows that there are two groups of codes in the film. The first group connects the codes of religion, gender and social status and links them to the code of family relations; this is the group of codes involved in the succession to the throne of Wakanda. The second, larger group connects the codes of technology, secrecy, space and time and again links them to the code of family relations: this is the group of codes that is activated in the plot to use Wakanda's secret technology to start a global revolution. The point of contact between the two groups of codes is the royal family of Wakanda and the struggle for power between the hero T'Challa and his cousin Erik Stevens.

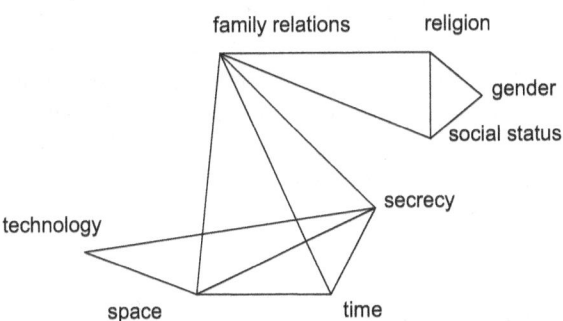

Figure 20: Final graph of the relations between codes in *Black panther* (Karagiannis 2019: 22; reproduced by permission of the author).

A very tight network of relations (Figure 21) between all main codes – in which case the whole graph essentially makes up the nucleus – is found in the film *The Da Vinci code* (2006), directed by Ron Howard. The graph, from a seminar paper by Athanasia Manazi (2019), shows the strong links between all the major codes

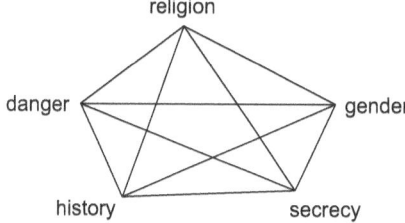

Figure 21: Final graph of the relations between codes in *The Da Vinci code* (Manazi 2019: 18; reproduced by permission of the author).

of the film: the code of religion (*religious* vs *scientific thought*) is closely related to the isotopies of danger, history, secrecy and gender, but these isotopies are also closely related to each other, since the danger derives from a secret, guarded for 2000 years and involving a particular woman. In order to arrive at such a tightly knit graph, several simple isotopies were considered as subordinate levels of the major codes of the film (the isotopies of art and of puzzles, for instance, were considered as parts of the code of secrecy).

1.9 The extended concept of isotopy

So far, our discussion of isotopies has been founded on the definition of isotopy as following from iterativity. However, Fontanille (1999: 1–5, 15–22, 35–40) offers a wider definition of isotopy. Fontanille starts from the principle that speech is neither a macro-sign nor a set of signs, but a process of signification assumed by an act of enunciation. He observes that semiotics evolved slowly into a theory of living speech, of speech in action, and points out that, while living speech draws its ingredients from the language system, it also invents its own forms and these are not limited to the forms it takes as enunciate, i.e., as text. This is why he argues that, in addition to the initial identification of isotopy based on the semantic categories offered by the language system, speech also develops other forms of isotopies, due to the dynamics of enunciation. Speech selects, combines, arranges, distorts and invents its own categories, isotopies in action.

Fontanille elaborates on two sets of concepts, each including three terms, which he connects by pairs. His first set are the "formal types of totality" (*types formelles de totalité*) which are founded on mereology, a branch of mathematical logic and philosophy which studies the meronomic, i.e., part-to-whole, relationships between elements. Fontanille focuses in respect to this set on three types of logical relationships, each of which gives its unity to a totality, following a specific rule of arrangement:

(a) the series (*série*), whose unity is due to the existence of a particular generic, common element (Fontanille gives the example of a flock of animals of the same kind);
(b) the agglomerate (*agglomérat*), a totality whose unity is due to only one of its parts, different from all other parts (for example, a river uniting different neighbourhoods); and
(c) the family (*famille*), which is a network acquiring its unity from local concatenations of parts, different from each other and connecting the parts at least by pairs (a totality formed by a river between the slopes of two hills, with a forest covering the slope of one of the hills and part of a plain and with a hamlet in the plain on the riverbank, etc.) – Figure 22.

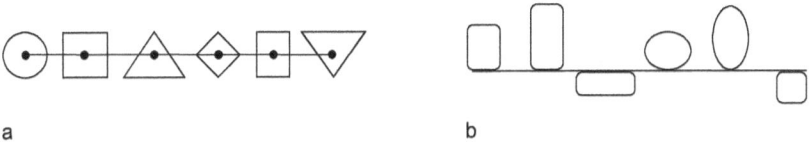

a   b

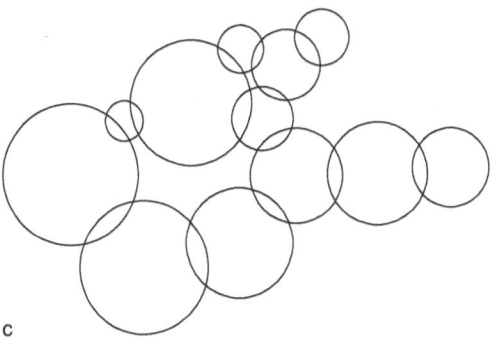

c

Figure 22: The three forms of logical relations between the parts of a whole. a: series. b: agglomerate. c: family.

Fontanille's second set is "the mode of construction of the semiotic totality" (*mode de construction de la totalité sémiotique*), that is, the organising principles which it follows. These principles are:
(a) cohesion, which is the organisation of a text into sequences and the processes, such as connection, overlapping, inclusion, parallelism or symmetry,

which locate each textual segment as dependent on other segments whether close or more distant[66];
(b) coherence, the subsuming of isotopies into a unified universe of discourse, in spite of their apparent lack of homogeneity; and
(c) congruence, referring to both the textual and the discursive perspective, which introduces in the text partial homologies (Fontanille's term) between isotopies (as in many rhetorical figures, such as metaphors).

Connecting by pairs the terms of each of the two sets according to the order above – (a) with (a), etc. – Fontanille arrives at the following conclusions:
(a) The series is produced by the linear analysis of a text. It is based on repetition as a semiotic mechanism and ensures textual unity in the form of cohesion, giving the impression that there is a continuous and progressive construction of the text. Referring to the isotopies of expression, Fontanille gives the example of rhyme and we would also add metre.
(b) The agglomerate consists of different parts constituting a whole through their connection with a common part, which ensures the coherence of discourse and its uniform comprehension. Fontanille once more uses rhyme as an example, this time from a semantic point of view, on the grounds that the resemblance on the level of expression imposes a certain interpretation of the content which would not take place under other circumstances. Fontanille also gives another semantic example from a text in which a seme of "degradation" deeply contaminates all narrative situations, in spite of their differences. Concerning the expression plane, he mentions prosody, and on our part we would refer to the alliterative metre of *Sir Gawain*, in which we also encounter the pattern of the agglomerate on the plane of expression, since the same set of stressed syllables alliterate in each line, but the phonemes that create the alliteration vary between lines (the different neighbourhoods), though they all follow the rule of "three-ness" (the river).
(c) The family is produced by a network constituted by consecutive local concatenations of different kinds between heterogeneous neighbouring parts; the relationship between parts is their common area of articulation. This network is not simply linear; it may be based on repetition, but of a more complex kind. It offers congruence, founds textual cohesion and relates it to coherence. Fontanille gives as example a rhyme scheme that is not simple but based on a play of rhymes grouped by two or three lines, consecutive or not.

---

[66] This definition does not coincide with the use of the same term by Greimas; Fontanille uses the term series for what Greimas calls cohesion.

He also refers to the connectors of an argumentation, metonymic transpositions, associations between ideas and metaphors.

Fontanille thus proposes a set of relations between isotopies at the textual macro-scale. In section 1.5 above, we discussed such relations at the micro-scale. As we can see, there is a close alignment of the two approaches: Fontanille's first type coincides with the typical definition of isotopy; our type (a), the systematic association of different isotopies with a particular element, coincides with Fontanille's second type; and our type (b), the appearance of a systematic sequence of groups including the same isotopies, coincides with Fontanille's third type.

2 Qualitative analysis of isotopies: Examples

2.1 Isotopies in prose: *The life of Saint Alexius*

In the previous chapter we analysed the narrative syntax of *The life of Saint Alexius*, starting from the discursive level in order to arrive at the level of narrative structure. The semantic analysis, the isotopies of the text, also starts from the level of discourse and works towards the second level, that of narrative semantics.

The life of Saint Alexius is technically a realistic narrative: it aims to depict events that are supposed to have actually happened in the real world. On the discursive level, we therefore encounter a relatively rich figurativisation, verbal elements that create the illusion of reality. We will not analyse every word of this figurativisation, but will focus on the isotopies that shape the semantic structure of the text, its thematisation. For example, when the text writes that Alexius in Rome goes to the harbour, takes a ship to Laodicea and then continues on foot to Edessa, we recognise on the figurative level an isotopy of *spaceness*, with references to Rome, the harbour, the sea, Laodicea and Edessa. Of these references, Rome and Edessa are nodes that articulate this isotopy with other isotopies in a manner that develops a central theme of the text. The harbour, the sea and Laodicea appear only contingently in the text and are important mainly for the creation of a reality effect: the realistic geography makes the text more persuasive, which is important for a text that purports to communicate true historical events, but is relatively unimportant for the analysis that interests us here.

2.1.1 Identifying the isotopies: Figurativisation

As we have already mentioned (section 1.8 above), the first step in identifying the isotopies of a text is empirical and consists in grouping together words and phrases that seem to have some common seme. A native speaker of the language of the text already has a good feeling for how to make these groups. However, we need to be careful to do so, to the extent that this is possible, on the basis of what is in the text and not on the basis of our own personal views or our modern sensibilities. For example, in our society, sexual relations are generally positively valued, but in an early medieval saint's legend, they are not.

We also need to remember that every isotopy is organised around an axis, a semantic category, such as *positive* vs *negative* or *presence* vs *absence*. That is, if the text includes references to men and women, we should not create a group of words referring to "man-ness" and another group of "woman-ness", but classify the references both to men and to women in the same group of "gender" and then see if the internal structure of this group allows us to identify a code of *male* vs *female*.

In *The life of Saint Alexius*, this empirical procedure leads us to identify the following groups:

(a) From the beginning of the text, we encounter a group of words referring to the Christian religion: God, good deeds, almsgiving, prayer, conversion, an icon, and later abstinence, waking, fasting, sainthood and miracles. For the moment, we shall not try to organize this set more precisely.
(b) We also very quickly encounter a group of words referring to the family: husband, wife, heir, son, father, mother, parents and later marriage and bride.
(c) The references to the family are accompanied by references to the noble birth of Alexius's parents and later of his bride, who is of the same family as the emperor. Noble birth is a form of social status. Thus, we can identify a group including all the forms of social status that are mentioned in the text: the eminent and powerful, such as emperors and archbishops, as well as the lowly, such as servants, churchwardens and common people.
(d) It also becomes obvious that the family of Alexius is wealthy. This gives us a group structured around the axis *rich* vs *poor*: the wealthy and the beggars.
(e) From the very beginning, the text places special emphasis on the concept of sexual abstinence. Together with abstinence, we need to take into account its opposite, which first appears in the text when Alexius's father urges him to consummate his marriage.
(f) With the episode of the marriage, we perceive that the text gives importance to the opposition *male* vs *female* and thus to a code of gender.

(g) Also from the beginning, we have a reference to a place, Rome. Immediately after the episode of the marriage, other geographical references appear: harbour, sea, Laodicea, Edessa, Syria. This group also includes architectural spaces: the house of Alexius's father, the church in Edessa, the church porch where the beggars sit, the small room in which the mother and bride of Alexius live enclosed, the church of Saint Bonifatius in Rome where Alexius is buried. Spatialisation, as we saw in the previous chapter, is part of the syntactic structure at the level of discourse, but space also plays a part in thematisation, as we shall see below.
(h) Temporalisation (the order of the episodes, the chronological organisation of the narrative) is also part of the syntactic discursive structure, but in this text (and in many others) time is also part of the thematisation, given the 17 years that Alexius lives hidden in Edessa and the further 17 years that he lives as a beggar in the house of his father.
(i) Finally, we need to note the textual references to the semantic axis *hidden* vs *eminent*. They appear for the first time when Alexius flees from his father's house and are repeated in each successive episode, often in the form of the opposition *recognised* vs *unrecognisable*.

We note that there are some elements that we cannot classify in any group, in particular the objects that Alexius gives to his bride on their wedding night: a ring, a cloth, and his belt. These objects are probably symbolic, but the text gives us no clues to their meaning, and we cannot interpret them unless we have more information on their significance for the society where the text was created.

2.1.2 The internal structure of the isotopies: The codes
So far, we have located a total of nine groups of words or phrases which we suspect are semantic isotopies of the text. The second step of the analysis is to identify the common semantic element (seme or set of semes) that creates each group, and then to discover their internal structure, that is, to organise them into codes.

We have already noted that group (a) has the common element of "religionness". It is more difficult to determine its internal structure. There seems to be a difference between the life of ordinary Christians and the especially demanding life of the ascetic saint, but the distinction appears to be quantitative rather than qualitative: all Christians must pray and do good deeds such as almsgiving, fasting, waking and abstaining from sexual relations, but the ascetic must do all of these things more severely and all the time. However, one difference is not simply a matter of quantity. Ordinary Christians live their life in the world and can have high social status, wealth and authority: they are eminent and powerful. The ascetic saint has deliberately divested himself of wealth and glory and lives a life that is hidden and humble. Thus, the religious code has at least one internal opposition (Figure 23).

```
              Religion
             almsgiving
              fasting
              waking
             abstinence
                etc.
               /    \
strict ascetic life    moderately virtuous life
```

Figure 23: First attempt at the internal structure of the religious code.

However, as we know (section 2.1.1 above), every isotopy is structured around an axis of opposition. If the religious code gathers together the elements of a virtuous Christian life, it logically presupposes the existence of the opposite form of life: not almsgiving but greed, not fasting but gluttony, not waking but sloth, not abstinence but lust. That is, the religious code has a negative pole, that of sinfulness, and in the case of a text such as this, which is monastic in origin, we are justified in concluding that this negative pole is implied, even though no obvious representative of the sinful life appears in the text. The characteristic quality of the semantic element that occupies the positive pole, the virtuous life, is that it tries to control the desires of the flesh, just as the characteristic quality of the sinful life is that it surrenders to the pleasures of the flesh. Thus, we can complete the internal structure of the religious code as seen in Figure 24.

Figure 24 shows that the religious code is composed of a positive pole (the virtuous life), represented in the text by a series of isomorphic isotopies (almsgiving, fasting, waking, abstinence, etc.) and a negative pole (the sinful life). But the code also has a second hierarchical level, concerning the degree of observance of these virtues: strict observance or asceticism, as opposed to moderate observance, both opposed to the lack of observance involved in the sinful life. The religious code is thus a composite hierarchical isotopy.

During the analysis of the internal structure of the isotopies, when we examine the semantic elements more closely, we may find that some elements that we had originally classified in one group should in fact be moved to another. What

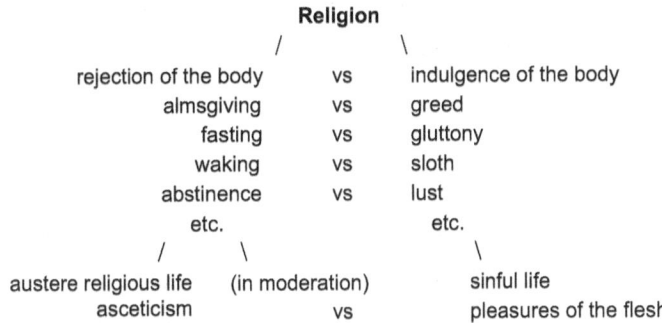

Figure 24: Final structure of the religious code.

we had originally identified as group (e) above, the isotopy of sexual relations, can be integrated into the religious code as *abstinence* vs *lust* (the specific role of abstinence in the narrative will become clear below, when we discuss the relations between isotopies that produce the thematic structure of the text).

Group (b), with the common seme of "family-ness", includes not only family relations, but also procreation, the perpetuation of the family in the next generation. From the beginning, the parents of Alexius desire to have not simply a child but specifically an heir. The marriage of Alexius is part of the effort of his father to ensure the perpetuation of the family. This brings the code of family into direct conflict with the strict form of the religious code, which prescribes abstinence.

This concern for the perpetuation of the family is explained by the relationship of the code of family to the next two codes, those of social status (c) and wealth (d).[67] Social status, public office and wealth, at the time when this text was written, all depend on noble birth. These two isotopies have a simple binary structure and are isomorphic, the two elements of the one corresponding exactly to the two elements of the other (Figure 25).

Group (g), the isotopy of space (Figure 26) is organised in a two-level hierarchy. On the first level, space is divided into the two geographical places of Rome and Edessa. Within each city, space is marked by churches; Rome in addition is marked by the particular role played by the house of Alexius's father, to which there is no corresponding element in Edessa. The sea is the medium of movement between the two cities. Because sea voyages in the tenth century

---

[67] It would be more correct to call these two codes "social status-ness" and "wealth-ness", but we simplify the terminology in order to avoid too many clumsy neologisms.

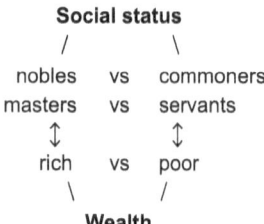

Figure 25: The isomorphic codes of social status and wealth.

were dangerous and unpredictable, they often function in contemporary narratives as expressions of the will of God. In particular the second sea voyage of Alexius, when he boards a ship going to Tarsus but ends up in Rome, is in this way related to the religious code and thus plays a small thematic role in the text.

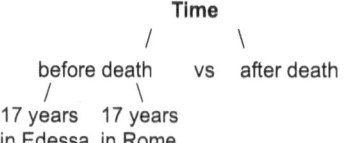

Figure 26: The spatial code.

Group (h), the isotopy of time (Figure 27), seems to have a structure also closely related to the code of religion: the lifetime of Alexius is divided into intervals of 17 years.

```
              Time
             /    \
      before death  vs  after death
         /    \
    17 years  17 years
    in Edessa in Rome
```

Figure 27: The temporal code.

Group (f), the code of gender (Figure 28) with the simple structure *male* vs *female*, is closely related to group (i), the code of "hidden-ness". For a man, the ascetic life initially implies flight outside and far away, while for a woman it implies enclosure inside the house. Only when asceticism has rendered him unrecognisable can the man continue his hidden life inside the house. This shows that the actual purpose of his flight into external space was to disappear, to become "hidden".

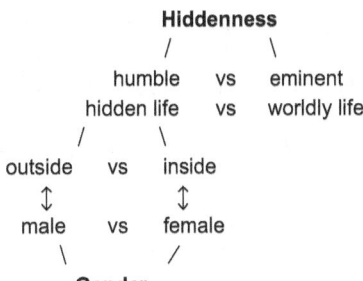

Figure 28: The articulation of the codes of hiddenness and gender.

2.1.3 Relations between codes: Thematisation

We have already discussed the relations between codes in section 1.8 above. The network of these relations produces the semantic structure of the text.

If we apply the technique of the graph to the relations between codes in *The life of Saint Alexius*, we can construct the matrix in Table 8 below. A relationship between two codes is marked with a + in the square where their rows and columns cross.

Table 8: Matrix of the relations between codes in *The life of Saint Alexius*.

Codes	religion	family	social	wealth	gender	hiddenness	spatial	temporal
religion		+			+	+	+	+
family	+		+	+		+		
social		+		+		+		
wealth		+	+			+		
gender	+					+	+	
hiddenness	+	+	+	+	+		+	+
spatial	+				+	+		+
temporal	+					+	+	

The code of religion is related to the code of family through the element of sexual relations: the perpetuation of the family necessitates marriage and hence sexual relations, but asceticism requires abstinence from sexual relations, creating an antithesis between the two codes. Sexuality thus has a very specific role in the thematisation of the text, because the need to avoid sexual relations is what forces the hero to flee from his family.

The code of religion is related to the codes of gender and space, because the ascetic life takes the form of flight into external space for men and enclosure in internal space for women. For the same reason, it is related to the code of hiddenness, to the need to disappear.

The code of family is directly related to the codes of social status and wealth, because (as we already noted) social status and wealth in this text are inherited, which creates the obligation of marrying and producing an heir. It is also related to the code of hiddenness, because in this text a noble family by definition leads an eminent, worldly life.

For the same reason, the codes of social status and wealth are related not only to the code of family but also to each other and to the code of hiddenness. The social status of a noble family is eminent, illustrious: the opposite of hidden.

The code of gender is related, as we saw, to the codes of religion, hiddenness, and space, because the ascetic life requires different forms of hiddenness for men and for women.

The codes of space and time are related to each other and to the code of hiddenness, because time in this text is divided into the two 17-year intervals during which Alexius's hidden life takes two different forms in two different places. No symbolic meaning or explanation of the number 17 is provided by the text, but these intervals of ascetic life create a relation between the temporal and the religious codes.[68] The code of space is also related to the religious code, because particular spaces are apparently required for the ascetic life.

If we count the number of relations of each code to other codes, it is clear that the code with the greatest number of relations is the code of hiddenness, which is connected to each of the other seven codes of the text. Then follow the codes of religion, family and space, each with four or five connections to other codes. The remaining codes, the codes of social status, wealth, gender and time, have three connections each to other codes.

Turning this matrix into a basic graph, we arrive at the form in Figure 29.

The central role of the code of hiddenness and its relation to the religious code govern the transformation of this basic graph into a final graph. The code of hiddenness takes the central position in the new graph and the religious code is positioned above it and slightly to the left. This gives us the graph in Figure 30.

---

[68] The two periods of 17 years add up to 17 + 17 = 34, very close to the 33 years that Christ is supposed to have lived on earth.

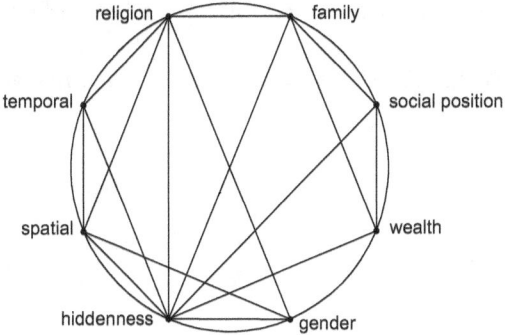

Figure 29: Basic graph of the relations between codes in *The life of Saint Alexius*.

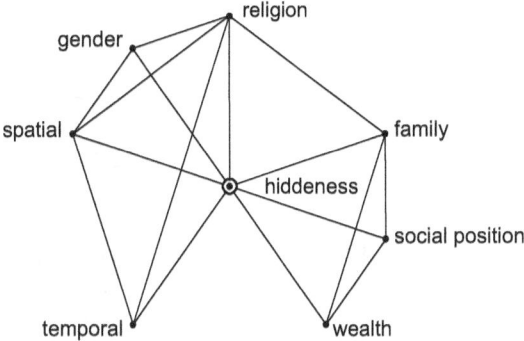

Figure 30: Final graph of the relations between codes in *The life of Saint Alexius*.

We can see that the graph is divided into two distinct groups of code, with close connections between the codes within each group: a religious group, which links the codes of hiddenness, religion, gender, space and time, and a second, worldly group which covers one pole of the code of family (its other pole is connected to the religious code) and the codes of social status and wealth. These two groups are linked by only two articulations. The first link is through the relation of all three codes of the worldly group with the code of hiddenness, but specifically with that pole of the code which is negatively valued by the text: the opposite of hiddenness, eminence. The second link comes from the only other relation of this group with codes external to it, namely the relation of the religious code to the worldly pole of the code of family, which again is a relation of opposition. In other words, the two groups of codes are related as antithetical to each other and the whole structuring of the isotopies of the text reflects this basic relation of opposition, *asceticism* vs *worldly life*.

If we examine specifically how the codes are linked together, we arrive at the diagram in Figure 31.

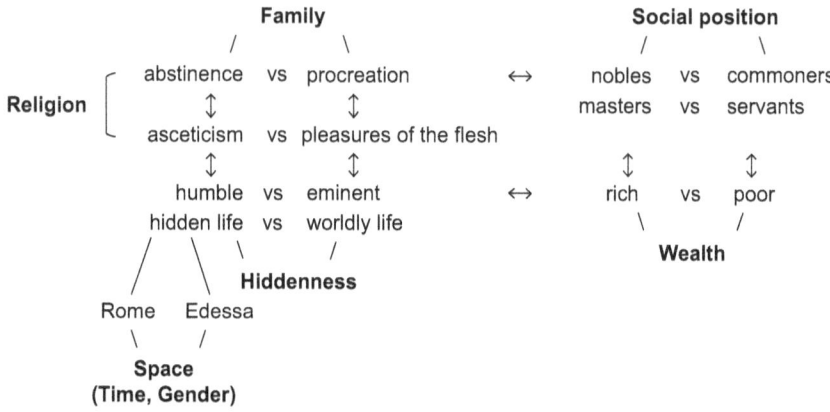

Figure 31: Structural diagram of the relations between codes in *The life of Saint Alexius*.

The structure of this diagram of the relations between codes leads, as expected, to the same conclusion as our interpretation of the final graph in Figure 30. The diagram can also be divided into the same two groups of codes: on the right side, the codes of social status and wealth are linked to the code of family and the negative pole of the code of hiddenness, and on the left, the positive pole of the codes of religion and hiddenness are linked to the remaining codes.

The diagram also shows how the major themes of the text are created. The choice of the ascetic life, which requires sexual abstinence, is antithetical to the need to ensure the perpetuation of the family through marriage. That opposition, in turn, creates the need for flight into external space and disappearance into a hidden life. The themes of the text are shaped by the interaction of its central isotopies.

2.1.4 The semiotic square

In the last chapter, starting from the level of discourse with its actors and spatial and temporal setting, we analysed the narrative syntax and arrived at the second level of the genetic trajectory, the level of actants and narrative structure. In this chapter, analysing the narrative semantics, we started from the figurativisation of the level of discourse and saw how the discursive isotopies of the text are woven together to create its themes, including the basic theme of the text, the hidden life. That theme has its source in the fundamental value of the narrative, sainthood: the thematisation of the text is the product of its fundamental semantics, in other words of the semiotic square that founds the genetic trajectory of the text.

It is not easy to identify the semiotic square of a text, the structure of oppositions that underlies both the narrative structure and the multiple figurative isotopies of the discursive level. Which of all the many isotopies is so significant that it can be said to determine the story? There is no mechanical method for finding the semiotic square, though in this chapter we have pointed out some techniques – the matrix, the graph, the diagram – that can be helpful. Essentially, they all amount to ways of identifying thematisation.

Thematisation is not created only through figurativisation, but occurs at all levels of the narrative. In *The life of Saint Alexius*, the basic theme of the text, the hidden life, determines the syntax as well as the semantics of the narrative. The theme has its source in the Object of the narrative, sainthood. Sainthood is defined by the text as antithetical to the worldly life of a noble family; this creates the need for the flight of Alexius, his family's unsuccessful attempt to find him, and his life as a beggar in his father's house; it also shapes the secondary narratives of his mother and bride (enclosure as an alternative form of the hidden life). The prominence of the theme of the hidden life in both the figurative discourse and the narrative syntax of the text is a strong indication that it forms part of the semiotic square.

The life of Saint Alexius also thematises its actants. We already noted that the Object of the narrative is sainthood. The Subject is a personified version of this theme, a "saint". Sainthood, in this text, implies the hidden life, because it implies asceticism. The religious code is deeply involved in the thematisation of the ascetic life, which requires the rejection of both the "world" and the "flesh". Rejection of the "world" implies rejection of the eminent position of his family and leads us to the theme of the hidden life. Rejection of the "flesh", in addition to abstinence and hence the refusal of marriage, involves the specific religious practices that Alexius engages in, but it also involves a particular definition of evil, of the sins that the saint must struggle against.[69] Thus, the role of Opponent is also thematised.

---

[69] Some later vernacular versions of the legend, without altering the narrative structure, attempt to create a different thematisation by emphasising the poverty of Alexius rather than his rejection of bodily pleasures. The same narrative can thus to some extent be given a different meaning through a different thematisation (wealth rather than "the flesh" becomes the source of evil).

Alexius struggles against two enemies. The first to appear in the text is the "flesh" (emblematically but not exclusively in the form of sexual pleasure). Rejection of the pleasures of the flesh implies refusal of marriage and resistance to the demands of the body for food, drink and sleep. This gives us the first contradiction of the semiotic square:

abstinence, privation vs *marriage, pleasure*

In a slightly more abstract form, we can rephrase this contradiction as:

asceticism vs *pleasure of the flesh*

The second enemy of Alexius is what in the course of our analysis we called the "world": glory, wealth, the power and authority that accompanies the life of a Roman nobleman. Rejection of the world, in this text, means choosing obscurity, poverty, humility. The second contradiction thus takes the following form:

obscurity, poverty, humility vs *eminence, wealth, power*

Here also, we can rephrase the contradiction more abstractly as:

hidden life vs *worldly life*

The text equates asceticism with the hidden life (in fact, the bodily disfigurement resulting from ascetic practice is the precondition for the hero's remaining "hidden"). Thus, it is likely that these two contradictions belong to the same semantic category. This leads us to the first-level semiotic square that appears as the inner square of Figure 32.

We observe that the horizontal axes, the axes of contraries, follow the requirements of the semiotic square: asceticism is contrary to the worldly life and the pleasure of the flesh is contrary to the hidden life. The perpendicular axes, the

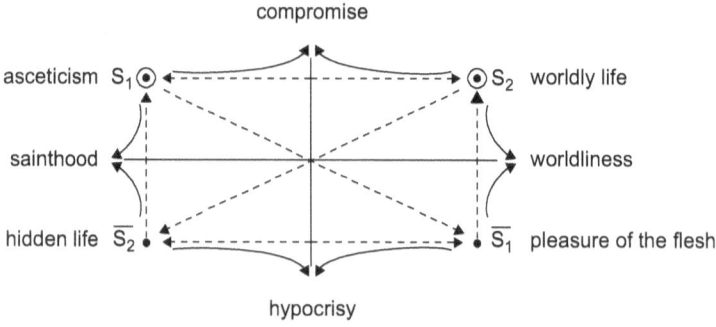

Figure 32: The semiotic square of *The life of Saint Alexius*.

axes of complementarity, are also correct: asceticism implies the hidden life and vice versa, just as the worldly life implies the pleasure of the flesh and the pleasure of the flesh presupposes a worldly life.

The external square of Figure 32 shows the semiotic square of the second hierarchical level. The two terms to the left of the square form the condition of "sainthood", while the two terms on the right compose "worldliness", two concepts that are related as contraries. That is the double semiotic square that produces the semantic universe of *The life of Saint Alexius*.

The external square also has other possible combinations. For example, we could combine the hidden life and the pleasure of the flesh, in order to produce a figure of *hypocrisy* (for example, "sinful prelates"). This combination is not realised in the text, but it is a possibility offered by its semantic universe. On the other hand, a combination of "worldliness" with asceticism could correspond to the life of Alexius's father, a wealthy nobleman who practices sexual continence and gives alms to the poor (Alexius among them). The text implies that this *compromise* of a moderately virtuous worldly life is a possible choice, though not the best one. The double semiotic square creates possibilities for other narratives, including further developments of the semantic universe of *The life of Saint Alexius*.

2.2 Isotopies in poetry

Lyric poems are very dense texts. The text tries to squeeze as much meaning as possible into few words, which means that poems will often exploit several different connotations of the same word. We can demonstrate this with an analysis of *The lake isle of Innisfree*, a short lyric poem published in 1890 by the Irish poet William Butler Yeats.

> *The lake isle of Innisfree*
>
> I will arise and go now, and go to Innisfree,
> And a small cabin build there, of clay and wattles made;
> Nine bean-rows will I have there, a hive for the honey-bee,
> And live alone in the bee-loud glade.
>
> And I shall have some peace there, for peace comes dropping slow,
> Dropping from the veils of the morning to where the cricket sings;
> There midnight's all a glimmer, and noon a purple glow,
> And evening full of the linnet's wings.

> I will arise and go now, for always night and day
> I hear lake water lapping with low sounds by the shore;
> While I stand on the roadway, or on the pavement grey,
> I hear it in the deep heart's core.

The title of the poem, *The lake isle of Innisfree*, is a reference to a real place: Innisfree is a small island in Lough Gill, near the town of Sligo in the west of Ireland. The title thus predisposes us to read the poem as a realistic description, though we might also note that an island in a lake is a rather isolated place.

The first word that we encounter in the text is the personal pronoun "I". It is the only personal pronoun in the text, and it is repeated seven times in twelve lines. We thus have a speaker (though we need to remember that the speaker in a lyric poem is as much a textual construct as is the narrator in a story), but apparently no addressee.

The phrase "I will arise and go now" opens the text and is repeated verbatim in the beginning of the last stanza. "Arise" used in the first person singular is an old-fashioned verb, vaguely biblical in its connotations; the phrase suggests a kind of sudden resolve, a "departure" in more than the literal sense. The suggestion is reinforced by the absence of a specific addressee: the speaker seems to be talking to himself. On the other hand, he is departing for a real place, Innisfree.

The following lines seem to confirm that we are dealing with a realistic setting: a cabin made of clay and wattles, a garden with beans and a beehive. But although the setting seems realistic, it is at the same time strikingly simple, even austere: clay and wattles are extremely simple, traditional construction materials, and living on beans and honey sounds positively monastic. Even the very specific number, "nine bean-rows", reinforces this sense of austerity. Our suspicions are confirmed when we get to line 4, "live alone" (both words heavily stressed in the rhythmic pattern of the poem). The simple life that the speaker envisions seems to be a kind of hermitage.

It is thus no surprise that the speaker expects to "have some peace there", though the second stanza warns us that "peace" is a slow process, falling in drops, in a gentle and rhythmical movement "from the veils of the morning to where the cricket sings". Crickets sing in the evening, in trees or bushes. The line describes a vertical movement, from sky to earth, and also a temporal movement, from morning to evening. The poem returns to the temporal isotopy with the changing times of day (midnight, noon, evening), first in terms of shifts in light and colour – glimmer, purple glow – and then in terms of the delicate movement of the wings of a small bird.

The third stanza, repeating verbatim the opening phrase of the poem, reinforces the sense of a sudden resolve and departure for a new life. The other main isotopies that have been established by the text are also repeated and reinforced in this stanza: "always night and day" belongs to the temporal isotopy; the lake water and the shore recall the other natural elements of Innisfree; "lapping with low sounds" gives us one more gentle, repetitive natural sound.

The sudden break comes in line 11, where the speaker stands "on the roadway, or on the pavements grey". This is the first and only appearance of an urban environment in the poem, and it is brought into sharp contrast with what the text has been describing so far. The most explicit contrast is in terms of light and colour: instead of glimmering light and glowing colour, we have dark, colourless "grey". But there are also other implications. The verb used, "I stand", is opposed to the verbs of the opening line, "I will arise and go now" as stasis is opposed to motion. The "roadway" and "pavements" imply horizontal movement, whereas in the second stanza peace descended in a vertical movement. They also imply crowds, in contrast to the speaker's resolution to "live alone", and perhaps also noise, as opposed to the soft natural sounds of Innisfree.

The final reversal of the poem begins with one of those sounds. The speaker tells us that "always night and day / I hear lake water lapping". That sound is what is calling him, leading to his resolution and departure ("I will arise and go now, *for* always . . . "). But the sound does not come from outside; he hears the sound of lake water "in the deep heart's core". In the final line, space is reversed: the lake is located inside the heart, external space becomes a part of internal identity, the real place becomes something mythical, or imaginary, or a dream.

This tension between the real and the symbolic is fundamental to the poem. From the first stanza, the *spatial* isotopy of the text is a complex isotopy (section 1.5 above), in which two or more isotopies coexist harmoniously in a single verbal unit. Innisfree is at the same time a real place and a spiritual state. This ambiguity retrospectively colours the whole poem, so that we look for and find echoes of spiritual meanings in expressions that at first seemed unambiguously realistic.

The complex spatial isotopy is present even in the title of the poem. Innisfree is, as we said, a real place, but the archaic form "isle" and the isolation implied by an island already introduce the potential of a seme of spirituality in addition to the realistic place name.

The isolation of the island participates in an isotopy of *solitude*, which appears in the exclusive use of the pronoun "I" and the speaker's determination to "live alone". The other pole of this isotopy is not actualised in the text, and thus we are not told what the text imagines would be the opposite of "alone" – friends and family or anonymous urban crowds? – though the grey pavements in stanza 3 make the second possibility more likely. It also tells us that the spatial opposite of Innisfree is the city.

There is an interesting isotopy of *motion* vs *stasis* in the text's choice of verbs: "arise and go" vs "stand" and "hear". Motion seems to be associated with Innisfree, and stasis with the city street (which is curious, since city streets are usually envisioned as bustling with people, but the speaker seems to be frozen motionless among them). The verbs "live" and "have peace", which are also associated with Innisfree, at first seem to imply stasis as well, but life on Innisfree is not static, though its motion is gentle: bees hum, lake water laps, and peace "comes dropping slow".

We have already noted the extreme *simplicity* of the objects that the text ascribes to Innisfree: a cabin of clay and wattles, nine bean-rows and a beehive, and we have seen how this simplicity potentially activates a seme of austerity linked to the spirituality that runs through the poem. The text does not seem to actualise an explicit opposite pole of complexity for this isotopy.

The text also mentions a series of natural elements that we could group together in an isotopy of *nature*: bean-rows, bees, crickets, linnets, lake water. The isotopy of nature seems to be parallel to the previous one of simplicity, in the sense that the very simple life envisioned by the poem would also be a life in nature. The other pole of the isotopy would probably be *urban*, as represented by the roadway and the pavements of the city in the third stanza, giving us an opposition of *natural* vs *urban*.

The poem is full of references to low, gentle *sounds*: the bee-loud glade, the cricket singing, the linnet's wings, the lake water lapping in the third stanza. Even peace comes in the form of dropping, a slow, gentle, repetitive sound. There is no obvious negative pole; the city streets are not marked by noise in the text.

There is an isotopy of *light*, with an opposition of *light and colour* (glimmer, glow, purple) vs *dull and colourless* (grey). We also already noted a *temporal* isotopy (related to the isotopy of motion, since the speaker will "arise and go now") or rather an isotopy of time passing (morning, midnight, noon, evening), but this is a cyclical, repetitive time, a sense reinforced by the timelessness of the "always night and day" of the third stanza. The sense of timelessness is related to the reversal in the last lines of the poem. The speaker hears the lake water of Innisfree as he stands in the urban space of the city, but he hears it *inside* himself, "in the deep heart's core". The place is calling to him, summoning him, not to a physical journey but to a kind of spiritual awakening. In the end, the space of Innisfree turns out to be an interior space, deeply embedded in his own identity. This, in retrospect, leads us to examine the poem for an isotopy of *identity*, which we find in the first person singular pronoun, and also in the fact that the speaker seems to be familiar with Innisfree: it is a place he knows well. This would imply that the opposite of Innisfree, the city streets, are an unfamiliar and foreign place.

Apart from the complex isotopy of space, the remaining isotopies of the poem are generally limited to a single semantic opposition, a simple code, with no additional hierarchical levels and often (as in the isotopies of solitude, simplicity and sound) with only one semantic pole actualised in the text. A diagram of their structure would be a fairly simple set of isomorphic pairs, as in Figure 33.

there (Innisfree)	vs	here (the city)
↓		↓
alone	vs	—
motion	vs	stasis
simple	vs	—
natural	vs	urban
low sounds	vs	—
light (and colour)	vs	grey
time passing	vs	timelessness
recovery of self	vs	loss of self

Figure 33: Isomorphic structure of the isotopies in *The lake isle of Innisfree.*

As we already noted, lyric poetry is a very dense discourse, and we see this immediately if we examine the isotopic structure of the text. Though it is only 128 words including the title, it is quite rich semantically, with more isotopies (9) than *The life of Saint Alexius*. The isotopies cover all the main lexemes, and many lexemes can be grouped in more than one isotopy; in other words, the text shows a high degree of semantic density. The isotopies are also very closely linked to each other, as we can see from Table 9 below:

The isotopy of space is, as we saw, a complex isotopy, with both literal and figurative meaning; in purely spatial terms, it is structured simply as *there* (Innisfree) vs *here* (the city), and its symbolic meaning is produced by the other isotopies gathered around the place of Innisfree. It is related to the isotopy of solitude literally (because Innisfree is an island) and figuratively (because solitude is part of the kind of spiritual life the speaker envisions there). It is also related to the isotopy of movement both literally (the speaker is resolved to "go" there, and Innisfree is full of small, delicate movements) and figuratively (going there is a form of spiritual awakening). Space is closely related to the isotopies of simplicity and nature, since these are what the speaker expects to find on Innisfree, as well as to the isotopies of sound, light and colour, and time (in the form of the times of day). It is also closely related to the isotopy of identity, because Innisfree is part

Table 9: Matrix of the relations between isotopies in *The lake isle of Innisfree*.

Isotopy	space	solitude	movement	simplicity	nature	sound	light	time	identity
space: real & spiritual		+	+	+	+	+	+	+	+
solitude	+		+	+	+	+			+
movement	+	+			+	+		+	+
simplicity	+	+							+
nature	+	+	+			+			+
sound	+	+	+		+			+	+
light & colour	+							+	+
time	+		+			+	+		+
identity	+	+	+	+	+	+	+	+	

of the speaker's identity ("the deep heart's core"), and the space of the city is apparently foreign to him.

The isotopy of solitude, in addition to space, is related to the simplicity and naturalness of life on Innisfree, and to the isotopy of sound (the sounds of crickets and lake water).

The isotopy of movement (*motion* vs *stasis*) is related to space and time (*stand* vs *arise and go now*) and to the isotopy of solitude ("live alone"). It is also related to the isotopies of nature and sound, because nature on Innisfree is full of small movements and sounds.

The isotopy of simplicity is related to space through the very simple objects that the speaker envisions having on Innisfree, and to the isotopy of solitude for the same reason.

The isotopy of nature is also related to space and solitude, but in addition it is related to the isotopies of movement and sound (the movements and sounds on Innisfree are all natural).

The isotopy of sound is related to space, movement and nature, and also to time (through the song of the cricket and the lapping of lake water). The isotopy of light and colour, in addition to space, is also related to time (the times of day have their own colours). The isotopy of time is related to space, movement, sound and light. Finally, the isotopy of identity is related to all the other isotopies, since they together constitute the symbolic space of Innisfree, which is central to the speaker's sense of self.

If we transform this table into a basic graph, we arrive at the shape in Figure 34.

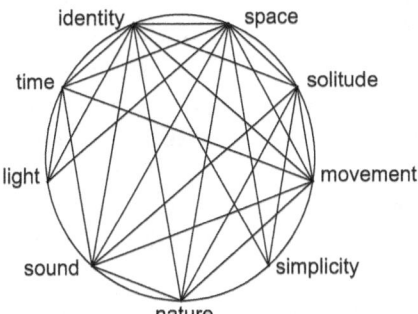

Figure 34: Basic graph of the relations between isotopies in *The lake isle of Innisfree*.

In order to see more clearly the network of isotopies in the poem, we transform this graph into the final graph of Figure 35.

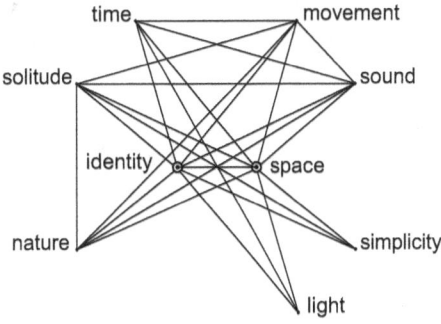

Figure 35: Final graph of the relations between isotopies in *The lake isle of Innisfree*.

As we can see, the semantic structure of the poem is centred on the relation between space (literal and symbolic) and identity. These two isotopies are strongly linked to each other, but at the same time linked to all the others, binding them together.

Most of the remaining isotopies are linked to each other as well as to the central pair of space and identity. The five isotopies of solitude, movement, nature, sound and time form a tightly knit group. A few isotopies (simplicity, light) are more peripheral, though still securely tied into the structure. Clearly, then, the pair of isotopies of space and identity must be involved in our construction of the semiotic square of the poem.

When determining the semiotic square of a text, it is worth remembering that, according to Greimas, behind any kind of discourse we can identify a narrative structure. Even short lyric poems incorporate a rudimentary narrative, though they do not always tell their story explicitly. In this poem, the narrative starts in the last lines of the text: the speaker, on the city streets, hears in his heart the lake water of Innisfree and resolves to "arise and go" there to live a simple life alone. We see that this rudimentary narrative activates the same basic isotopies that we have identified as central to the poem, the spatial isotopy and the isotopy of identity.

In the spatial isotopy, the antithetical poles would be Innisfree and the city, or in more abstract terms, *there* vs *here*. We have seen that Innisfree (*there*) is felt by the speaker to be a part of himself ("in the deep heart's core"), while living in the city seems to lead to a loss of identity. Going to Innisfree would then be the equivalent of recovering one's identity. This would give us a semiotic square like the one in Figure 36.

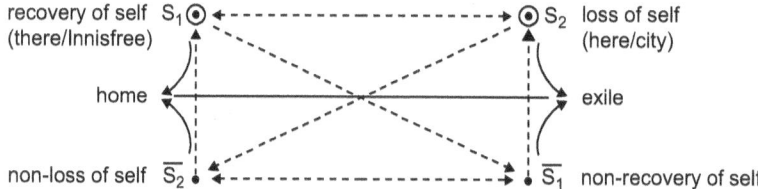

Figure 36: The semiotic square of *The lake isle of Innisfree*.

The external square is incomplete. We can see on the meta-axis of contraries that living in the city is a kind of exile, and returning to Innisfree is a return to the speaker's own place, home. The positions on the meta-axis of contradiction of the second square are empty. It does not seem possible, in this text, to recover one's self while living in the city, or to lose one's identity on Innisfree.

Now that we have analysed the internal structure of the text, it might be interesting to note that in his autobiography (1956: 153), Yeats gives the following account of how he came to write this poem:

> I had still the ambition, formed in Sligo in my teens, of living in imitation of Thoreau on Innisfree [. . .] and when walking through Fleet Street [in London] very homesick I heard a little tinkle of water and saw a fountain in a shop-window which balanced a little ball

upon its jet, and began to remember lake water. From the sudden remembrance came my poem Innisfree [. . .].

2.3 The use of isotopies for the analysis of ideology

Up to now, we have encountered the concept of isotopy as a fundamental tool for narrative analysis. However, Greimas and Courtés apply the same concept beyond narrative, to the wider field of sociosemiotics, thus touching upon sociology (as approached from the point of view of meaning). The authors see sociosemiotics as having two objects of study, social systems of classification and communication. Given that we shall deal with communication extensively in chapter 8, we shall limit ourselves here to the first issue.

The study of social classification systems is an inquiry into the universe of ideology, which Greimas and Courtés conceive as structured by two registers. The first is "sociolect", a collective semiotic register associated with a particular social group. The second is "idiolect", an individual semiotic register attached to a particular actor. The individual register orders the collective according to its own terms, but the collective also manipulates the individual in its own way, that is, each register is articulated with the other from its own perspective.

Greimas and Courtés support the hypothesis that the individual register revolves around the semantic category *life* vs *death*, while the collective register around the category *nature* vs *culture*, both presumed to be a universal metalinguistic tool. The first opposition, *life* vs *death*, referring to individual actors who have integrated the second opposition *nature* vs *culture*, rules their semiotic activities and all the texts they produce, i.e., their idiolect, while the second, *nature* vs *culture*, integrating the first, is assumed by social groups and rules their attitudes to the crucial issues they face, i.e., their sociolect. All major sub-discourses of a social group express its sociolect and their analysis reveals the cultural classification system of the group, which is diffused throughout its semiotic activities and texts.

According to Greimas and Courtés, the main object of the analysis of sociolect is the connotative level of values, which has as point of departure the fundamental semantics invested in the semiotic square, that is, the deep paradigmatic structuring of values, accompanied by the study of the syntactic component. It focuses on the classification of cultural texts; in the case of texts of a historical nature, on classifications such as that into sacred and profane discourses, and in the case of contemporary texts, on the division of, for example, sacred discourses into religious, philosophical, poetic, etc., and the appearance of new textual genres, such as detective stories, Westerns, etc. (Greimas and Courtés 1979: Axiologie, Collectif, Idiolecte, Sociolecte, Sociosémiotique).

We mentioned earlier (chapter 3: 11.1) Foucault's concept of *épistémè*, the epistemological field that governs the knowledge of a particular historical period. *Épistémè* is, for him, the background against which a culture conceives of the world. The everyday empirical conception of the world orders things, classifying them and creating a system with them, on the basis of spontaneous primary codes which organise language, perception and values. At the other extreme, sciences and philosophy, as reflexive knowledge, attempt to explain the existence of this empirical order. Foucault places *épistémè* between these two as a mediation of a fundamental nature, but actually we can better understand it as superior to both, because it is, according to him, the order *par excellence*, anterior to language and perception, which supports both the empirical order and the reflexions on it (Foucault 1966: 11–14).

If we compare the idea of *épistémè* to Greimas and Courtés's universals of *life* vs *death* and *nature* vs *culture* (the latter borrowed from Lévi-Strauss), we understand how bold it is to attempt to find a general regulator for the whole set of *épistémès* that have appeared in the course of human history. However, on a less ambitious and more specific level we can indeed delimit the classification systems ruling a culture's conception of the world.

A classification system is the condensed cultural expression of *épistémè*. In precapitalist societies, it is essential for the structuring of signification and constitutes the backbone of their practical, intellectual and emotional culture, supporting their worldview or ideology. Its centrality for the comprehension of the cultural/semiotic sphere has been repeatedly emphasised by anthropological research, from the classic essay by Émile Durkheim and Marcel Mauss (1903) to the work of Claude Lévi-Strauss and beyond.

Although the classification system is incorporated into the culture, it is not formulated by precapitalist societies as a whole in an explicit form, but is metalinguistically reconstructed by the anthropologist. It includes and orders all major isotopies conceived by the culture, thus also incorporating all its key concepts, and shapes its perspective for understanding the cultural and natural world. The typical form of the classification system is that of a vast set of semantic categories, of the form *a* vs *b* (see, for example, Middleton 1973: 369). We also frequently find the form of the triadic code *a* vs *O* vs *b*, where *a* and *b* are part of a binary opposition *a* vs *b* and *O* is the medium term between the contraries, usually of a neutral, unmarked nature as opposed to the marked nature of the two poles of the code.[70] The codes of the classification system are

---

[70] Lévi-Strauss (1958: 248–251) identifies a similar intermediary term in a binary pair, having the function of mediating between irreconcilable poles.

isomorphic, with as a result that the set of their first terms is conceived as homologous to the set of their second terms. Classification systems are structured by the specific nature of their codes, by the internal structure of each code, and by the structuring of and the hierarchies established between the whole set of codes.

We would like to stress here the concept "specific nature" of an isotopy. An isotopy may have both a general and a specific nature. Its general nature follows the metalinguistic category according to which it is classified and which allows direct comparisons between texts. If this isotopy is a value of the fundamental semantics of a text, it is actualised in the narrative semantics of the text and in its discursive semantics first takes the form of an abstract theme, which then becomes specified with figurativisation. On this last, discursive, level, the isotopy acquires its specific nature expressing the particular text to which it belongs, and this nature is no longer the same as that of another text starting from the same general isotopy. The issue of the general and the specific nature of an isotopy is an instance of a "bone–flesh" relation. "Cosmicness", for example, is detected as an isotopy in ancient India, ancient Greece, among the Navajos and the Fali Kangu in North Cameroon, allowing a general – and relevant – comparison and the general conclusion that all four societies use the same cultural isotopy; however, the specific conception of the cosmos in these cultures is revealed to be totally different at the discursive level. And, if "ecologicalness" is today prominent in a set of texts, allowing them to be grouped as ecologically oriented, in one text "ecology" may focus on the protection of natural resources, in another on pollution and in a third on recycling.

A system of classification is not homogeneous, but includes a nucleus or central part and a periphery. A certain code or group of codes is dominant, certain other codes are closely related to them, while the rest are of lesser importance and frame the previous codes. Domination establishes value hierarchies between codes. We should not, however, reify the formal expressions of classification systems, because, being metalinguistic, they are an abstraction, and in spite of their actual operation underpinning cultures, they are manifested in practice with greater or lesser fidelity according to the case.

Here we shall discuss the classification systems of three precapitalist societies: Ancient Greece, the Amhara of Ethiopia, and the Lugbara of Congo and Uganda.

From the end of the sixth century BCE, prominent in the culture of ancient Greece was the Pythagorean concept of the order of the cosmos, from which the key concept of *symmetria* was derived. *Symmetria* indicated the commensurability, i.e., proportional relations, between the various parts of a whole, and between the parts and the whole. Each of the major isotopies of the Greek classification system, as revealed by their projection on the urban space of the polis, was structured according to *symmetria* as an overarching principle. These isotopies are: the cosmic/religious isotopy (the cosmos is ruled by proportional relations); the social isotopy (the reciprocity of relations among citizens, that is, the principle of democracy, expressing social equilibrium, the latter concept ruled by the right proportions of *symmetria*); the political isotopy (the equality of political rights among citizens, again democracy, expressing equilibrium); the anthropomorphic isotopy with its two sub-isotopies of the shape of the human body (ruled by proportional relations and organised around its navel projected on the city as its cosmic *omphalos*) and bodily health (due to the correct proportion and equilibrium of the four humours, which acquired an urban dimension as the health of the city); and a *sui generis* aesthetic isotopy (ruled by the most complex forms of *symmetria*). These isotopies represent the deep structure of the dominant ancient Greek ideology.

Symmetria as a concept derives from a new form of economy, namely monetary economy (implying the proportional relations of the values of all goods), which emerged at the end of the seventh century BCE (Lagopoulos 2012b: 33–65, 73–75). The ancient Greek case reveals an interesting semiotic phenomenon. *Symmetria* as product of a cosmic isotopy became the cement of the whole classification system or – to use Fontanille's types of isotopy structures, *symmetria* is the common element of the classification system which forms it as an agglomerate. Each isotopy became structurally isomorphic with all other isotopies, because it was structured by the concept of *symmetria*, and thus the whole classification system is ruled by the cosmic isotopy.

Our second example comes from the Amhara ethnic group, which gained control over a large area of the Abyssinian plateau at the beginning of the 14th century and founded the Kingdom of Shoa (flourished until the mid-16th century). The main legal document of the Amhara, considered as the oldest Ethiopian constitution, is the *Ser'ata Mangest* [*The order of the kingdom*], a systematic account of the Amhara classification system already in existence in the early 14th century. All the codes of this system follow a ternary structure with the familiar form *a* vs *0* vs *b*, where *a* and *b* are contrary terms equilibrating around a prominent middle term *0*, and all the codes are isomorphic to each other.

Amhara Ethiopia is comparable to ancient Greece in that here also there is a common element holding together the totality of the classification system, but here it is the semantic category of *left* vs *right* (manifestly rooted in the human body), operating on both sides of a regulatory centre which is the most highly valued. Unusually, left is valued positively and opposed to the negatively valued right; left is closely connected to the centre. The two dominant and strongly related codes of the system are the cosmic/religious and the royal code, both structured according to the *left* vs *right* opposition. In general, the other codes, major or not, are isomorphic to the *left* vs *right* pair and thus also with each other. The cosmic code appears as *cosmos* vs *centre* vs *chaos* and is closely connected to *order* vs *disorder*. The "King of the Kings" (i.e., emperor) occupies the zero point of the cosmos, its centre and simultaneously its highest point, because from the centre–emperor passes the cosmic axis, allowing communication with God. The geographical centre occupied by the emperor is not actually on earth at all; it is divine and belongs to the heavenly space.

The other major codes of the Amhara classification system are: the prominent legal code, with judges of the left and judges of the right; the administrative code, with officials of the left and officials of the right; and the military, similarly structured. These codes have as centre the emperor. There are codes of gender, of space, of time, etc., as found also in ancient Greece and many other cultures.

The hierarchy of the codes of this system displays as dominant code the religious, while the royal code is explicitly subordinated to it. In terms of power, the emperor is below the power of God. However, simultaneously the emperor, an autocratic ruler, adopts a legitimising strategy projected on the classification system, by investing himself with the main attributes of the cosmic/religious code: he is divine, he occupies the cosmic centre, he communicates directly with God. The emperor and his court stand higher than any official of the church. He and his court are an image of God and the heavens respectively and mirror the celestial order on earth. This strategy offers him symbolic power, but this is not his final goal, since power is not only, not even primarily, symbolic. What is at stake is to secure with the help of symbolic power his actual, material, that is, socio-economic and political, power (Lagopoulos and Stylianoudi 2004: 50–53).

Our final example is a tribal society, the Lugbara, a Sudanese-speaking people of NE Congo and NW Uganda. Their ideology is organised according to a long and elaborate binary and isomorphic classification system. Its pairs refer to people, events and things, to directions and relations, and to abstract concepts; all of them go back to the fundamental opposition of the system *order* vs *disorder*, explained by their cosmogonic myth and implying that of *good* vs *evil*. According to this myth, in the beginning there was no order or social and moral authority. These virtues were only later constituted as permanent ideal principles: order arose from disorder and authority from the lack of it. The opposition *order* vs *disorder*, of a cosmological origin, permeates their views on the cosmos and society – it is the common element of their classification system – and this binary structure is indispensable for understanding not only their cosmology, but also their actual social structure, which moreover seems to be the source of their cosmology. In actual social relations, the senior man of each elementary lineage has full authority over its members. Thus, the myth acts as an instrument of legitimation and stabilisation of the actual relations of power, and this is the deeper function of the classification system (Middleton 1973: 369–370, 372–373, 377, 378, 386–389).

Within the Lugbara system, the *right* vs *left* pair is present, but only occasionally. It does not play any important role, but is used by the overarching opposition *order* vs *disorder*. We observe a comparable case in ancient Greece, where the importance of this pair was weak and limited to the intellectual level, and had no impact on social organisation.

These few examples allow us to proceed to certain generalisations. There are similarities and dissimilarities between classification systems, but the similarities are found on a rather high level of abstraction, the metalinguistic denomination of the codes, though it still provides crucial information. On the other hand, there are dissimilarities both on this level of abstraction and on the next level of cultural specificities, because the nature and structure even of the same codes and the structuring of the systems as a whole are different and depend on the particularities of each culture.

What we found in the classification systems discussed above, something that seems to be universal in the cosmogonic myths of precapitalist societies which are the core of their existence, is the fundamental conception that the created cosmos emerged from a primeval chaos, as these two are conceived by each culture. This was also the case in ancient Greece. The first known Greek cosmogony is the *Theogony* of Hesiod (c. 700 BCE), which describes the origin and genealogy of the gods. The cosmos, for Hesiod, emanated from the generation of four beings: first emerged *Chaos* (chasm), followed by *Gaia* (earth), *Tartarus* (a deep abyss) and *Eros* (desire). Gaia gave birth to the sky, the mountains and the seas (Hesiod 2007, *Theogony*: 116–133). In this case, then, the natural cosmos (earth, with its mountains and seas, covered by the sky) – together with one imaginary being, *Tartarus*, and what is for us an abstract concept, desire – emerged from, and manifestly as an opposition to, a primeval chaos.

We began this section with the view of Greimas and Courtés that the sociolect, the collective ideology, is founded on the metalinguistic semantic category *nature* vs *culture*. But the anthropological material seems to be pointing in a different direction – at least in the case of precapitalist societies – because what emerges as the foundational codes are the twin oppositions *cosmos* vs. *chaos* – in more abstract terms, *formed* vs *unformed* – and *order* vs *disorder*. Actually, they correspond to one and the same code, (formed) *cosmic order* vs (unformed) *disorder of cosmic chaos*. It is not simply a static logical opposition, but always incorporates the temporal dimension, because – as Hesiod states –

in the beginning there is chaos and then the cosmos rises from it. It is interesting that precapitalist cultures provide the above codes (and by extension the pair *formed* vs *unformed*), because they can be used directly for metalinguistic analysis, without the need to have recourse to further abstraction (as can the pair *nature* vs *culture*, which also occurs in spontaneous semiotics). If we follow the general logic of precapitalist cosmologies, the cosmic order includes more than nature – as we saw in the *Theogony* – and it is within the framework of nature that culture emerges.

To conclude, the semantic category *nature* vs *culture* seems weaker than *order* vs *disorder* as a foundation for the analysis of sociolect, because the precapitalist cosmogonies reveal it to be too anthropomorphically oriented. They also offer a deeper and more abstract code, with and under which *nature* vs *culture* can be articulated. In other words, *order* vs *disorder* (not *nature* vs *culture*) is the cement of precapitalist classification systems and offers an interesting metalinguistic tool.

Chapter 6
Paradigmatic analysis: Isotopies, quantitative approach

1 Theoretical background

1.1 The quantitative approach in semiotics

In the previous chapter, we studied isotopies and their relations through a qualitative approach. We shall try in this chapter to show that a different, quantitative, approach to isotopies is possible, focusing on their quantitative presence and hierarchy. To have recourse to a quantitative methodology in semiotics may seem iconoclastic, because semiotics usually operates only with qualitative data. This attitude has deep roots in the social sciences, which are traditionally divided into two camps: one camp, including semiotics and social anthropology, defends the exclusive use of qualitative data, methodology and techniques, while the other, including sociology and demography, tends to give priority to their quantitative counterparts.

Our conviction is that these conflicting views result from the direct theorisation of empirical knowledge about the nature and requirements of the object of research. They first reflect primary research needs and only as a consequence become scientific credos. For example, social anthropology studies relatively small social groups, and structuralist methodology in anthropology operates with small-scale structural relations within these groups, which are of a qualitative nature; the small groups invite the adoption of participant observation and qualitative procedures. On the other hand, sociology studies macro-groups, excluding the use of participant observation as a methodology and inviting reliance on quantitative data and statistical operations. The radical division between camps derives from the fact that each camp theorises its experiences, without concerning itself further with the question of widening its perspective. We believe that this division of the social sciences is without epistemological justification. Each side would be more balanced if it reflected on the possible methodological merits offered by the other side.[71] The conflict between qualitative and quantitative

---

[71] Anthropology was founded on participant observation and this is still its cornerstone. However, more recently many anthropologists also use quantitative data, though without adopting any explicit methodology.

methodology is epistemologically baseless; the two methodologies may well be combined, of course in proportion dictated by the specificities of each field.

We would like to point out that the very definition of isotopy by Greimas is based on the *repetitive* occurrence of the same seme, and this definition implicitly entails a quantitative dimension. When "repetitive" is given the more precise form of "how many times", then we are dealing with the explicitly quantitative concept of "frequency". There is thus no obstacle to measuring, once an isotopy has been detected, the number of sememes or larger units that are its vehicles.

Measuring the occurrences of an isotopy delivers a number that in mathematics is a positive integer (1, 2, 3 . . .) and reflects the absolute frequency of the isotopy. When we want to assess this absolute weight of the presence of an isotopy in a text, absolute frequency – what Rastier (2009: 114–115) calls density – offers an empirical image of it. Let us suppose that we are analysing a text in which the total number of occurrences of all isotopies in the text is 76; isotopy *a* occurs 5 times, isotopy *b* occurs 8 times, isotopy *c* 9 times, isotopy *d* 14 times, isotopy *e* 15 times, etc. This gives us an empirical image of the presence of each isotopy in the text, but the image has meaning only for this text. On the other hand, the sum of the occurrences of all the isotopies of a text, that is, of all its absolute frequencies, can be compared to the corresponding sum of another text. The same is the case with the absolute number of isotopies, the "semantic richness" of a text.

However, if we want to compare the frequencies of occurrence of the isotopies of the above text with another text, where the total number of occurrences of all isotopies is, for example, 136, and if isotopy *a* in this second text also presents 5 occurrences, its relative frequency is obviously less than in the first text (5 occurrences in a total of 136 is a smaller proportion of the whole than 5 occurrences in a total of 76), which implies that the use of integers is not satisfactory. We cannot judge the comparative presence of an isotopy in two texts by using absolute frequency, because the same number of occurrences in different texts has a different weight in each text.

The way out of this difficulty is to use the concept of relative frequency – the percentage of relative density, according to Rastier (2009: 114–115) – which is the assessment of the occurrence of an individual isotopy in a text in relative terms, by connecting it to the total number of occurrences of all isotopies in the text, that is, by formulating it in terms of a percentage. In this way, all isotopies acquire the same point of reference. This connection takes the form of a percentage, and the 5 occurrences of *a* in the first text take the form of 5 : 76 = 7% (more precisely 6.6%, but decimal numbers in percentages is generally an excessive detail for the needs of a semiotic analysis), while the same number in the second text is converted into 4% (3.7%). These percentages, which represent the relative frequency of an isotopy, give a clear image both of the quantitative structure of isotopies and their hierarchy within a text and their comparative importance in different texts.[72] To display this hierarchy clearly, the relative frequencies of the isotopies are written in descending order, whether in a text or in a table; i.e., for the second text, *e* 11%, *d* 10%, *c* 6.5%, *b* 6%, *a* 4%.[73]

1.2 Techniques for the quantitative analysis of isotopies

The quantification of isotopies poses certain technical problems. One lexeme may have an ambiguous signification: "a beautiful forest", for example, may refer to either ecology or aesthetics or both. The occurrence of similar expressions in the text either disambiguates the isotopy, showing, for example, that the reference is to ecology, or shows that both isotopies are simultaneously activated, in which case we have a pluri-isotopy and thus need to count two isotopies in the same expression. This also occurs in the case of connotative isotopies: for example, in a Gothic novel, an isotopy of "fire" may carry a connotation of "purification", and both the connotative isotopy and the denotation supporting it need to be identified and counted each time they occur. It goes without saying that we never analyse a text quantitatively without a previous careful reading and qualitative analysis of it, during which the connotations should have been identified. We emphasise that qualitative analysis *always* precedes its quantitative counterpart.

Let us return to the twelve isotopies in the matrix presented in the previous chapter (Table 7, section 1.8) and let us suppose that Table 10 records the absolute and the relative frequencies of occurrence of each of its isotopies.

How should we interpret this table? The simplest way is as follows: We see that hierarchically the most frequent isotopy is isotopy 1 (18%), then follows isotopy 8 (15%), third is isotopy 2 (11%), etc. Such a reading is a simple repetition of the table, but does not explain it, in the sense of adding any new information. There is a more pertinent reading, allowing a deeper understanding of the table. We observe that the relative frequencies may be grouped into different categories. A first attempt at a grouping shows that the first category A consists of isotopies 1 and 8 (15%–18%), the second category B of isotopies 2, 11, 10, 5, 4, 7, 3, 6 (5%–11%) and the third category C of isotopies 12 and 9 (1%–2%). Then, we

---

[72] Oddly, Rastier (2009: 115) chooses absolute frequencies for the comparison of isotopies.
[73] When decimal numbers are rounded up or down, we need to check that the final sum of the frequencies equals 100% (plus or minus 1%).

Table 10: Absolute and relative frequency of occurrence of the twelve isotopies.

Isotopy	Frequency	
	absolute	relative, %
1	34	18
8	28	15
2	21	11
11	19	10
10	17	9
5	15	8
4	15	8
7	13	7
3	11	6
6	9	5
12	4	2
9	2	1
Total	188	100

observe upon closer inspection that the second category could be split into two, a higher category B_1 consisting of isotopies 2, 11, 10, 5, 4 (8%–11%) and a lower one B_2, consisting of isotopies 7, 3, 6 (5%–7%), because the repetition of 8% twice suggests a kind of continuity with the higher frequencies of the B category and discontinuity with the lower frequencies of the same category. The result is that we detect a quantitative polarisation between a major category A, consisting of the two dominant isotopies 1 and 8, and a marginal category C, with isotopies 12 and 9, having as intermediate a category B, itself split into a middle category B_1 and a peripheral category B_2.

In the previous chapter, we ended with the final graph of the qualitative relations between isotopies (Figure 19, section 1.8). We can now take a further step and combine this graph with the frequencies of the isotopies presented in Table 10. This combination is shown in Figure 37.

In this manner, the vertices of the graph lose their neutral character and become weighted. This combination leads to new conclusions about the four categories of isotopies. The frequencies of the two dominant isotopies 1 and 8,

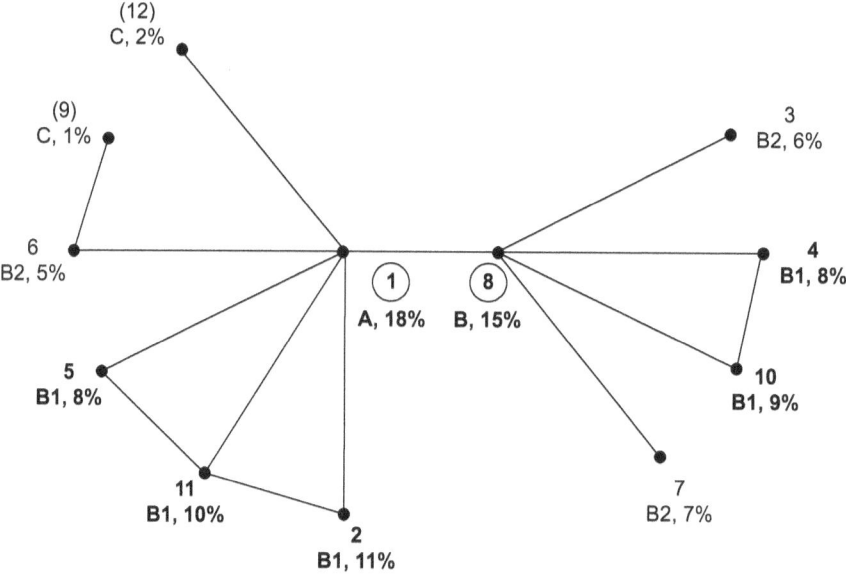

Figure 37: Projection of frequencies on the final graph. Numbers in bold in a circle: dominant isotopies. Plain numbers in bold: middle category of isotopies. Plain numbers: peripheral category of isotopies. Plain numbers in parenthesis: marginal category of isotopies.

closely related and organising the totality of the text, amount to a remarkable 33% (one-third) of the total number of occurrences of isotopies in the text. The isotopies of the middle category of frequencies are not only interrelated (5 with 11 and 11 with 2, as well as 10 with 4), but they are also directly related to the dominant isotopies. The frequencies of the sub-network of isotopies 5, 11 and 2, which are related to isotopy 1, amount together to 29% of the total occurrences, while the frequencies of 4 and 10 amount to 17%, whence we conclude that there is a stronger grouping of isotopies around isotopy 1 – which also has the most frequent occurrence among the two dominant isotopies.

Thus, we observe that the text presents a nucleus that is doubly dominant (both qualitatively and quantitatively), consisting of the dominant isotopies, and a strong double framework revolving around it. If we add the relative frequencies of the isotopies of the middle category sub-network around isotopy 1 to the frequency of 1, their total amounts to 47%, almost half of the total frequencies, while the middle category sub-network around isotopy 8 together with its own frequency amounts to 32% (almost one-third) of the total. Thus, the stronger middle category sub-network is the network around the stronger of the dominant isotopies.

1 Theoretical background — 195

The isotopies of the next two categories are divided into those that are related to 1 (6, 9, 12), with a sum of frequencies amounting to 8% of the total, and those that are related to 8 (3, 7), with frequencies amounting to 13%. As a whole, then, the whole sub-network around 1 gathers 55%, while the whole sub-network around 8 gathers 45%; that is, although the former is of greater weight than the latter, as also isotopy 1 has a greater relative frequency than 8, the text incorporates the hierarchy of isotopies in a more or less balanced manner – which does not exclude a balanced opposition.

The graph examined above is rather simple and shows a neat matching between the positions of the vertices of the graph and the frequencies corresponding to them. We should have a more or less comparable matching in the case of mono-isotopic nuclei, such as those of *Saint Alexius* and *Black panther*, with the nucleus presenting the greater number of relations. In the case of a tight network of connections between all main isotopies, as we encountered with *The Da Vinci code*, we can expect that they will function together as a collective nucleus and will have comparable individual relative frequencies, though not necessarily the same. A similar pattern can be expected in the case in which each isotopy is connected to all or nearly all others, as in the poem by Yeats. There is no guarantee that there will be a direct matching of this sort in every case, and there can be greater or lesser discrepancies, but we can say that there is a notable tendency for qualitative and quantitative data to converge. In each case, a careful interpretation is needed both of the qualitative form of the graph and of its relation to the frequencies.

We just made the hypothesis that there is a tendency for convergence between the hierarchical position of an isotopy in the graph, reflecting its qualitative importance in a text, and the frequency of occurrence of the isotopy. We shall try to support this hypothesis below. Analysing Honoré de Balzac's short story *Sarrasine* in his *S/Z* (1970: 23–27), Barthes identifies five major "codes" (technically isotopies) which produce the unity of the text. He observes that these codes appear from the very beginning of the text, in its title and first sentence, and though initially he seems to consider this fact as random, he ultimately questions its random character. With this observation Barthes adds to the structural characteristics that make an isotopy important, namely its order of appearance in a text. He may also have implicitly assessed the importance of the story's isotopies with the help of something like their frequency and thus this observation indicates the possibility that there may be a relation between the qualitative importance of an isotopy, its frequency of occurrence, and the order of its appearance in a text.

We examined the issue of the relation between relative frequency and order of appearance in our study, mentioned in the previous chapter (section 1.4), of the conception of regional space in Greece (Lagopoulos and Boklund-Lagopoulou 1992: 225–227). The study was based on field research, during which a stratified sample of 144 subjects answered a questionnaire in the form of a structured interview. Due to the questionnaire form, the answers of each respondent delivered what could be considered as a fragmented text, which was then subject to analysis, response by response. The central goal of the analysis revolved around the minute study of isotopies. After a qualitative analysis identifying the isotopies, we continued with a quantification of the isotopies on the basis of their relative frequencies, and finally with statistical correlations using cross-tabulation. With this latter technique it was possible to examine statistically the issue in question.

More specifically, for each sub-corpus of a very large set, we correlated, through cross-tabulations, the isotopies occurring in the three first positions in each response with their relative frequencies in the sub-corpus as a whole. In spite of the fact that the discourse of the respondents was oral, spontaneous and fragmented, and thus unprocessed,[74] the statistical results showed a clear tendency for the greater relative frequencies to converge with the first orders of appearance. There were, of course, exceptions in some of the sub-corpora examined and there are no doubt also individual exceptions, but most of the cross-tabulations showed the existence of very significant correlations (as a rule at the .0000 level of significance). If, coming back to Barthes, we consider that the first isotopies that appear in a text also tend to be its major isotopies in qualitative terms, we can conclude that these isotopies also tend to present higher frequencies of occurrence. Given that the major isotopies of discourse are the strategic viewpoints that it adopts on the world, this conclusion suggests that a written text or an oral discourse returns insistently to its core ideology, thus revealing it during the development of the discourse.

We repeat that this is a statistical tendency, not a structural regularity. However, as was shown from the above study, the probability of convergence between the main isotopies and their frequencies tends to certainty, to the extent that we pass from individual texts to a large corpus. We also find other instances of this tendency. Gary W. Evans (1980: 264) mentions a study of sketch maps elicited from different subjects which showed, this time in respect to individual subjects, that the elements first drawn on their sketch maps were also the ones most frequently recognised in a picture-recognition test.

---

[74] In contrast to literary discourse and particularly the discourse of poetry, which as we saw in the previous chapter (2.2) is extremely dense and coherent.

In conclusion, there is a great probability, with reference to the final graph of the main isotopies of a text and the relative frequencies accorded to its vertices, that there will be a convergence between the positions of the vertices of the graph and these frequencies, as well as a further convergence of both with the order of appearance of the most prominent among them.

1.3 The utility of graphs for other operations

Graphs such as the one described above may be useful in other cases as well. Below we present an example of a graph which attempts to describe a different textual structure, more superficial than that identified through Greimasian narratology or the graph described in the last chapter, but nevertheless enlightening. Our example comes from the analysis by Betty (Despoina) Kaklamanidou (2005: 95–96, 102–106) of the epistolary novel *Les liaisons dangereuses* [*Dangerous liaisons*] by Pierre Choderlos de Laclos, published in 1782 and filmed in several versions. Kaklamanidou's graph investigates the narrative structure of the text as shown by the number of letters exchanged between the characters. It is possible to apply the same method to other forms of communication in fiction, such as the number of dialogues between two characters, or the number of scenes in which they both appear. This operation is totally independent from any reading of the novel, since it only presupposes the recording of the names of the actors and their communicative interaction.

The plot of Laclos's novel is based on the machinations of the Marquise de Merteuil and her former lover the Vicomte de Valmont. Merteuil asks Valmont to seduce the innocent fifteen-year-old Cécile, daughter of Madame de Volanges, a virtuous widow of strict morals. Cécile was educated in a convent, from which her mother has recently removed her in preparation for her marriage to Vicomte Gercourt, on whom Merteuil wants to avenge herself because he has abandoned her. Valmont initially refuses, because he is planning to seduce Madame de Tourvel, a young married woman of strict principles. Finally, Valmont and Merteuil make a bet that, if Valmont succeeds in conquering Tourvel and gives Merteuil written proof of this, then Merteuil will spend a night with him.

While Valmont starts his seduction of Tourvel, Merteuil pursues her revenge against Gercourt by introducing Cécile to the Chevalier Danceny, but the sexual relation she wishes to establish does not materialise due to the innocence and politeness of the young Chevalier. Valmont learns that Cécile's mother has informed Tourvel about his bad reputation and to avenge himself seduces Cécile. However, he actually falls in love with Tourvel and they begin an affair.

198 — Chapter 6 Paradigmatic analysis: Isotopies, quantitative approach

Merteuil is furious with this turn of events and pressures Valmomt to end the relation, which he accepts in order to preserve his reputation as a Casanova. However, although Valmont won their wager, Merteuil refuses him, resulting in a conflict between them. Merteuil reveals to Danceny that Valmont has seduced Cécile, the two men duel and Valmont is fatally wounded, but before he dies he gives Danceny his correspondence with Merteuil, with the aim of exposing her in Parisian society.

On the day of his death, Tourvel succumbs to a fever and dies. Danceny discloses the letters and Merteuil's reputation is ruined. She falls ill with smallpox, is horribly disfigured and finally flees to the Netherlands. Cécile, also ruined, returns to the convent for good and Danceny leaves for Malta.

Since this is an epistolary novel, a first approach to its narrative structure is to examine the exchange of letters between the actors, that is, the communication network between them. The graph constructed by Kaklamanidou (Figure 38) shows the

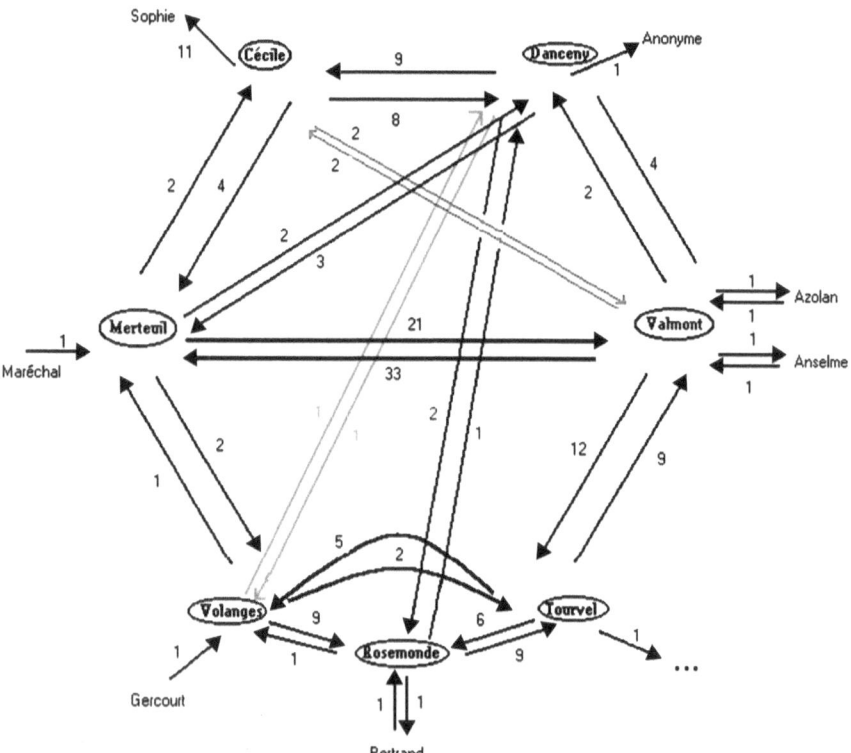

Figure 38: The flow of letters between actors in *Les liaisons dangereuses* (Kaklamanidou 2005: 104; reproduced by permission of the author).

flow of letters to and from each actor in terms of absolute frequency. The vertices of the graph are here occupied by all actors, primary or secondary, in the novel. Thus, the relations depicted in the graph are not relations between isotopies, but relations due to the exchange of letters, the total number of which amounts to 175.

Using the data provided by Kaklamanidou, we calculated (a) what we call the "epistolary weight" of each actor, as a function of the sum of all letters sent and received by them (actor A sent and received x letters in total), and (b) the "epistolary intensity" between pairs of actors (with the exception of Sophie, Cécile's friend from the convent), as a function of the total number of letters exchanged between them (actors B and C exchanged a total of z letters).[75] This calculation delivers the absolute frequency for each case, from which we then calculated the relative frequency in the form of a percentage. In the first case, we calculated the epistolary weight of an actor as a proportion of the total epistolary weights of all actors in the novel (175 letters, each exchanged between two actors, 175 x 2 = 350), and in the second the epistolary intensity between pairs of actors as a proportion of the total epistolary intensities between all pairs (still 350). These frequencies are shown in Figure 39 (very low frequencies are not included):

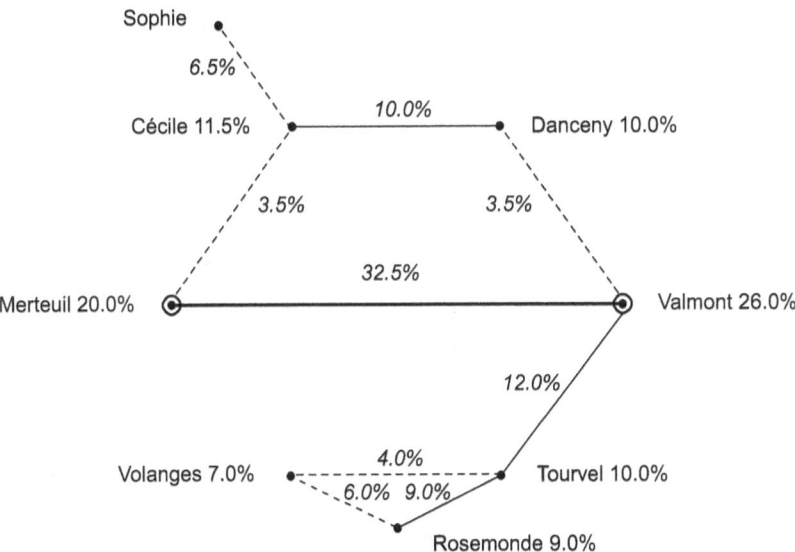

Figure 39: Epistolary weight (plain letters) of the main actors and epistolary intensity (italics) between pairs of actors in *Les liaisons dangeureuses*. ——: first category of epistolary weight. ——: second category. ---: third category.

---

75 As Kaklamanidou notes, it is also possible to calculate separately letters sent and letters received.

We can draw certain conclusions from this graph even before we read the novel. We observe the existence of three categories of epistolary weight: the first includes the field of values 20.0–26.0 and is due to Valmont and Merteuil, the second and much lower category includes the field 9.0–11.5 (in descending order, Cécile–Danceny and Tourvel–Rosemonde), closely followed by the third field 6.5–7.0% (Volanges and Sophie). For epistolary intensity, we also observe three categories: the first covers the value of 32.0% and is again due to Valmont and Merteuil, the second and much lower includes the field 9.0–12.0% (in descending order Valmont–Tourvel, Cécile–Danceny, Tourvel–Rosemonde), and the even lower third includes the field 3.5–6.5% (Cécile–Sophie, Rosemonde–Volanges, Tourvel–Volanges, Merteuil–Cécile, Valmont–Danceny).

These data leave no doubt that the central actors are Valmont and Merteuil. The sum of their epistolary weights is almost half (46%) of the total epistolary weights and is far higher than the weights of any other pair. Their epistolary intensity amounts to almost one-third (32%) of the total epistolary intensities and is also much greater than any other pair. If we compare the structural positions of Valmont and Merteuil, Valmont has a greater weight than Merteuil and is surrounded by a larger sub-network of exchanges, which shows that he is the actor with the greatest epistolary activity – but the graph does not reveal the actantial role of Merteuil as Sender.

The actors in the second weight category, Cécile, Danceny, Tourvel and Rosemonde, are also connected with the strongest epistolary exchanges after the protagonist couple. Even without further reading, we could assume that the novel revolves around the personal relations between the couples Valmont–Merteuil, Valmont–Tourvel and Cécile–Danceny. The couples Valmont–Merteuil and Valmont–Tourvel have Valmont as their only common contact, which shows the lack of contact between the two women. This reflects a real situation in the novel, but does not reveal Merteuil's promise. The epistolary intensity of the couple Cécile–Danceny is quite comparable to that of the couple Valmont–Tourvel. The graph shows that there is very low epistolary intensity between Valmont and Danceny on the one hand, and Merteuil and Cécile on the other, and this fact could give the impression that the couple Cécile–Danceny is acting independently from the other actors. However, if we want to assess the relations between couples, we must pass over these individual relations and consider their sum. We then observe that the relations between Valmont–Merteuil and Cécile–Danceny amount to 3.5% + 3.5% = 7%, an intensity which becomes stronger if we consider the low intensities between Valmont and Cécile, as well as between Merteuil and Danceny (which are not shown in the graph). This intensity gives us a feeling for the relation between the two couples, but underestimates its role in the novel and does not reveal the key role of Merteuil's plot.

We also cannot know from the graph the nature of the relation within the couple Tourvel–Rosemonde. We understand that the two women have at least a relation of friendship. If to the minimal information of the names of the actors we add their age in the novel, we could infer that the elder Rosemonde supports the younger Tourvel, which accurately reflects the relation, since Rosemonde treats Tourvel as her protégée.

Concerning the three first couples, we discover when we read the novel something that we could guess from the graph, namely that all three relations are erotic. On the other hand, we cannot infer the novel's moral position: after their erotic relation, both actors of the protagonist couple have a tragic end; Valmont and Tourvel find true love, but also a tragic end; and the love of the young couple Cécile and Danceny is ruined.

2 Examples of quantitative analysis of isotopies

2.1 The discourse on space

The analysis of isotopies so far has mainly concerned narrative prose and lyric poetry, with a brief extension to the analysis of responses to questionnaires. In this section we shall look more closely at the last issue, because this kind of material delivers the most spontaneous form of discourse and has only rarely been studied. Below, we present concrete analyses of isotopies found in the responses elicited from standardised questionnaires based on field work. We start with our own work, which focused on the semiotics of urban and regional space in Greece.

Our questionnaire was very long and our sample of 144 subjects was stratified according to social class, gender and age. Most of the questions were open-ended, allowing the respondents to express their views spontaneously. The responses were carefully analysed. Both researchers analysed the responses for each interview and identified the isotopies; agreement was usually automatic but sometimes required discussion. After a first randomly selected sample of six or seven interviews, we had defined almost all isotopies we found in the corpus, though some were redefined as a result of the accumulation of further material. A relative uniformity can probably be attributed to the orientation of the questionnaire, which insured a uniform register of discourse. This qualitative analysis provided the data for the quantitative part of the study.[76]

---

[76] The quantitative analysis of the data was done with the help of the SPSS (Statistical Package for the Social Sciences) software package.

In this manner, we identified 32 isotopies[77] ruling the conception of space, which we grouped into eight categories: (a) economic (economic-ness); (b) social (social-ness); (c) functional (referring to services, service-ness); (d) ecological (ecological-ness); (e) topographical (topographic-ness); (f) category of the built environment (building-ness) or spatial category; (g) historical (historical-ness); and (h) personal (individual-ness). These categories are composite, made up of simpler, semantically related isotopies. The simple isotopies are presented below within their respective categories (Lagopoulos and Boklund-Lagopoulou 1992: 209–217).

(a) Economic isotopies:
   (1) *Isotopy of economic activities.* This isotopy underlies references to and descriptions of any kind of economic activity: for example, "Most people live off of tourism"; "Krini had a lot of sheep and cattle-raising"; "A lot of people work in the mines in Gerakini".
   (2) *Isotopy of economic development.* This is used for references to the level of economic development of a region: "Yes, there's a lot of money in Ormylia, it's a very rich place".
   (3) *Isotopy of natural resources.* This covers references to the fertility of the soil – "Badlands, like, they're not productive" – and to other natural resources: "There's quite a lot of metals there".
   (4) *Isotopy of the cost of living.* This covers references to the cost of living: "In Moudania it's easier to find a place to rent, but it's awfully expensive". The frequency of this isotopy in the whole corpus is very low.

(b) Social isotopies:
   (5) *General social isotopy.* We considered that this isotopy was used when there were observations of a social nature without further specifications: "The people around here, they're okay, I'm happy". It is not an umbrella isotopy for others belonging to the category of social isotopies, since it corresponds only to unspecified references to society.
   (6) *Isotopy of social groups.* The isotopy covers statements about any kind of social group, i.e., social class, profession, gender, age group and so on: "In Ormylia there are farmers and a lot of workers"; "The old people still speak the dialect"; "Foreigners have bought land, built houses – lawyers, that kind". Not infrequently, when we asked a question concerning economic activities ("How do people make a living?"), the respondent answered by referring to a profession ("They're farmers"). In these cases,

---

77 Isotopy is a more exact term than the term "code" that we used in the original study.

we considered that the respondents were using both the isotopy of economic activities and that of social groups – and in fact there is logically an overlapping between the two.

(7) *Isotopy of social origin.* This is also an isotopy related to social groups, but the focus here is on the origins of the people referred to. In our case, the great majority of these references were to ethnic groups: "Here we're locals. Over there they're refugees". But there are also references to migration groups related to the respondent: "Because of the mines, they come from all over Chalkidiki". Strictly speaking, both this and the previous isotopy are sub-isotopies of the isotopy of social groups.

(8) *Isotopy of wealth.* This is another isotopy related to social groups, focusing specifically on the income or wealth of *people* (as opposed to the wealth of a region as a whole, which is covered by the code of economic development): "People generally are pretty well off".

(9) *Isotopy of lifestyle.* The isotopy concerns statements touching upon any aspect of the way of living: "There isn't so much movement there, they're more quiet areas; in the city there's much more pressure"; "People here, they believe in hospitality".

(10) *Isotopy of mentality.* This refers to the character of people and their way of thinking (also presumably expressed in their behaviour): "More educated people, who raise the level with cultural activities"; "They're good people, polite"; "The other guy is friendly with you because there's something in it for him".

(11) *Political isotopy.* This relates to statements about the political positions of people, political parties and the political situation: "In Chalkidiki, we consider Ormylia the most progressive village"; "But unfortunately we're divided by the parties"; "When the Conservatives were in power, it was the same, and now it's just the same".

(12) *Isotopy of property.* In another study, this isotopy might have been grouped with an independent legal isotopy. But for our needs, and given its very low frequency, it was grouped with the social codes. It frequently referred to land ownership: "That [stretch of land] belongs to the community, or maybe . . . [78] it belongs to some ministry and that's why it can't be divided up like they say".

---

[78] Three dots indicate a hesitation pause.

(c) Functional isotopies:
   (13) *General functional isotopy*. Like the general social isotopy, this isotopy is used for general observations of a functional nature: "Within Ormylia, things are equally convenient for everybody. But in all of Chalkidiki, things aren't as convenient for everybody as they are for us in Ormylia".
   (14) *Isotopy of shopping*. This refers to statements concerning commerce as a consumer activity, a service, and not as an economic activity (in which case the isotopy of economic activities is used): "In Ormylia you can find most anything you need"; "They've got lots of stores, it's really convenient in Moudania"; "You have to go to Thessaloniki to go shopping".
   (15) *Isotopy of leisure*. Statements using this isotopy are related to leisure, entertainment and cultural activities: "We'd go swimming there in the afternoons"; "That's the only place where there's a disco"; "The last two years we've even had a film club, but the trouble is, the club won't work unless the movies are a bit more . . . people want them really easy".
   (16) *Isotopy of administration*. From a certain point of view, this isotopy could be classified as related to government activities, but in our case the statements, due to the orientation given by the questionnaire, concerned the services provided by government agencies: "Everything's in Polygyros. Everybody goes to Polygyros. Law courts . . . of course it's a problem . . . courts, government agencies, eveything's in Polygyros".
   (17) *Isotopy of education*. As in the previous case, in another study this isotopy could be classified as referring to the educational system as such, but here the references were to education as a service provided: "It used to be we were really badly off for schools . . . but now the secondary school's finished"; "There's a technical school there".
   (18) *Isotopy of health*. The references here concern the system of health care, once again as a service: "And then, we haven't got a hospital here, just the rural health service".
   (19) *Isotopy of transport*. The references covered by this isotopy are to public transport: "Then there's Vatopedi, a little village here really isolated, hardly even the bus goes by there".
   (20) *Isotopy of housing*. This isotopy underlies statements on the availability and the quality of housing: "In Ormylia, if you're looking for a place to live, you won't find a place to rent"; "Houses are comfortable".

(d) Ecological isotopy
   (21) *Ecological isotopy*. In a study designed to elicit statements concerning the environment, this isotopy would be split into a number of different isotopies. However, we estimated that such a differentiation would not

change the nature of our results and we grouped into a single isotopy all statements concerning the natural environment and environmental pollution: "We have about the same climate with Gerakini, but not with Vrasta, it's much colder there, it's more mountainous"; "The first thing I think of is the sea, the ocean here"; "In Chalkidona you can find fresh air, on the other side there's the smog, the exhaust that the cars bring with them. Like in Diavata, because the industrial zone's over there. Those people really have a hard time".

(e) Topographical isotopies[79]
(22) *Topological isotopy*. This includes topological notions such as the semantic categories *here* vs *there*, *inside* vs *outside*, *up* vs *down*, *centre* vs. *periphery*: "Up there"; "Down by the beach"; "All around there's mountains".
(23) *Toponymic isotopy*. This covers references to locations made by using place names: "Ormylia, Vatopedi, Nikiti, Vrastama, all these villages, I know them inside and out".

(f) Isotopies of the built environment
(24) *Isotopy of building morphology*. While the isotopy of housing considers buildings as objects of use, the isotopy of building morphology concentrates on architectural form: "Look, the villages by the seashore, like Nikiti, like Metamorphosi, even the houses they've built, they're all a different style from Ormylia"; "It's got apartment houses and that sort of thing, which I don't like much".
(25) *Isotopy of historical monuments*. This isotopy is related to the previous isotopy, but concerns archaeological sites and what the respondents consider as monuments, old or recent: "Olynthos has other attractions, they've got the archaeological site that reminds them of their history"; "Down there, I don't know if they told you, is the ancient city of Sermyli"; "The village hasn't got any sights for the tourists to see".
(26) *Isotopy of technical networks*. It covers the references to infrastructural networks (roads, water supply, sewage disposal, electricity, etc.): "There's just a dirt road between Vrasta and Polygyros".

---

[79] Due to the geographical orientation of our study, these two isotopies were frequently overrepresented in the respondents' discourse. In order to avoid an undue statistical emphasis on these isotopies, during the quantification stage we did not evaluate their weight in a mechanical manner.

(27) *Urban isotopy*. It underlies all references to the settlement as build environment: "Vatopedi ... is a new village, it was built with regular roads, with a plan ... but Ormylia is old, and you'll find very narrow roads, very densely, one house on top of another"; "They've done a lot of construction there"; "They can't build because they aren't included in the [city] plan".

(28) *Regional isotopy*. The differentiation between urban and regional reflects our specific interests; a study less focused on space would unify these two isotopies. The regional isotopy corresponds to statements concerning regional organisation and the relations between settlements, administrative relations included: "Chalkidiki, the place where we live ... there's no city. It's all villages"; "It's the most central place in all of Sithonia ... Ormylia is a crossroads"; "Gerakini belongs to the City of Polygyros".

(29) *Demographic isotopy*. This isotopy does not literally refer to space, but to a particular characteristic of urban or regional space.[80] It covers the population characteristics of settlements and regions, as well as population movements when seen from a demographic point of view: "It has to do with the population in that area. Vatopedi is too small"; "All the young people are leaving from here"; "They are coming back from Germany now"; "There's a lot of foreigners, they rent houses, it doubles the population".

(g) Historical isotopy

(30) *Historical isotopy*. With this isotopy we have references to the past, whether social or geographical (which may be in the form of a personal memory): "Of course things were different then"; "Ormylia used to belong to the monks [of Mt. Athos] ... that's why there was very little Turkish influence here".

(h) Personal isotopies

(31) *Aesthetic isotopy*. This covers references to the aesthetics of the natural or built environment: "As far as I'm concerned, it's the most beautiful place"; "The houses are nicer-looking there".

(32) *Experiential isotopy*. Here, the references explicitly concern the subject. The isotopy functions as a catch-all for any reference to the individual or to the individual in his or her relation to persons and space, and

---

[80] The isotopy is of such a low presence in the corpus that the creation of a separate category is not justified, and in any case it does not alter the character of the built environment category.

covers anything from personal feelings, experiences and memories to personal attachments: "We have a good time there"; "My sister-in-law is from Chanioti"; "The people I know, my relatives, the neighbours, all that sort of thing"; "I've never been there"; "I was born here, my memories are here, I married here, I had my children here – it's our whole life, this place".

It has probably become clear from our observations above that the identification of isotopies is strictly guided each time by the text (in this case, by the corpus) and their exact definition follows from a continuous reflection on the text. Our corpus had the peculiarity that the perspective to adopt for the analysis had been set from the beginning, since it was constructed to correspond to the spatial perspective. The 32 isotopies defined correspond to the degree of abstraction adopted for the analysis, namely the third level of the hierarchy of semantic categories, and cover all the isotopies that interested the perspective we had adopted (the corpus also contains isotopies that have no bearing on the conception of space, and that were therefore left out of the analysis). For two isotopies, the historical and the experiential, we relaxed the prerequisite of strict reference to space, because of their particular nature.

Thus, the analysis of the corpus was subject to a set of criteria, among which the most important criterion, the selection of the strategic point of view to approach the corpus, constituted a given due to the perspective of the questionnaire that led to the constitution of the corpus. There is no doubt that some other researcher, for example a linguist, could proceed to a totally different analysis of the material. But a semiotician, interested in the signification of space and its structuring in the discourses of the corpus, would proceed in a way similar to ours. Not necessarily the same, because they might be interested in some other level of analysis (for example the level immediately superior to ours), which could, however, be directly articulated with our analysis.

If some other researchers had selected the third-level analysis as we did, they would probably come to results closely comparable to ours. Of course, even if different researchers adopt a common perspective and end up with similar results, we cannot claim that we have discovered the objective meaning of the text; that claim is too ambitious. The result of a thoughtful analysis is undoubtedly better than an intuitive approach, but is still subject to the limitations of the methodology used and the inescapable intrusion of a certain degree of subjectivity on the part of the researcher. We can, however, consider that it can achieve a relative objectivity, which is strengthened when researcher and text share a common cultural background and a more or less common historical period. A systematic, theoretically and methodologically grounded analysis also offers itself for an intelligent dialogue between researchers, unlike subjective approaches. The intuitive interpretations of a competent reader or native speaker are certainly not to be rejected, but they represent the responses of the spontaneous subjects of semiosis – and their non-scientific semiotics, to recall Hjelmslev – rather than the metalanguage required of a theoretician.[81]

This distinction can help us to clarify certain issues concerning the elicitation of responses, the resulting texts and their semiotic analysis. First, the spontaneous semiotic world of the respondents is in fact the semiotician's goal, which is why techniques such as Charles E. Osgood's semantic differential are to be avoided. Osgood's psychological approach is designed to study people's connotative "experiential continuum", activated to describe or judge a given word or concept. To achieve this aim, Osgood asked his respondents to evaluate the given element according to a set of semantic scales, each one considered as corresponding to a different experiential (sub)continuum. Each scale extends between two polar adjectival terms (for example, *good* vs *evil*, *adequate* vs *inadequate*) and is divided into seven grades, showing the direction and intensity of the description or judgement. According to Osgood, the whole of these scales represents a multiple semantic space and corresponds to the experiential continuum. Osgood's final target is extremely abstract – the definition of the universal semantic space underlying human thought in general – and he pursues it with the statistical treatment through factor analysis of the responses of groups of subjects. He concludes that each concept can be transformed into an abstract quantified semantic structure, with its own percentage composition consisting mainly of three main factors (Osgood 1952: 222–237; Osgood, Suci and Tannenbaum [1957] 1975).[82] This technique is research-oriented, but not subject-oriented, and does not reveal anything about the respondents' semiotic world, because it imposes on them predefined and standardised isotopies, ignoring their spontaneous response to the concepts presented and consequently their actual experiential continuum.

Second, there is no doubt that, when a standardised questionnaire is used, the nature of each question posed to a respondent tends to orient them towards a specific but flexible field of isotopies. During field work, it is important to maintain the exact formulation of each question, without any alteration or personal clarification on the part of the researcher, because any reformulation could lead the respondents to a different course that the one they would spontaneously

---

[81] Ideally, however, a theoretically informed and skilful analysis should both correspond to the intuitive interpretation of competent readers and offer a deeper penetration into a text.
[82] This is the so-called EPA (Evaluation, Potency, Activity) structure.

adopt.[83] There is also a technical reason involved in this neutrality, namely the comparability of the responses to the questionnaire. The way to avoid enclosing the respondents within the narrow framework offered by each question is to formulate a balanced questionnaire, including a large number of questions which attempt to catch as far as possible the totality of some aspect of the semiotic world of the respondents, which in our case was their spatial semiotic world.

Next, the flexibility of the responses to the questions posed was revealed to be greater than expected. We concluded that in reality there is a real interaction between the predefined question and the perspective adopted by the respondents. The great majority of them were enthusiastically involved, because they were presenting their own place. They had probably never been asked about this before, and thus had to think creatively. What was more astonishing is that their discourse was far from superficial, as we had the opportunity to check in the many instances where we had to contact our respondents months later to clarify something in their responses: they repeated the same views without hesitation.

Fourth, the response to each question is a semi-isolated micro-discourse; the whole set of responses delivers a complete discourse, but it is discontinuous, stitched together. However, we hoped that the coherence of the questionnaire would offer a scaffolding for semantic coherence, and the persistence of the views of the respondents corroborated our expectations.

There can also be technical issues with the use of questionnaires. We expected that the spatial orientation of our study would tend to produce responses with an overemphasis on the topographical category of isotopies, i.e., the topological and the toponymic isotopy. This was indeed the case, and we compensated for this in our processing of the data, but nevertheless there was important variance, both between respondents and between the responses of the same individual respondent.

The examples we gave above for each of the 32 isotopies that we identified in our corpus were meant to demonstrate the isotopy in question, but also frequently included other isotopies as well. For instance, one of the examples we gave for the ecological isotopy was "We have about the same climate with Gerakini, but not with Vrasta, it's much colder there, it's more mountainous". A minute analysis of the isotopies included in this statement would be as follows:

---

83 There are certain techniques that can be used to maintain neutrality. For example, the first question of the questionnaire was "What comes to your mind when you think of your region?" The respondents would frequently hesitate and ask "What do you mean?" The interviewers were instructed to repeat the question, verbatim but more slowly. In all cases the response was "Oh. Well . . . " and the communication channel would open.

"We have [*experiential* isotopy] about the same climate [*ecological*] with Gerakini [*toponymic*], but not with Vrasta [*toponymic*], it's much colder [*ecological*] there [*topological*], it's more mountainous [*ecological*]". Below, we present a series of concrete and detailed analysis of several responses to the questionnaire by inhabitants of the city of Veria (population about 45,000), which both display the technical part of the qualitative characterisation of isotopies and indicate the possibilities offered by their quantification.

Our first example (Table 11) comes from a sixty-year-old woman worker. It is her response to the first question, "What comes to your mind when you think of your region?"

Table 11: Isotopies of the response by a woman worker in Veria to the question concerning the first and spontaneous conception of her region.

Answer	Isotopies
I mean . . . about *Veria*, it's	toponymic
a *very wealthy place, around here*	development, topological
all the villages are . . . *rich*, because	regional, development
they have rich fields, they have . . . fruit	economic activities, resources
trees that . . . you know, that	economic activities
set them very high, like,	wealth
on *the level of . . . money.*	wealth

On the left, the table shows in italics the part of the discourse to which an isotopy corresponds, while on the right we record the isotopy. The isotopies detected and their absolute frequencies are one reference to the toponymic isotopy, two to economic development, one to the topological isotopy, one to the regional, two to economic activities, one to natural resources and two to wealth, which makes ten occurrences of a total of seven different isotopies. This response is thus quite rich semantically, with seven isotopies in a response of 39 words.

The articulations of the isotopies in the discourse are clearly expressed through explicit logical relationships (*"because"* they have, *"that"* sets them very high, *"like"*). If we leave out the toponymic, topological and regional isotopies, we might describe the isotopy sequence on the syntagmatic axis of this discourse as:

(a) development – (b) natural resources – (c) economic activities – (d) wealth

We could group the structure of the syntagmatic chain of the segment as:

a / b / c / d,

where / stands for an articulation, in this case an explicit one: the area is economically developed because the natural environment is particularly favourable, and this allows the inhabitants to practice fruit farming, with the result that they become wealthy.

If we consider the logical argument of the same segment, we could render its semantic structure as:

c / b / d / a,

which gives us an explicit and complex logical relation of cause-and-effect: the fields are fertile, due to this fact the inhabitants are fruit farmers, hence their income is high, therefore the place is economically developed.

The major orientation of the discourse becomes clear if we pass from the simple isotopies to the categories to which they belong and calculate their frequencies, as shown in Table 12.

Table 12: Frequencies of the isotopies in the response by the woman worker in Veria.

Category of isotopies	Frequency	
	absolute	%
economic	5	50
social	2	20
topographical	2	20
of the built environment	1	10
Total	10	100

We see from this table that the economic category of isotopies (economic development, economic activities and natural resources) dominates half of this passage (frequency 50%), followed at a significant distance (20%) by the social category (wealth) and the topographical category (also 20%), while the category of the built environment is weakly represented (10%). This sub-discourse, then, adopts a social register (70%), with clear emphasis on economic matters. We also observe a characteristic quite general throughout our corpus, namely the use of value judgements: "*very* wealthy place", "*rich*", "*very* high". To record evaluations, we used a scale consisting of six grades; each isotopy that was evaluated was marked with the corresponding grade.

Not all respondents produce a discourse so rich semantically. Our next example (Table 13) is from a middle-aged man, owner of a hotel, who is responding to a question about social differences in his region.

Table 13: Isotopies of the response by a male hotel owner in Veria to the question concerning social differences.

Answer	Isotopies
Well, like . . . like *intellectually* you know	mentality
the *people in the villages* you might say still haven't reached the degree where . . .	social groups, regional
like the *intellectual level*, you know,	mentality
of the *people in the cities*. Mostly	social groups, regional
it's *lower than what you'd expect*.	mentality

This respondent uses only three isotopies: the isotopy of mentality, that of social groups and the regional isotopy, and mentality is the pivot of this segment, while the social groups and the region are the field with which mentality is articulated, giving the segment the form of an agglomerate. There are also plenty of neutral fillers between isotopies ("you know", "mostly"), which do not add any substantial information. The basic articulation of the isotopies is:

(a) mentality / (b) social groups/ (c) regional

This sequence is repeated twice, first in reference to the villages, then to the city, and it is this opposition that leads to the classification of the isotopy not as urban but as regional. The three isotopies are organised isomorphically, and indeed the social and the regional isotopy tend to coincide, because the groups are defined by their regional location: *group a = villagers* vs *group b = urbanites*. The isotopy of mentality is also isomorphic with the above; it takes the form of a code, the two contrary terms of which are defined by evaluations: "still haven't reached the degree", "lower" (negative evaluation) as opposed to "intellectual level" (positive evaluation). Here the code is not structured into logical contraries, but *the opposition is created through evaluations*; as we shall see, this is not an exception, but a case frequently encountered.

Thus, the repetition of the above articulation is not a simple repetition, because its two parts are related by opposition:

$$a/b/c \text{ vs } a/b/c$$

If we compare this discourse to our first example, we see that it has a totally different discursive orientation. Given that the isotopies of mentality and social groups belong to the same category of social isotopies, the frequency of this category amounts to more than two-thirds of the total, diverging from the economic orientation of the first example. The semantic richness is lower in the second example, and the connection between isotopies is also simpler, because the previous cause-and-effect micro-discourse becomes here a simple binary opposition.

Both examples explicitly use the syntagmatic axis to articulate isotopies. This is not always the case, as we shall see with the following example, from the response of a young woman married to a businessman, who answers the same question as the first respondent (Table 14).

Table 14: Isotopies of the response by the wife of a businessman in Veria to the question concerning her spontaneous conception of her region.

Answer	Isotopies
Like *it used to be, mulberry trees,*	historical, ecological
bicycles, flowers, sea – and like it is	networks, ecological (2)
now, noisy, smelling of souvlaki, pizza,	historical, networks, ecological (3)
lots of cars . . . like that.	networks

The discourse is syntactically simple and built by juxtaposing words and alternating isotopies, but it shows considerable semantic richness. The ecological isotopy dominates by 60% and this is the strategic selection of the respondent, but the discourse is organised on the basis of the historical code, in the form *used to be* vs *now*. The ecological isotopy is a structured code, as we can see from the references to it: *mulberry trees, flowers, the ocean* vs *noisy, smelling, pizza*, and this is also the case with the isotopy of technical networks: *bicycles* vs *cars*. These codes become fully isomorphic from the isomorphic relation of each one separately with the historical code. Behind these codes there is also another, latent code. What "used to be" was the old image of the city of Veria, with low houses and gardens (and an extension, "the sea"), as opposed to the "now" of the modern city; that is, the latent code is that of building morphology.

If we include this implicit connotative and evaluated code in the calculation – which would classify the discourse in the type of the agglomerate – the ecological code would still dominate, but by 50%, and the category of the built environment (technical networks and building morphology) would be promoted from one-fifth to one-third of the total frequencies. Thus, the added data would not alter the ecological orientation of the discourse, but would add an important dimension. What is not stated explicitly, then, is the historical change in the image of the city, something that the respondent approaches through the register of the senses (sight, hearing and smell) and by focusing explicitly on the ecological environment. It is a romantic reaction to modernisation, in which the ecological code becomes a metaphor for the urban.

This metaphorical discourse is also found in our last example, part of the response of a middle-aged woman, employed as a public servant, to one of the last questions of the questionnaire, asking the respondents what they would like to change in their region (Table 15).

Table 15: Isotopies of the response by a woman public servant in Veria to the question concerning desirable changes in her region.

Answer	Isotopies
And the *brick roof tiles had – have* an important role in *the city*. When I say	building morphology, historical urban
roof tiles . . . the *neighbourhood* and the	building morphology, urban
area . . . the *apartment houses* I mean . . . there's a huge difference . . .	urban, building morphology

In all cases, the full understanding of each response has to draw on the context of all the responses in each interview, since many of the respondent's references and value judgements become evident only in the course of the whole interview. The above passage comes at the end of a lengthy nostalgic description of the city where the speaker has lived all her life and the changes it has undergone. Aside from a single reference to the historical isotopy, the segment uses only two isotopies, building morphology and the urban isotopy, morphology being quantitatively in first place (57%, with an absolute frequency of 7). The respondent first makes reference to an element of building morphology ("roof tiles") which she evaluates very positively ("an important role to play"). She first says that they "had" an important role, but she immediately corrects this to "have", extending their importance from the past to the present; she explains her view in the next phrase, which is a metalinguistic reference to her own discourse ("When I say"). The importance of the roof tiles is thus emphasised twice, each time in a different manner.

The reference to the "area" would remain unclear if the speaker did not explain it further with "the apartment houses, that is". The apartment houses in the "area" are opposed to the "neighbourhood", which like the area belongs to the urban code. The opposition (the "huge difference") is between the old "neighbourhood", with its low houses and red tile roofs, and the new, impersonal "area" with its high-rise apartment buildings, which replaced the neighbourhood as a consequence of urban development. Two codes emerge, then: *old houses with tile roofs* vs *apartment houses* and *(traditional) neighbourhood vs (modern) area*.

In this case, the image of the city is the explicit topic of the discourse, both in its morphological and its urban dimension. As in the previous case, the discourse is organised according to the historical code *past* vs *present*, in reference to which the other two codes are isomorphically organised. In the previous case, building morphology was an implied connotative code; in this case it is explicit, but both the code of morphology and the urban code seem to be a metaphor for an implicit social code, that of lifestyle. The "huge difference" lies in the new way of life which has come with the apartment buildings. The semantic structure of this discourse is based on a series of metaphors: the brick roof tiles for the traditional low houses, the houses for the old neighborhood and that in turn for the traditional lifestyle which is now lost with the anonymity of the modern city. Poetry is not the only form of discourse that can be metaphorically structured; as Jakobson pointed out (chapter 8: 2.6), the poetic function of language is not the exclusive property of poetry.

2.2 The spatial discourses on the city of Thessaloniki

The above examples were short excerpts from the total discourse of four respondents to our questionnaire. In this section we shall pass to an analysis of individual discourses. The material that will be discussed in this section comes from four papers by students in our postgraduate classes on semiotics, which we use here as a mini-corpus. The object of each paper was the semiotic conception of the city of Thessaloniki in northern Greece, based on an interview with one of its inhabitants. The students conducted the fieldwork with the help of a small standardised questionnaire noting the respondent's gender, age, marital status, profession, education, and years of residence in the city, followed by an interview consisting of eight open questions. They chose their own respondents following a sociological matrix prepared by us.[84]

We have already pointed out the impressive convergence between the relative frequency and the order of appearance of isotopies. This was corroborated by the students' results (Nikolaou 2007; Rigopoulou 2007), indicating that even spontaneous oral discourse is coherently organised on the semantic level.

We have also already noted that in the responses to the questionnaire of our own study, the topographical category of isotopies was overrepresented due to the nature of the questions (the specific orientation towards the conception of space), but that these isotopies did not have the same importance in all cases. The variance in the relative frequency of these isotopies is clearly displayed in the present mini-corpus. In one of the student papers (Nikolaou 2007), the toponymic isotopy is first or second in terms of relative frequency in all the individual responses and prominent in the whole interview. In another paper (Rigopoulou 2007), the topological isotopy comes first in only two of the eight responses (followed by the toponymic isotopy in one of them) and comes second in one more response. In the other responses, the first place is occupied twice by the isotopy of leisure (functional category), twice by the ecological isotopy and once by the urban isotopy (built environment category) and the isotopy of lifestyle (social category). In spite of this variance, both isotopies of the topographical category are prominent in the whole interview. In a third paper (Apostolopoulou 2005), the topological and the toponymic isotopies occupy the second place in two questions, while in the interview as a whole they rank far behind the dominant isotopies, which are the urban and the experiential.

In spite of the emphasis on space in the questionnaires, we see that there is a marked variance in the occurrence of the topographical isotopies, which suggests that, although the respondents felt this bias, they to some extent balanced the pressure through their creativity. Nevertheless, the bias is inherent in the

---

84 The open questions concerned the respondents' views (cf. Table 6.17) on (a) the city as a whole; (b) the character of the city; (c) the most prominent elements of the city; (d) possible differences between its areas; (e) its most pleasant places; (f) its most unpleasant places; (g) what they would like to change to make the city better and (h) their ideal city. There were also three questions concerning the mental map of the respondents, who were asked to draw a sketch map of their city.

questionnaire, which is why the data for the topographical category were not taken at face value but treated as complementary.

We implied above that the number of isotopies used is a criterion for the semantic richness of discourse. The comparison between the student papers shows that certain responses had a very low semantic richness, that is, a very limited number of isotopies – four or fewer (Apostolopoulou 2005: 11) – while other responses included as many as 15–20 (Pontosidou 2007: 29). There is a comparable variance of semantic richness in respect to the responses to the same question by different respondents. Concerning the interview as a whole, all four cases proved to be multi-isotopic, activating at least two-thirds of the 32 isotopies of space. However, this conclusion is not generalisable, because in our own study we encountered cases with a much lower number of isotopies.

Another interesting issue is the variance in the frequency of isotopies within each response. We shall start with the response to the first question of the questionnaire, concerning the spontaneous conception of her region by a seventy-year-old woman worker who had lived in Thessaloniki for 50 years. Table 16 shows the frequency of isotopies detected in her response.

Table 16: Frequency of isotopies in the response by a woman worker in Thessaloniki to the question concerning the spontaneous conception of her region (Nikolaou 2007: 4). First column of percentages: all isotopies. Second column: without the topographical isotopies. Numbers in bold: frequency of main isotopies.

Isotopy	Frequency		
	absolute	%	
		all isotopies	w/out topogr.
1. experiential	16	**45**	**64**
2. toponymic	8	23	–
3. lifestyle	5	14	**20**
4. regional	2	6	8
5. topological	2	6	–
6. urban	1	3	4
7. leisure	1	3	4
Total	35	100	100

The table reveals the deep experiential connection of this woman to her city (the experiential isotopy accounts for 45% of the total, 64% if we do not include the topographical isotopies), a connection that recurs throughout the whole interview with expressions such as "I like Thessaloniki" (experiential and toponymic isotopies), and the relation of this experience to her lifestyle (14% and 20% respectively).

We already discussed the variance in the relative frequency of the topographical isotopies between the responses to questionnaires. Table 16 shows the variance of isotopies within one response. In Table 17 (Nikolaou 2007: 25–27) we can follow this variance in each of the answers of the woman worker. In the table, isotopies are represented in the rows and the code number of the responses in the columns.

First, we will briefly discuss the issue of the variance of one isotopy *across* responses. This can be done for any isotopy in the table, but we will take as an example the urban isotopy. We can find this variance through a horizontal reading of this row in the main body of the matrix of Table 17 (the total 100% should normally be shown at the end of the row). It appeared in the responses with the following absolute frequencies (which are not shown in the table): in response (a) with 1 reference, in response (b) with 6 references, in (c) with 5, in (d) with 6, in (e) with 5, in (f) with 2, in (g) with 3 and in (h) with 1, a total of 29 references. On this total the relative frequency of this isotopy (presented in the table in parenthesis in italics) is as follows: response (a) relative frequency 3.5%, response (b) relative frequency 21%, (c) 17%, (d) 21%, (e) 17%, (f) 7%, (g) 10% and (h) 3.5%, total 100%.

The other operation is the variance of each isotopy *within* each response, which corresponds to a perpendicular reading of each column within the main body of the matrix (in which case the total 100% is shown at the bottom of the column). In the second column of the table, to the left of the main matrix, the frequency of each isotopy in the questionnaire as a whole is given.

The isotopies of Table 17 are individual isotopies, but, as we saw, they can be grouped into eight categories. If we group the individual isotopies into categories, we obtain the frequencies in Table 18 (Nikolaou 2007: 25), which derives from the grouping of the isotopies presented in the second column of the previous table.

Table 17: Frequency of isotopies in each response by the woman worker in Thessaloniki. 2nd column: frequency of each isotopy in the questionnaire as a whole. Numbers in bold in the 2nd column: frequency of main isotopies. Numbers in bold in the main matrix: frequency of main isotopies. Numbers in parenthesis: variance of the urban isotopy across responses.

Isotopy \ Question		a	b	c	d	e	f	g	h
		% of isotopy by question							
1. toponymic	27%	23	40	33	21	19	21	31	25
2. urban	10%	3 (3,5)	30 (21)	7 (17)	21 (21)	14 (17)	7 (7)	7 (10)	5 (3,5)
3. aesthetic	9%	–	10	18	7	14	17	–	–
4. experiential	8%	45	–	3	7	3	3,5	–	5
5. leisure	8%	3	5	10	–	21	–	9	5
6. topological	8%	6	–	6	21	5	3,5	16	–
7. lifestyle	5%	14	–	–	–	11	–	–	30
8. ecological	4,5%	–	–	3	3	5	14	2	15
9. services	3%	–	–	4	3	–	–	13	–
10. political	3%	–	–	6	–	–	17	–	–
11. networks	3%	–	–	–	–	–	10	7	10
12. regional	2%	6	15	–	–	–	–	–	5
13. social groups	2%	–	–	–	–	3	3,5	9	–
14. monuments	2%	–	–	7	–	–	–	–	–
15. development	1%	–	–	–	10	–	–	–	–
16. econ. activities	1%	–	–	1,5	–	5	–	–	–
17. mentality	1%	–	–	–	7	–	–	–	–
18. gen. functional	1%	–	–	–	–	–	3,5	2	–
19. transport	1%	–	–	–	–	–	–	4	–
20. education	0,5%	–	–	1,5	–	–	–	–	–
Total	100	100	100	100	100	100	100	100	100

Table 18: Frequency of categories of isotopies in the questionnaire as a whole for the woman worker in Thessaloniki. 2nd column: absolute frequencies. 3rd column: relative frequencies in the whole sample. 4th column: relative frequencies without the topographical category. Numbers in bold: frequency of main categories of isotopies.

Category of isotopies	Frequency		
	absolute	%	
		whole sample	w/out topogr.
1. topographical	99	35	–
2. personal	49	17	26.5
3. built environment	48	17	26
4. functional	37	13	20
5. social	32	11	17.5
6. ecological	13	5	7
7. economic	6	2	3
Total	**284**	**100**	**100**

We can now compare the data from the three preceding tables, all originating from the same questionnaire of the woman worker, and demonstrate their utility for the understanding of this woman's semiotic conception of Thessaloniki. On the basis of Table 17, we can group the frequencies of individual isotopies (second column of the table), leaving out the toponymic and topological isotopies, into three categories as a function of their relative frequencies: 1st category (8–10%), urban, aesthetic, experiential and leisure isotopies; 2nd category (4.5–5%), lifestyle and ecological isotopies; and 3rd category (0.5–3%), the remaining twelve isotopies. The urban, aesthetic, experiential and leisure isotopies dominate, followed by the isotopies of lifestyle and ecology. The importance of the experiential isotopy was already evident from the very first response of this woman, where it predominated by 45% (64%, Table 16).

We observe in Table 17 that the aesthetic and experiential isotopies occur in five and six responses respectively and at least one of them occurs in every response but one; the urban isotopy runs across all eight responses; and the leisure isotopy occurs in six. From this point of view, the importance of the lifestyle isotopy is not fully displayed, because it has fewer occurrences than the ecological isotopy. Topographical isotopies excepted, almost all of the dominant isotopies (in bold in the main body of the matrix) belong to the urban, aesthetic, experiential, leisure and lifestyle isotopies. We conclude that the distribution of isotopies within each question displays as prominent about the same isotopies which are prominent in the whole questionnaire.

Now, let us investigate the data of Table 18. We can group the categories of isotopies as follows, putting into parenthesis the topographical category (35%, in which case the total number of references becomes 284 - 99 = 185): 1st group, personal (aesthetic and experiential isotopies) and built environment (urban isotopy, etc.), from 17% of the total to 26% without the topographical category; 2nd group, functional and social, from 11–13% to 17.5–20% respectively; and 3rd, ecological and economic, from 2–5% to 3–7% respectively. The second group is not very distant from the first, and the third is far behind both of the others.

Table 18 offers complementary information to Table 17, because it unifies the aesthetic and experiential isotopies within the framework of the personality of the woman and integrates the urban isotopy within the wider framework of the built environment (though dominated by the urban isotopy). There follow the orientation towards the functionality of the city (with great emphasis on leisure) and the social dimension (with emphasis on lifestyle).

The urban ideology of this respondent now becomes transparent. The importance of the personal category and the category of the built environment, founded on the urban (the two together amount to about half of the frequencies), shows the close dialogue between her and her city. Her ideology is founded on her personal views and preferences, integrates urban space, and emphasises leisure and lifestyle, matters directly related to her as an individual.

The relation of isotopies through their relative frequencies is an indirect relation, and is only one of the possible ways of relating isotopies. In both this and the previous chapter, we have discussed different types of direct relation between isotopies, which when systematically reiterated are of major importance for the interpretation of a text. Below we will refer to examples showing some of the modes of qualitative association between isotopies, taken from the responses to the student questionnaire. However, this time we will discuss these qualitative relations in conjunction with their quantitative counterparts.

In the response of the woman worker to the first question (Nikolaou 2007: 6, 13), we encounter a wording displaying her very positive attitude towards her city (Table 19).

In another of her responses, the isotopy of leisure is identified with that of lifestyle, while both refer to their common background, the experiential isotopy (Table 20).

Table 19: Relations between isotopies in the first response of the woman worker in Thessaloniki.

When I hear "Thessaloniki" . . .	experiential (A), (toponymic) & urban (B)
I feel, like, *pleased*,	experiential (A)
because *I live in Thessaloniki*,	experiential (A), (toponymic) & urban (B)
I like Thessaloniki.	experiential (A), (toponymic) & urban (B)

Table 20: Relations between isotopies in another response of the woman worker in Thessaloniki.

To go for a walk along the sea	experiential (A), lifestyle (C), urban (B)
to go there for a coffee,	experiential (A),(topological), lifestyle & leisure (C & D)
to have a coffee,	experiential (A), lifestyle & leisure (C & D)
to have an ice-cream	experiential (A), lifestyle & leisure (C & D)

We observe in these two quotations a systematic relation of isotopies effected through description. In Table 19, we observe that the relation A∩B is repeated thrice; in Table 20 we again find an equivalent relation, A∩C∩B, together with the relation A∩C & D repeated three times. The discourse is simple and marked by juxtaposition, but the connections are deliberate and create a quite systematic sequence. There is also one occurrence of a cause-and-effect relation with the conjunction "because" ("because I live in Thessaloniki"), but this is not generally characteristic of the discourse in these quotations.

These passages show the complementarity of quantitative and qualitative analysis. They reveal both the importance of these isotopies and the mode of their connection within the context of the woman's urban ideology. However, they are fragments of discourse selected by us, not integrated into the network of relations between isotopies in the discourse as a whole. In the next example we will try to penetrate further into this network.

This example comes from the responses of a forty-year-old woman working as a public servant, who has lived in Thessaloniki for about 30 years (Pontosidou

2007).[85] The quotations below are characteristic of her discourse and allow the reconstruction of the major network of her isotopies.

The response of this woman to the first question of the interview (question a, "What comes to your mind when you think of your city?") was: "[Thessaloniki is] my home [. . .]. A place that I could not live far away from." We can identify the isotopies and their evaluation as follows: "[. . .] my [*experiential* isotopy] home [*social groups*, very positive evaluation] [. . .]. A place [*urban* and *topological*] that I could not live far away from [*experiential*, very positive evaluation; *topological*]". In her response to the next question (b), she starts by comparing the city where "I lived [*experiential*] twenty years ago [*historical*, positive evaluation]" with today's city "which has become a classical urban centre [*urban*, negative evaluation]". "It was [*historical*] [. . .] a city [*urban*] where at any moment you could find [*experiential* and *historical*] something to stimulate your interests [*experiential* and *lifestyle*, very positive evaluations]". This is "the Thessaloniki [*toponymic* and *urban*] where I grew up [*historical* and *experiential*, positive evaluation], not the Thessaloniki [*toponymic* and *urban*] where you [*social groups*] are growing up [*historical*, negative evaluations]. The Thessaloniki [*toponymic* and *urban*] where you are growing up [*social groups* and *historical*] is what I wouldn't want to have lived myself [*experiential*, very negative evaluation]". The "degeneration" of the city (very negative evaluation) is due "to the Thessalonikians themselves [*social groups*]" and to "the large number of immigrants [*social groups*]"; "you don't hear only Greek [*mentality*], or even the Greek you hear [*experiential* and *mentality*] . . . is the Greek [*mentality*] you learn on the streets [*lifestyle*, very negative evaluations]".

In a question (c) about the most prominent elements in the city, this woman refers in a very positive manner to the central area of the city, where "you see [*experiential*] more handsome [*aesthetic*] people around [*social groups*], usually better dressed [*aesthetic*], more well-groomed [*aesthetic*], the people [*social groups*] that you would like to be with [*experiential*] and socialise [*experiential*] with [*social groups*] all the time". She believes that there, "the everyday life [*lifestyle*]" of the city "is completely different [very positive evaluation], you can breathe [*experiential*]". This very positive Thessaloniki is the projection in present time of "the years [*historical*] of my youth [*experiential*]". Integrated into these responses is a brief historical narrative which praises the city's history and arrives at "Oh, you modern Greeks [*social groups*], what has become of you today

---

85 For the purpose of the present discussion we made a few modifications in the classification of isotopies made by the author of the paper and the definition of isotopies in textual analysis. We also, as in the previous analysis, rounded up some percentages of the weight of isotopies for reasons of simplicity.

[*historical*] and you have forgotten where you come from [*historical*, very negative evaluations]".

In the next question (d), concerning the differences between various areas of the city, we see the respondent's semiotic geography of the city. Her explicit reference is to an east and a west Thessaloniki, that is, an axial division of the city,[86] but as we shall see, her urban semiotics reorganises this into a concentric pattern. Urban space derives its character from the social groups inhabiting it. In eastern Thessaloniki, there are social groups of various origins, including the inhabitants of Kalamaria: "These people [*social groups*], who were [*historical*] sleeping in the mud [*lifestyle*, very negative evaluation], found themselves [*historical*] very well off economically [*wealth*, very positive evaluation], something the native Thessalonikians [*social groups*] don't have [*wealth*, negative evaluation], a person [*social groups*] living [*historical*] in the centre of the city [*urban*]". Eastern Thessaloniki as a whole is characterised by negative evaluations. Western Thessaloniki is also seen through the lenses of history and negativity. Thus, in the axial model both east and west Thessaloniki are negatively evaluated.

At this point the respondent shifts to a concentric model, *centre* vs *periphery*. Within the walls (the city *intra muros*, within the ancient walls, the historical core of the city) were the Thessalonikians, outside "were [*historical*] those who were not Thessalonikians [*social groups*] . . . they were not even Greeks [*social groups*], they were Turks [*social groups*], they were Albanians [*social groups*], they were people who [*social groups*] did not have the Greek element [*mentality*] in them [*social groups*, negative evaluation]". The Greek element is shared by the Jewish population of Thessaloniki, inhabitants of the centre of the city, also for historical reasons. Finally, "what we call Thessalonikians [*social groups*]" are "those [*social groups*] who lived [historical] in the area of the centre [*urban*] and around [*topological*] the centre [*urban*, positive evaluation]".

In her response to a question (f) about the most unpleasant places of the city, the woman begins "Well, I feel we are losing our [*experiential*] identity [*mentality*]. As Thessalonikians [*social groups*, very negative evaluation] [. . .]. The solution is to say that, since this [*topological*] is my [*experiential*] place [*topological*], this is where [*topological*] I was born [*experiential*], this is where [*topological*] I grew up [*experiential*] and this is where [*topological*] I chose to live [*experiential*], to be able to make your life liveable [*experiential*, very positive evaluations]". She opposes to this view the perspective of "the new generation

---

[86] This conception is typical among the inhabitants of Thessaloniki and follows from the actual geographical form of the city, since its central area develops along a relatively narrow stretch of land between the hills and the sea.

[*social groups*]", with special reference to the students, for whom Thessaloniki is "a place of escape [*lifestyle*, negative evaluation]" and she also differentiates from it the "foreign immigrants who [*social groups*] are coming here [*urban, topological*] . . . without really feeling [*experiential*] that they are Greeks [*social groups*, negative evaluation]". Closing her response, she mentions that "What troubles me most [*experiential*] is . . . that the Greek element [*mentality*] is dying out [very negative evaluation]".

In the next question (g), about what kind of changes should be made to improve the city, the religious element, which surfaces here and there in previous responses, reappears. She wants the public to be better informed about scientific studies of the city and its role in history, social issues and the Greek Orthodox religion. After referring to a variety of subjects, she concludes that "we ourselves [*social groups, experiential*] do not know our real roots [*experiential, social origin*, very negative evaluation]" and she is worried that "in the end, we'll end up [*experiential, social groups*] a minority [*social groups*] in our own place [*experiential, social groups*]".

In Table 21 below, we present most of the response of this woman to the last question of the questionnaire – (h), on the ideal city – in which she returns to some of her previous thoughts, coming full circle back to her first response.

The woman's discourse is definitely multi-isotopic, and very rich, since it uses 25 out of the 32 isotopies of spatial discourse that we defined. The relations

Table 21: Isotopies of the response by a woman public servant in Thessaloniki to the last question of the questionnaire.

[I would like to live in the city] *I live in*	experiential
and *in the one I would like to change*	urban, experiential
its *ingredients*	(hypothesis) social groups
Whatever I said up to now, it is the city	experiential, urban
that I want to live in. [. . .]	experiential
Where I can live as a Thessalonikian.	experiential & lifestyle, social groups
And *as a Greek. I could not live*	social groups, experiential
in *another city.*	urban
This is why *I say*	experiential
that *Thessaloniki is my homeland*	toponymic & urban, experiential, social groups

between isotopies are expressed both explicitly and implicitly. Her discourse delivers a set of isomorphic codes – a frequent mode of association between isotopies – structured according to a simple binary scheme of the form *a* vs *b*, as shown in Table 22 (the plus sign (+) covers the two positive grades of our scale and the minus sign (–) covers our two negative grades). Together with the qualitative conclusions from her interview, this table also includes the quantitative aspects, by showing the relative frequencies of the dominant codes as they resulted from the quantitative analysis (second column of the table); it thus gives us the opportunity to stress once more the complementarity of the two approaches.

Table 22: The binary scheme ruling the isomorphic codes in the discourse of the woman public servant in Thessaloniki.

Isotopy	% of total	Semantic categories	
		+ vs –	
1. historical	12,5	old times (and very old times)	today
2. social groups	9.7	local Thessalonikians	rest of Thessalonikians, foreigners, Greek immigrants, youth and students
3. experiential	9,5	positive feeling	negative feeling
4. mentality	9,3	local Thessalonikians	foreigners, youth and students
5. urban	9,0	city centre (and area around it)	city periphery
6. lifestyle	8,5	Thessalonikians of the city centre	immigrants, youth and students
Total	58,5		

We shall start our discussion with the qualitative aspects of the codes in the table. Of the codes of the category of the built environment, we find the urban code; the other codes in the category have a minimal presence (there are references to the isotopies of networks and of building morphology). However, the city as urban space is not important *per se*, it is not the essential element in the discourse. Instead, it is used as a receptacle in order for her to articulate the other codes shown in Table 22.

The relations between codes are systematic and reiterated across all the responses, showing that the respondent has established and strong views. The very first phrase of the interview, "My home", creates a solid connection between the experiential and the social codes (with a strong patriotic dimension). Later, in the answer to question (c) and elsewhere, we encounter the same connection. Her first answer continues "A place that I could not live far away from", associating the urban with the experiential. These three codes, experiential, social groups and urban, compose a very tightly knit complex already in the woman's introductory response. The same complex, with the same codes and adding the code of lifestyle, emerges in her final response, this time with a stronger emphasis: the connection of her personal experience to the specific urban space is repeated thrice, her connection of the same experience to her social group is repeated twice, while the code of lifestyle is connected both to her experience and the social groups.

The same codes participate in the isomorphic set that structures the relations between them. In this set, all the first members of the codes are strongly related to each other, as are all the second members. On the basis of Table 22, we conclude that the semiotics of the respondent can be summed up as follows: her experiential world is identified with the mentality and the lifestyle of native Thessalonikians who live in the central city, while she is negative vis-à-vis all other Thessalonikians who live outside the central city, whether Greek immigrants or foreigners, including their mentality and lifestyle. The urban code shows that the "Thessaloniki" of this woman is not the city of Thessaloniki, but just the central city, downtown Thessaloniki – which coincides with the old *intra muros* city. Her negativity to the "others" extends to the lifestyle of young people and students, but with a slightly different shade: she believes that they do not live in the real Thessaloniki. The city for them is "a place of escape": they may live in the centre, but they do not belong there, they belong to a social periphery; the geographical margins of the city become a metaphor for the social marginality of the students.

The analysis of the responses of this woman reveals, without deeper examination, not only her urban ideology but more generally her worldview. If we look at her use of the historical code, we may have the impression that it is contradictory, because it is negatively evaluated in the matrix, while she evaluates it positively in the present. But this is a contradiction only if her feelings for the city are viewed on logical, not semiotic grounds. There is, for her, a positive Thessaloniki even today, but it is in reality the city "where I grew up, not the Thessaloniki where you are growing up". This positive Thessaloniki is the projection today of the city of her youth, a projection that allows her to feel attached to her city in spite of the negative changes. We detect an anchoring point of the past and the present: in the centre, "you see more handsome people around, usually better dressed, more well-groomed, the people that you would like to be with and socialise with all the time". This projection of the past onto the present, a selective and idealised present identified with the past, allows the link between past and present. It is the connection with a collectivity within which she integrates herself, a collectivity that extends beyond the limits of the city to the level of the Greek nation.

Table 22 presents, in addition to these qualitative data, the frequencies of the most frequently used codes (in hierarchical order) in the discourse of the respondent as a whole. There are in total 776 occurrences of codes. There is a group of codes with higher numbers of occurrences, ranging from 7.3–12.5% of the total, and a group of codes with lower numbers of occurrences, ranging from 3.5% to only one reference. Table 22 presents the first group, with the exception of the topological (8.6%) and the toponymic (7.3%) codes which are among the lowest occurrences of the first group.

In section 1.2 of the present chapter, we gave an example of the combination of the final graph, representing the qualitative structure of the network of isotopies, with the relative frequency of each isotopy. A striking characteristic of this combination was the close connection between the structure of the network and the distribution of the relative frequencies of the isotopies. That example was fabricated, though based on our experience. In Table 22 we have the results of the analysis of an actual discourse.

We can see in Table 22 that the historical code is prominent in the high group (12.5%) and this importance is in line with the main, and major, intellectual acrobatics of the respondent to unify past and present. As is clear from the previous qualitative analysis, her semiotics is summed up in a close association of the experiential dimension (9.5% in the matrix) with social groups (9.7%), mentality (9.3%), lifestyle (8.5%) and the city (9.0%). There is a complete alignment between qualitative and quantitative data. The major codes displayed in the discourse, composing a tight complex of binary oppositions, are also the isotopies having the greatest relative frequency. Quality and quantity go together.

2.3 The semiotic square revisited

One of the most difficult aspects of Greimasian narrative theory is the formulation of the semiotic square of a text. How do we define it? This question is actually misleading, because there are many semiotic squares in a text, and we can find them at every level of the generative trajectory in respect to both the syntactic and the semantic component. As we saw, in the surface narrative syntax, each actant can be developed into a semiotic square (chapter 4: 1.4.3), as can the modalities and the combinations of modalities; we gave as example the semiotic square of the modality of wanting-to-do (chapter 4: 1.4.2). We saw (chapter 4: 1.3) that fundamental semantics is not necessarily structured by a single semiotic square only, but may derive from two interrelated squares; as we shall see below (chapter 7: 1), in the more recent developments of Greimasian theory, fundamental semantics by definition includes more than one semiotic square.

This being said, the definition of the final semiotic square(s) of fundamental semantics remains a difficult issue. We must keep in mind that it is a heuristic tool and as such sometimes offers only useful indications and other times demands less austere operations. We shall attempt below to suggest some possible approaches, starting with a point which has not been satisfactorily clarified in the theory: on what level of abstraction should we look for this square? This is obviously the same issue as the one we encountered concerning the level of analysis of isotopies (chapter 5: 1.4). In that discussion we tried to clarify these levels as a function of their degree of abstraction. As we saw, Greimas and Courtés believe that there exists a small number of universal semantic categories of a very high level of abstraction, and they also propose a next level, based on classemes of great generality and constituting the basis for the classification of the world, the specific semantic organisation of which varies for different cultures and can be identified with the cultural world view. This seems to be their favourite level of analysis. We observed in that discussion that these levels are still too abstract. We presented operations with two hierarchically lower levels, dictated by the particular characteristics of the text being analysed, and we argued for the operational advantages of the third level of analysis.

The issue of different levels emerges in our presentation of the double semiotic squares of the binary pair *life* vs *death* (chapter 4: 1.3, Figure 13), a semantic category belonging to the Greimasian universals. When we linked the two terms of the axis of contraries, life + death, we named the new term in a more concrete manner "resurrected" instead of the more abstract "resurrection", thus passing to the third level of analysis, which corresponds more closely to textual phenomena.

We may better understand the advantages of operating at this lower level of abstraction by taking as example the story of *Cinderella*. In the traditional European versions of the tale, from the Brothers Grimm to the film by Walt Disney, a crucial role in the story is played by the fact that Cinderella has no dress to wear to the ball; her dress and shoes are provided for her by a magical agent (a dove that represents the spirit of her dead mother in the Grimm version, a fairy godmother in the version by Charles Perrault). It is thus possible to formulate the semiotic square of the story as *being* vs *seeming* (chapter 4: 1.3, Figure 12): Cinderella *is* beautiful, but *appears* ugly, and the plot of the story is to make her appearance match what she really is. However, although this semiotic square does represent the structure of the story, it could equally well apply to any number of other narratives in which the central issue is one of deceptive appearances, from Plato's Allegory of the Cave to contemporary detective novels. Formulating the semiotic square of Cinderella on such an abstract level ignores the specificity of this particular narrative, what most readers or audiences would feel is the central point of the plot, namely her clothes.

Cinderella is a member of a wealthy family, as demonstrated by the fact that her two stepsisters have the resources to dress appropriately for the ball. However, she has been unjustly relegated from daughter of the house to servant, and her clothing is dirty and ragged as a result. Her actual social position is contrary to this poor dress, which instead implies a low social position. When she is magically dressed in rich clothing, her new dress implies a high social position and thus restores her to the status that she should have.

The difficulty with this is that we are dealing with two related but slightly different isotopies (dress is an aspect of social position, but the two cannot be conflated into the same isotopy). It is clear that the fundamental semantics of the narrative revolve around two isomorphic semantic categories: *high social position* vs *low social position* and *rich clothing* vs *poor clothing*. If we construct two parallel semiotic squares starting from the above contraries, these semiotic squares offer no significant information. The same is the case with their second-level semiotic squares, because both monotonously deliver (if we use anthropomorphic terms) aspects of Cinderella: Cinderella as being, Cinderella as seeming and Cinderella as being and seeming.

There is no commonly accepted methodology for combining two different semiotic squares, but we propose to proceed to a semiotic-square-like construction starting from an empirically meaningful, but non-logical, opposition, combining one member from each isotopy: *high social position* vs *poor clothing* (Figure 40). This will not give us an orthodox semiotic square, since the two contraries are not members of the same isotopy, but it has the advantage of bringing out the specific elements of this particular narrative. It also demonstrates rather explicitly the ideology that lies behind the story: appearance ("beauty") is a function of social position.

We believe that this semiotic square, constructed on a lower level of abstraction, demonstrates better the particularity of the Cinderella story, which is lost when we operate with the superior hierarchical level *being* vs *seeming*. On the other hand, the superior level is also important, because it reveals the relationship of the Cinderella story with a great number of other texts and thus allows us to define a specific sub-group of texts. This is of course useful information, but it

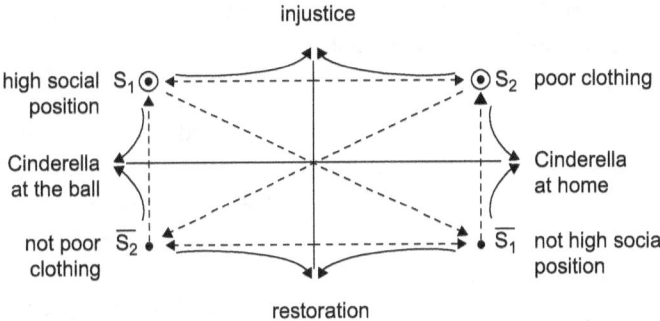

Figure 40: The empirical semiotic square of Cinderella.

levels out the marked difference of the story with, for example, *Les liaisons dangereuses* (which also has a plot based on the opposition *being* vs *seeming*).

Independently from the level of analysis we select, however, the question remains of how we construct the fundamental semiotic square (or squares) of a text. In the previous chapter (2.1.4), we pointed out that there is no mechanical method for doing this. It requires practice and analytical sensitivity, and will usually involve a good deal of trial and error. The various techniques, qualitative and quantitative, that we proposed in this and the previous chapter, and that we summarise below, are designed to complement and facilitate this procedure.

Qualitative techniques:
(a) *Identifying the themes* (chapter 5: 2.1.3). The fundamental semiotic square represents the fundamental values that underlie the semantic structure of a text, and the techniques that we have proposed all have the purpose of identifying that semantic structure and its most important isotopies, on the hypothesis that these should form the basis for the semiotic square. However, we have already pointed out that the semiotic square founds the *whole* generative trajectory of the text. In other words, it underpins not only the semantics but also the syntax of the text, and the basic themes formed by the interweaving of isotopies will occur at *all* levels of the narrative: actantial structure, plot episodes, values, motivations, descriptions, from the deepest to the most superficial level. Strictly speaking, then, it should be possible to construct the semiotic square of a text by locating the themes that run through both its syntactic and semantic structure and identifying the isotopies that form these themes.
(b) *The use of graphs* (chapter 5: 1.8). We formulated a technique for identifying the structure of relations between isotopies. It starts from a matrix of these relations as presented by the text, continues with their visualisation through a

basic graph and ends with the formulation of a final graph, which displays in relief the dominant isotopies and the way they are connected.

Quantitative techniques:

(c) *The weighting of isotopies* (section 1.1 above). We argued that the occurrence of an isotopy can be measured and that this measurement is reflected in its relative frequency (%). The isotopies with higher frequency are the most important quantitatively. We then posed the question whether there is any relation between quantitative weight and qualitative dominance of isotopies. In the present chapter (section 2.2) we discussed some examples of the spatial discourses on the city of Thessaloniki, based on date from our students. One was the discourse of a woman worker and we were able to identify her urban ideology on the basis of the quantitative analysis of her isotopies. Another example was the discourse of a woman public servant, and we concluded that her major codes coincided with the isotopies having the greatest relative frequency. So there seems to be a relation between relative frequency and qualitative dominance of isotopies, and thus the former seems to be a reliable indication of the latter, and vice versa. The two approaches strengthen each other.

(d) *The relation between the order of appearance of the isotopies and their relative frequency* (sections 1.2 and 2.2 above). Based on our research on the conception of regional space in Greece, we concluded that the first three isotopies that occur in a text tend also to be the ones with the greatest relative frequency; this conclusion was generally corroborated by our students' results. More broadly, we concluded that this tendency reveals a convergence of the qualitative importance of isotopies, their relative frequency and their order of appearance.

(e) *The combination of the relative frequency of the isotopies and the final graph* (section 1.2 above). We gave a theoretical example of the projection of the relative frequencies of isotopies on the final graph of the relations between them. This allowed us to observe the matching between the structure of the graph and the distribution of the relative frequencies of the isotopies. Since this was just a theoretical example, it did not lead to any definite conclusions, but we assumed that a tendency of this kind exists. This hypothesis is now reinforced by the conclusion above, since the qualitative importance of isotopies is reflected in the graph and this importance was just shown to be related to their relative frequencies.[87]

---

[87] How to define a dominant isotopy – or isotopies – is a riddle for semiotic theory. Rastier believes that the principal criteria of dominance are qualitative. He first considers as dominant

To conclude, the identification of the semiotic square need not necessarily be left solely to close semantic analysis. This operation can be combined with the three quantitative techniques suggested above, which allow us to define it with greater precision. Since quantitative analysis of an extensive text needs a considerable amount of time, at least with the use of traditional means, even the graph alone may give the necessary complementary information for the formation of the semiotic square.

---

the isotopy that (a) is characterised by the marks of enunciation and (b) defines the referential impression. He then adds the isotopy that (c) is most extended and (d) presents the most complex interpretative trajectory (Rastier 2009: 202, 211). However, he does not explain why (a) is of so great importance as to exceed all other structural elements of the text, nor why (d) also exceeds the other structural elements and how it is to be evaluated. As to cases (b) and (c), it seems to us that they are essentially quantitative and thus may be advantageously treated in the manner described in this chapter – given that Rastier also accepts a quantitative approach – as long as they are considered as complementary to the qualitative relations.

Chapter 7
Late and post-Greimasian theory

1 The second Dictionary

Our account of Greimasian theory in the previous chapters was based mainly on the 1979 Dictionary by Greimas and Courtés, together with Greimas's *Sémantique structurale* (1966) and *Du sens II* (1983). Seven years later, a second volume of the Dictionary was published under the same title (Greimas and Courtés 1986). Its purpose was to deepen narrative theory, to add new entries and to offer a stage for debate; that is, it has a pluralistic and frequently confrontational character. We have not based our account of Greimasian theory on this more recent bibliography, partly because it is frequently unclear which proposals are generally accepted and which are clearly personal, and partly because many proposals present such a degree of complexity that they do not seem to follow one of the major principles of scientific description, namely that of the greatest possible simplicity.

Though we personally have doubts as to whether the developments in the second Dictionary represent a logical extension of Greimasian theory, a deformation of it or a paradigm shift, we feel we owe it to the Paris School to present at least the very general lines of the new generative trajectory proposed.

The basic principles of the new generative trajectory are in line with the canonical theory. They are three: the existence of a deep level of a semiotic text, the coexistence of a syntactic and a semantic component and the gradation of the levels of the trajectory, linked through the mechanism of conversion. However, there is also a marked difference, because the logico-semantic dimension of the original trajectory is completed by, or rather subsumed under, an affective (*thymique*) semantic dimension, for which the term now proposed is *tensal/tensif* (which we may translate as "tensile/tensive"). The affective is in turn subsumed under a wider axiological category, proprioceptivity, articulated by the semantic category *euphoria* vs *dysphoria*. In addition to the affective, proprioceptivity also covers the "veridical" (*véridictoire*), articulated by the semantic category *being* vs *seeming*. For this new approach, then, fundamental semantics is ruled by proprioceptivity.

There are also other novelties enhancing the impression of a radical extension of the original theory. First, there is a multiplication of the levels of the trajectory. Instead of three levels (the fundamental level, the semio-narrative level and the discursive level), the semio-narrative level is split into a deep level, an intermediary level and a surface level, with each successive level receiving the data from the previous level. Second, each level is split into two interrelated sub-levels, as reflected in the double characterisation of tensiveness: *tens-al / tens-if*. The sub-level of type

-al is that which is "presupposed" (*présupposé*), while that of type *-if* is that which follows from the "presupposition" (*présupposant*), i.e., the realisation of type *-if* presupposes the level of type *-al*. Within this framework, the generative trajectory is traversed by two parallel sets of influences from superior to inferior level, one set from *-al* to *-al* and another from *-if* to *-if*.

Fundamental semantics is thus placed under the umbrella of proprioceptivity, now combined with the binary pairs *life* vs *death* and *nature* vs *culture*. It is constituted by an abstract "elementary axiological structure" (*structure axiologique élémentaire*), a virtual structure of a paradigmatic nature. It is composite, a network of hierarchical relations, embracing both the affective and the veridical semiotic squares. On the other hand, the fundamental syntax constitutes a virtual "elementary syntactic structure" (*structure syntaxique élémentaire*), which presupposes, but also transforms, fundamental semantics.

The three levels of the semio-narrative syntax convert and actualise the fundamental syntax. The deep narrative syntax (*syntaxe narrative profonde*) is the first step toward actualising the fundamental syntax and is completed with the surface narrative syntax (see below). The "intermediate narrative syntax" (*syntaxe narrative intermédiaire*) poses the primordial, not yet completed, utterances of doing and of state, which install the actants: the Subject of doing, the Object of value and the Recipient. While the Object and the Recipient are fully actualised, the Subject, as Subject of state and in junction with the Object, has not yet been invested with modal competence. Finally, the "surface narrative syntax" (*syntaxe narrative de surface*) actualises both the deep narrative syntax and the intermediate narrative syntax. Its unit is the narrative programme and these programmes are related to each other, obeying a polemical syntagmatic structure and thus constituting a set of oppositions. The typology of narrative programmes depends on their position and function inside this structure. It is only on this surface level that the utterances of doing and of state take shape.

Semio-narrative semantics is a proprioceptive system that actualises fundamental semantics, following from only one of the possible choices deriving from it; it is constituted by a set of axiological semiotic squares hierarchically ordered and enters into the world of human experience. We would like to point out that the same logic accompanies the initial theory; that is, the semiotic square, as a major semiotic analytical tool, is not limited to the fundamental level, but reappears on every level and in fact traverses the whole of the generative trajectory. On each lower level it takes more specific forms, all of which, however, stem from the fundamental level. The trajectory from fundamental to discursive semantics is accompanied by the continuous expansion of signification.

Discursive syntax includes the processes of actorialisation, temporalisation and spatialisation that we are already familiar with. These processes create our impression of the world, which is interpreted as reality. Discursive semantics include the equally familiar processes of thematisation and figurativisation. This is the realisation of the actualised narrative structure of the previous level.[88] With the second Dictionary, the three levels of the generative trajectory become ten. This number is already large for any semiotician attempting the analysis of a text, but additionally they will have to deal with two kinds (the -*ifs* and -*als*) of four causal conversions between sub-levels – and consequently levels. The schema covers all kinds of abstract theoretical gaps, but it ends up being a theoretical exercise of dubious operational value. To recall Hjelmslev (1961: 10–11), the last of the three conditions governing scientific description is the greatest possible simplicity.

2 Greimas and the semiotics of passions

The above search for affectivity and proprioceptivity reflects a malaise of Greimas and his followers with the exclusive focusing on the development of action and the acts of actants and actors. They felt that what was missing from the theory were the emotional states of the Subjects, which in fact are frequently an important dimension of both oral and written discourse. The definitive answer on the part of Greimas on this issue came eight years after the second Dictionary, when he proposed a new kind of semiotics, which would be a "semiotics of passions" (*sémiotique des passions*, see Greimas and Fontanille 1991), that is, of the affective states of Subjects. With this turn of Greimasian semiotics, there is a shift from doing to being.

Greimas's concern with this issue is evident already in *Du sens II*, which he published a few years before the second Dictionary. There, he sees emotional states as belonging to the order of "affective modalisation" (*modalisation affective*), which refers to the states of mind of a Subject and results, at least partly, from the positive or negative assessment of a state or object, i.e., from axiological systems. Aesthetic pleasure, according to Greimas, belongs to the same modality. With this modality, the affective world takes the form of a language (Greimas 1983: 93–102, 225–246). To come back to our old friend Mary, if instead of describing and analysing Mary's acts, we choose to turn to her affective state as a modality, we might learn (according to one scenario) that because her father refused to give her a ball when she was little, ever since she has *passionately* desired to have her own ball. According to another scenario, in which football is a family tradition, when she succeeds in taking the ball

---

[88] For the above, see Greimas and Courtés 1986: Génératif (parcours), Proprioceptives (catégories), Sémantique discursive, Sémantique fondamentale, Sémantique narrative, Syntaxe discursive, Syntaxe fondamentale, Syntaxe narrative intermédiaire, Syntaxe narrative profonde, Syntaxe narrative de surface.

from John, she feels *absolutely triumphant* (or, if she does not succeed, she feels *horribly disappointed*). Two affective states are described, both in their highest tension.

We note that there is a discrepancy between Greimas's 1983 presentation and the second Dictionary on the position of affect in the generative trajectory. Greimas locates it on the second, semio-narrative, level of the trajectory, while the second Dictionary gives the affective–semantic dimension and its superior category of proprioceptivity the defining role in fundamental semantics. However, eight years after *Du sens II* Greimas confirmed his agreement with the position of the second Dictionary by orienting semiotics to the study of substance. Greimas's *Sémiotique des passions* of 1991, co-authored with Fontanille, established firmly this new approach to semiotics, already prefigured in the second Dictionary, which drastically disrupted the theoretical framework of the Paris School and led after the death of Greimas to its dispersion in different, even radically different directions.

The semiotics of passions represent a retreat from the form (the relation between a plane of expression and a plane of content) to the substance (Saussure's amorphous mass of confused ideas and Hjelmslev's substance of the content), that is, to an "ontic horizon" (*horizon ontique*,[89] Greimas and Fontanille 1991: 10–11) and thus to ontology. The new approach is systematically opposed to classical semiotics, the main contrast being the new foundation on continuity as opposed to the previous structuralist discontinuity. Discontinuity is considered as the "manifested" order, as belonging to seeming, and as following a "topological" logic, the domain of signification, categorisation and discretisation (in the mathematical sense). But this is now seen as the product of a preceding domain of continuity, of a "manifesting" (in the sense of determining; Hjelmslev's terminology) order of being, governing the generative trajectory.

All the concepts of this domain are of a vague nature. The Subject is a proto-actant, an "almost Subject", a sensing potential Subject, a "tensive Subject", in a state of flux before the polarisation *euphoria* vs *dysphoria*, that is, with a body in a state of "'phoric' tensivity", which is the precondition of signification. It emerges only in the fundamental level of the generative trajectory. The Object is ambivalent, an "almost Object"; that is, neither Subject nor Object are fully formed. The Subject is in a state of potentiality of doing, from which later will emerge doing and action; it has not yet decided on conjunction with the Object. In this domain, values (as "shadows of values") and axiologies are vaguely shaped. Modalities also find in this first level their pre-modal foundation, a "metamodalisation" according to which the subsequent differentiation of modalities into virtualising, actualising and realising is supplemented with a preceding "potential" level of the "modulations of passions".

---

89 Heidegger's idea of the concrete being of experience.

The guarantor of the anchoring of continuity and of the transition from continuity to discontinuity is considered to be the body. It achieves this transition through proprioceptivity in the sense of "global feeling" (*sentir global*, Greimas and Fontanille 1991: 18), the perception that a person has of the substance of their own body (a role for which Greimas and Courtés had initially proposed the affective; see 1979: Proprioceptivité). This is where the semiotics of passions encounters the phenomenological project. To overcome the dualism of mental and physical, semiotic existence needs to be homogenous; this is considered to be achieved through proprioceptivity, with the mediation of the "feeling body" (*corps sentant*, Greimas and Fontanille 1991: 13). The idea is that the external world of the "state of things" can be reduced to the internal world of the "state of the Subject", a formal equivalence being created between the two states.

This approach allows us to understand the two major epistemological shifts in the new proposal. First, the shift from discontinuity to continuity represents a movement away from the static quality of structuralism and an attempt to give semiotics a dynamic dimension. Second, there is an attempt to achieve this dynamism with reference to the body and affect.

With the introduction of continuity, there is a doubling of semiosis according to which each component of the narrative structure is connected to another in the domain of preconditions. The two domains, of continuity (the imaginary, inaccessible through the text alone) and discontinuity, are considered as coexisting and completing each other, and in fact the only access to the former is through the latter (on the semiotics of passions, see Greimas and Fontanille 1991: 7–110; Ablali 2003: mainly 115–117, 166, 178–235).

On a more concrete level, Greimas and Fontanille attempt to construct a first sketch of a system of passions,[90] based on the definitions given in a French dictionary, while being aware that their proposal is culturally bounded and many theoretical problems remain unsolved. They select the following seven notions: "feeling" (*sentiment*), "emotion" (*émotion*), "inclination" (*inclination*), "penchant" (*penchant*), "temperament" (*tempérament*), "character" (*caractère*) and "mood" (*humeur*). They use these notions as the columns of a matrix, on the lines of which appear three variables. The first and more important is "aspectualisation" (not to be confused with the same term in discursive syntax), which includes two dimensions: affective duration, which is classified as permanent (such as temperament or character), durable (such as feeling) or passing (emotion), and the acts due to these affective conditions, which can be continuous (due to temperament or character),

---

[90] They give examples of passions such as anger, despair, amazement, terror, admiration, astonishment, stupor, greed, jealousy, hatred.

episodic (due to mood) or isolated (due to feeling or emotion). The second variable covers the three modalities of knowing, being-able and wanting, and the third relates to competence. Each grid cell of an affective term is marked if there is a relation to one of these variables and not marked in the opposite case (Greimas and Fontanille 1991: 92–96).

Following a similar logic, Fontanille formulates a "modal apparatus" (*dispositif modal*), including two modalities, in the form of oriented scales on a pair of Cartesian coordinates, which start from "little" and gradually increase. These are two "tensive exponents" (*exposant tensifs*), showing the different degrees of affective presence. The horizontal coordinate axis represents the affective duration of an affective state, since it corresponds to the temporal extension or quality, graduating from weak to continuously more important. The perpendicular coordinate axis corresponds to the perceived tension, that is, the perception of the intensity of an affect, which gradates from dull (unstressed) to continuously stronger (stressed). The different affective states (four of which – feeling, emotion, inclination and mood – coincide with the list above) are determined by the relation between extension and tension, that is, the space between the two axes represents a continuum showing the distribution of the possible affective states (Fontanille (1999: 63–81). For example, a crisis (upper left part of the diagram) has a minimal duration but a maximal intensity, while an inclination (lower right part of the diagram) is a permanent attribute of low intensity (Figure 41).

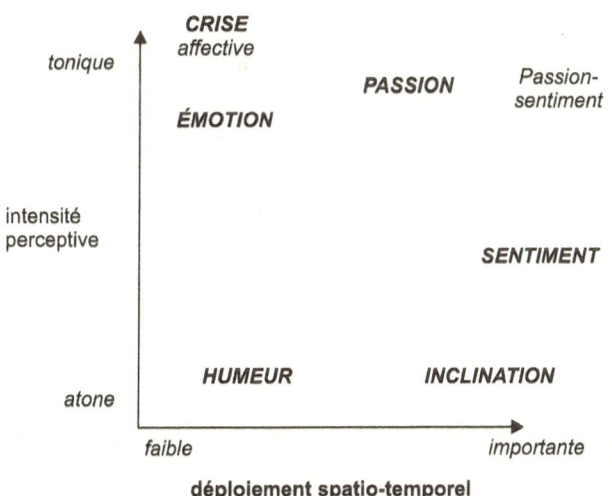

Figure 41: The affective states as a function of the two tensive exponents of the modal apparatus (Fontanille 1999: 78; reproduced by permission of Presses Universitaires de France).

3 Fontanille and the semiotics of passions

Recently Fontanille, without abandoning the general outlines of the semiotics of passions, has advanced a fresh approach to it, an approach which does not invoke the depths of ontology but focuses on the substance levels of Hjelmslev. In a paper with Didier Tsala-Effa (2017) they stress the need to relate epistemology, theory and methodology (posing the latter as the operational epicentre of semiotic analysis), to link semiotics with anthropology as science of meaning, and to account for the cultural singularity of the semiotic objects of study. The authors closely follow Hjelmslev's approach and emphasise his two different interpretations of purport, concluding that the form is not isolated from existential realities, which, as we shall see below, are of major importance for their argumentation.

The anthropological part of the paper relies heavily on Albert Piette's existential anthropology, which Piette himself considers to be the empirical aspect of phenomenology; they also refer to Clifford Geertz's "thick description". Fontanille and Tsala-Effa agree with Piette's view on the need to focus, not on the central and structured part of a task or interaction, on the grounds that this would reduce the diversity of cultural production, but on the part resisting this dominant structuration, due to elements belonging to a surrounding situation. Fontanille and Tsala-Effa assume that, while this different focusing reveals particular behavioural residues, it nonetheless shows the *specificity* of each situation. They consider that this phenomenon reflects, from an existential perspective, a mode of existence in a semiotic situation; the latter is of the nature of a phenomenological field, whose object of study are the variations in extension and intensity of the inner world of the actors (we recognise here the two tensive exponents of Fontanille's modal apparatus). The authors call the central part of a practice (the structuration of the form) "major" and the peripheral (the residue due to the substance) "passive", and consider that focusing on the latter implies a permutation of the actantial roles.

At this point, Fontanille and Tsala-Effa reach the core of their methodological proposal. They consider each corpus studied as heterogeneous and not *a priori* definable but continuously enriched – due to the information coming from the substance levels – and they include in the corpus this "passive" mode as participating in the specific meaning of a situation. The argument is that, while current orthodoxy homogenises the corpus, eliminating the marks of subjectivity and enunciation, their inclusion anchors the textual structure in a unique, non-reproducible situation. Enunciation is conceived no longer just as traces in a text, but as a matter worthy of analysis in itself, inseparable from and an explanatory factor for the analysis of a text. The aim of this methodology – and here there is a return to Hjelmslev – is to sort out from the primary ontological purport the semiotic substance that is relevant for accessing the form; in other words, to focus on the three levels presented in Figure 3 (chapter 3: 8).

This approach is specialised in an operational manner, which we shall follow by briefly presenting Fontanille's proposal for a set of "methodological regimes" of semiosis corresponding to different "levels of immanence" (*plans d'immanence*). Each level is composed of a structured form and a substance of a "residual" nature, assumed by another level in which it is analysed as form; these levels are not independent but articulated. We observe in this approach a new connection to Hjelmslev, who writes: "*La substance semble donc demander une base d'analyse différente de celle exigée par la forme sémiotique propre* [. . .] *les diverses substances peuvent bien présenter des structures très différentes entre elles*" [Thus, substance seems to call for a basis of analysis different from the one required by the semiotic form itself [. . .] different substances may well present very different structures], but "*il y a une certaine correspondance de structure interne dans les différents niveaux*" [there is a certain correspondence between the internal structure of the different levels] and this relationship between neighbouring levels should follow a principle "*qui reste encore à trouver*" [which remains to be found] (Hjelmslev 1971: 68); "'substance' [. . .] can only designate a whole that is in itself functional and that is related to a given 'form' in a certain way" (1961: 80). It is the levels of immanence and their articulation that Fontanille and Tsala-Effa attempt to define with the typology that follows, including the formalisation of the behavioural residues according to the rationale that the *explanatory* foundation of signification follows from (semiotic) conditions preceding its manifestation (see also Ablali 2003: 116). In this manner, semiotics is operationally extended to include factors preceding form, which become the very foundation of semiotics.

A first typology of the levels is presented by the authors: (a_1) signs–figures, (a_2) texts–utterances, (a_3) objects–supports, (a_4) practices–strategies and (a_5) forms of living[91]–modes of existence; this is followed by a second one: (b_1) figures (signs), (b_2) works (texts and objects), (b_3) flux (practices and forms of

---

[91] The concept of "forms of life" was used already by Greimas, for example when, referring to the reader of the city, he equates the content structure (not to be identified with the Anglo-Saxon "mental image" of behavioural geography) of this actant-Recipient to a "life model", which he specifies as the semantic representation of their lifestyle (Greimas 1976: 154). In the entry on sociosemiotics in his first Dictionary (Greimas and Courtés 1979), the concept also covers signifying practices.

living) and (b_4) existences (modes of existence, anthropological modes). If we closely compare these two taxonomies, we observe that:
(i) (b_1) is identical to (a_1);
(ii) the "objects" of (a_3) are removed from it and added to (b_2);
(iii) the "practices" of (a_4) and the "forms of living" of (a_5) are grouped together as (b_3);
(iv) the "modes of existence" of (a_5) are made independent and become (b_4); and
(v) as a result, and given that the "supports" of (a_3) and the "strategies" of (a_4) are no longer used in the terminology, (a_3) is eliminated and (a_4) and (a_5) are mutually restructured.

Signs are created by a "process of segmentation" which produces signifiers and signifieds; texts and objects relate to a "process of totalisation" of meaning akin to paradigmatic analysis, and are differentiated only by the topological dimension of their expression plane (the former are bi-dimensional, the latter three-dimensional); strategies are covered by practices and, together with the forms of living, refer to a "process of regulation of flux" akin to syntagmatic analysis; and modes of existence refer to an "existential process" related to enunciation (Fontanille and Couégnas 2018: 234–237, 243–244, 252).

The above levels of immanence, starting from what we could consider as the surface level and continuously retreating towards deeper substance levels, develop according to a chain down to the founding cause. We can understand this process with two examples given by Fontanille and Tsala-Effa. The first, following the second typology, concerns painting. They start from the level of "works", where the painting is analysed as a text, that is, as a structured form, the traditional object of semiotic analysis. But, they argue, it is accompanied by plastic (touch) and gestural (brushstroke) properties, which are the residual remains of this level. These unstructured remains acquire their structured form on the following and deeper level of immanence, that of "flux".

The second example, following the first typology, comes from workers' cooperatives.[92] Starting from their socio-economic practices, it focuses the analysis of

---

[92] The book by Fontanille and Couégnas includes a study of cooperatives which focuses on two specific cooperatives integrated into the institution Économie Sociale et Solidaire (ESS). The corpus for this study was formed by the International Statement on the Co-operative Identity, statutes of one of the cooperatives studied, books and articles on ESS and cooperatives, views of the founders of the cooperatives studied published in books and articles, published interviews with members of the cooperatives studied and films on cooperatives (Fontanille and Couégnas 2018: 156–158, 172, 190–194, 198–219).

the narrative and actantial structure on actantial syncretism, since the Sender is a collective actant including a set of Subjects–members who are beneficiaries of the value produced; the modality of wanting-to-join, the foundation of the equality between members, predominates. This focusing, concerning the structured part of the level, is according to the authors dictated by the political factor and the contrast to the capitalist model. But they argue that there are residual remains which point to cooperative life; the latter is structured as form on the deeper level of the causative chain of the substance. This last analysis is based on the principle of "generalised reciprocity", which constitutes a collective actant composed of "others", through the fulfilment of "oneself as other".

We can draw certain theoretical conclusions from this approach. Fontanille and Tsala-Effa attempt to anchor the text in its ultimate cause in an explanatory manner, and in this course we should be able to follow the dynamics of the proto-actants, almost-Objects and shadows-of-values before their formalisation as semiotic planes. The authors want to pass from a static analysis to a situational dynamic analysis by articulating form with substance. From a theoretical viewpoint, the concepts with which they operate for the analysis of substance are those that have been formulated for narrative analysis; indeed, we have followed the same procedure in our analysis of pragmatics (chapter 8: 2.12).

The methodological principles of Fontanille and Tsala-Effa and the fundamental concepts they propose together constitute what they call "anthroposemiotics". Their aim is displaced from text to practices and the values attached to them, and these practices are no longer "on paper" but are practices of real people seen from a semiotic point of view. In this case, practices are studied as texts and the corpus used is the means for, no longer the object of, semiotic analysis. What is proposed is essentially a new branch of semiotics, founded on a specific trend in anthropology and akin to but not coinciding with pragmatics and proxemics, a branch which Fontanille and Nicholas Couégnas (2018: 156) consider as distinct from sociosemiotics. This is is a radical epistemological leap in respect to the French semiotic tradition. The model for French semiotics – as for Lévi-Strauss's structural anthropology – has always been linguistics, a science of meaning. Fontanille and his associates propose a displacement of the model to anthropology, a field not restricted to the study of meaning. However, from the different tendencies in this field, they choose the phenomenological approach, which identifies the whole anthropological enterprise with the search for meaning.

An approach very close to that of Fontanille is adopted by Eric Landowski (2017). He criticises the Greimasian canonical model on the basis that it is culturally bounded, as it corresponds to only one regime of meaning while there are four of them, each with its own actantial and relational characteristics; that the idea of exchange reduces life to only one of its dimensions, the economic dimension; that the logic of junction is inadequate and that subjects are not only "motivated subjects", but also "affect-experiencing subjects" (*sujets éprouvants*). Landowski is in quest of an interpretative sociosemiotics along the lines of the tensive semiotics of the second Dictionary, that is, of the logic of continuity, which he sees as one aspect of the opposition *continuity* vs *discontinuity*. The foundation of this attempt is throughout Greimasian, but the Greimasian concepts are used within a different framework. In the anti-systemic spirit, Landowski wants to include within the closed "text" the foundations in discourses and practices that make it an object of "meaning". He thus wants to pass to a semiotics of situations, dealing with action, with processual dynamics understood as interactional relations. What is at stake is the conception of lived, sensory (esthesic) experience, of the meaning of our being in the world, of a semiotics of experience.[93]

4 Some critical thoughts

The motives behind the semiotics of passions – the dissatisfaction with what was felt to be the static and formalist nature of structuralism and the desire for a more dynamic approach – were common to a number of different theoretical tendencies in the 1980s and 1990s, our own approach included. However, there are six points in this new turn with which we are uncomfortable.

First, the social sciences have in the past shown a certain sense of inferiority in respect to the positivist natural sciences, frequently attempting to copy their models. However, in the last several decades positivism has been severely criticised and today positivist *epistemology* is marginalised even in the natural sciences, though this is not the case with many of its theoretical and methodological insights, which are foundational not only for the natural sciences but are also integrated in social sciences such as linguistics, economics, sociology or demography.

Formalism, including Greimasian semiotics, is a positivist approach, but formalism and its concepts of structure and system need not be rejected on *a priori*

---

[93] There has also been an attempt to formulate a canonical passional schema, imitating the canonical narrative schema and composed of five stages, but it is presented as tentative, flexible and open to restructuring (Biglari 2017: 210–213). Couégnas, Fontanille's collaborator, attempting to enrich their common approach, concludes that the formulation of a new semiotic theory still has some way to go (Couégnas and Famy 2017: 453). This situation of flux parallels the many variants of the semiotics of passion – and the limited accumulation of case studies (Biglari 2017: 215–216) which would offer an occasion to check and improve the theory, as well as select among its variants.

grounds. Formalism is not necessarily static, as a look at systems theory will corroborate, but Saussurean linguistics and Greimasian semiotics are static, and the semiotics of passions attempts to introduce a focus on process. However, any such attempt needs to proceed with great caution. One reason is that, at the present stage of our theoretical knowledge, we do not dispose of a single unified theory that can deal with both these dimensions together. For example, Marxism has developed a powerful processual theory, but has no means of analysing a text structurally, i.e., formally. Thus, any processual dimension attempted for semiotics is not in a position to replace structural analysis. Rather, the epistemological issue is posed in terms of an articulation between processual and formal analysis (chapter 9: 2 and 3). In other words, we do not believe that the theory of process should alter the premises of semiotic theory beyond some possible adjustments. We have the feeling, however, that the semiotics of passions is in search of an entirely new epistemological grounding for semiotics.

Second, the new level proposed by Greimas, Fontanille and Landowski undoubtedly attempts to give greater depth to semiotic analysis and may be considered as an interesting complement to previous semiotic theory, but this depth is too deep and disorienting for the usual need to understand the structuring of a text. This is why we have opted in this book for the analytical presentation of canonical Greimasian theory as the direct descendant and extension of Saussurean structural linguistics. It is certainly not perfect, but, taken seriously, it can be transformed from abstract theory into a reliable methodological tool of analysis. In spite of the more recent views of the Paris School, we think that the affective dimension would be more manageable operationally if it were integrated as a new type of modality, as was Greimas's first insight.

Third, the centrality given to the body brings late and post-Greimasian semiotics very close to phenomenology, though one should not forget that the roots of Greimasian semiotics have from the beginning had contacts with phenomenology (a fact also acknowledged by Driss Ablali, 2003: 119–137). Phenomenology is the order of the day for the followers of the semiotics of passions; Göran Sonesson (2017: 94), working in the direction of cognitive semiotics, states unambiguously that "phenomenology is the only foundation on which it will be possible to erect semiotic theory". The semiotics of passions was from the beginning set by Greimas in the framework of phenomenology, a framework still used by the semioticians of the former Paris School who are working on the various branches of this theory.[94]

---

[94] One of these orientations is due to the work of Jean-Claude Coquet, who in order to escape the limitations of static structuralism and approach texts in a dynamic way attempts to widen the perspective of semiotics from the text to the conditions of communication of the two instances of "origin" and "reception" (Kharbouch 2017: 8, 14, 18 n. 96). Enunciation is the stratum behind, above

Ablali acknowledges that this convergence with phenomenology – a philosophy close to idealism – could raise fears that semiotics might lose its autonomy, but is optimistic that this is not the case. Independently, however, from the question of autonomy, this enclosure within the semiotic, when we are in a search of the origin of systems of signification, leads semiotics directly to idealism. Arguments are put forward about the materiality of the body justifying the anchoring of signification in "the material", but the approach to this "materiality" remains subject to the semiotic law of relevance. There are different ways to approach the body epistemologically – consider how many different classes are taught on it in the schools of medicine – but the semiotics of passions, together with phenomenology, selects only one of these approaches, the purely semiotic one. As Rastier points out (2017: 8), this is "*un Corps absolutisé, comme jadis l'Esprit absolu*" [an absolutised Body, as formerly the absolute Spirit].

Fourth, this choice is purely psychologising, as is clear from the system of passions. This is a traditional habit of semioticians, who systematically turn their backs on the social sciences dealing with materiality. For example, Fontanille and Tsala-Effa deal with socio-economic practices (semiotically approached) in the next-to-last substance level from a point of view dictated by political relations and the capitalist model. We believe that this level could open the road for the actual foundation of the phenomenon the authors analyse. But then they opt to abandon society and culture and find its foundation not in institutional practices based on democratic relations or ideological formations, but in the phenomenological psychologising concept of fulfilment of oneself-as-other. The specific political strength of semiotics, the study and unveiling of ideology, is replaced by the study of personal feelings in interaction.

Semiotic theory is by definition open to any major isotopy detectable in a text, but the new passional super-level is a Procrustean bed prescribing the category of isotopies that should be given exclusivity. A work like Marcel Proust's *À la recherche du temps perdu* is a good candidate for such an approach, as Ahmed Kharbouch shows with his analysis of a small passage from *Du côté de chez Swann*, the first volume of Proust's work. In this passage, the narrator passes from a state of deep sadness to one of sudden pleasure as the effect of

---

and before the structuring of the enunciate and displays the direct, lived, phenomenological contact of the body of the "enunciating" (intra-textual) actant with the world. The next superior stratum is composed of the above two (extra-textual) instances, that of the origin, speaker or author as the first enunciating instance, and that of reception. According to Coquet's semiotics of continuity, both strata are founded by the body as substance – the impassioned body, the suffering body, the speaking body – and by body relations as the fundamental structure from which meaning emerges (Kharbouch 2017: 11–12, 14, 17 n. 93; Ablali 2003: 225, 227–228).

the feeling caused by the taste of a piece of Madeleine cake dipped in tea. According to Kharbouch, the singularity of this text, lost in the canonical approach, is the narrator's unique corporeal experience (Kharbouch 2017: 16–18). We shall not comment here on the degree to which the canonical theory is able to approximate such an analysis, but we would like to point out that the effectiveness of an analysis based on the body and affect depends, in this case, very much on the selection of the text analysed. It is unlikely to be equally effective when analysing a text such as *Rambo* or the *Odyssey*. There is also a bias in the isolation of this passage from its intra-textual context (see the discussion of this issue with reference to Vitruvius's *De architectura* in chapter 8: 2.7), because the problematics of passion, interesting as it is, obscures Proust's reflections on the aristocracy and the bourgeoisie, their ideology and the incentives to social ascension.

Finally, we come to our fifth point. The semiotics of passions seeks the interpretation of the semiotic in a subjective world of pre-signification and attempts to explain action through this same world, indeed in psychological terms. We consider as unfortunate the foundation of situation on the affective dimension (or even on the cognitive dimension) alone. This is a strong epistemological position, closely related to the idea of voluntarism. Philosophically, the theory of voluntarism argues that will is the dominant factor in experience or action; it is a subjectivist and idealist conception of action which harmonises well with the desire of semiotics to observe at all costs and in all cases the law of relevance. Sociologically, voluntary action implies the freedom to choose goals and how to achieve them.[95] However, sociological voluntarism avoids strict subjectivity, because it situates voluntary action *within* the framework of societal and cultural constraints, part of which is no longer of a semiotic nature but tied to extra-semiotic material processes. Sociological voluntarism thus has recourse to the extra-semiotic, if only as a constraint. The semiotics of passions, however, is the victim of a radical misunderstanding, because it transfers Greimasian theory from paper to real actors. Semiotic texts, because they are "on paper", are products of ideology: the motives and actions of their actors are explained ideologically *within* the system of the text. But in real life, *outside* the text, actants are subject to social constraints understood even by sociological voluntarism.

Ultimately, the situation delimited by the semiotics of passions is a microsituation, another habit of semioticians, in a relation of mutual attraction to psychologism. Fontanille and Tsala-Effa are right to search for the uniqueness of a situation, but we believe that this idiographic approach should not be

---

[95] We note in passing that free market advocates, libertarians and anarchists opt for voluntary action to replace most of the apparatus of government.

transformed into an epistemological choice. Any micro-situation is a specific – and of course interesting in its specificity – token of a more general pattern, which, moreover, is not formulated in the structured elements of the substance levels. The approach adopted by the authors does not allow them to catch the interplay between specificity and generality.

Anne Hénault chooses a different approach in her 1994 study of an early seventeenth-century diary. She is interested in identifying traces in the text of the affects experienced (*l'éprouvé*) by the author, Robert Arnauld d'Andilly, the young scion of a distinguished family setting out on a career in royal service and subject to the precipitous ups and downs of court favouritism and intrigue. Diaries were kept at the time as a memory aid in view of the all-too-likely possibility of being accused of dereliction of duty if one fell out of favour, and for that reason the diary writers avoid expressing personal feelings or opinions. Hénault thus does not look for obvious rhetorical expressions of affect (which, she points out, Arnauld was quite capable of producing, as his letters and memoirs testify), but searches for "disturbances" in the text, very slight changes in language that can be interpreted as the signs of an affective tension: expectation, enthusiasm, pride, disappointment. As Fontanille observes, this is the first time in the study of passion that the passional dimension of discourse is identified without a reconstruction based on conventional signs and explicit verbal references in a text, but through penetration into the text as such. He finds that the innovative concept of "*l'éprouver*", the experiencing of affects, also used by Landowski, essentially replaces that of "feeling" (Fontanille 2017: 15, 19).

Hénault's work is inscribed within the semiotics of passion, but she also makes liberal use of contemporary historical sources to throw light on both the political situation and the discursive conventions of the period. Inevitably, she encounters the material social conditions of the times and she does not hesitate to include them in her interpretation of the psychology of her "hero".

Contestations from inside the group concerning parts of Greimasian theory had appeared already during Greimas's lifetime and multiplied after his death. They follow different orientations, maintaining a greater or lesser number of common or similar elements from the theory, but not generally sharing the same set of elements. Some attempt to define the dynamics behind the text that lead to its creation; here, the aim is to study situational factors and either preserve the possibility of articulation with the generative trajectory, or propose a structurally comparable trajectory with totally different levels, anchored in phenomenology or biology. Another orientation rejects the generative trajectory and operates on a single level of analysis. All these attempts operate within the semiotic relevance, except those that try to anchor semiotics in biology.

However, when semiotics turns to situation, not as a micro-semiotic factor, but as a material macro-factor, the social is lurking in every corner, and there is need for some original theoretical acrobatics if one desires to evade it. For us, the productive cause of the semiotic is in the extra-semiotic (as material, not only semiotic situation) and our social semiotics attempt to offer a causal explanation of semiotic structures based in material society; contrary to the semiotics of passions, the "state of the Subject" is determined by the "state of things" (chapter 9).

Part IV: **The semiotics of communication**

Chapter 8
A global model of communication

1 The field of communication

In chapter 3, we examined the structure of the language system and semiotic systems in general, in chapters 4, 5 and 6 we delved as deeply as possible into the structure of the texts presupposing and built with these systems, and in chapter 7 we discussed the new semiotics of continuity in the form of the semiotics of passions. Texts, of course, are not self-made: they are constructed with the purpose of arriving at a destination, and when they do arrive they are incorporated into a circuit of communication. This circuit – which is only schematically elaborated by Saussure – is an essential factor for the comprehension of the dynamics of speech. From the moment that semiotic analysis moves from text to communication, there is a parallel shift from mainstream semiotics to sociosemiotics and further, as we shall see, to social semiotics.

Semiotic systems are used in association with cultural practices, which according to Greimas and Courtés (1979: Communication, Production) may have two different orientations: they can relate to action on things, which aims at the transformation of nature and which they call *production*, or represent action upon human subjects, which they call *communication*. For Greimas and Courtés, communicative exchanges are of two kinds: transfer of objects of value (which they define not in substantial terms but as a formal position) and communication between subjects. They give as example (Greimas and Courtés 1979: Communication) what Lévi-Strauss has identified as the three fundamental systems of communication in any society: the kinship system, consisting in the exchange of women; the economic system, involving exchanges of goods and services; and the linguistic system, covering the exchange of messages (Lévi-Strauss 1958: 95, 327).

However, we need to remember that the product of production already embodies signification and may also involve an intention to communicate on the part of its producers; in any case, with or without such intentions, it always becomes a source of signification for its user–readers, not necessarily the same signification as it was intended to have in production. In this case, the practice of the users is the "consumption" of signification, which rests on the signification

---

Note: An earlier version of this chapter, by Alexandros Ph. Lagopoulos, was published as A global model of communication, *Semiotica* 131 (1/2). 45–77, 2000 and republished with the same title in Paul Cobley, ed., *Communication theories: Critical concepts in media and cultural theories*, 1, pp. 389–419 (London and New York: Routledge, 2006).

that they ascribe to the product. A similar process emerges in the case of the semiotic consumption of natural products; for example, a natural landscape can be meaningful to us, although nobody sent it to us as a message (unless we believe in supernatural forces).

The structural components of the communication circuit and their relations appear to be few and simple, but a more detailed approach reveals a far greater richness and complexity, and the elaboration of all the dimensions of communication involves, as we will see, a large part of semiotic theory. We will examine fourteen aspects of the communication model, referring to its components, their nature, their dynamics, their relation and interaction, and their structure; to the functions and environments of the message; and finally to the types of semiotic systems used for communication. Each aspect is considered as a (sub-)model of a global communication model. The aim of the discussion is to reveal to the greatest possible extent the complexity involved in the analysis of communication.

As we shall see, subjects of several types may occupy the two positions of addresser and addressee: they can be real individuals, textual constructs (as in fictional narratives), or mythical and religious beings (in sacred narratives). In all cases, with the partial exception of Model 14, we shall study the aspects of the communication circuit strictly as cultural phenomena, *sub specie communicationis*, not from a practical point of view (for example with reference to the wealth of the communicating individuals).

2 Fourteen models of communication

2.1 Model 1: Saussure's circuit of *parole*

As our starting point, we propose to revisit the circuit of *parole* as described by Saussure (1971: 27–31, 98–100), which represents the elementary form of communication.[96] The circuit of *parole* depends, for Saussure, on an individual act, though his aim in formulating the model was to identify the language system, *langue*. The Saussurean communication circuit takes the form shown in Figure 42.

---

[96] This model also appears in communication theory, where a sender A codifies his ideas and sends them as a message to a receiver B; the message is transmitted through a medium. There is, however, a radical difference between Claude E. Shannon's information theory, where communication theory belongs, and semiotics. The purpose of information theory is the technical and quantitative study of the transmission of information through technical media, while semiotics is primarily interested in the qualitative analysis of the processes of semiosis in cultural, rather than technical, communication.

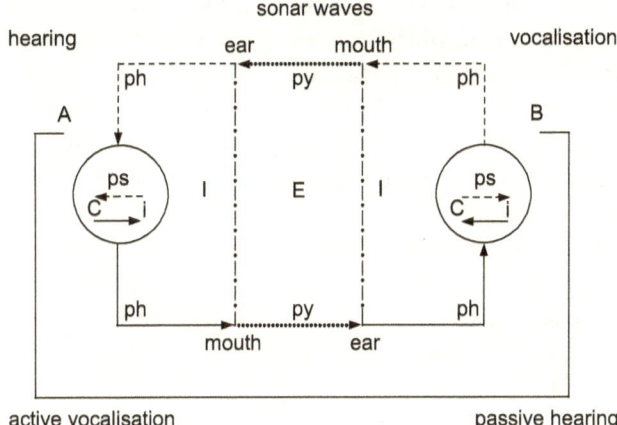

Figure 42: Saussure's circuit of parole. A, B: individuals. c: concept (signified). i: acoustic image (signifier). ps: psychic process (in the mind). ph: physiological process. py: physical process. I: internal circuit. E: external circuit.

The two structural positions in this elementary circuit, as Saussure presents it, are occupied by two individuals, A and B, who communicate with each other.[97]

The circuit starts in A's mind, where there are concepts, the signifieds (facts of consciousness) linked to linguistic representations or acoustic images, the signifiers expressing them. The concept activates the acoustic image corresponding to it, a process which is psychic (mental) in nature, as is the concept itself. Then A's brain transmits an impulse relative to the acoustic image to the vocal organs, which is a physiological process. Transmission from the mouth of A (vocalisation) to the ear of B (hearing) is a physical process based on sound waves. In Saussure's approach the medium is the air, through which the sound waves are transmitted. The psychic and the physiological processes constitute

---

[97] Jakobson uses the term "addresser" for position A and "addressee" for B. Greimas and Courtés use the equivalent pair *Destinateur–Destinataire*, with a capital first letter, to indicate the two actantial positions within a text that we named Sender and Recipient. They also refer to another set of communicative positions involving the text as a whole; for them, a text as an object of study is an *énoncé* [utterance], the existence of which presupposes an act of *énonciation* [enunciation]. This act leads to two interrelated intra-textual positions: position A, the *énonciateur* [enunciator], is logically implied and corresponds to the external enunciator (the author), being the author's textual *alter ego*, while position B is the *énonciataire* [enunciatee], once more not the external addressee (the actual reader), but the intra-textual subject that the enunciator addresses. The term "subject of enunciation" covers both these positions of intra-textual communication (Greimas and Courtés 1979: Énoncé, Énonciateur/Énonciataire, Énonciation).

the part of the circuit which is internal to the individual, while the physical process constitutes the part of the circuit which is external to the individual. From this point on, the circuit encounters the individual B and functions in inverse order: from B's ear to his or her mind, and in the mind linking the acoustic image with the corresponding concept. If B speaks in reply, this new process, from B's mind to A's mind, will follow exactly the same course in reverse order (shown in the figure with dashed lines). The process is more complex in reality, writes Saussure, but these are its essential elements. The sub-circuit extending from A's concept to B's ear he calls active, the rest of the circuit passive. A's psychic part (c–i) of the active sub-circuit is the executive part and B's psychic part (i–c) of the passive sub-circuit is the receptive part.

2.2 Model 2: The positions of communication

Saussure's model of communication is founded on the following assumptions:
(a) each of the two communicating positions A and B is occupied by one individual subject;
(b) each of the two positions is occupied by a different individual subject;
(c) each of these subjects is a living human individual;
(d) these individuals coexist in the same space and in the same time, i.e., they communicate synchronically;
(e) these individuals have a conscious intention to communicate; and
(f) they communicate using oral natural language.

These assumptions are certainly satisfactory for Saussure's theoretical needs, but they do not correspond to the general aims of linguistics, even less for those of semiotics. None of them is a prerequisite for the communication circuit to function. We shall try below to broaden our perspective in respect to each one of them.

First, communication can take place between *collective* subjects. The positions of the communication circuit are not necessarily occupied by single subjects. Greimas gives an example of a collective addresser in reference to urban planning. He observes that an urban plan is produced by a subject of enunciation, which is a collective actant including both collective (for example administrative agencies) and individual actors (for example the planner, the economist, the mayor) and possibly automated substitutes for them. According to Greimas, the structure of the actant does not follow simply from the modalities of knowing-how-to-do (Model 11 below), wanting-to-do and being-able-to-do, but also includes ideological investments. The actors assume different syntactic roles and in the planning process an amalgamation of views – sometimes contradictory – takes place from which emerges an implicit ideological model of the city. The study of this dynamics allows the description of the decision-making process, ending with the building of the city (Greimas 1976: 152–153). Equally collective, but on another level of analysis, is the addressee (Model 3 below), since it includes the future residents of the city.

The second issue concerns the *relation* between positions. The positions of the communication circuit are not necessarily occupied by different subjects, nor is it even necessary for both of them to be occupied. When a subject A communicates, he or she does not necessarily communicate with another subject B: communication may take place with one's self, that is, have the form of a monologue (B = A).

A monologue is not necessarily individual; we can also find cases of collective monologues. Edmund Leach discusses ritual performances from the perspective of communication. Inspired by Lévi-Strauss, he refers to the "composer" of a rite and identifies them with the mythical ancestors; that is, the rite itself is considered as a message passed down from the ancestors. In this manner, the ancestors become the ultimate addressers (the final Sender) of the rite. However, the rite-as-message is in each performance the product of actual performers, who are in reality the actual addressers. Leach points out that there is a "conductor", a master of ceremonies or a chief priest, and that the addressees are the same people as the performers. As he writes: "When we participate in ritual we 'say' things to ourselves", we "transmit collective messages to ourselves" (Leach 1976: 43, 45). In this case, positions A and B are collective (A = Σ_α and B = Σ_b), but also B = A. We can extend Leach's position, because there is another collective addressee beyond the performers, which is the whole of the community; in the case of narratives, this is the final Recipient.

It is also possible for one of the positions of communication to be empty. When someone is in danger and screams "Help!" or a castaway on a deserted island throws into the sea a note in a bottle, or when someone writes a letter of recommendation "to whom it may concern", they quite consciously send a message, an utterance, to a virtual addressee, which may never be received by an actual addressee: if this happens, the position of the addressee is empty, that is, B = 0.

Is it possible to have an empty addresser's position, A = 0? Let us suppose that someone sees the face of a sleeping person, or a natural object, for instance a seashell or a coloured pebble. The observer may well find signification in what they see, but it is not a case of communication. A natural object signifies denotatively ("seashell") and probably connotatively ("What a wonderful seashell!") for the subject seeing it, but natural objects are not messages sent by some addresser – unless they are considered as the creation of a supernatural being, who in that case would occupy the position of the addresser of the message. In cases like these, signification is "communicated" to the addressee, but there is neither real communication nor a communication circuit. When the addresser's position is empty, i.e., when there is no addresser, when A = 0, there can be signification, but no message and no communication.

Raymond Ledrut believes that the process of semiosis relating to the city is such a process of non-communication. In a study published in French in 1973, he compares the signification of the city to that of a forest (a whole with individual trees): though the city is not the product of an addresser in the strict sense, it is nevertheless a kind of text, acquiring signification in the interpretation of the addressees (like the seashell). Actually, however, Ledrut integrates circuits of communication in the semiotic perspective on urban space, because he believes that there are literal addressers (frequently more than one) producing the city-as-text, but they are authors of only fragments of the city,[98] and thus the city is not a single coherent text, unlike a building or a costume that constitutes a single message. That is, Ledrut does not deny that in the last instance there is a semiotic production of the city and thus the opening of a communication channel, but he asserts that this does not hold for the city *as a whole*; instead, it is the addressees who produce the semiotics of the city. Position A is occupied by many addressers communicating only parts of the city, but in respect to the whole city A = 0, while in both cases position B is occupied by a collectivity.

For Ledrut, the city is both the product of a collective "pseudo-speaker" and a "pseudo-text", because it is the addressees who make it a text and invest it with signification through their own urban experience. He considers that these observations are valid for both precapitalist and contemporary settlements. He believes that even in precapitalist settlements there is no conscious or subconscious collective intention to communicate a specific message. It is not a collectivity that speaks, but only its spokesmen, who express the tendencies of the collectivity; there is only a collective "quasi-intention" (1986: 118–124).

Ledrut sees contemporary cities as a super-text constructed by the addressees, with separate islands of signification due to various and different urban planning projects. He is probably thinking of the connotative, symbolic level, and if this is so, we would concede that he has a point. But, as we know, signification is not only connotative. Even the most trivial producer when building

---

[98] Manifestly Ledrut is thinking of the many urban planning projects for different parts of the city, each one conceived as a whole and intended to communicate a specific message.

any kind of house uses the culturally patterned elements that communicate "house", and the same holds for "shop" or "street"; all these are messages immediately understood by any addressee belonging to the same culture. Thus, there are a plethora of denotative elements which unify semiotically the fragmentary nature of the city. In the case of contemporary settlements, we are indeed dealing with a text without a unified semiotic producer, but denotatively it is not really a pseudo-text. Instead we have a "patchwork" text, a complex message sent by a plurality of both synchronically and diachronically heterogeneous addressers (who as a rule do not interest the addressees). It is read denotatively as a whole composed of distinct elements; connotatively, it is fragmented on the production side, but unified by the elaboration of the addressees based on their urban experience, as Ledrut concludes.

However, neither the perspective of connotation taken by Ledrut nor our own perspective of denotation ever delivers the semiotic conception of the whole city. Today's cities at least have become too large for a holistic conception. Any individual has only a very limited view of the urban space of their city and our conception of it consists of a limited number of areas, each with their own signification and positively or negatively evaluated, but also of a series of blank, non-significant spaces, corresponding to the areas of the city that escape our perception – and our social routines.

Finally, Ledrut's observations are not valid for precapitalist societies. In these societies there is always a culturally formulated semiotic model governing the organisation and form of space, a model known at different levels of sophistication to all the members of the community. During the foundation of a settlement, a small group of religious and possibly technical specialists are responsible for the foundation rite itself, but they voice the knowledge and feelings of the whole community, which is to a greater or lesser extent present and participates in the event. The communication pattern is identical with that of ritual performances discussed above: the head of the religious group is the "conductor" of the rite and the community holds both positions of communication, engaged in a monologue with itself. Contrary to Ledrut's views, there is a culturally sanctioned semiotic urban model to be communicated and there is a conscious collective intention to communicate it (Lagopoulos 1995).

What of the third assumption behind Saussure's model of communication, the *nature* of the subjects of communication? In Saussure's model the two communicating subjects are living human individuals. However, neither A nor B are necessarily living, human or individuals. This is just one case among a wide spectrum of possible cases. First, the subjects of communication can be real, fictional or mythical beings; in addition to real persons, the subjects of communication may be a divine or semi-divine being, a saint, a dead ancestor, an animal, an object, a mechanical apparatus or even a concept (see also Greimas and Courtés 1979: Actant; Eco 1976: 8–9). In the computer-animated film *Ratatouille*, we encounter rats speaking to people. The addressers may also be implicit. For example, in the case of the contemporary city discussed above, the analyst knows metalinguistically that there are different synchronic and diachronic addressers of the denotative urban messages, but most of the addressees do not think of the existence of addressers and are not aware that they are in a communication situation. We shall see in Model 11 below that the subjects of communication are not some sort of instantaneous subjects coextensive with the duration of the communication act, but integrated subjects existing before and after each singular act and constituted as actants by their competence.

Second, an addresser or addressee as actant may be composite and manifested through different actors, who may compose a small group of subjects or larger cultural groups, as was the case with the planning processes leading to the conception of a modern city or the ritual performances discussed above. In the case of the collective addresser, or even in the case of a television presenter, we are not dealing with inter-individual, person-to-person communication, but with "communication of diffusion" (Moles and Zeltmann 1973: 125–129).

Third, the two communication positions need not be occupied by subjects of the same nature. The participants in the rite consider as its addresser the imaginary dead ancestors. The practice of augury, which in ancient Rome involved the observation and interpretation of the flight of birds or the reading of the entrails of sacrificed animals, was considered as delivering auspices sent by the gods. Birds and entrails were treated as messages sent by a divine addresser to the human addressees: real B, imaginary A. In the case of sacrifice, an imagined relationship is established between a real addresser A and a deity B of another world. The power is in the other world and the rite of sacrifice aims, through a gift to the addressee, at establishing a bridge, an imagined channel of communication, whether the blood of animal or human sacrifice, the smoke of the burning sacrificial animal, other foods or objects. This channel allows a mutual relationship: through it as medium, the human request in one direction and the divine power in the opposite direction are transmitted (cf. Leach 1976: 81–83).

Saussure's fourth assumption is that A and B coexist in the same space and in the same time, i.e., they communicate synchronically. But communication can equally well be *diachronic*. The communicating subjects do not necessarily coexist in space and time: a letter is not read at the moment of its writing and a book can be read long – sometimes very long – after it has been published. Thus, communication may be diachronic, either in the sense of not being strictly synchronic (the letter) – in which case, however, it is considered as synchronic from a semiotic perspective – or in the broader sense of extending through a number of years or even historical periods. It goes without saying that in diachronic communication in the last sense, the addresser is physically absent relative to the addressee.

Writing on architecture, Eco (1972: 279–287) observes that in the course of history the architectural signifieds both of denotation and connotation, as those of art forms in general, are subject to various losses, recuperations and substitutions. In fact, de- and re-semantisation processes are the rule in history. We can think of the different conceptions of the Parthenon, the temple of Athena on the Athens Acropolis, held by modern Greeks and the Greeks of the classical period. In ancient Greece, what we consider as aesthetics was an integral part of cosmological ideas that were embodied in the temple, while today the Parthenon, due to its integration within a different framework of cultural representations and values, is conceived against the background of modern (Kantian) ideas on aesthetics as a more or less pure aesthetic artefact. This deviation becomes sharper if we think of the conception of the Parthenon by persons of a totally different cultural origin. Japanese visitors to the Parthenon will assimilate the temple within their own tradition of values (more or less influenced by Western culture), in which aesthetics may or may not be present and, if it is, will probably be accompanied by isotopies foreign to ancient Greek thought.

The diachronic dimension of communication displays a major fact which also applies to synchronic communication. Saussure considers that A's signified is directly comprehensible to B, and the same assumption is implicitly present in Jakobson. Both positions presuppose a passive addressee, which as we shall see with the next model is far from being true.

Saussure's fifth assumption concerns the *intention* to communicate. According to Saussure, speech is an act of will, that is, intentional. In fact, when a subject as addresser opens a circuit of communication, he or she has an intention to do so, indeed to communicate what it communicates. However, when the message is not elementary, the addresser also frequently communicates an unintentional message, because he or she is not conscious of the full meaning of the message communicated. Behind the intention to communicate and any conscious discourse, there are as a rule deeper structures operating, and these are also communicated – a communication of which the addresser is usually unaware, but which is also the object of semiotic analysis (this is the essence, for example, of Lévi-Strauss's analysis of myth). These are subconscious messages expressing the deeper thoughts, values and feelings of an individual or a collectivity. The subconscious level also takes other forms: the addressers of ritual performances are not aware that they transmit messages to themselves, but they do so nonetheless.

Frequently, subconscious messages are activated by a subconscious intention to communicate, without any conscious awareness on the part of the addresser.

Psychoanalysis provides us with a multiplicity of such examples. Imagine a plausible scenario: he is cheating on her and she does not know how to react and hides her feelings. One day, he comes into the kitchen as she is washing the dishes. She turns towards him with a plate in her hands and breaks it on the floor. Nothing is said, she does not know that she has just communicated her anger, but she has done so, in a symbolic form, because of a subconscious intention. He is surprised by this reaction, so communication there is, but he misinterprets the message and asks "what's wrong with you?"

Whether communication is conscious or subconscious, the addresser has the intention to communicate; without intention, message and communication do not exist, only text and signification (unless the addressee takes the initiative to integrate the text received within a communication circuit of their own creation, for example as a supernatural sign). In the case of direct communication, the intention to communicate also characterises the addressee, provided he or she does not turn their back on the addresser. Frequently, as Saussure believes, there is intention in both communication positions, but this view does not necessarily imply that the intention is chronologically simultaneous (for example, writing the answer to a letter involves a certain delay in time). From the moment that a message is conceptualised on the part of the addressee as something meaningful sent by the addresser, attention is turned to it and attention goes together with intention.

It may happen that this attention is turned to a message which was not sent specifically to the addressee, but received by chance or usurped; nonetheless, there is still intention to communicate. In this case, we have intention in both positions of communication, but their directions do not converge and A is transformed into an addresser of B, which was not A's specific intention. We encounter the same case when B reacts to a manifestation of some kind by A which was not due to an intention to communicate; B's reaction transforms A's manifestation *a posteriori* into an object of communication, whence the quality of addressee assumed by B, simultaneously installing A as an involuntary addresser. We frequently encounter cases of this kind: for example, A sneezes and a bystander turns to her and says "Bless you", to which she answers "Thank you".

Intention, then, is the prerequisite for the functioning of the communication circuit. When messages are not elementary, the conscious message becomes the vehicle of a subconscious message. And the addresser of a message may be constructed by the addressee.

Saussure's final assumption concerns the nature of the *message*. A message is not necessarily coded in terms of natural language, more specifically oral language. The domain of signification is coextensive with a society's culture; culture is composed of a great number of semiotic systems and sub-systems, and elements of any one of them may enter a communication circuit. This is true for the verbal products of intellectual and everyday culture, as well as for those of verbal and non-verbal artistic products. It is also true for the objects of material culture, namely use objects, such as clothing or buildings, and any possible object defined by narratives (Model 4 below) or intellectual systems, such as the objects for sacrifice. It also holds for behavioural culture, that is, the part of culture that is imprinted in behavioural patterns and custom (cf. Leach 1976: 6, 15–16) or, to use the relevant semiotic term, signifying practices (Model 12 below).

2.3 Model 3: The active semiotic labour of the dialogists and their interaction

In the discussion of the previous model we presented the founding factor of communication, intention; the nature of the positions of communication; and their relations through a static perspective. We shall now adopt a dynamic view on these relations, analysing them in process and in their interrelationship.

In order to send a message, the addresser must accomplish a semiotic labour of encoding. Saussure acknowledges that this work is active. A comparable point was made by Mikhail Bakhtin in 1926 (Bakhtin 1989: 403), who in discussing art observes that with the manipulation of the artistic form, the artist adopts an active position relative to its content.

Two of Saussure's positions are open to serious criticism. First, objections can be made to the individual nature of the message, which essentially demotes it to the realm of contingency and impedes attempts at generalisation or typological approaches; such objections were already raised by Vološinov ([1929] 1977: 119, 124). Second, and this is the point we would like to make in reference to the communication circuit, the reception of the message is not the passive event that Saussure describes. This is a fallacy due to the apparent transparency of language, which is in reality deceptive. Other types of communication do not leave room for such a misconception.

A good example of the active semiotic labour required in consumption is given by the semiotic system of space. In contemporary societies, the production of buildings or urban space is largely de-semantised, due to the preponderance of economic, technological and utilitarian factors.[99] Still, meaning there is. If it is patterned, as happens with the established, commonly known and

---

[99] Postmodernism reacted to this by trying to bring back meaning, in the sense of connotation, to architectural and urban forms.

accepted architectural styles, that is, with semiotic systems that have been socialised, the semiotic labour on the part of the addressee is not very demanding, though it is never passive. On the other hand, when richer and original meanings are intended on the part of the producers of built space (as we saw in the case of Brasilia), it is far from certain that understanding of the meaning inscribed will be transparent to the addressees. For most of them, spontaneous interpretation will be quite limited and partial, and they usually need both an active semiotic labour of deciphering – and, inescapably, reinterpretation – and probably additional information to make sense of it.

Both in circumstances of patterned semantisation and in the case of the use of an original system, and whether a greater or a lesser part of the message is understood, the active semiotic labour of the addressee, more or less demanding according to the case, is present and the semiotic conception of space usually diverges to a significant degree from the message sent by the addresser. Even if we assume complete knowledge of the intentions of the addresser, and although the message is not independent of the addresser's intentions, from the moment it acquires its own existence in space, it also acquires its own dynamics of signification and offers itself for interpretations not dependent on the intentions of its producer.[100] In other words, intentions are far from being unequivocally and linearly reflected in the message, even if certain bridges with it may be found; the message acquires its own reality and the addressee makes his or her own interpretation of it, depending on a series of semiotic and extra-semiotic factors.

Thus, not only the "executive" part of the communication circuit, which we would call the "production" of signification, but the receptive part, the "consumption" (conception, reading) of signification, is also active. This is explicitly acknowledged by Eco. For him, both the production and the interpretation (in consumption) of signs, messages or texts presuppose semiotic *labour*. During consumption, the addressee has to observe the rules of the system used, mobilise complex inferential processes in order to interpret a message, establish the correct interpretation of the message and check if the message refers to the actual properties of the things mentioned (Eco 1976: 151–156). Even in the case of natural language, transparency disappears as soon as we deal with something beyond trivial exchanges, plain denotation and surface comprehension. In

---

[100] This is the point made about poetry in the famous essay "The intentional fallacy" by W. K. Wimsatt and M. C. Beardsley: the poem "is detached from the author at birth and goes about the world beyond his power to intend about it or control it" (Wimsatt and Beardsley 1946: 470).

certain cases, even denotation may be received by the addressee in a manner not intended by the addresser (Eco 1976: 140).

Whether or not in a communication situation, the emergence of signification on the part of the addressee is founded on an active semiotic labour. As we saw with the questionnaire analysis, the semiotic user of space identifies significations in space by selecting, organising and interpreting signs, thus literally re-constituting the external space internally. Reconstructed space is invested by its consumer with cultural values, constituting part of the consumer's ideology. In this manner, there is an active involvement with space achieved through semiotic labour, a labour of investing signs in space intellectually and emotionally; this process leads to the appropriation and recuperation of space or to its rejection (Lagopoulos 1996: 594–595).

Let us now look at the possible interactions between A and B. Saussure presents a kind of additive model of communication. A addresses B, then B addresses A, and so on. We shall not dwell on the fact that frequently both A and B may speak partly at the same time. What should be noted is that Saussure's model does not show us the possible *dialogical* connection, or degrees of closeness, between A and B, particularly in the sense of the interference of B in the production of A's message. B and A remain external to each other. This is the most distant of the possible interactions of B with A, but there are two other types of interaction which bring B successively closer to A. We can describe these three types of interaction as follows:

(a) *Distant non-participatory interaction*. B remains external to the structure of the message. Distant interaction occurs, for example, with films or traditional theatrical performances. Here, we can distinguish two types of message structure: the structure of the performance (the actual message) and its background structure, the initial text on which the performance is based. The audience may have some influence on the actual message, as when an enthusiastic audience encourages a better performance, but no matter how great the psychological involvement of the public may be, it remains outside the play or film and does not alter the structure of the initial text of the production.

(b) *Closer participatory interaction*. B remains external to the initial structure but interferes with the performance of the message. An example of this would be contemporary participatory theatre. Avant-garde theatre since the 1960s has been oriented towards the idea of an open and participatory work. Toward the end of this decade, a play entitled *1789* (the year of the French Revolution) was staged in Paris by the company of Ariane Mnouchkine. The work had a definite plot, but in certain scenes the theatre-goers were called on stage (or the actors would mingle with the audience) to make them participate in the play as "the French people". However, in spite of the different dynamics of the audience of each particular performance, only surface elements of the play were altered, because the addressees did not have access during the performance to the initial structure of the message, which remained unaltered.

An extreme case of such participation is exemplified by ritual performances, where, as we saw, there is complete participation on the part of the addressees in the production of the message, since the addressee coincides with the actual addresser, but in each case the structure of the message remains, and metaphysically must remain, unaltered (as it was initially formulated by the ultimate addresser), that is, each particular performance must be a faithful copy of the initial divine text.

(c) *Dialogical interaction.* B interferes with the initial structure of the message. In the case of the play discussed above, we observed that the addressees did not have access to the structure of the message *during the performance*. They could, however, influence the structure *before* the actual performance, during the very composition of the message, an issue we shall examine immediately below.

The interactive presence of the addressee in the message produced by the addresser is convincingly demonstrated by Bakhtin. Writing about poetry as one case of aesthetic production, he observes that the real addressee ("listener"), in the sense of belonging to the addresser's own social group, is an immanent participant and intrinsic factor in the poetic message, independently of the poet's intention. Bakhtin tries to distinguish between this addressee and another kind of addressee, the reading public. He relates the latter to the capitalist supply-and-demand economy, which as he sees it "regulates" writers, and influences them in a conscious and external manner. The poet's vulnerability to this social group, which is for Bakhtin foreign to the poet, influences the message intrinsically, degrades the artistic quality of the message and divorces the poet from the actual listener and his own social group. If we ignore the rather elitist dichotomy between a "pure" and a "contaminated" addressee, we would like to retain the interactive presence of the addressee – an addressee who thus has a double aspect for Bakhtin – in the addresser.

For Bakhtin, the utterances produced by poets, their "external speech", should be in harmony with their "inner speech" (a concept closely related to that of ideology, see Model 11 below), which is itself a product of their whole social life (Model 14 below and chapter 9: 2 and 3). The true artistic message springs from this background, as do other forms besides poetry, each of them preserving its uniqueness. Every utterance in natural language, verbal or written, in everyday communication is for Bakhtin the product of an interaction between the addresser and the addressee, a process of social interaction in which all of social life becomes an intrinsic factor (Bakhtin 1989: see, for example, 393–395, 401, 408–409).

Quite independently from Bakhtin's purism, he prophetically foresaw the extreme vulnerability of cultural production to capitalism, a pressure which was already felt before the recent integration of the whole of culture into the movement of capital but which really took off with the new possibilities offered by the Internet. In the fields of cinema and television, communities of fans – i.e., consumers – entertain a continuous, multimedia dialogue with the production companies around a particular audiovisual work. These networks have been called "joint brand management" (Petridis 2019) and the audiovisual brand communities created mark a new kind of "participatory culture". What is of direct interest to the present model is that the fan communities influence the nature of the characters and interact with or even alter the plot narrative: the fans invested Jon Snow with a noble pedigree in the television drama series *Game of thrones* and pressured the latest sequel to *Ghostbusters* to follow the canon and return to the male heroes of 1984 (Petridis 2019).

2.4 Model 4: Communication through objects

Saussure's circuit is a linguistic one, i.e., A and B interact verbally, more specifically orally. Manifestly we may imagine a case in which A and B interact in writing, exchanging notes or letters. Oral and written communication both constitute verbal communication, and verbal communication is one of the three fundamental systems of communication for Lévi-Strauss; for both Lévi-Strauss and Greimas and Courtés, verbal communication is one form of the more general communication between subjects, the other form being, for Greimas and Courtés, the *transfer of objects* of value.

For an object to become communicative, it must first be semantised. The semantisation of use objects is clearly described by Barthes (1964a: 106), who observes that *"dès qu'il y a société, tout usage est converti en signe de cet usage"* [as soon as society exists, every usage is converted into a sign of that usage]. For Barthes, such a sign is a "sign-function", which we can understand as a sign whose substance of expression is not primarily related to signification, but serves utilitarian and functional aims and fulfils material functions. For him, the systems composed of such signs are used by society to signify in a derivative way.

This view of the signifying dimension of use systems constitutes the foundation of Eco's architectural semiotics. For Eco, architectural objects are primarily functional – that is, non-signifying, material objects – but by this very fact they also secondarily become vehicles of signification – that is, they are transformed into material *culture* – and constitute a communication system (Eco 1972: 262–266, 269, 271, 295). In fact use objects, functional as they are, are material objects and display their materiality, a fact distinguishing them from signs, which are also anchored in the material world through their substance of expression, but which do not foreground this materiality.

Between these two extremes of communication – on the one hand, the use of spoken language for the simple exchange of messages without further intellectual or artistic elaboration, and on the other communication as a by-product of the semantisation of use objects – lie all other modes of communication. We have already made reference to many of them and we shall now focus, based on Greimas's account (Greimas 1983: 19–48; also Greimas and Courtés 1979: Don, Échange), on communication through objects of value (including humans), which may be of very different nature but are always axiologically invested.

Greimas does not analyse real-life situations but a corpus of narratives. We can see, however, both from his text and contextual evidence, that he extrapolates the basic patterns he finds to real-life situations. For Greimas, magical objects, goods or services are invested with collective or individual cultural values, which are values for some subject. A narrative is a transformation or a series of transformations that start with a specific relation of a Subject to an Object of value and conclude with a different relation between them; the relation may be described as either conjunction or disjunction, two opposed terms of the same semantic category.

These transformations, which form the foundation of the Greimasian narrative model, follow from the transfer of objects of value, which constitute the Greimasian model of communication. The subjects involved in the transformations may be considered as participating in an act of communication, and thus as occupying the positions A and B. Narrative discourse can thus be seen as a sequence of communicative acts. Greimas observes that he uses the term communication in a very wide sense, allowing it to cover all cases of relationships between human or humanised Subjects; the value through which this relationship is achieved is an "exchange value".

Greimas formulates four cases of communication through only one Object:
(a) *appropriation*: the acquisition of an Object by a Subject disjoined from it, through the Subject's own action;
(b) *attribution*: the acquisition of the Object through the mediation of another Subject (who is also a Subject of doing);
(c) *renunciation*, deprivation of the Object with the consent of the Subject; and
(d) *dispossession*: deprivation of the Object through the action of another Subject.

Cases (a) and (d) are called by Greimas "tests" and (b) and (c) "gifts". There may be reciprocal gifts involving the same object, in which case gift and counter-gift coincide. There can also be cases in which gift and counter-gift are not identical but equivalent, and then they belong to an exchange circuit of communication. Leach (1976: 6), formulating the anthropological view on the gift and drawing on Marcel Mauss's classical study, points out that the sense of reciprocal obligation created through gift communication is the expression of a common feeling of belonging to the same society.

Greimas also examines the case of the transfer of two objects of value, which he feels is comparable to the previous case in that it consists of two operations of transfer. It is a structure of exchange, a reciprocal operation which now involves a double performance; it presents two aspects, both of which presuppose the conjunction of a Subject with an Object and the disjunction of the latter from a different Subject. Exchange follows the implicit or explicit establishment of a contract and therefore involves a Sender and a Recipient, whence his conclusion that the canonical narrative schema follows the structure of the exchange, in other words of communication in its widest sense.

Finally, Greimas discusses the case of "participatory communication", in which the attribution of an Object to a Recipient–addressee does not imply its renunciation on the part of the Sender–addresser and the Object still remains in conjunction with him or her. This may happen, for example, with the transfer of knowledge or of inexhaustible magical objects. In the case of knowledge, the transfer to the addressee of the knowledge of the addresser in verbal communication, i.e., the conjunction of the addressee with a verbal object of value, leads to a sharing without deprivation of the addresser, that is, without their disjunction from the Object.

On the basis of the above, it becomes clear that verbal communication is just one kind of communication and that communication may be achieved through all the means existing in a society (even through what Lévi-Strauss called the exchange of women).

Jacques Fontanille and Nicolas Couégnas criticize this approach (2018: 35–38, 45–46). They argue that Greimas's canonical schema is Eurocentric and confining and adopt the view that exchange is not the only form of social relations. They focus on these relations and their properties and argue that Subjects, Objects and values are not given *a priori*, but constituted at a later moment from a previous network of interactions. This perspective repeats the order of manifestation ruling the generative trajectory according to the semiotics of passions (chapter 7: 2). As to the widening of the anthropological horizons concerning relations in society – a widening accomplished by Marx long ago – no epistemological argument is presented why a theory of narrative should reproduce anthropological theory.

On a more concrete level, the criticism of Fontanille and Couégnas is addressed to the statistically dominant patterns of the canonical schema and ignores its potential for application to less familiar cases, something we can also see from the analysis of cooperatives discussed in the previous chapter (7: 3). However, they offer a fresh view when they point out a kind of conflation between competence, performance and sanction (214), which in the canonical model are three distinct stages of the narrative structure. The issue emerges from real-life situations, but it is possible that such a pattern may appear in a narrative. The use by Fontanille and Couégnas of the concepts of "competence", "performance" and "sanction" demonstrates that these dimensions were useful for their analysis, something that shows that their approach is structurally founded on canonical narrative theory, but offers a possibility of enlarging it – not refuting it – by adding possible variants, thus making it more flexible.

2.5 Model 5: The channel of communication and signification

We know that the form of a message can remain the same while the substance of expression, that is, the material part of the message as the vehicle of the form of expression, can vary. The material, the ontological substance to which the substance of the expression belongs, defines the channel of communication. That channel may be simple, as in the case of sound waves, painting or sculpture, or composite, involving the transformation of one substance into another, as in the case of radio or television transmissions, in which case the final substance becomes the substance of the expression, that is, of the sensible message reaching the addressee.

We could make the argument that, in the case of humans, the definition of the channel should be extended to include not only Saussure's physical process, but also his physiological processes. There are also other such processes in the human organism, such as the functioning of the human senses (Moles and Zeltmann 1973: 123, 132–133). The physiological study of these channels falls outside the interests of semiotics, but of course the messages communicated through them are as much an object of semiotics as verbal messages are.

We may distinguish three broad categories of channels. The first includes *natural* channels, such as sound waves, electromagnetic waves or the above physiological processes; the second *artificial* channels, constituted by technological systems, such as the telephone (functioning on the basis of electromagnetic waves); and the third cultural channels, such as the imaginary channels of the sacrifice. Cultural channels can be studied through direct semiotic analysis, while natural and artificial channels are not generally suitable for semiotic analysis. There are, however, exceptions, which require a widening of mainstream semiotic research.

Given that the field of semiotics proper is the universe of meaning, it usually does not deal with the materiality of the channel. However, the materiality of the channel, its ontological substance, may place constraints on both planes of the form of the message or enrich them; in either case, it does not leave the form unaltered. The ontological substance, natural or artificial, may have an impact on the nature of the substance of expression, resulting in the production of connotations. This becomes apparent in the case of sculpture, for example, where the natural properties of the material, including its volume and texture, may have an essential influence on the message, including its aesthetics. The same statue has a different meaning if it is carved in marble, in wood or in grey stone.

Eco, writing about iconic messages, identifies this dimension with his "transmission codes", such as the grain of a photograph, a characteristic of its ontological aspect. Eco observes that the role of such transmission codes is not limited to simple perception, studied by information theory, but they have an impact on the aesthetics of the image – that is, on its connotative level. He adds that they influence the "tonal codes", such as "power" and "tension", which he considers suprasegmental features, and established systems of connotation, such as "graceful" or "expressionist" (Eco 1972: 215). Such significations are an indication of the essential difference between semiotics and information theory, because for information theory, a quality such as the grain of a photograph not only does not constitute part of the message, but is considered as a noise in the message that should be eliminated.

When sending a message, the addresser may use redundancy for the sake of clarity or for rhetorical reasons. But they may also have recourse to redundancy as a way to counteract semiotic *noise*, which causes a loss of information. Noise may appear during encoding or decoding, but it may also be an effect of the channel itself. In information theory it is defined on a strictly technical level, but it can be given a wider definition in semiotics (for example damage to a painting).

The concept of noise may be extended to cover phenomena such as the loss of known information, that is, information which the addresser is conscious of, but certain internal or external factors prevent it from being accurately formulated, received or interpreted. It could also be extended, admittedly in a loose way, to account for resistance to information which is considered objectionable or incomprehensible, more specifically information which for social or semiotic reasons (which function as noise in a very wide sense) is not acceptable or cannot be conceptualised by some addressees. Comparable issues will be discussed in relation to Model 10.

We should not underestimate the importance of channels in communication. Certain senses are physiologically privileged compared to others and a particular sense may dominate culturally; they are also related to technologies which may have an impact on culture. An obvious example are the views of Marshal McLuhan, who sees technological media (alphabetic writing, the printing press, electronic media) as the extension of our senses and functions. For him, the media and the modes of our relation to them are much more important than the messages produced through them, whence his fundamental idea that, more than the message, the nature of the medium itself subconsciously shapes our ideas (McLuhan and Fiore 1967: 8, 40–41, 125). This approach, then, relates the technology of the channel directly to ideas (the semiotic) through the physiological channel of the senses. Interpreting McLuhan, the focus is not the specific technology of the channel, the message carried by it or the physiological processes as such, but their receptor sense, for example the cultural predominance of vision, as the mediator for the shaping of ideas which in turn alter social organisation.

The relation between technology and the shaping of ideas has concerned semiotics. It has been argued, in this line of thought, that the new possibilities offered by television for the annihilation and conflation of space and time (quick alteration and collage of images relating to quite different geographical settings and historical periods) present a fragmented, eclectic and technically constructed world in which the actual referents disappear in favour of semiotic constructs. This world of *simulacra*, to use Baudrillard's term, is central to the views of postmodernism.

Baudrillard's basic argument is that the functional nature of objects is an illusion and their existence as referents is a cultural myth. The real object, the referent of the sign, is just part of lived experience. Denotative meaning does not refer to any reality, but is in fact the most subtle and ideological form of connotation (Baudrillard 1972: 8, 60, 185–186, 191–194).

According to Baudrillard, until recently the object was a sign heavily loaded with signification by people, but today people no longer project themselves psychologically and mentally into objects. Today is the era of the *simulacrum*, in which simulation does not refer to a (supposed) referent, but generates a reality through models of the real, transforming it into the hyperreal. In the era of the *simulacrum*, of the "hyperrealism of simulation", reality is dissolved and artificially contained within sign systems, the signs of the real substituting for the (supposed) real. Previously, the signification with which an object was loaded was experienced as metaphor, but now this signification is projected into reality without being felt as metaphorical, resulting in the replacement of reality with a simulation of it.

We are living in the "'protean' era of networks". All other functions are effaced by the function of communication, and all spaces and scenes vanish under information. The ultimate instrument of communication in the new era is television, because through the televised image our body and its environment are transformed into a terminal of multiple networks, into a screen (this situation is even more obvious in the case of computer-generated virtual space). According to Baudrillard, television is today the central tool for the shaping of our worldview (Baudrillard 1981 and 1992: 151–153, 155).

Model 4 above led us from the specific issue of communication to a large-scale generalisation, since we concluded that the canonical narrative schema is adapted to the structure of communication. The present model leads us to the perspective of another large-scale generalisation, namely that the communication channel may contribute to the nature of the messages it transmits at its end-point to shape the most general level of signification, that belonging to Foucault's *épistémè*. The views held by McLuhan and Baudrillard on the channel of communication converge in that the channel is the very factor shaping the *épistémè* of our historical period, an overstatement in the tradition of American technological materialism which nevertheless includes a portion of truth.

2.6 Model 6: Jakobson's functions of language and the message

Starting from information theory, Jakobson elaborated a famous model of the factors in any act of verbal communication (Jakobson 1963: 213–220), which can be generalised for any kind of communication. There are six factors. Saussure's A is the "addresser" and B the "addressee", and A is sending a "message" to B through a "channel". The message takes place in a "context", refers to a "referent" (the signification it is intended to convey), and requires a "code" wholly or partially known to A and B. The transmission of the message presupposes a double contact between A and B: a physical channel and a psychological connection. These factors are shown in plain letters in Figure 43.

To each of these factors corresponds a different function of the message, shown in italics in Figure 43. Jakobson clarifies that it is difficult to find messages having only one of these linguistic functions. A single message usually has more than one function, but one is predominant, creating a hierarchy of functions leading to a typology of messages. The verbal structure of a message follows mainly from its predominant function. This is an interesting point, because it correlates the internal structure of a message with its external functions, thus articulating textual analysis with the communicational function. It

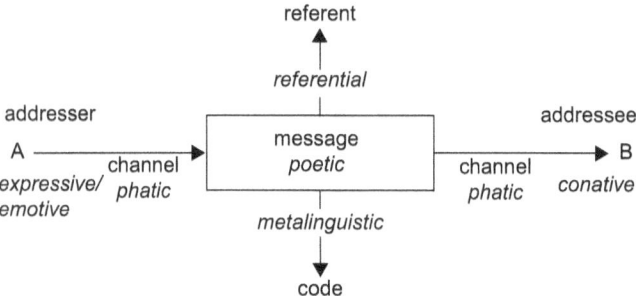

Figure 43: The factors and functions of the message according to Jakobson. Plain letters: factors of communication. Letters in italics: functions of the message.

is actually a sociolinguistic view, pioneered in the West by Jakobson in the essay referred to above (first published in 1960), and a few years later taken up by sociolinguists (see chapter 3: 12), among them Dell Hymes, who as we saw explicitly refers to Jakobson's functions.

The orientation of a message towards the referent results in the "referential" function (we may add that the effect of this function on the message is to focus on denotation).

The "expressive" or "emotive" function is oriented towards manifesting the attitude of the addresser *vis-à-vis* their message, and is thus centred on the addresser. It communicates an emotion, real or faked. Jakobson tells the story of an actor auditioning for the theatre director Constantin Stanislavski; Stanislavski asked him to create forty different messages from the expression "Tonight". The actor made a list of forty emotional situations and then rendered them with different phonic forms – manifestly of a suprasegmental nature – of the phrase. The effect of this function on the message is to load it with connotation.

Orientation towards the addressee creates the "conative" function, finding expression, for instance, in the imperative. This function may be addressed either to the intellect (in the case of military commands, for example) or to the sentiment of the addressee (see also Guiraud 1971: 11); we may add that it is expressed either on the denotative level or through connotative investments. In magic, writes Jakobson, a conative message is addressed to an absent or inanimate "person", a kind of communication that we have already discussed.

One of the aims of the conative function is persuasion. Persuasion, according to Eco, functions not only on the conscious level but also on that of the subconscious. Speaking generally about the iconic message, he refers to "codes of the unconscious"; such codes structure the components of the image, the visual signifiers, the denotative and connotative signifieds, the argumentation and rhetorical figures and the stylistic aspect; they are attached culturally to psychological situations, allow specific projections, lead to identifications through the image and stimulate specific (pragmatic) actions (Eco 1972: 217, 241–242, 252, 256–257).

Another function of the message follows from an orientation towards the channel and aims at establishing, maintaining or interrupting communication. That is, the aim of this function is to verify that the communication circuit is functioning (for example "Hello" when answering the telephone), attract the attention of the addressee ("Have you heard what happened to so-and-so?"), secure that communication will continue ("Mmm" at the other end of the line) or end communication ("Go to hell"). Such messages have a "phatic" function, a term Jakobson borrowed from the anthropologist Bronislaw Malinowski. The function centres on the channel of communication itself.

The phatic function is very central, as Pierre Guiraud (1971: 12) notes, in many modes of communication, such as communication between lovers or rites and ceremonies, where it is important to stress the belonging to a group. We can think of the way a fairytale starts: "Once upon a time [. . .]", indicating a particular form of communication, or the refrains of poems and songs, where repetition, in addition to creating an aesthetic rhythm, emphasises continuity and the unity of the message as a whole. A good example is Edgar Allan Poe's poem *Annabel Lee*. Below, we emphasise with italics the parts of the poem relevant to the phatic function:

> It was many and many a year ago,
>   In a *kingdom by the sea*,
> That a maiden there lived whom you may know
>   By the name of *Annabel Lee*;
> And this maiden she lived with no other thought
>   Than to love and be loved by me.
>
> I was a child and she was a child,
>   In this *kingdom by the sea*,
> But we loved with a love that was more than love –
>   I and my *Annabel Lee* –
> With a love that the wingèd seraphs of Heaven
>   Coveted her and me.
>
> And this was the reason that, long ago,
>   In this *kingdom by the sea*,
> A wind blew out of a cloud, chilling
>   My beautiful *Annabel Lee*;
> So that her highborn kinsmen came
>   And bore her away from me,

> To shut her up in a sepulchre
>   In this *kingdom by the sea*.
>
> The angels, not half so happy in Heaven,
>   Went envying her and me –
> Yes! – that was the reason (as all men know,
>   In this *kingdom by the sea*)
> That the wind came out of the cloud by night,
>   Chilling and killing my *Annabel Lee*.
>
> But our love it was stronger by far than the love
>   Of those who were older than we –
>   Of many far wiser than we –
> And neither the angels in Heaven above
>   Nor the demons *down under the sea*
> Can ever dissever my soul from the soul
>   Of the beautiful *Annabel Lee*;
>
> For the moon never beams, without bringing me dreams
>   Of the beautiful *Annabel Lee*;
> And the stars never rise, but I feel the bright eyes
>   Of the beautiful *Annabel Lee*;
> And so, all the night-tide, I lie down by the side
>   Of my darling – my darling – my life and my bride,
> In *her sepulchre there by the sea* –
>   In *her tomb by the sounding sea*.

The poem has six stanzas, with six to eight lines per stanza, and in every stanza we find repeated the rhyming phrases "(kingdom) by the sea" and the name "Annabel Lee", frequently more than once in the same stanza, so that these expressions function as internal refrains binding the poem together. In the last two stanzas, especially in the last, the repetition becomes more insistent and small variations are introduced ("the demons *down under* the sea [. . .] In *her sepulchre there* by the sea [. . .] In *her tomb by the sounding* sea") that signal the closing of the poem. These repetitions give the poem a double rhythm; in addition, their end words rhyme (Lee–sea), an echoing that critics have considered "hypnotic".

The two repeated phrases represent two major isotopies of the poem. "Annabel Lee" is the central one, as the poem's title shows, and also the richest, embracing a number of figurative elements (maiden, highborn, ensouled, love, beauty, bride, illness, death) on the discursive level. It is a personal name (onomastics), as the "kingdom by the sea" is a toponym.[101] The "kingdom by

---

[101] The "many and many a year ago" of the opening line situates the events of the poem in the past, but does not specify when they occur, so there is no true chrononym.

the sea" is actually composed of two isotopies ("kingdom" and "sea") that generally only appear in this phrase; they are very slightly developed, though the "highborn kinsmen" can be seen as elaborating the notion of "kingdom" and the "sea" is given further elaboration as the home of demons and as the location of the sepulchre where Annabel Lee is buried.

In the discussion of isotopies in chapter 5, we presented isotopies of both the plane of content and the plane of expression. In the two repeated phrases of Poe's poem we find a combination of isotopies of content and of expression as a result not only of the rhyme, but also of the transformation of the content into an acoustic pattern, a kind of transformation that can be generalised to all refrains.

We have already examined rhythm as one of the suprasegmental features, and we connected it to the iteration of acoustic patterns of stressed and unstressed sounds and to alliteration. We see now that the iteration of isotopies in *Annabel Lee* is also an iteration of acoustic patterns, hence a rhythmic one created by an internal refrain; rhythm can also be created through verbal units (such as refrains) greater than suprasegmental features. Simultaneously, however, the two isotopies have a phatic function, because they repeatedly ascertain that the channel of the message remains open during the whole poem and thus secure the continuity and unity of the message, its homogeneity.

Thus, the phatic function may fulfil three different tasks: it acts as an opening for a text; it can mark the continuity of the text; and it can define its closure, as is the case with the small variations of ". . . by the sea" at the end of *Annabel Lee*.

The next function of the message that Jakobson identifies is due to an orientation towards the code. This is the "metalinguistic" function. Jakobson considers metalanguage as a scientific language applied to an object-language – which coincides with Hjelmslev's definition – but argues that it is also frequent in everyday language, appearing every time the addresser or the addressee wants to verify if they are making use of the same code; he also mentions the process of language learning, mainly by children. We can add the case of clarifications during a discussion that do not refer to elements of the code but to the issues discussed. For example, if we say to someone "The city centre needs to be upgraded", they may ask "What do you mean by the city centre", and we may answer "I mean the area from the rail terminal in the west to the airport in the east and from the hills in the south to the courthouse in the north", then we have used a metalanguage. In other words, the metalinguistic function does not follow only from an orientation to the code, i.e., *langue*, but also from one to the discursive content of the message, i.e., *parole*. Metalanguage is essentially of a denotative nature, though it may also comment on a connotative discourse or may be itself invested with connotations.

Finally, the orientation towards the message as such produces the "poetic" (aesthetic) function, always loading the message with connotations. As we saw, for Jakobson a message rarely if ever has only one function, and the poetic function may appear in non-poetic messages. He gives as example the old political slogan "I like Ike" and observes that it consists of three monosyllable words, all of which include the diphthong [aɪ] ("*I líke Íke*"); each diphthong is followed by a consonant and the first word has no consonant, the second has one consonant on both sides of the diphthong and the third has one consonant at the end. He points out that the second and third word rhyme with each other (-ike) and the first and third alliterate ("I"). Finally, he identifies two paronomastic images: of the two words that rhyme, the third word ("Ike"), is completely incorporated within the second ("like"), expressing the feeling of a subject that totally incorporates its object, and among the two alliterating words, the first word ("I") is included in the third ("Ike"), showing the wish of the loving subject to be incorporated in the beloved object.

Jakobson's conclusion is both that the linguistic analysis of the poetic function must be extended beyond poetry, and that the linguistic analysis of poetry cannot be limited to the poetic function. He adds that in poetry the poetic function predominates, but other functions are also in play, in variable hierarchical order depending on the poetic genre. This view, controversial even today in some philosophical circles, liberates us to seek in a work of art the other elements constituting it beyond aesthetics. We note, however, that while the poetic function implies the elaboration of a message for its own sake, the reverse is not necessarily the case, i.e., such elaboration does not always imply poeticity, because, as Hymes (1974: 23) remarks, editing a book or correcting proofs are also forms of elaboration of a message for its own sake.

Greimas and Courtés believe that Jakobson's functions are partial, focusing only on the transmission of information and not generalisable to semiotic systems other than natural language. They observe that communication includes not only "informative doing", but also "persuasive doing" and "interpretative doing".[102] As they state, informative doing is about the transmission of knowledge, while the goal of persuasive doing is to make the addressee accept something proposed by the addresser, and interpretative doing is the semiotic labour on the part of the addressee on the message received (Model 3 above) – Greimas and Courtés 1979: Cognitif, Communication, Faire, Informatif (faire), Interprétatif (faire), Persuasif (faire), Pragmatique.

---

[102] These three forms of doing together constitute "cognitive doing", which in turn is one of two kinds of doing, the other being "pragmatic doing" (Model 12 below).

We cannot agree with Greimas and Courtés about the lack of persuasive doing in Jakobsons's model, because persuasion is an essential aim of the conative function. On the other hand, they are right about the lack of interpretative doing, because Jakobson's model is a non-interactive, one-way model, which however does not make it any less valid (nor does the criticism of Greimas and Courtés have such an intention). As to their argument that Jakobson's model is not generalisable to other semiotic systems, once more we do not think that they are vindicated. A convincing generalisation of Jakobson's functions is given by Eco in a discussion of the semiotic system of advertising and also, more briefly, of a semiotic system very different from natural language, namely architecture (Eco 1972: 235–257, note p. 271).

Eco points out the close connection in advertising between persuasion, argumentation, rhetoric, connotation and consumer ideology. He emphasises that the main function of advertising is persuasion, mainly in its emotional aspect (the appeal to the sentiment of the addressee), but also in its imperative aspect (the appeal to the intellect), both of which correspond to the conative function.[103] He also points out that the most important component of the advertising message after persuasion is the aesthetic, corresponding to Jakobson's poetic function. In fact, this component is obvious in most elaborated advertisements, often in the form of an aesthetic composition or the image of a beautiful woman (frequently combined with a connotation of sexuality). For example, the Unilever company, producing cosmetics and toiletries, has advertised its Lux soap using prominent actresses, from the Indian Leela Chitnis in 1929 to the Italian Rosanna Podesta in 1963 to Scarlett Johansson more recently.

Eco's views verify Jakobson's position about the reflection of the hierarchy of functions in the type of the message. In his discussion of advertising he mentions almost all of Jakobson's functions, including the phatic (though in a rather farfetched manner), the metalinguistic and the referential, but it is clear that they are secondary to the conative and the poetic. Advertising certainly makes use of the referential function, as we can see from a 2009 Volkswagen advertisement, which consists of a picture of a very small car and the following text:

> ... In fact, some people who drive our little flivver don't even think 32 miles to the gallon is going any great guns. Or using five pints of oil instead of five quarts. Or never needing

---

103 In his discussion of advertising, Eco takes a bold step from semiotics to social semiotics. He argues that it is not the persuasive nature of the message that persuades the addressee, but persuasion rests on the fact that the proposed objects of consumption are already wanted by the addressee. Advertising does not depend on the possibilities of persuasive discourse, but on economic conditions: it is these conditions that regulate the advertising message.

anti-freeze. Or racking up 40,000 miles on a set of tires. That's because once you get used to some of our economies, you don't even think about them any more. Except when you squeeze into a small parking spot. Or renew your small insurance. Or pay a small repair bill. Or trade in your old VW for a new one. Think it over.

This advertisement gives us plenty of referential information, but envelops it in rhetoric through the repetition of the initial "Or", and both the referential and the poetic functions are integrated by the umbrella of the conative function in its imperative aspect: "Think it over".

Advertising can be directly compared to political discourse in that in both these types of discourse the conative function predominates in both its imperative and emotional aspects. In both types of discourse, the referential function is of secondary importance; it is only activated as an alibi. They differ, however, in their use of the metalinguistic function, which is less frequent in advertising but central in political discourse.

The presence of the poetic function creates a certain overlapping between advertising and poetry, but there are important differences between them. In poetry, the poetic function predominates; in advertising it is second in the hierarchical order of functions. In advertising the conative function predominates; in poetry it comes second and the focus is on its emotional aspect. The poetic function is in advertising simply a means for the conative function to promote an object – and to lead to the very pragmatic goal of purchasing it – while in poetry the poetic function is in itself the goal of the message; thus, the aesthetic plays a very different role in the two cases.

In poetry, the expressive function appears to be at least as important as the conative, the poet being a vibrant addresser, while the advertiser is a cold-blooded executioner, hiding personal emotions as non-relevant to the message. In political discourse the expressive function is also important, but here it is probably secondary to the conative.

Eco also discusses the Jakobsonian functions in relation to architecture. In addition to the aesthetic, he notes that architecture also fulfils the other functions: the conative, both in its emotional aspect – for which he refers to the feeling of calm created by Greek temples and that of excitement created by the Baroque church – and its imperative aspect, because it makes people inhabit space in a certain manner; the phatic, for which he gives as examples arches, tympana and obelisks, as well as recurring elements in urban space; the metalinguistic, shaping the facades of the buildings surrounding a museum so as to convey the message "This building over here is a museum"; and the referential, which is, for him, literally the architectural object itself. However, he shifts from the issue of the referent to the architectural object as signifier of a functional denotative signified, a shift constituting the foundation of Eco's architectural semiotics.

Eco is well aware that architecture is primarily a system of uses, and in this sense the functions of architecture are primarily material, but when discussing the semiotics of architecture he approaches them *sub specie communicationis*. All messages carried by use objects show the same semiotic functions as any other message.

Messages are specific instances of *parole*, the use of semiotic systems, but the systems themselves also have functions. Maurice Godelier (1978: 172–173) mentions four general functions of thought and its representations, in other words of semiotic systems. The first is the *conceptualisation* of things, visible or invisible, material or not, concrete or imaginary, external or internal to humans, that is, the representation of the world in its widest sense. This representation also implies *interpretation*. Representation presupposes signification, and signification involves interpretation. Godelier's conceptualisation and interpretation aim at rendering the way in which social subjects understand the world and situate themselves in it.

The third function is, for Godelier, *organisation*, namely the use of the products of representation and interpretation to conceive ways to organise relationships between people and between people and nature, in the form of principles for action, rules of behaviour, rights, prohibitions, etc. The fourth function of semiotic systems is *legitimation* or *delegitimation* of these relationships.[104]

Godelier's last two functions of the semiotic systems are not limited to the semiotic domain, but have an impact – a new function – on the surrounding extra-semiotic material processes of society.[105] The function of organisation, among other things, establishes symbolic power relations between people which

---

104 We may have the impression that there are parallels between Godelier's first three social semiotic functions and Sebeok's hypothesis of the phylogenetically original function of language. Sebeok argues that language, prior to its development with *homo sapiens* into communicable speech, from the time of the earliest hominids was initially a "mute verbal modelling device" fulfilling the function of modelling the perception of reality. He observes that the survival of an organism depended on the correspondence of the representation achieved through modelling to the species' possible perception of reality and on the alignment of its behavioural resources with this model (Sebeok 1988: 73–77). Sebeok's function of representation, that is, the modelling of reality, might seem to correspond to Godelier's functions of representation and interpretation, and representation's function of guiding behaviour to Godelier's third function of organisation, since it presupposes social action. However, the parallels are of terminology only, because they belong to two different and conflicting paradigms: Sebeok adopts a biological and universalising paradigm, while Godelier a socio-historical one. The only conclusion compatible with Saussurean semiotics is that signification and action are biological capacities of humans.

105 The same processes that Eco encountered in their economic aspect with his analysis of advertising.

reinforce actual social power relations, and the function of legitimation or delegitimation leads to the perpetuation (that is, reproduction) or political contestation of the existing social relations and thus of the *status quo*. These functions are achieved through the medium of everyday communication.

We see that communication is not necessarily neutral, but may – in fact frequently does – involve symbolic power relations, and in these cases the act of communication is simultaneously an act of power, of communication-as-power (Models 11 and 14 below).

2.7 Model 7: The intra-textual contexts of the text

In this and the following model, a text is approached within the framework of communication. Both models concern the context of a text. Greimas and Courtés (1979: Contexte) divide the context into a linguistic context and an extra-linguistic or situational one. We can generalise their linguistic context to any kind of semiotic context, and we shall use the term "situation" for any kind of extra-textual semiotic environment, that is, the semiotic environment surrounding the subjects of communication (Model 10 below). There are two types of context: the "intra-textual context" (or "intra-textual environment") and the "extra-textual semiotic context" (or "extra-textual semiotic environment"). In this section we shall discuss the first type.

A typical form of context is the text that precedes or follows or surrounds a target text; the target text is a part of the initial text, selected for some reason from the latter. The initial text is the intra-textual context of the target text. These two levels of a text are syntagmatically related as part to whole. Examples of this form are the chapters of a book; we might read one chapter of the book each day and thus receive that chapter as a (relatively) isolated target text, but it would still be understood as an integral part of the previous chapters we read, enriched by the active semiotic labour of the reader in the form of extrapolations and anticipations (cf. Iser 1972). This is of course even more true for the author. Target text and intra-textual context are not always as precise as the chapters of a book and the book itself; they are flexible entities, frequently with vague contours, something that shows the relative arbitrariness of their delimitation.

A particular form of relation between text and intra-textual context appears in anthologies and in edited series or complete works of an author (a writer, a poet, a painter). Anthologies collect in a single volume different types of texts – poems, short stories, plays or excerpts from novels – selected according to some criterion, such as theme; often they are organised chronologically, grouping texts according to the period when they were written into a kind of brief history of literature. The mere fact of putting together independent texts in this kind of collection implies for each individual text a new interpretation differing from its interpretation as autonomous text. There is a mutual exchange of signification between texts and between them and their new and common intra-textual context which influences the meaning of each work. From the viewpoint of communication, there is a doubling of the addresser: each individual text has an author-addresser, but the editor of the anthology functions as the final addresser, unifying and thus manipulating a collective set of previous addressers, that is, $A \supseteq \Sigma_A$.

The concept of context also applies at a lower level than that of the target text. We saw earlier in this book that a lexeme, together with its stable nuclear semes, includes the variable classemes, the contextual semes, whose presence creates isotopies running throughout the text. The classemes are a context for the nuclear semes, but their activation depends on the intra-textual context. We can consider the classeme as the "elementary intra-textual context". The variation of classemes is limited and thus the influence of the intra-textual context is constrained within a certain range.

The intra-textual context is not a simple accompaniment of the target text, because the complete understanding of the latter depends on this context. Let us imagine an elevated ground floor flat with an open window on a hot summer night. Two people inside are having an argument. One of them says with bitterness "You know I adore you. Why have you suddenly become so cold and distant? [pause] You're killing me! [pause] Isn't it time we became a real couple?" Someone walking along the street passes under the window in the middle of the discussion and overhears "You're killing me!" – the target text. If they continue walking and do not here the rest of the discussion – the intra-textual context – they might well start wondering if they should call the police. De-contextualisation leads to a poorer understanding of the target text; indeed, dissociation from the context – quoting someone "out of context" – may produce a deliberate distortion of meaning, making it a favourite tactic of politicians and news media.

Forgetting or ignoring the intra-textual context is also important when attempting a scholarly metalinguistic analysis of a text. In his ten-volume classical work *De architectura*,[106] the Roman architect Vitruvius dedicates chapters IV to VII of Book I to urban planning theory. In the central chapter VI, the city is inscribed within a circular windrose, and Vitruvius relates the healthiness of the city environment to the direction of the winds. Modern (Western) analysts read the target text literally and, given their culture, are predisposed to a practical and rational

---

106 Written before 27 BCE; see Vitruvius 1983, 1985.

interpretation. Thus, since the Renaissance, the interpretation given to the Vitruvian city focuses on and is limited to this issue of salubrity.

This is not at all the case if we read the urban target text in its intra-textual context, the complete ten books of *De architectura*. In the two preceding chapters Vitruvius discusses the characteristics of a site and makes reference to topography and pastures (corresponding to the cosmic element "earth"), to fog, frost and marshes ("water"), to heat ("fire"), and to breezes ("air"). This correspondence follows from the fact that he presents and adopts the Greek theory of the four cosmic elements (IV: 9–12), which he also considers as ingredients of all living organisms, whose characteristics are determined by the mixture of the elements according to precise mathematical proportions varying with the nature of the organism.

This context, which precedes chapter VI, shows that wind is not, for Vitruvius, simply a natural element, but also and mainly a cosmological element. This isotopy is corroborated in chapter VI, in which he relates the winds to the course of the sun and gives a description of the cosmos identical to the form of his windrose. That is, the windrose as denotation, on which modern readers focus, is simply the vehicle of a deeper, connotative cosmological isotopy.

The idea of proportion, which we encountered in reference to the cosmological elements, has already been introduced by Vitruvius in connection with a totally different issue. In chapter II of Book I, he establishes his fundamental architectural concepts, based on the Pythagorean concept of *symmetria*. *Symmetria* means the proportional relation of the parts of a work to each other and to the work as a whole. Vitruvius writes in chapter I of Book III that a temple is ruled by *symmetria*, which also rules the relations between the bodily members of a normally shaped man; man was shaped by nature according to the rules of *symmetria*. Architectural *symmetria*, directly borrowed from ancient Greece, is the foundation of whatever kind of aesthetics we may attribute to Vitruvius.

We learn from chapter I of Book X that all machines are constructed having nature as their model and their principles derive from the rotation of the universe. In chapters X and XI of the same book, Vitruvius mentions that scorpions (a torsion catapult) and ballistae are ruled by *symmetria*. For Vitruvius, the cosmos, nature, the four elements, the human body and all human constructions are ruled by numbers and proportions, i.e., *symmetria*; the mathematical and the cosmological isotopy are inextricably linked.

This concept is the key to understanding Vituvius's urban planning proposal. This connection is not revealed in chapter VI of Book I, but becomes manifest if we turn to his description of the relation between temple and body. He writes that, if a man lies on his back with hands and legs spread diagonally, and we consider his navel as the centre of a circle, the circumference of this circle will pass from the extremities of his fingers and toes. But also, writes Vitruvius, we discover a square: the height from the soles of the feet to the top of the head is equal to the width of the outstretched hands. Here, Vitruvius establishes an implicit relation of equivalence between these two geometrical figures, the circle and the square, and the body, vehicle of *symmetria*, is inscribed within these two "perfect" geometrical figures.

It is precisely these perfect figures that are involved in Vitruvius's planning proposal. His city has a square plan (not a radial-concentric one[107]) inscribed within the circular windrose. The Vitruvian windrose-cum-city is the product of *symmetria* and concentrates major isotopies of classical antiquity: mathematics, cosmology, the body, salubrity and beauty.

In conclusion, our target text, chapter VI of Book I, does contain the most precise technical description of the Vitruvian city, but if we read it in isolation, it traps us within denotation and the salubrity isotopy. However, if we read it in the intra-textual context of the whole work, we see that this practical (and substantial) aim is not autonomous, because it is a by-product of a superior reality, hidden in connotation, which establishes the grounds for its efficacy. We do not have access to this hidden reality if we do not pass from the target text of chapter VI to the intra-textual context of the other chapters of Book I and the other books of *De architectura*. Then, we realise that the natural winds are indeed salubrious when they are well-balanced in their relation to the city and its inhabitants, but this takes place when the cosmic element "air" is in equilibrium, that is, when it is ruled by *symmetria*. This equilibrium is achieved within Vitruvius's cosmic city, which offers a well-balanced background founded on *symmetria*, the external and practical effects of which is protection from excessive winds. Protection allows a site and an organism to be healthy – it allows the equilibrium of cosmic "air" – and is achieved by tracing the avenues and alleys of the city according to specific directions. The city is the reflection of, and a part of the workings of, the cosmos (for the above, see Lagopoulos 2009).

2.8 Model 8: The extra-textual contexts of the text: Intertextuality

The second type of context, the extra-textual context, is related to a text through intertextuality, a term derived from Bakhtin. No text appears by parthenogenesis; every text draws elements from a pool of texts external to it, elements which then become integral parts of it. Intertextuality is a process of enrichment of a text, a

---

[107] This was the *doxa* concerning the Vitruvian city plan from the Renaissance until recently.

process that expands its boundaries. It creates a paradigmatic relation between the recipient text and the source text, and may appear within the same semiotic system or between different semiotic systems. It is present in all semiotic systems, and myths, folktales, literature or cinema offer rich examples of it. The concept re-emerged in the late 1960s in the circle of the journal *Tel Quel*, where Julia Kristeva was on the editorial board and which published work by many distinguished structuralists, semioticians and poststructuralists.

Greimas and Courtés give a quite narrow definition of intertextuality, trying to avoid the vague concept of influence. They consider that it appears as a function of the processes of reproducing, transforming or building more or less implicit models internal to particular autonomous semiotics. Having as model Lévi-Strauss, they identify intertextuality with formal correlations and relate it to the typologies of comparatist studies. They do not include in this concept the existence in a text of semantic and/or syntactic structures common to types of discourse such as intra-individual communication, and obviously not the transformations of content within one and the same text (Greimas and Courtés 1979: Intertextualité).

Barthes in his poststructuralist phase relates intertextuality to the idea of the death of the author. Writing in 1968, he takes the position that a text does not express a specific meaning (a "theological" meaning, as he calls it) created by a "Writer–God", but is a multidimensional space characterised by the mixture of a multiplicity of writings emanating from innumerable cultural centres, no one of which is original. This textual space is not, according to Barthes, the close formal space of one of the currents of structuralism (structuralist analysis), but the object of its other current, the space of "significance" (*signifiance*), that of the text as production in process and flexible structuration connected to other texts. Barthes here takes up the view of Derrida, discussed below, that intertextuality makes the text. For him, the only contribution of the author is the fact that he or she mixes writings, without, however, founding their work on any particular writing. The author only ever imitates something that has preceded, which itself is not original. Finally, for Barthes, the idea of decoding a text is illusory, given that a text consists of a multiplicity of texts, the author is erased and only the reader constitutes the text as a whole (Barthes 1988a: 170–171 and 1988b: 172–174).

We saw in Model 2 that when the position of the addresser is empty (when $A = 0$) there can be signification, but no message and no communication. But the texts to which Barthes refers are objects of communication and thus messages, and their existence is not possible without an addresser, that is, always $A \neq 0$. Position A cannot be totally inactive, with all the semiotic labour attributed to B and only B. If we follow Barthes, the text that A creates is a kind of compilation, but it is nonetheless a unique and thus original text, and, since it is not meaningless in itself, it is by definition loaded with meaning that may be flexible or fragmented, but not chaotic.

Derrida pushes the interpretation of intertextuality to the extreme, integrating it within his highly abstract deconstruction. For him, as we saw, signification arises from differential effects running through the totality of semiotic systems, differences produced by the structuring process of "differance" (*différance*, or *gramme*). We have also seen that for Saussure, on the very abstract level of value, since any element of the linguistic system is constituted by the traces in it of the other absent elements of the system, the element itself is not actually present. Derrida extends this pattern of structuring of the linguistic elements to the relations between texts, stating that each text is produced by its differential relation to other texts. Because of these interconnections, no text has signification in itself and every text is different from itself before even being posited (Derrida 1972b: 17–18, 28, 37–39, 45–46). This is the extreme conception of intertextuality, every text as a whole following from the differential integration into it of all other texts, but none of them present as a text.

Kristeva adopts Bakhtin's more down-to-earth concept of intertextuality, which she elaborates as follows. She describes the literary text as having three "dimensions": that of the writing of the text (due to the intra-textual author, the enunciator), that of the enunciatee (the reader implied by the text), and, finally, the dimension of connection to other literary texts, chronologically antecedent or contemporary to the recipient text, which constitute its context. As a consequence, the position of poetic discourse – Bakhtin refers to the "word" – is, according to Kristeva, at the intersection of two axes: a horizontal axis connecting the subject of writing with the (implied) reader and a second, vertical axis connecting the text with the relevant literary corpus. Bakhtin conceives of intertextuality as incorporating history and society in a text. Kristeva relates it to the "doubleness" (horizontal and vertical), which she considers as the specificity of poetic language. She classifies all texts into two groups. The first, the "monological" group, includes texts which try to hide the double nature of language, as is the case with scientific and historical texts and realist representational narratives. The texts of the second, "dialogical" group display the multiplicity of intertextuality, as in the polyphonic novel, Menippean satire and the texts that Bakhtin calls "carnivalesque" (Kristeva [1969] 1978: 82–112, 195–196).

Kristeva attributes her idea of the two axes to Bakhtin's two concepts of "dialogue" and "ambiguity", but she believes that he does not differentiate them clearly. She believes that by ambiguity Bakhtin means that every text originates from the absorption and transformation of some other text, and she concludes that this idea should lead to a new science of texts, "translinguistics" which, starting from linguistics, would study intertextuality as a "signifying act" (*acte signifiant*, Kristeva 1978: 84–85). Bakhtin's ambiguity, Barthes's "significance" as a process of production and Kristeva's doubleness of poetic language converge to define the profile of intertextuality.

Through the intersection of her two axes, the poetic signified for Kristeva refers to other signifieds, with the result that it incorporates many discourses, leading to the organisation of a multiple textual space around it. Due to this process of intertextuality, a poetic utterance becomes a subset of a wider set. This is, for her, the locus of the birth of poetry. She uses the Saussurean concept of "paragramme" to indicate this quality of poetic language to absorb a multiplicity of texts. The literary text is not linear but a system with multiple connections, more specifically a structure of paragrammatic networks which can be given the form of a graph. On this basis, she concludes that language creates meaning rather than expressing it (Kristeva 1978: 123, 194–196).

Intertextuality has thus been subject to many different interpretations since its revival as a concept. Barthes's approach is a restatement of Derrida's philosophy and, though interesting theoretically, does not offer any operational guidelines for application. Greimas and Courtés's view is more useful for what it excludes from intertextuality than for what it includes: they exclude trivial forms of repetition and transformations occurring within the same text, and this helps. However, they become extremely severe when, with too strict theoretical criteria, they consider the existence of particular autonomous semiotics and formal correlations as preconditions for intertextuality, thus excessively limiting the possible spectrum of this concept and excluding phenomena at a smaller scale, for which we would need to invent a new name if we cannot consider them as intertextual. Bakhtin, Kristeva and Barthes allow a greater spectrum for intertextuality by considering it as the relation of a text with a multiplicity of texts. However, an intertextual relation can appear, as we shall see, in reference to only one text and even to only one part of it.

We can think of intertextuality as involving three levels of expansion: an "extra-textual context", referring to conscious or subconscious specific borrowings in a recipient text from texts by other addressers; a "wider extra-textual context", from genre and style up to groupings such as literary, political or religious discourse; and the "widest extra-textual context", the whole of culture. In all these cases, when an addresser produces a work, he or she incorporates in it elements they have received in the past as addressees, that is, $\Sigma_A \to B = A$; thus, intertextuality is a case of communication, not between addresser and addressee, but between texts through the intermediary of an addresser. This is an expanded definition of communication.

The simplest level of intertextuality, the extra-textual context, covers two different categories of intertextual phenomena: on the one hand, citation and plagiarism, and on the other re-elaboration, implying transformation. Citation is a literal and explicit relation to a source text, a direct and unaltered transfer from it to the recipient text: their articulation is a passage for an element that remains the same, without transformation of any kind. Plagiarism is also a literal relation, but a concealed one. We shall call the category including citation and plagiarism "citational intertextuality" and focus below on citation, noting that this discussion is also valid for plagiarism. We may distinguish the following four types of citational intertextuality (Table 23):

In the first type (a_1), the recipient text includes one citation or a series of heterogeneous citations from one or more source texts, of a purely local character as regards their extent and range and unrelated to each other. An example of heterogeneous citation in cinema is the use in a recipient text of one or more unconnected scenes from previous films or documentaries (for example the explosion of the atomic bomb in Hiroshima, Marilyn Monroe, the coast of North Africa), without integrating them into a whole. We can consider these cases as the extreme lower limit of citational intertextuality.

In the above example, the citations have a purely local presence, but in the second type of citation (a_2) a series of unrelated citations (some may coincide with the whole of the source text) are connected into a new meaningful whole, independently of the initial meaning of each citation in its original source text. This is the artistic technique of collage, dating from the early 20th century; it is typically found in the visual arts, though there are also collage novels. It consists in the assemblage of heterogeneous borrowings of all sorts (for example, parts of other paintings, photographs, magazine clippings, even objects) with the aim of creating a new artistic whole with its own meaning, marginalising the meaning of the borrowings in their original source. We may consider this type as "free intertextuality".

In the third type of citation (a_3), the source text plays an organic role for the recipient text. In this type, there is a direct connection of the citation with the totality of the recipient text such that the citation functions as a part incorporating the general logic of a whole, or in other words the general meaning of the source text is diffused within the recipient text through that connection. This would be the case, for example, with the incorporation of actual news footage of the assassination of Kennedy into a docu-drama about the events before, during and after the assassination. While this citation has a local character, it marks the whole recipient text, that is, it is diffused throughout the recipient text, connecting it with the totality of the source text and with other similar texts. The borrowed news footage also has a metalinguistic function, stating:

Table 23: Categories and types of intertextuality.

Relation between texts		Recipient text					Source text(s)	
Category of intertextuality	Type of intertextuality	one local	series of local and homogeneous transformations	series of local and heterogeneous transformations	diffusion in recipient text	whole recipient text	local borrowing(s)	total borrowing
Citational	type a_1: lower limit	+					+	
	type a_2: free (collage)			+			+	+
	type a_3: intense	+			+		+	
	type a_4: integrated		+		+		+	
Transformational	type b_1: lower limit	+		+			+	
	type b_2: juxtaposed		+				+	
	type b_3: part to whole	+	+				+	
	type b_4: integrated part to integrated part	+	+				+	
	type b_5: whole to whole		+			+		+
	type b_6: micro-systemic					+		+
	type b_7: macro-systemic					+		+

"This is the main theme". This type of intertextuality is "intense citational intertextuality".

The fourth type (a_4) of citation differs from the previous type only in degree; it consists in a series of homogeneous citations of this kind.[108] The docu-drama concerning Kennedy would now include many citations, scattered throughout the film, multiplying the parts borrowed from news footage. Another example would be a novel beginning each chapter with a half-title in italics, borrowed from one or more source texts; the assumption would be that each half-title reflects in a condensed manner the meaning of the corresponding chapter, and we might also think that each half-title is significantly related to all other half-titles, and each in some way reflects the totality of the novel because of this unity. These relations operate within the recipient text. On the other hand, all the half-titles depend on the external source text or texts, incorporating their meaning to a greater or lesser degree. This is "integrated citational intertextuality".

The second category of intertextuality, re-elaboration, is unlike simple citation in that it implies the transformation of the borrowed element, and transformation involves a reworking, a restructuring that fits the element into its new intra-textual context. This creates a paradigmatic relation, which turns into a connotative relation between the recipient text and its source texts. We shall call this category "transformational intertextuality" (Table 23) and its seven types are discussed below. They do not necessarily appear in isolation and different combinations are possible.

The first type (b_1) of transformational intertextuality is a local semiotic transformation or a series of local heterogeneous juxtaposed transformations in the recipient text from a source text; this type is comparable to the first type of citational intertextuality. The assassination of Kennedy, for example, could be used as a model to recreate a comparable scene in a thriller. Cinema often imitates an impressive shot or scene from a previous film and recomposes it in an explicit or disguised new manner, adapting it to the needs of the new film and changing characters, space and time.

---

108 A parallel phenomenon appears in scientific texts, in which references are made to other scientific authors in order to support or reject a certain argument. We may think, for example, of a book on semiotics which on the page after the title page has the dedication "'*Dans la langue il n'y a que des différences*', F. de Saussure", or, alternatively, at the beginning of each chapter a half-title in italics with a quotation from Saussure. In both cases, the relation of the citations as part to whole of the recipient text and the close relation of the recipient text to Saussure's theory are beyond doubt, the only difference between these two cases being one of degree.

Similar phenomena appear in all semiotic systems. The film *Limelight*, which appeared in 1952, was produced and directed by Charlie Chaplin, who also acted in the film. We discover with some attention that the main musical theme of the film, *Terry's theme*, also known as *Eternally*, is related to Tchaikovsky's piano concerto no. 1 (op. 23).[109] The beginning of the melody of the song reminds us acoustically of the first bars of the theme of the first part of the concerto. Common to both compositions is a series of six comparable notes, with the highest note of longer duration. Chaplin slightly slows the tempo and removes Tchaikovsky's intense rhythmic elements, making the melody more lyrical. The result is that in Chaplin's composition a sort of "echo" is created, which momentarily reminds the listener of Tchaikovsky's melody.

Intertextuality in the above examples concerns a very partial borrowing from the source text and is of a purely local character. This is why we consider it as the "lower limit of transformational intertextuality".

The second type (b_2) of transformational intertextuality is a series of homogeneous local transformations of a part of the source text, creating a sequence in the recipient text in the form of rhythmic repetition, thus also fulfilling a phatic function. We encounter this pattern in the film *Il mio nome è Nessuno* [*My name is Nobody*], produced in 1973 and directed by Tonino Valerii, with the participation of Sergio Leone. It is a spaghetti Western with many elements of parody. The narrative is about a leading gunfighter, Jack Beauregard (actor b), now middle-aged, who wants to retire to Europe in an attempt to avoid constant challenges on the part of young and ambitious gunfighters. Against him stands the "wild bunch" (a collective actor c), a large gang of about 150 robbers, who have killed people close to Beauregard. Beauregard encounters the other hero of the film, Nobody, (actor a), who behaves in a carefree and odd manner but is a first-class gunfighter. Nobody urges Beauregard to confront the wild bunch alone, which he decides to do after repeatedly refusing. He succeeds in blowing up most of the gang, stages his own death in a mock fight with Nobody and is free to leave for Europe.

---

[109] Chaplin's mother was a music-hall singer, and he himself was a self-taught musician who played piano, violin and cello and was deeply fond of classical music. Before the arrival of recorded soundtracks, Chaplin himself selected the music to accompany his films in cinemas, and after the introduction of sound he wanted to have complete control over the music in his films, which often paraphrases the music of other composers but is marked by his individuality. The relation of *Terry's theme* to Tchaikovsky's first piano concerto has been observed by several commentators, recently in Greece by the composer and pianist Christos Papageorgiou, in his radio programme "The lady with the strychnine". However, since we are not musicologists, we asked for help from friends with a better knowledge of the theory of music. We want to warmly thank Dimitris Tsoukas, Dr of composition and musical technology, and Anna Vafeiadou, piano teacher and musical educator, for their help which is reflected in the text that follows.

For six scenes of the film, Ennio Morricone's music borrows a theme, *The ride of the valkyries*, from the prelude to act 3 of *The valkyrie*, the second opera of Wagner's *Ring of the Niebelungs*. The theme is performed in a light way, proper to the parodic character of the film, and is combined with another musical theme by Morricone himself. With the single exception of a scene near the end of the film in which Nobody is getting a shave, all five occurrences of the *Ride of the valkyries* accompany scenes of men riding galloping horses, one with an individual rider, the four others with the wild bunch, and it is in one of these that the theme is used for the first time. Intertextuality consists here in a transmedia connection between sound and image, achieved through the concept of riding. The importance of the *Ride* for Morricone is also shown by the trailer of the film: it starts with the hierarchical presentation of the three main actors (a)–(b)–(c) and (c), the wild bunch, appears against the musical background of the *Ride*. Six years later Francis Ford Coppola, in his *Apocalypse now*, uses the same theme for an attack by helicopters, replacing the image of the horses with that of the helicopters and thus creating a metaphor.[110]

We shall call the cases examined above "juxtaposed transformational intertextuality".

The two previous types rest on one or more purely local transformations from the source to the recipient text. The third type (b_3) of transformational intertextuality, on the other hand, refers to the intertextual relation of the totality of the recipient text with one or more homogeneous parts of the source text, due to the diffusion of the meaning of the source text in the recipient text (cf. types a_3 and a_4 of citational intertextuality). An example of this is a 90-second VW video advertisement which shows a child, dressed in Darth Vader's uniform from *Star wars*, admiring his father's 2012 Passat. The whole sequence is accompanied by Darth Vader's musical theme. Intertextuality here has a multimedia basis, visual and musical, and is diffused throughout the recipient text, which nevertheless narrates a story completely different from the source text. We encounter the same phenomenon with, for example, Santana's song *Love of my life*, in which the composer uses a theme from Brahms's Symphony no. 3 (op. 90), transposed to another key with variations having their own rhythmic background.[111]

---

[110] We note that this impressive connection of horses and helicopters with the "*Ride*" is in disagreement with the narrative of act 3 of Wagner's opera. The act does not involve the Valkyries riding horses, but gathering at the top of a mountain and preparing to bring heroes fallen in battle to Valhalla.

[111] We thank Konstantinos Papaspyrou, composer, musician and teacher of jazz and harmony, for pointing out this connection.

We shall call this case of intertextuality "part-to-whole transformational intertextuality".

The fourth type (b_4) refers to the intertextual relation of one or more key parts of the recipient text to one or more key parts of the source text (or texts) which are so closely linked with the rest of it that the result is the integration and diffusion of the source text as a whole in the recipient text (cf. type a_4 of citation). The hero of the film *Ferris Bueller's day off* (1986), directed by John Hughes, is a high school senior who fakes being ill to skip school for a day. He persuades his best friend to borrow his father's Ferrari, which is taken for a ride by some parking garage attendants and later ends up in a ravine. The actor who plays the hero, Matthew Broderick, also made a video advertisement for Honda, which shows him driving a car, a marked element of the film, but in this case the car is a Honda, while in the film the car was a Ferrari. The image of the same actor and the marked element of him driving draws with it into the advertisement the whole original story of the film.[112]

In this example intertextuality does not follow only from the similarity of contents, because another factor also intervenes: metonymy. The hero of the advertisement is the protagonist of the film and has a metonymic relation with it as part to whole, so close that his presence driving the car recalls the film as a whole. We find the same semiotic function in Martin Scorsese's film *Cape Fear* (1991), a remake of the successful film of 1962 by the same name; both films are based on the novel *The executioners* by John D. MacDonald. Scorsese's film has an intertextual relation as a whole to both the original film and the book, and this relation belongs typologically to the following type b_5.

The two protagonists of the first film, Gregory Peck and Robert Mitchum, appear in the new film in small roles quite different from their roles in the original film. Nevertheless, their visual presence as Peck and Mitchum recalls their very successful roles (as enemies) in the original film and, given their tight metonymic relation to the whole of the original film, makes them the medium for the integration of the original film within its remake. Through the personalised element of the presence of these two actors, the source text is metonymically related to the recipient text as a whole. Thus, Scorsese's film belongs simultaneously to types b_4 and b_5; as we already noted, intertextual relations are not necessarily limited to one type.

---

[112] The advertiser calculated that the intertextuality would be highly recognisable due to the success of the film. The film received generally positive reviews and was a box office success, ranking as the tenth highest-grossing film of 1987.

We shall call this type "integrated-part-to-integrated-part transformational intertextuality".

With the fifth type (b_5), we have a complete intertextual transformation, due to homogeneous local transformations, the source text or texts being transformed as a whole in the totality of the recipient text. Morricone connected the theme from the *Ride of the valkyries* with the wild bunch riding its horses. This was done purely locally and without any other effect on the film as a whole. We may contrast with this the use of music in Prokofiev's *Peter and the wolf*, the children's story that he rewrote and for which he composed the music. The story is presented by a narrator and the narration is accompanied by an orchestra. The narrative consists of seven actors: Peter, the wolf, Peter's grandfather, three small animals and the hunters, to each one of which corresponds a different musical theme and a different instrument. Not only is there a direct correspondence between the music and the actors, but the narrator also connects the musical parts syntagmatically during the narration of the story. In this manner, Prokofiev's music transforms musically and in detail the whole of the original story.

Advertising often draws on a traditional pool of art, including such artists as Leonardo da Vinci, Vincent van Gogh, Pablo Picasso, René Magritte, Salvador Dali and Andy Warhol. The publicity image is usually a transformation of the original; for example, an advertisement by Pizza Hut shows Mona Lisa eating pizza. Individual remakes of films also entail what we would call "whole-to-whole transformational intertextuality".

With type (b_6), we encounter a more complex form of intertextuality. Here, the totalising intertextuality of the previous type does not refer to a simple source text–recipient text couple, but to the intertextual relation of the recipient text with a relatively limited corpus of source texts. This may occur if, for example, a novel is adapted for cinema not only once but several times, resulting in a series of film or other media versions. Laclos's novel *Les liaisons dangereuses* was first filmed in 1959 by director Roger Vadim, who situated it in his contemporary France, the film having a rather loose relation to the novel. However, the landmark for the snowball effect of the novel was its staging in 1985 by the Royal Shakespeare Company. This was followed by two consecutive films, Stephen Frears's *Dangerous liaisons* in 1988 and Miloš Forman's *Valmont* in 1989, both preserving the characters and historical period of the book. Ten years later, Roger Kumble directed a remake, with the title *Cruel intentions*, situated in New York in the 1990s. In 2003 a mini-series with the original title, directed by Josée Dayan, was shown on French television. Also in 2003, E J-yong directed *Scandal: The love story of men and women in Joseon*, situated in the same period as the novel, but in Korea under the Joseon dynasty, and in 2012 a version was released, filmed by the Korean director Hu Jin-ho and situated in the Shanghai of the 1930s. Between these two films, in 2005, the director and producer Michael Lucas released his *Dangerous liaisons*, a hardcore gay pornographic film situated in contemporary New York. There have also been different theatrical performances of the novel, including on Broadway.

The cinematic subset of *Les liaisons dangereuses* is impressive in itself, but it also belongs to a wider set of adaptations including television, theatrical performances, two operas and a ballet. The set originated in literature and expanded into a series of visual media, thus creating a micro-corpus larger than the intermedia adaptation from literature to cinema. As we can see from the films, intertextuality is not a matter of copying; it displays great transformational creativity, and multiple adaptations of the same text may start a dynamic interaction between the different versions of the story. Micro-corpora of this kind are also created in modern mainstream music.

This intertextuality with its complex combinatorial composition may be called "micro-systemic transformational intertextuality".

Finally, the most complex form of intertextuality is type (b_7), in which the recipient text is related to a macro-corpus, a kind of system. This is a common phenomenon with theatre, given that many classical works are staged repeatedly throughout the world – we have only to think of ancient Greek tragedy or the works by Shakespeare, Corneille, Racine, Ibsen, Strindberg or Tennessee Williams. Given that the performances of the same work take place along a wide geographical and temporal spectrum, not all versions interact with all other versions, though there are many partial interactions; this is why the concept of system should be understood here in a loose sense.

This is not the case with the kind of macro-corpus defined by formal correlations, such as the corpus studied by Lévi-Strauss in his four-volume *Mythologiques*. Lévi-Strauss follows the transformations of a single myth through different indigenous groups from the tip of South America via Central America to the very north of the American continent, focusing (in a typically structuralist way) not on the content of the myth, but on the underlying structural elements.

Type (b_7) is "macro-systemic transformational intertextuality".

So far, we have presented examples of intertextuality within a simple extra-textual context; a recipient text interacts with one or several other texts in increasingly complex ways. But, as we noted above, there are two other levels of intertextuality. When discussing Russian Formalism, we noted its turn towards the extra-textual contexts of a literary text, notably the genre to which it belongs, and ultimately to the whole of culture. Textual genre is related to style. Genre and style concern the levels of both expression and content, but genre is characterised in terms of form and content, while style by an emphasis on expression. Genre and style, the wider textual context, become endogenous elements of the recipient text (as do intertextual elements in general), but they are not usually produced by it, since they are products of a wider collective dynamics.

The intertextual relation of a recipient text with a certain genre or style is a common phenomenon and generally well understood. More complex forms of intertextuality are created by the mixing of genres and styles. In Menippean satire different kinds of discourse, such as news, letters and poetry, are combined into a new whole (cf. Kristeva 1978: see, for example 72–75). Postmodernism, as we saw (chapter 2: 9), represents the extreme case of the conscious effort to create "hybrid" texts by shifting and mixing different literary genres. This is also a common phenomenon in contemporary cinema: *Punch-drunk love* (2002) is a romantic comedy drama, *Let the right one in* (2008) is a romantic horror (vampire) film, *Personal shopper* (2016) is a supernatural psychological thriller drama, *A girl walks home alone at night* (2014) is a horror (vampire) Western romance and *The lure* (2015) is a horror musical fantasy comedy drama.

Postmodern architecture, however, and mainstream music since the Beatles do not mix genres but styles. A characteristic example is given by Charles Moore's *Piazza d'Italia*. Its design is a circular piazza within a city block and this piazza is cut across by a representation of the Italian peninsula (a denotation) which culminates in a monumental architectural scenery connoting the Italian Alps. The complex includes an iconoclastic reinterpretation of the five orders of Italian columns that culminates in a new order invented by the architect; Moore humorously called it the "Deli Order", since it marks the entrance to a restaurant (Jencks [1977] 1991: 115, 116–118, 138, 166–170).

Model (b_6) that we discussed above concerned a micro-corpus revolving around a common theme. There is a comparable case in which the bond uniting a series of works is not a particular theme, but a thematic pattern. This is the case, for example in cinema or television, when this pattern is constructed on the same hero or group of heroes, integrated each time into a different story. In this manner, a sub-genre is created. The individual hero in cinema can be a Superman, more commonly a Tarzan and quite regularly a Dracula or an Emmanuelle (the "classical" Emmanuelle with Sylvia Kristel, the black Emmanuelle with Laura Gemser and Emmanuelle in space with Krista Allen[113]). Typical examples of hero groups in cinema are the *Star wars* films and in television series *Mission impossible* and *Charlie's angels*.

---

[113] There are times when one wonders about the coherence of this pattern, as for example in the case of *Emmanuelle vs Dracula* (2004).

Beyond genre and style, finally, there is the widest extra-textual environment of a text, culture as a whole (including influences from other cultures). Any text is immersed in its culture, the level from which it derives its fundamental structural traits. Culture is the all-embracing historically defined supersystem which is the shared background of all semiotic systems and all texts included in them; it is the ultimate semiotic limit of a text.

Jakobson's six functions of a message result from the articulation between the orientation of the message towards the factors of communication and the elements internal to the message. The term "function" refers to the relation of an element to its environment, which in Jakobson's model is constituted by the factors of communication. We pointed out that, besides these functions which concern the individual message, there are also other functions of a more general nature, the four general functions of semiotic systems. The last two models above, concerning the intra-textual and extra-textual context of a text, remind us that a message also has a function in relation to its context, the function of intertextuality. This addition does not invalidate Jakobson's model, since he refers to the orientations of the message, while intertextuality concerns the impact on the message of its textual environment, that is, movements towards the message.

2.9 Model 9: Simple, accompanying and complex semiotic systems

Messages belong to semiotic systems, and these systems may be simple or complex. The classification below is an attempt at a typology of semiotic systems from the point of view of their substance of expression and with emphasis on their communicative interaction.

By simple semiotic systems we mean systems composed of one primary, predominant system which may be accompanied by secondary systems, as is the case with natural language. The complex (multimedia or multimodal) systems are composed of more than one system, as happens with theatre or cinema. We saw that in the case of intertextuality a communication takes place between texts orchestrated by the addresser. In the case of complex systems, a similar communication takes place, not between separate texts but between interacting semiotic systems. In a manner comparable to intertextuality, the mediator handling the communication between systems is the addresser, but as the regulator of their interaction rather than as the receiver of the source text and sender of the new text.

In simple systems with secondary accompanying systems, the signification of the message is achieved mainly on the basis of the predominant system, though with the assistance of the accompanying systems. The addresser or the addressee has to manipulate these systems simultaneously in order to achieve a synthesis. In the case of natural spoken language, there are three accompanying systems: the *prosodic* system, which is integrated into language and includes the suprasegmental features; the *kinesic* system, which is not only a semiotic system in itself – as in the case of dance or pantomime – but also acts as an accompanying system for language through posture, gestures and mimicry; and lastly the *proxemic* system, which in its aspect as an accompanying system of language refers to the significations emerging from the distance and relative position of the speakers (Hall [1966] 1982: see, for example, 113–129; Guiraud 1971: 59–61, 103; see also Eco 1976: 141).

Written language also has accompanying secondary systems. The signification of a book is not limited to the written text. It also resides partly in traits of the channel, the ontological expression substance, such as the size of the page or the type and colour of the paper (literary books are not printed on glossy paper, and in some countries, white velvet paper is considered more suitable for scientific books and ivory-coloured chamois paper for literature). The signification of a book also resides in other accompanying systems, such as the type of print and the design of the pages; if illustrations are added, the book becomes a complex system in which verbal language predominates.

In the above systems, the accompanying systems are so conventionalised as to be more or less structurally given. But complex systems depend on combinations due to more recent cultural inventions. Complex systems start from the combination of two independent semiotic systems, as in illustrated books, comics or advertising, where image and natural language coexist in different proportions. A special case of this combination is presented by concrete poetry, which forms a printed image using the letters and words of natural language and various typographical devices.

There are also more composite forms of complex systems. Cinema, for example, is composed of two broad systems, visual and auditory, each of which includes other partial systems. The visual includes first and foremost the moving image, the dominant medium, itself including other semiotic systems, such as signifying practices and objects; it also includes the written form of natural language (in subtitles for example). The auditory includes oral language, usually central to the plot; the musical soundtrack, an important complement to the image; and background noises. Each of the above is a separate system and the cinematic text is a synthesis of all of them.

An even more composite form of complex systems is transmedia storytelling, a concept popularised by Henry Jenkins. Using the *Matrix* trilogy as his example, Jenkins writes that it was conceived from the start as a project "integrating multiple texts to create a narrative so large that it cannot be contained within a single medium", but spills over into other forms such as "television, novels, and comics" or is "explored through game play or experienced as an amusement park attraction" (Jenkins 2006: 95–96). Though few films have, like *The matrix*, been planned from the beginning as transmedia franchises, film studios and television networks have been quick to exploit the commercial opportunities offered by this combination of franchising and online promotion, and some of these franchises have turned into something very like the phenomenon Jenkins describes. The HBO *Game of thrones* franchise includes video games, podcasts, interviews, pre-shows, after-shows, companion books, record albums and a concert tour of the musical soundtrack. Transmedia storytelling, in which a single "storyworld" is exploited by different media, is a semiotic super-system, composed of a set of semiotic systems interrelated through intertextuality.

2.10 Model 10: Text and (micro-)situation

It is important to differentiate situation (or circumstance) from context. Context, whether intra-textual or extra-textual, refers to the textual environment of a text, while situation refers to the extra-textual but still semiotic environment, that which surrounds the subjects of communication. We shall call this the micro-situation, to distinguish it from the macro-situation discussed below as Model 14. Situation may be considered from two different points of view, a linguistic/semantic and a pragmatic one. Here we shall discuss the first point of view, according to which this particular external environment acts as the setting for verbal communication and is composed of semiotic systems that may be of the same nature as, or different from, the one used for communication, and, while not themselves part of the communication, nevertheless penetrate semantically into it. The second point of view will be presented in connection with Model 12.

An act of communication does not take place in a void, but in a concrete environment that may include, beyond the interlocutors, other individuals, actions and natural and artificial objects. Not all the elements that happen to be in this environment are relevant for the semiotic analysis of the communicative situation, but only those that are semantised during the communicative interaction, that is, that acquire meaning relative to the particular communicative exchange.

Let us consider the following example. Two cinema fans, A and B, are sitting in B's living room talking (verbal communication circuit) about the soundtrack of a film. At the same time, the soundtrack is playing on B's stereo installation (a musical semiotic system belonging to the situation, different in nature from the linguistic system of their verbal communication). At one point A, who is sentimental and has the synaesthetic capability of combining music with colours, cries out enthusiastically "Did you hear that? Those high notes are harmoniously connected to your red wall!" The musical system that formed part of the situation led to an association with the architectural environment in such a manner that, of the set of walls of the living room, only the red wall was semantised, i.e., was transformed into a sign, while the other walls remained outside semiosis.

A comparable phenomenon occurs with popular television drama series or sports events. While watching such programmes, the social groups who form their audience (family, football fans, etc.) are typically involved in certain activities within a broader environment of people and activities, which evolve in different places (home, coffee shop, bar, etc.). The total signification of the programme exceeds its actual content in the sense that the signification of the television text is interwoven with situational significations. Watching a television series together as a family may lead to the emergence of euphoric connotative signifieds such as "family reunion", "relaxing at the end of the working day", etc. Watching a football game may imply the gathering of friends supporting the same team and the collective consumption of large quantities of beer, pizza and, in non-politically-correct company, cigarettes, giving rise to the euphoric signifieds of "fun", "camaraderie", etc.

We can understand the situational factor theoretically with the help of Eco's semantic model, based on Katz, Fodor and Postal's compositional analysis that we encountered earlier (chapter 5: 1.1). Eco's Revised Model shows how the direct and coded denotations and connotations of a sememe are enriched through contextual[114] and situational selections of semantic markers; these selections lead to different possible significations (Figure 44). Contextual selections give instructions for certain denotations and connotations to be activated when the initial sememe is contextually associated with another particular sememe; the significations activated are those which are customary in that context. Circumstantial[115] selections give such instructions when the signifier of the initial sememe is circumstantially accompanied by signifiers relating to events or objects belonging to a semiotic system other than language; as in the previous case, the significations produced are the usual ones (Eco 1976: 105–106).

Eco considers this as an encyclopedic representation of the sememe, as opposed to the use of meta-theoretical markers in the tree structure, dictionary-like representations that he considers as too narrow. Though he still uses a tree

---

114 What we have called the intra-textual context.
115 What we have called situational.

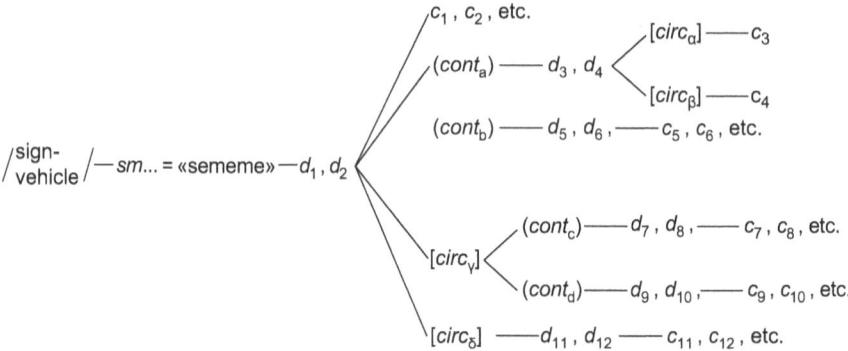

Figure 44: Eco's compositional tree (Eco 1976: 105, Table 17).

structure, he incorporates into it "coded circumstantial and contextual occurrences" (Eco 1986: 69) of a relativistic, transitory and cultural nature. He is clear on the fact that this structure is of a "local" level, because on the global level each interpretant is connected with all other interpretants, with as a result a virtually infinite network of interpretants – encountering thus the consequences of Saussure's concept of value. Eco believes that this structuring may be rendered by Gilles Deleuze and Félix Guattari's metaphor of the rhizome (Eco 1986: 46–86).

Two further points are stressed by Eco. First – and this is clear from the above definitions – even in the case of circumstances we are dealing with cultural units (signifieds), that is, circumstances are formulated within the domain of semiotic and linguistic communication. Second – and this is the rationale for the expression "the usual ones" above – not all possible contexts and circumstances for a sememe can be accounted for, but only those that are statistically most probable on the basis of given cultural conventions, whence the local nature of his tree structure (Eco 1976: see, for example, 96–98, 105–114, 155).

For Eco, the compositional tree accounting for the possible significations of a sememe is only a temporary device, because beyond the statistically known relations, there are relations not yet conventional but to be conventionalised. To deal with this possibility, he defines two semiotic operations of "extracoding": "overcoding", the operation starting from the existing rules to establish new ones that are more analytical; and "undercoding", used in the absence of recognisable rules and implying the invention of unknown rules on the basis of different relations considered as eligible (Eco 1976: 124, 126–127, 129–136, 155).

This is the dynamics surrounding a simple sememe within the language system. On the other hand, on the level of discourse, in the case of any particular text or part of a text, we are no longer dealing with a tree of possibilities, but with an actual, realised entity. A sememe in a text acquires signification with the mediation of context and circumstance; the context is manageable, but circumstances can hardly be predicted. The above environment of the message led Eco (1976: 139–142) to propose the model of communication shown in Figure 45.

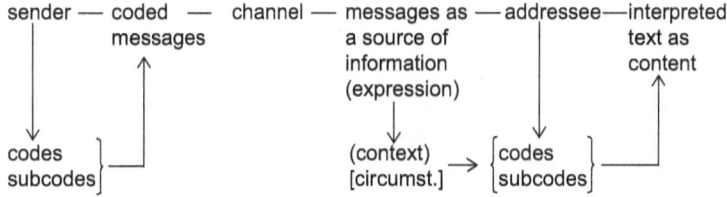

Figure 45: The communication model according to Eco (1976: 141, Table 29).

This model attempts to render the complexity of communication to the greatest possible degree. Jakobson's model, like Saussure's, presupposes transparency of comprehension between addresser and addressee. As we saw with Model 3, such a transparency is out of the question. It is this pitfall that Eco avoids. He states that the semiotic analysis of the message of mass communication media "at the moment of emission" is expressed with a fixed code, but "at the moment of reception" it is subject to filtration or distortion and semantised with new meanings. We also see that, contrary to Iser's persistence with the text's "implied reader" (1972), aligned with the semioticians' focus on immanent analysis, Eco is aware that "every semiotic study [of a message] should be complemented by a *field research*" (our emphasis), bringing thus a sociological logic to semiotics (Eco [1979] 1984: 141).

Eco specifies this approach with his communication model above. It starts with the addresser, who codifies a message using a set of codes and sub-codes. By code, Eco means what we have called Code, the language system, and by sub-codes probably what he considers as one of the content levels of the message, which he equates with the Greimasian isotopy, considered by him as an autonomous level of signification. Once the message is encoded, it is sent by means of a channel, but, as for Saussure, it is represented only by its expression. This is mediated by contextual and situational factors and then, reaching the addressee, it is subject to his or her codes and sub-codes, through which it is interpreted as content.

Eco reminds us that the reading of a message has as starting point only the expression plane. In this manner, he seems to agree with Barthes's idea that a text has no meaning in production, but only acquires meaning when received by the addressee. This possible interpretation of Eco could be reinforced by his statement that, due to the variety of circumstances and the interplay of codes and sub-codes "the message (or the text) appear [sic] as an *empty form to which can be attributed various possible senses*". But this statement in isolation is misleading, as can be seen from the statements which follow it: "Thus the message as source constitutes a sort of network of constraints which allow certain optional results [. . .]. The multiplicity of codes, contexts, and circumstances shows us that the same message can be decoded from different points of view and by reference to diverse systems of convention [. . .]. Sometimes the addressee's entire system of cultural units (as well as the concrete circumstances in which he lives) legitimate an interpretation that the sender would have never foreseen" (Eco 1976: 139, 141). The message in its production is not without meaning, but it is not limited to one and only one interpretation, because it is open for the addressee. We may add that, even if the decoding corresponds to the message on the level of denotation, the connotations can differ if the addressee follows a different path of the tree diagram, equally acceptable culturally.

Eco's position is in fact totally different from Barthes's. He wants to push to the limit the openness of the message, but within the framework of the pair coding–decoding; Eco doe not eliminate coding in the name of decoding. In other words, during the decoding of a message, and after the mediation of the contextual and situational factors, a spectrum of possible semantic interpretations is offered to the addressee and an optional field of codes and sub-codes is activated by him or her, converging to a greater or lesser degree with those of the addresser.

This is the process of communication of an open message. Eco completes this concept with a case in which the message is received as totally opaque. In this case, for Eco, the addressees are either unable to locate the codes of the message or replace them with their own codes, idiosyncratic or collective. The result is that the message is received as pure noise. When discussing the channel of communication in Model 5, we extended the concept of noise to cover not only disturbances in the channel, but also the communication gaps between addresser and addressee, and we just saw that Eco also adopts such a view. We shall encounter the same issue in the discussion of the following model.

2.11 Model 11: A and B as competent cultural subjects

So far, distancing ourselves from the static semiotic view of a text and in the dynamic framework of sociosemiotics, we have examined the positions of communication and their interaction, the means and the channel of communication, the functions and contexts of the message and the structural typology of semiotic systems. We would characterise all these models as socio*semiotic*, with the emphasis on the second term. From this point of view, they are close to mainstream semiotics, while the models that follow are *socio*semiotic, adopting a cultural orientation.

Greimas and Courtés do not conceive of the two positions of communication A and B in the same way as communication theory, which they feel impoverishes these two positions of emission and reception to abstractions transmitting neutral information. A and B, they tell us, are *competent* subjects, possessing multiple cultural codes. Competence – a term introduced by Chomsky – is very close to the concept of Saussure's *langue*; it refers to the implicit knowledge a subject has of language and the faculty of producing and understanding utterances. For Greimas and Courtés, linguistic competence is part of a wider competence, which is a knowing-how-to-do, constituting a subject as actant (Greimas and Courtés 1979: Compétence).

As competent subjects, A and B are not seen as abstract and instantaneous subjects of communication, but as concrete and integral cultural subjects. Competence articulates an individual semiotic universe. Using terminology from political economy, Ferruccio Rossi-Landi (1983: 47) considers linguistic competence as a form of "constant capital". In the same framework, Pierre Bourdieu (1977: 646–647) extends linguistic competence to the concept of "symbolic capital". Whether in verbal or other forms of communication, the concept of competence points to a relation between the semiotic and the cultural, by establishing A and B as cultural subjects (Greimas and Courtés 1979: Sociosémiotique).

The linguistic concept of competence refers to the positive structuring of a subject's semiotic universe, conscious and subconscious. This concept, however, should be complemented by another concept of Marxist origin, namely the concept of "possible consciousness". It was introduced by Lucien Goldmann (1971; see also Lukács [1923] 1971: 46–55) as part of a typology of attitudes towards received information. He is particularly interested in why some social groups seem to resist or refuse certain kinds of information. Goldmann discusses two different spheres of collective consciousness: real and possible consciousness. He believes that in respect to information, real consciousness is of only marginal interest to sociology (though this is not the case for semiotics, which covers the whole of the ideological domain) on the grounds that the phenomenon of resistance to information may appear, but the reception of information is nevertheless possible as long as it does not threaten the existence of the social group.

Goldmann then introduces the concept of possible consciousness. The limits of possible consciousness define what kinds of new information can and cannot be assimilated and understood by social subjects. Possible consciousness allows the reception of new information even if it is upsetting for real consciousness, as long as the resulting restructuring of consciousness does not challenge the essential characteristics of the social group. Beyond the limits of possible consciousness, social subjects are unable to assimilate information, because it is incompatible with their essential characteristics and threatens their existence as a group (Goldmann 1971: 7–24).

At the end of the discussion of the previous model, we presented Eco's view on the opaque message. His explanation is, as we saw, the inability of the addressee to locate the codes of the message or the decision to replace them with other, collective or idiosyncratic codes. In the discussion of Model 5, we presented the idea of the resistance to information considered as objectionable or incomprehensible. Goldmann's approach offers a semiotic and sociological framework for these views. The background he uses is the protection of the material existence of a social group from ideological threats. Information which is not *per se* incomprehensible, but which the addressees perceive as threatening the existence of their social group, falls outside the limits of the group's collective possible consciousness and is resisted or refused.

This corresponds to what Eco sees as the inability of the addressee to understand the codes of the message, resulting in their replacement with different codes to the addressee's liking. Commenting on the incomprehensibility of a message received as pure noise, Eco takes the radical step of articulating semiotics with the material dynamics of society, writing that this "frequently happens with the circulation of messages from the centers of communicational power to the extreme subproletarian peripheries of the world" (Eco 1976: 142) – a rare epistemological convergence of semiotics with Marxist sociology.

The concept of possible consciousness has two aspects. The positive aspect is that it is the structure within which new information can be creatively absorbed by a given social group, resulting in a restructuring and expansion of real consciousness and possibly the emergence of a fresh worldview. The negative aspect is that it imposes a limit beyond which there is a semiotic sphere inaccessible for historical reasons to the consciousness of a social group and thus beyond its cultural competence. More generally, while for Chomsky competence is a quality of the individual, Greimasian semiotics allows us to consider the competent actant as a collective actant. The Marxist concepts of constant capital, symbolic capital and possible consciousness promote competence to a cultural quality akin to worldview and related to the material existence of society.

The concept of cultural competence undermines the cultural neutrality of A and B. If they have a more or less structurally similar and hence equivalent competence, this creates a communicative balance but does not guarantee a balanced communicative output, and in this case communication is not neutral. But it is also possible that A and B may have different competences, a different symbolic capital, as happens between a company director and his employees or between the clients and waiters of a restaurant. Here, it becomes clear that there is no structural balance of communication: this is a case of *communication-as-power*, which we already encountered in Model 11 and shall encounter again in Model 14. In fact, the relation of communication is inseparable from power relations.

2.12 Model 12: Pragmatics: A and B as overtly acting subjects

Jakobson's functions refer to verbal action but not to non-verbal signifying practices. His conative function covers the imperative message from A to B "Please give me that bottle", but not the signifying reaction of B giving A the bottle. Eco also refers to signifying practices when he links verbal persuasion to an ensuing action. We saw in Model 6 that Greimas and Courtés differentiate pragmatic doing, i.e., actions as signifying practices, from the three modal dimensions of cognitive doing. They do not, however, use the term "pragmatic" in the same sense in which it is used in linguistics.

Cognitive doing and pragmatic doing are in psychological terms behaviours, and in sociological and cultural terms practices, and the acts of producing a message and of consuming it are also behaviours or signifying practices. But pragmatics, as understood by Morris and the American tradition, refers specifically to the conditions of *verbal* communication, such as the manner in which two interlocutors interact verbally. This approach focuses on the influence of situation on verbal communication and on the cultural competence of the communicating interlocutors, which is expressed among other things in the extent of their previous knowledge of the attitude of their interlocutor and their successful assumptions about his or her intentions. This is an extended definition of competence which includes *pragmatic* competence.

Such an understanding of pragmatics is epistemologically identical to the sociolinguistic approaches we discussed earlier (chapter 3: 12): Hymes proposes the study of the *use of language* in situation; Halliday identifies situation with those features of the environment of speech that *concern speech*; Bernstein extends his approach to social roles in their interactional situation, considering them as the foundation of *verbal meaning*; Labov focuses on the non-linguistic variables of situation *influencing speech*; and Fairclough's CDA broadens the range of situation to include the material social conditions *influencing texts*, thus aligning with the Marxist tradition in sociolinguistics. Eco adopts a similar logic, identifying pragmatics with the integration of context and situation into *linguistic* communication (Eco 1976: 108, 143).

However, although they broaden the limits of situation, the above approaches still remain within what Greimas and Courtés call "cognitive doing": they are pragmatic approaches focusing on the use of language, while the other kind of Greimasian doing, pragmatic doing, lies outside their field of vision. Pragmatic doing is not pragmatic competence but action – action, we would add, within a particular situation. Greimas and Courtés understand pragmatics as dealing with chains of "signifying corporal behaviours" (*comportements somatiques signifiants*), organised into programmes ranging from simple cultural stereotypes to complex structures (Greimas and Courtés 1979: Faire, Pragmatique, Pratiques sémiotiques). In this case, situation is seen as including pragmatic doing, as opposed to the semantic/linguistic view of situation that we discussed in Model 10.[116]

Thus, pragmatics in the Greimasian sense does not refer to mental processes but to signifying practices. This is an important distinction, because not all practices are of a semiotic nature, nor do all pragmatic practices take place within a communication circuit. A subject may perform an action mechanically, for example when going to sleep or mounting a staircase. Only when an action conveys meaning does it become a signifying practice.

Practical practices are of a functional nature and also cover actions that follow from technical instructions, such as those involved in an industrial production line or a military drill. The range of such functional practices is very wide. Taking care not to break a plate while washing the dishes is a functional practice and does not involve any symbolic conception of the plate, such as the aesthetic pleasure of looking at its nice design.

Simple pragmatic practices cover everyday routines, such as showering and shaving in the morning, tidying up the office or washing the dishes. This functional extra-semiotic dimension frequently coexists with a semiotic, communicative aspect. Showering in the morning may be a purely functional action, but shaving before going to the office in order to present what is considered an appropriate appearance in the public domain is clearly an action with a view to communication. Taking care not to break a plate while washing the dishes acquires a symbolic component when the breaking of your late grandmother's beloved teapot brings tears to your eyes.

---

[116] We believe that the concept of action is more indicative of the nature of pragmatics than the phenomenological concept of bodily behaviour as conceived by Greimas and Courtés. It also shows the theoretical bridge between extra-textual pragmatic doing and the intra-textual components of the narrative programme, the utterances of doing and of state, since we can analyse pragmatic doing in terms of narrative theory.

An example of non-communicational pragmatic semiotics is the "mental map" of behavioural geography. During our diachronic interaction with the external environment, we assimilate it in our mind by constructing a mental map – a product of interpretative doing. This map is a semiotic system that guides us in our pragmatic, overt movements in the city and our use of existing places. It is a generalised complex programme, though with many routine elements. A simpler but still complex programme involving signifying practices but not necessarily communication would be, for example, an art lover who has acquired a painting of great value by a well-known painter and arranges to hang it in a specially designed space, purely in order to contemplate it for private aesthetic pleasure.

Communicational pragmatics start from very simple cultural stereotypes, such as greetings: "Hello, I'm your new neighbour", to which the addressee answers "Glad to meet you" and simultaneously offers to shake hands. If the boss asks her secretary "Can you bring me a cup of coffee?", the secretary walks to the coffee machine, comes back with a cup of coffee and hands it to the boss, thus executing a simple, semi-stereotypical pragmatic programme of signifying practices (unless he answers "Go and get it yourself!", in which case communication remains within the limits of cognitive doing). These simple programmes are not limited only to oral communication. A television advertisement for a new shampoo or a new model car may convince the addressee that this is what is missing from their life and trigger the pragmatic programme of buying the product.

If during an intense oral quarrel the addresser pushes the addressee or assaults him, she performs a simple non-stereotypical communicative pragmatic programme. If the person who bought the precious painting is not an art lover but a millionaire, he invites friends and acquaintances to show off, champagne glass in hand, the painting in its designed space. In this complex programme, the pragmatics of displaying are deeply linked to the identity the person wants to be invested with by others.

Showering and shaving are daily routines, assault presumably is not; this and the display of the painting are non-stereotypical complex pragmatic communicative programmes. There are also stereotypical complex programmes. A society hostess has invited important people to dinner. The day before, she sees to it that the house is cleaned down to the last detail. On the day of the event, she goes to her display case to take out her silver tableware and the crystal glasses. She inspects them to make sure that they are clean and in good condition, and the tablecloth and linen napkins are impeccable. The cutlery on the dinner table must cover all the needs of the meal: soup, salad, fish, meat, fruit, cheese and dessert. In the evening she goes to dress and put on her makeup. She is now ready to communicate with her guests in view of the opening of the communication circuit. During the evening she, her husband and the guests will speak about everything under the sun, but the verbal communication will be of secondary importance. The pragmatic setting has prepared the central connotations: "rich house", "well-prepared formal dinner", "wealthy and well-mannered hosts", "useful business allies".

In the above examples we placed emphasis on one of the communicative positions, but the other may also be active. If in greeting his new neighbour the addresser offers his own hand, it is not only the addressee who is pragmatically active and both positions are involved in pragmatic exchange. In Model 4, we discussed the process of communication through objects possessing an exchange value. This process is part of Greimasian narrative theory, where it is described in terms of performance, according to the abstract terms of conjunction and disjunction. The pragmatic view, on the other hand, focuses on the concrete actions of gift-giving. The giving and receiving of gifts often involves simple stereotypical programmes. On your birthday, family and friends come to visit and there is a repetition of the same pattern: greeting, offering of the gift on their part, thanks and acceptance on your part, opening of the gift box, exclamations of pleasure and warm thanks. Another such programme is the stereotypical marriage proposal: he kneels in front of her, offers his gift in a fancy small box containing the engagement ring and anxiously asks "Will you marry me?" to which she (hopefully) responds "Yes!".

If we return to the case of the millionaire displaying his new work of art and follow it in its full pragmatic development, we can imagine that he gives a small speech in front of the painting, explaining the difficulties encountered in acquiring it and the artistic value of the painter and the painting. A discussion starts between the addresser and his addressees and then continues among small groups of guests, creating a complex network of linguistic communication, but also of movements in space, sitting down and standing up, all according to the patterned rules of polite behaviour. Parts of the performance are stereotypical structures, but the whole of the event is of a complex and each time particular nature. The same thing happens at the formal dinner party, as the guests rise from the table and the evening evolves. In both of these cases, the complex structure develops from an elementary initial pattern.

A simple collective programme is the Sunday liturgy in a Catholic or Orthodox church. The faithful are conservatively dressed (the women traditionally cover their heads). They enter the church, make the sign of the cross, light a candle in front of a sacred image and take a seat. During the liturgy, there is a patterned spoken and/or chanted interchange between the priest and the congregation and at the end the congregation leaves the church. The ceremony is marked by the ritual pragmatic signifying practices of the priest, while the patterned pragmatic signifying practices of the congregation are limited.

The Japanese tea ceremony[117] is a communicational signifying practice that develops into a very complex pragmatic structure. The Way of Tea is part of Zen, one of the schools of Mahayana Buddhism. It may be performed at home, but may also take place in special teahouses. The master of ceremonies, usually a man but sometimes a woman, is the addresser and central actant of the ceremony, given his quality as host, but he is in continuous interaction with his guests, who as addressees form a collective actant. The nature of the ceremony, the vessels used, even the disposition of the tatami mats (used as flooring material) in space vary according to the two seasons (cooler and warmer) into which the tea professionals divide the year. The nature of the ceremony also depends on the tea school. The most frequent form of the ceremony is the noon performance with a very limited number of guests (from one to five); its duration is from thirty minutes to four hours.

The guests first enter a waiting room, with a niche and a floor covered with tatami mats. In the niche hang paper scrolls with calligraphy, from words and sentences referring to proverbs or to the tea ceremony to poems and descriptions of famous places. A typical scroll would refer to the four basic principles of the ceremony: harmony, respect, purity and peace. The practice of drinking tea is associated with Zen meditation, revolving around the idea that the foundation of life should be Buddhist practice, which implies these principles. Calligraphy may be replaced by paintings or the two may coexist. The content of the scrolls changes in accordance to the seasons and the identity of the guests.

The waiting room thus presents a carefully structured situation, depending on semiotic (identity of the guests) and extra-semiotic factors (the seasons). It includes both verbal and pragmatic elements. The situational stimuli may intrude into the linguistic communication between the guests, but their main function is to act as spiritual preparation for the participation in the ensuing ceremony; that is, the guests begin to participate virtually in the pragmatics of the ceremony. In the waiting room, a cup of hot water and tea are offered to each guest.

Next, the guests pass to the garden, where they meet the master of ceremonies, greet him by bowing, and are led to a pool to be purified by washing their hands and mouth. They then enter the tea room, decorated with a flower arrangement; if this is just a single blossom, it must lean towards or face the

---

117 Our analysis of the Japanese tea ceremony follows the description in the entry of the same title in *Wikipedia*.

guests. They examine, as they must, the scroll in the room and the vessels for the preparation of tea and afterwards take their seats on the tatami (or on chairs at a table) according to their status, a proxemic arrangement. The door closes loudly, so that the master of ceremonies is informed that all guests are present and that he can now enter the room, after which he welcomes his guests and opens a dialogue with the most prominent guest. The master of ceremonies sits on the central tatami.

This is followed by the central meal in consecutive stages, accompanied by sake and a small sweet. Special attention is given to the types of dishes, which are arranged in a complex manner. Seasonal and fresh materials are always used. Dishes are often decorated with edible leaves, enhancing the flavour of the food, and flowers, combining the visual aspect with the experience of eating – an object of both visual semiotics and the semiotics of food. After the meal, there is a break and the guests go back to the waiting room. During the break, the room is swept, the scroll is replaced by a composition of seasonal flowers and the preparation of tea starts.

The guests are called back, are once more purified in the garden and, when they enter the tea room, examine its new items. The master of ceremonies reappears and ceremonially cleans the vessels following a precise order and using prescribed movements, simultaneously inspecting them, and then places them in strictly defined places. It is time for "thick tea", prepared from the tea leaves of better quality. Bowing, he offers the tea bowl to the most prominent guest, who bows in response. This guest then bows to the second most prominent guest (with certain modifications if the master of ceremonies has a helper), raises the bowl towards the master of ceremonies as a sign of respect, rotates it so as not to drink from the front, takes a sip, congratulates the master of ceremonies, takes a few more sips and passes the bowl to the next guest. The bowl is passed around the circle until all guests have drunk their tea.

At the end of the circulation of the tea, the bowl is given back to the master of ceremonies, who cleans the vessels and leaves the room. He comes back in a while and revives the stove to heat water. His return signifies the transition from the formal part of the ceremony to a more informal aspect. He now offers another bowl of tea, this time "thin" tea, to each guest. He again starts from his most prominent guest, with whom there is a new formal dialogue, but subsequently the guests start a free dialogue between them. The master of ceremonies cleans the vessels and the most prominent guest asks that the guests be allowed to examine some of the vessels, which they must do with respect and admiration as if they were unique. At the end, the master of ceremonies collects the vessels, the guests depart and the master of ceremonies greets them at the door of the room.

We can now understand the structure of the tea ceremony. The guests are the Subject, searching for what is achieved through meditation: the harmonisation of their life with the Zen principles. The Object of value is the acquisition of this harmony, achieved through the tea ceremony, and thus they are also the Recipients of this Object. They acquire it through the mediation of the master of ceremonies acting as Helper.

Taking the tea ceremony as a whole, the first conclusion is that it is a programme of symbolic pragmatics with a complex structure, encompassing a multiplicity of semiotic systems and situational influences. There is a coexistence of the linguistic system with the visual (in the form of flowers, images and the calligraphy of written language), the proxemic and the gustatory, without predominance of the linguistic. We observe the importance of situation as a factor penetrating semantically into communication, but also and mainly closely connected to pragmatic action. The situation, in all of its forms as scrolls, flowers, food or vessels, guides the guests in certain actions. They perform a programme pre-planned by the master of ceremonies, who arranges scrolls and flowers and the environmental setting of both these and the guests, and during the ceremony manipulates the vessels and the tea. The semiotic factor that embraces all these semiotic systems and the situation and holds them together is symbolic signifying practice.[118] There is an incessant pragmatic dialogue between the situation and the guests and the host and his guests, which imposes itself on the linguistic dialogue.

When we extend communication to the pragmatic dimension, communication is transformed into *communication-as-action*.

2.13 Model 13: Communication micro-networks and their structures

The communication circuit between A and B is the "atom" of communication. In group, cultural and social dynamics, this atom is constitutive of wider structures of communication networks. Group dynamics involves interaction between a small number of individuals. Applied socio-psychological studies of the communicative relations between five individuals engaged in a number of problem-solving tasks arrived at five structures of communication networks (Figure 46). Below we shall briefly discuss these micro-structures and their main characteristics (Mullins [1985] 2010: 344–346).

---

[118] We can imagine cases in which pragmatic action may be guided by situation, as happens with the movements in a labyrinth.

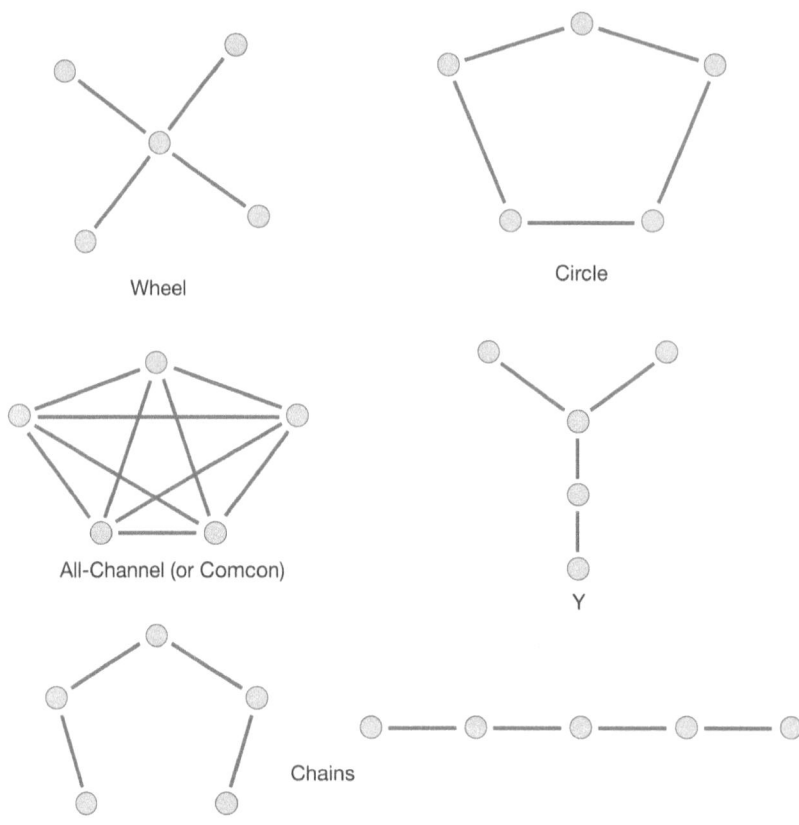

Figure 46: The five structures of the communication networks in small groups (Mullins 2010: 345, Fig. 9.1; reproduced by permission of Pearson Education).

The wheel or star structure. This is the most centralised structure, in that it reserves a position for leadership at its centre, allowing the link person to act as a focus of information flows and activities and the coordinator of group tasks. The leader is largely independent and experiences a great degree of satisfaction, while the periphery, the rest of the group, does not participate and shows the lowest degree of satisfaction of all the structures. Interaction is low and information flow minimal, as are the mistakes made in the tasks to accomplish. Efficiency and speed of performance are maximal for simple tasks, but poor for complex ones.

The "Y" and the chain structures. These structures are more centralised than the following structures; leadership predictability is high to moderate. As with the wheel structure, interaction among the members is low and their satisfaction is low to moderate. Performance is relatively good for simple tasks.

The circle structure. This structure is more decentralised than the wheel structure. Interaction is higher, but the group is not organised and there is low leadership predictability. The members of the group are moderately dependent upon each other and enjoy some degree of participation. They show the highest degree of satisfaction of all the structures. Performance tends to be slow and erratic; overall efficiency is lower than the wheel for complex problems but higher when coping with new tasks and change.

The all-channel or "comcon" structure. This is the most decentralised of all communication structures and shows the highest degree of interaction among members, but leadership predictability is very low. Satisfaction is fairly high for all members. Performance is poor for simple tasks, but good for complex ones.

It is tempting to compare these structures with the social macro-scale of types of governance, in which case the relations are also of a practical nature but include a semiotic component. We may connect the wheel structure to autocratic forms of governance, in which information flows from the centre to the periphery, and the all-channel structure to the anarchist utopia of direct democracy, if the vertices of the pattern are taken to represent individuals. But if they represent institutions and we want to formulate the structure of parliamentary democracy, we should combine the all-channel structure, as a framework for possible relations in the periphery, with a wheel, the radii of which channel flows in both directions, those from the centre being stronger.

In chapter 6 we presented a graph of the communication network between the actors of *Les liaisons dangereuses* (chapter 6: 1.3, Figure 39), and now we have the opportunity to compare it with the structures discussed above. The comparison cannot be direct, because the actors of the novel are not all collaborating to achieve a task; only the central couple Valmont–Merteuil collaborate and use the other actors to achieve their plans. Nevertheless, the comparison allows us to formulate some thoughts on the general structures of communication networks.

We see that there is no direct matching of this graph with any of the above structures, but it seems to be close to the Y structure. If we place in the central node of the Y not a single person but the couple Valmont–Merteuil, then we can locate Tourvel in the node below it and Rosemonde in the bottom node. There is a very close fit of the *Liaisons* graph with the lower part of the Y structure; an addition of secondary importance is the triangle created when we add the vertex of Volanges to the vertices of Tourvel and Rosemonde.

The *Liaisons* graph presents a divergence from the upper part of the Y structure: the connections represented by the two arms of the Y are weaker in the

Liaisons graph, and there is a new connection between the two summits of the Y due to the couple Cécile–Danceny. If the central node were not connected through these arms with this new connection, the graph would show an independent sub-network. However, the arms of the Y structure are linked to the central node, though with a lower degree of connection than that between their two summits, and from this point of view the Y structure is still valid as a background structure for the graph. Without the upper connection, we would have a loose Y structure, but this connection adds an important element and poses the question whether we should consider it as a variant of the Y structure or a new type.

Based on the above examples, we can draw some tentative conclusions on the typology of small-scale communication networks. It is clear that a number of variables are involved: at the least, the fundamental nature of the networks, which differentiates them into practical task-oriented and semiotically-oriented; the nature, scale and number of the unitary elements; the direction and intensity of flows. We cannot know on the basis of the above examples if there is a limited number of fundamental structures with many variants and combinations, in which case a typology is possible, or a continuous addition of *ad hoc* variants. On the other hand, we have seen that there seem to be similarities between practical and symbolic networks, as well as between the micro- and the macro-scale, which indicate that the types of communication networks are not radically different, each possessing its own unique structure, a fact indicating the possibility of a typology.

2.14 Model 14: From sociosemiotics to social semiotics: A and B as material social subjects in a macro-situation

Our last model ultimately presupposes a materialist conception of society. Such a viewpoint distinguishes between *material* socio-economic processes and semiotic (cultural, ideological) processes, and is theorised by the Marxist paradigm. Saussure used the principle of relevance in order to define the object of linguistics, an object included in the domain of signification, and we have said that this is a necessary epistemological presupposition for the constitution of any scientific domain. On the other hand, his external linguistics, corresponding to the influence on the language system of such external factors as society, history and geography, indicates that he extends the study of linguistics to the articulation of language with the material extra-semiotic domain, but this was not the direction taken by mainstream Saussurean linguistics.

Saussure's epistemological position concerning linguistics was extrapolated by semiotics to all kinds of scientific analysis. Semioticians, with very few exceptions, proceed on the assumption that every object of study in the human sciences is defined according to the relevance of signification. Such a position excludes, even negates, any orientation towards the study of material processes.

This general semiotic approach, in addition to reducing the study of society to its signifying aspect only, also reduces the interpretation of action. By its very presuppositions, it attempts to explain action by cognitive factors alone, whether conscious or subconscious. Contrary to this, the Marxist paradigm inserts the cognitive factors of action into, and in the last analysis explains them by, the material processes shaping society.

This articulation of the semiotic and the material does not, of course, only concern action; it applies to the semiotic systems as a whole. There is no doubt that the principle of relevance must be respected when semiotic systems are analysed in and for themselves, but if we ignore their articulation with the domain studying material society, the articulation leading to social semiotics, we end up with semiotic imperialism.

The communication circuit between A and B, indeed the communication networks between any number of addresser–addressee positions, must be seen against the material relations between the communicating subjects. These relations are to a certain extent psychological, and surely cultural, but they are primarily social, because they are inseparable from the structural positions of these subjects in the material dynamics of society. In Model 3 we pointed out that the addressee intrinsically influences the addresser's message. Bakhtin also situates everyday communication within this environment: during the process of social interaction, addresser and addressee both assimilate and evaluate the external situation, which enters the structure and the content of the utterances they exchange as an essential part of them – a view later rediscovered by sociolinguistics. For Bakhtin, the interlocutors become co-participants in the (micro-)situation; even further, their utterances depend on their material belonging to a common reality (the macro-situation), in the form of family life, profession, social class and other social groups, as well as a particular time and place, and thus all of social life becomes an intrinsic factor in their communication (Bakhtin 1989: 396–401, 408–409).

With this last step in the definition of the communication circuit we pass from the individual act of communication (culture-dependent, cf. Leach 1976: 96), the communicational micro-situation and cultural competence, all dependent on the *cultural micro-situation*, to the *social macro-situation*; and simultaneously from semiotics and sociosemiotics to *social semiotics*.

We can clarify what this passage implies by discussing the views of Pierre Bourdieu, first on linguistic communication and then on cultural production.

Bourdieu (1971) considers the relation between two speakers as a linguistic relation of production – by analogy with the Marxist social relations of production – that is, as a dynamic relation. Each speaker possesses a linguistic competence, including the capability of appropriate linguistic production, which is only a part, and not the most important one, of their cultural competence. There are many structured fields of linguistic production and circulation, and communication in each field depends on acceptability criteria and censorship, in combination with the expressive interests of the interlocutors. The linguistic relation of production involves power relations between the two speakers, who occupy specific positions in a market of symbolic power relations – which implies, we would add, that any such relation between two speakers is part of the whole set of relations between all speakers of the communication network of this market.

So far we are in the domain of sociosemiotics, though sociosemiotics of a special kind to the extent that its metalanguage originates to a great degree in political economy, a science studying material society. Bourdieu transcends mainstream sociosemiotics by taking the next step of grounding the sociosemiotic processes in material society, thus arriving at a theory of social semiotics. According to him, the market of symbolic power relations is structured by the material class relations constituting social structure as a whole and its partial specialised fields. The production of the social structure itself is governed by laws related to the material conditions of existence. The ultimate cause, then, of a specific discursive form and content in communication is material social structure. Language, for Bourdieu, does not only have a communicative function, but is an instrument of action and power, and is used in strategies having all possible functions.

The market of symbolic power relations constitutes the cultural field. The cultural field and the material social structure together make up the totality of the social field, and their dynamics create what Bourdieu calls *habitus*. This key concept indicates a historical system encompassing both signifying and material practices, and in both cases connecting dialectically systems, that is, structural determinations, and actual practices. On the one hand, the structuring of *habitus* by the structures governing it imposes limits on it and results in a tendency to stabilise it and its associated practices, but on the other the structures themselves are activated through practices; although these practices are subject to the specific logic of *habitus*, the process leads – due to a certain indeterminacy of practices – to the restructuring of structures and their transformation (Bourdieu 1980: for example, 88–96, 101–102). This is the general framework of Bourdieu's approach, an example of which is his analysis of the intellectual and artistic fields (Bourdieu 1971).

According to Bourdieu, in Western societies there have been constituted relatively autonomous symbolic fields of relations of production, circulation and consumption of symbolic, that is, intellectual and artistic, goods, which are commodities integrating symbolic value.[119] In each field, various cultural values and cultural perspectives are attached not only to the goods themselves, but also to their functions and the symbolic practices accompanying them (cf. the pragmatic programmes accompanying the painting in Model 12), and this variation depends on the position – that is, status – the goods occupy within their symbolic field. This position in turn depends on the cultural position in the field of the groups of agents handling the goods. These agents activate the cultural network, consisting in cultural relations; they have cultural, but also material, interests and compete, using power strategies, for cultural legitimation. The cultural perspectives of the agents arise from their interests and both their perspectives and their cultural positions follow from the material social position of the agents in the field: symbolic fields present their own logic, but are founded on (material) class relations.

Thus, Bourdieu shows the maximum complexity of communication networks, demonstrating how communication-as-action turns into communication-as-power and how the cultural networks find their foundation in material processes.

We started this chapter with Saussure's minimal model of face-to-face communication and ended with Bourdieu's maximal network communication model. We close this chapter with Figure 47, showing the set of our fourteen models of communication.

---

[119] Mainstream economic theory attributes to commodities two types of value: their use value (their utility) and their exchange value (their monetary value, which does not exist in non-monetary societies); both concern commodities as material objects. Bourdieu, like other Marxists, adds a third aspect of value: the symbolic (semiotic) value of commodities, valid for any kind of society.

320 — Chapter 8 A global model of communication

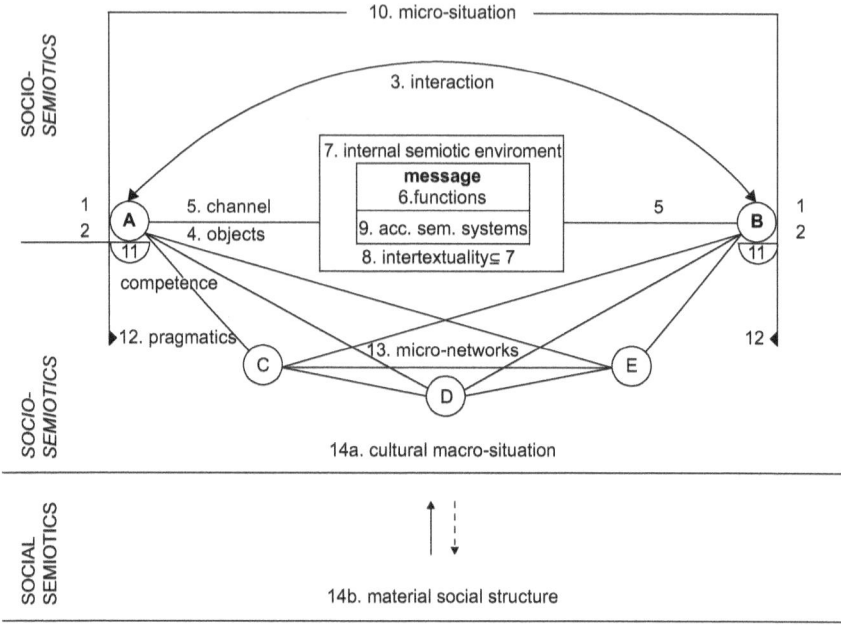

Figure 47: The fourteen models of communication.

Chapter 9
Social semiotics

1 School of Paris vs sociology

In Model 14 of the previous chapter, we encountered cultural networks, consisting of cultural relations between the agents activating them. From a semiotic perspective, such relations include linguistic communication and the communication of goods, but Bourdieu founds these semiotic fields on class relations by adding the material interests of the agents – in simple words, to acquire profit – thus bringing forward the material aspect of society as an explanatory factor. The agents communicate by using semiotic systems, but these systems have not been created *ex nihilo*; they are themselves products of social interaction, and this interaction also has the same double aspect, semiotic and extra-semiotic, in fact is founded, according to Bourdieu, on the latter. Thus, the issue of communication leads us to that of the social origin of semiotic systems.

The issue of the foundations of semiotic systems led the Paris School to contradictory positions, because it tried to protect the semiotic relevance. The Paris School is aware of a domain that escapes the scope of the Tartu–Moscow School, namely the social sciences. In the entry on sociosemiotics in the first volume of their Dictionary, Greimas and Courtés (1979: Sociosémiotique) start by stating that there is no doubt that language can be correlated with the traditional social classes (the aristocracy, the bourgeoisie, the people), but in modern industrial societies the criteria for social stratification shift to forms of living (vestimentary and culinary behaviour, dwelling, etc.), which are signifying practices appertaining to the domain of non-linguistic semiotics. According to Greimas and Courtés, seen from this angle, the correlation of semiotics with the social sciences would no longer result in an interdisciplinary sociosemiotics, that is, the bringing together of two heterogeneous fields, but would remain pure semiotic intertextuality (a position that raises the question of the correlation of language with "the traditional social classes", which presumably would require an interdisciplinary perspective). Similarly, the authors argue that, given that communication activates the complex articulation of semiotic systems undertaken by competent subjects, enunciation can be better studied through the utterance than through random sociological variables. They choose methodological coherence over interdisciplinarity.

The two options above are clearly presented in the second volume of the Dictionary (Greimas and Courtés 1986: Sociosémiotique). The authors state that the current stage of research reveals two tendencies. The first is to accept that social facts are irreducible to purely semiotic ones and are studied by a set of special theories, such as sociology, economics and political science; in this case, semiotics would be limited to investing these external realities. Greimas and Courtés opt, however, for the second approach, that of a sociosemiotics revolving within general semiotics, which conceives of the social in semiotic terms. They now propose for sociosemiotics a shift away from taxonomies to the discourses and practices constituting or transforming the interaction between individual or collective subjects, to be studied on the basis of narrative grammar. This is a broader and more dynamic view of the communication circuit, incorporating pragmatic doing.

A few years later, Courtés again expressed such a view on the relationship between semiotics and the social sciences, rejecting the perspective of the subjugation of sociosemiotics to the social sciences and defending its enclosure within the semiotic relevance, but accepting both approaches. He observes that there are approaches which study enunciation emphasising the external (social, economic, religious, etc.) conditions of production of an utterance (a text), and through them explain its composition and characteristics; this is, for Courtés, the "secondary signification" of the text. He himself adopts the view that enunciation is a purely semiotic instance, logically presupposed by and incorporated as traces within the utterance. According to Courtés, this maximum extension of the semiotic level, still in its infancy, delivers the "primary signification" of the text. He observes that the production of a text is something that involves all the human sciences, but he himself chooses "not to go outside the text", "prohibiting himself methodologically" from searching for an origin external to the text. This view, he believes, is much more modest and limited than the ambition of the social sciences to reach a deeper level of analysis, and does not contradict other approaches (Courtés 1991: 245–246).

Enclosure within the semiotic relevance is also defended by Greimas and Courtés in the case of psychosemiotics, an area of semiotics which they consider should be constituted in the future, although psycholinguistics has been in existence for decades. According to the authors, semiotics and psychology use independent methodologies and the illusion of interdisciplinarity only leads to the domination of the one over the other. They argue that by isolating *langue* as the unique object of linguistics, Saussure abandoned *parole* to psychologists and sociologists. Just as the sociolect is the articulation of the collective and the individual universes for a collective subject, so the idiolect is such an articulation for an individual subject; and just as the social and the sociological are thus absorbed by semiotics, so also the individual and the psychological are subject to the same absorption (Greimas and Courtés 1979: Idiolecte, Psychosémiotique).

However, this defence of the semiotic relevance is not without contradictions. In the entry on sociolect of the first volume of their Dictionary, Greimas and Courtés accept the existence of social stratification into classes, strata or social groupings as "phénomènes *extra-sémiotiques*" [*extra-semiotic* phenomena, our emphasis] and state that there are semiotic configurations *corresponding* to them. They thus end up with two contradictory epistemologies: interdisciplinarity when dealing with the "traditional social classes" and intertextuality for modern societies.

Courtés in his 1991 discussion levels out the difference between the objects of semiotics and the social sciences, which allows him to criticise the "ambition" of the latter. He argues – and this is semiotic imperialism – that sociological analysis is in search of a deeper "signification" of a text, thus confusing the study of spontaneous semiotic systems, the object of semiotics, with that of non-signification systems,[120] the object of social sciences: the social sciences do not study cultural signification, but the social processes of production of signification.

These ambiguities make it obvious that semiotics, in order to respond to a part of its own problematics, is *under pressure* to go beyond the boundary of its relevance, but that the tradition of the domain acts as a restraint against this transcendence. There is a limit beyond which the insistence to remain enclosed within the semiotic leads to an extrapolation from the known to the unknown and to the explanation with semiotic tools of phenomena belonging to a heterogeneous domain, resulting, in the best case, in partial conclusions, and in the worst (not so infrequent) case in erroneous conclusions. This attitude ends in "pansemiotism", semiotic imperialism and finally idealism.

2 Semiotics and sociology

The relation of semiotic phenomena to society has preoccupied not only sociologists, but also scholars with a different formation, and it is to some of them that we owe especially enlightening views. We shall start with the work of two philosophers, Louis Althusser and Étienne Balibar, who elaborated the branch of Marxism known as structural Marxism. They identify three major "instances" (societal components), internally structured and mutually structuring through their interrelations, which together compose the complex structured whole of

---

[120] There is actually a sociological orientation according to which the whole structure of society is created by beliefs and values. This semiotic conception of society shows that there is a sociological idealism as well as a philosophical one.

society. Two of these structures belong to the superstructure of society, namely on the one hand, the political and legal instance, and on the other ideologies and "theoretical formations" (philosophy and the sciences); the third structure is the economic one. To solve the epistemological issue of the coexistence of determination and social flexibility, Althusser and Balibar combine two concepts: there is a "structural causality", on the basis of which the economic structure is determinant of the other two social structures, but it is only determinant "in the last instance". This means that derivation is mediated in multiple ways and the superstructural structures are "relatively autonomous" (Althusser and Balibar 1968: 120–125). Our Figure 48 is based to a large extent on this theoretical perspective.

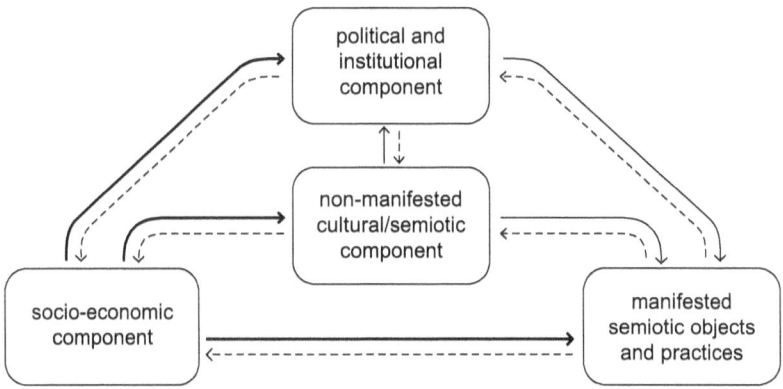

Figure 48: Social structure and the production of manifested culture. ——: major influence. —: influence. ---: secondary influence.

So far, the above components form an abstract Marxist theory of society, abstract in the sense that they are still not invested with actual existence, which, since the object of analysis is society as a whole, is their manifestation in geographical space. This task was undertaken by Manuel Castells. Castells adopted the above three instances in his initial analysis of the social production of urban space.[121] They become the three components, economic, political, and ideological, interpreting the production of urban space. Castells considers that the spatial manifestation of the ideological component of urban space is a sign system, with as

---

[121] Castells later considered this position premature.

signifiers the spatial forms and as signifieds the ideology they convey (Castells 1972: 165–280) – cf. the component of manifestation in Figure 48.[122]

Henri Lefebvre follows a logic comparable to Castells's. According to Lefevbre, the aspects of social space produced by a social formation are three. The first is "spatial practice", which refers to the spaces of the social formation related to its production and reproduction. Lefevbre uses for this the misleading term "perceived space" (*espace perçu*), but it is clear that he means the socio-economic aspect of space. He is referring to the product of the socio-economic production of space, produced socio-economic space; if our Figure 48 were oriented towards the production of urban space, this produced socio-economic space would take the place of the manifested semiotic objects and practices in the figure. This space coexists, for Lefebvre, with the aspect of "conceived space" (*espace conçu*), namely the "representations of space" held by scientists, urban planners and technocrats; the concepts of this space are formulated through linguistic signs intellectually elaborated. This is manifestly space as conceived by social theories, as well as by those responsible for urban planning, and thus resulting from the political and ideological production of space. Finally, the third aspect is "lived space" (*espace vécu*), the "space of representation" of the users of space and some artists, writers and philosophers, emerging from more or less coherent systems of symbols and non-linguistic signs and subordinate to the other two aspects (Lefebvre 1974: 40–43, 48–49, 283–284). This is experiential space, the "place" of personal bonds with a locality; it is not related to the production of space, but to its consumption.

With this third aspect, Lefebvre bypasses the semiotic production of space to replace it with its semiotic consumption, with how space is conceived by the people who use it. The semiotic consumption of space results in a spontaneous (not a scientific) semiotics which includes conceptions of the natural and the built environment (as in the mental image of space) and semiotic practices related to space.

We are now in a position to use these views to theorise the social production of the semiotic. To do so, we posit three components on the production side: the socio-economic, the political–institutional and the ideological component. Since our object is not only the production of space but of semiotic systems in general, we put in the place of space in Figure 48 all manifested semiotic objects and

---

[122] This political economy approach shows that the attempt of many semioticians of space to analyse an existing city solely in semiotic terms is a dead end. From the moment that space is not only semiotically produced, how is it possible to ignore the influence of, for example, land prices on city development? No semiotic product can be approached only as a semiotic phenomenon, since it is also always subject to material influences.

practices, that is, the products of the production process. The ideological component is defined as the non-manifested (ideological) cultural/semiotic domain, which includes the general ideological–axiological system of a society, that is, its worldview (Foucault's *épistémè*). The domain of manifested (produced) semiotic objects and practices includes:
(a) The explicitly formulated intellectual–axiological systems, such as mythology, religion and legislation.
(b) The artistic communicative systems, such as literature, painting, the theatre and the circus.
(c) The ideological part of philosophical and scientific texts.
(d) Signifying practices, everyday or ceremonial, secular or ritual, including the rules of polite behaviour and games.
(e) Material culture (material products seen from a semiotic viewpoint), including dress, small-scale objects of use, architectural and urban forms, as well as ritual objects, such as the sacrificial animal.
(f) Spontaneous notions about aspects of material society that are not cultural in nature, such as technology, economic development, social stratification or the natural environment.

We note that the nature of the socio-economic and political–institutional components is radically different from that of the semiotic component. The socio-economic component covers the means of production, including technology, demographic dynamics, the technical and social division of labour, and social differentiation or stratification. The political–institutional component includes the political institutions which revolve around government, the administrative and judiciary systems, and the system of political parties, as well as a great number of other institutions, such as the family, the school system, religious institutions and the media. This simple listing of some of the elements of material society displays what is missing from a stubborn semiotics of relevance: the many factors whose influence cannot be ignored when dealing with the semiotic domain.

After the preceding discussion of the nature of the social components, the diagrammatic nature of Figure 48 acquires a certain depth.[123] This figure is simplified and analytical, representing as separate analytical components and elements that cannot be isolated empirically but in practice constitute an indivisible and dynamic simultaneous whole. It also shows the dialectical interrelationships between these components and the intensity of these relationships in each direction.

---

[123] The figure does not include the consumption side.

Thus, the major influence on the whole social structure is that of the socio-economic component, a fact that holds not only for capitalist societies but also for societies without a monetary economy (Godelier 1978: 156–162, 168–173). It is this component that fundamentally structures the cultural (that is, the non-manifested semiotic) domain – while subject to its feedback and within the network of the above dialectical interrelationships. The influence of the socio-economic component on a manifested text is mediated by the non-manifested semiotic domain, producing the major semiotic axes structuring the manifested text. This is how the text is related to the socio-economic component as its material environment.[124]

The material environment also includes two further elements which we have already encountered. The first is the referent (chapter 3: 9), which as we saw is, and should remain, external to the text. The second derives from the projection of the text on the substance of the expression. The presence of the expression substance is not indifferent, as is the case with the referent, because it presents resistances and may create textual connotations (chapter 8: 2.5 and 2.9). This articulation of the text, not in its production but in its projection onto the expression substance, opens a new field that we could call "material semiotics".

Figure 48 demonstrates the statement by Althusser and Balibar that determination by the socio-economic component is only "in the last instance". There is continuous interaction and mediation between all components, so that the determining component is itself determined, though in a secondary manner. In spite of this dense network of influences, every component preserves a relative autonomy, due to its internal dynamics. This implies, with reference to the semiotic component, that there are semiotic phenomena that cannot be explained by external influences, but are generated by the internal dynamics of the component itself.

The question of what is meant by "determination" has been a central one for modern Marxist theory. The cultural materialism of Raymond Williams, for example, starts from the premise that "social being determines consciousness", in the sense of setting limits and exerting pressures on how humans conceive of themselves, their world and their possibilities for action (Williams 1977: 3–4). Williams supplements this "negative", as he calls it, determination with a "positive" one, originating from the pressure of social subjects on society and

---

[124] The mediation of ideology implies the semiotic world of the producer of the text, not in his or her trivial, day-to-day psychological individuality, but as a social being integrated within a particular social *habitus*. The focusing on the impact of the individual particularities, practical, cognitive or emotional, of a producer on the text produced reflects either an extra-semiotic interest – the intention of the author – or, if semiotically oriented, remains within the limited micro-scale of the phenomenological psychological level.

consciousness. Thus, he advocates a dialectical production of culture by socio-economic life. These two kinds of determination are strongly reminiscent of Bourdieu's dialectics between structural determinations and actual practices.

The tension between them leads Williams to conceive of a doubly structured cultural component, distinguishing between an "official consciousness" of fixed, "formally held and systematic beliefs" constituting the worldview or ideology of a society, and a "practical consciousness", a "structure of feeling" or "structure of experience" that is constituted by meanings and values as they are experienced in process, actively in everyday life (Williams 1977: see, for example, 83–89, 130–134). When we add to this concept the semiotic practices of everyday life, we arrive at what Greimas calls a life model and Fontanille and Tsala-Effa forms of living.

Williams's view brings out an issue concerning culture that should not pass unnoticed. Culture is not monolithic, but diversified according to social stratification; thus, culture is composed of a set of sub-cultures. In all except the so-called primitive societies, there is a dominant culture, representing the social class in power, which permeates all sub-cultures and exercises a cultural hegemony parallel to the socio-economic hegemony. There is a dialectics between dominant culture and dominated sub-cultures, the result of which is a strong imprint of the dominant culture on the sub-cultures, limiting their tendency to acquire autonomous expression.

The production of culture by socio-economic forces in capitalist societies has been meticulously studied by David Harvey. Harvey argues that the central process of capitalism, the accumulation of capital, is continually oriented towards the annihilation of space through time (through, for example, the invention of faster means of transportation) in order to reduce the turnover time of capital, whence a series of time–space compressions. Time and space are shaped by the social practices regulating commodity production.

But, as Harvey observes, capitalism is subject to periodic crises, which he relates to the over-accumulation of capital resulting in its inability to realise the expected rate of profit. He identifies a first crisis of over-accumulation in the mid-nineteenth century and considers that the oil crisis, starting in the late 1960s and reaching its peak in 1973, led to a new regime of capitalist accumulation which opened the period of postmodernity.

Still according to Harvey, these crises lead to a search for new spatial and temporal resolutions, upsetting the organisation of society and creating a strong experience of time–space compression, that is, a sense of the shrinking of world space and the shortening of time horizons to the present time. The new experience takes the form of radical transformations of philosophical thought, systems of representation and cultural formations, where by culture

Harvey means the "complex of signs and significations (including language) that mesh into codes of transmission of social values and meanings" (299).

This is also the framework for Harvey's approach to postmodern culture, which he sees as the result of a new process of circulation of capital, accompanied by the extension of the market over cultural production as a whole. Goods, including aesthetic production, are now integrated within the process of circulation of capital: in postmodernity, culture has become commodified. The result is that "money and commodities are themselves the primary bearers of cultural codes" (299). An important aspect of postmodernity is the construction of new types of imagery which both promote commodities, as in the case of advertising, and in a sense are themselves a commodity. Images are also used as a major strategy in a variety of areas, including economic competition, where they are used for brand-name recognition and image building (through, for example, sponsoring the arts), and the political arena, where they contribute to a profile of authority and power (Harvey 1989: 62, 124, 239–240, 287–288, 298–299, 305–307, 327–328).

In the discussion of Model 3, we mentioned the new phenomenon of joint brand management, i.e., the interaction between fan communities and production companies in respect to a particular audiovisual work. In contemporary capitalist conditions, films or television series are no longer works of art but "brands". Sotiris Petridis refers to the argument by Daragh O'Reilly and Finola Kerrigan that audiovisual works can be considered as brands both artistically and commercially, and these aspects are intermingled. They are brands because they "have a symbolic dimension; are the subject of capital and technological investment; are offered for sale [. . .] and are strategic assets for their production studios' brand portfolios" (as quoted in Petridis 2019: 3).

Harvey clearly aligns himself with Fredric Jameson, according to whom postmodern society does not represent a totally new type of social formation, but a new stage of capitalism that he calls late capitalism, and the postmodern culture produced by it is its cultural logic. However, in postmodern society the relation of culture to the economic system, and in general to the social formation, is different from the one that modern culture previously had. The previous relative autonomy of culture has disappeared and culture is now much more directly controlled by the economy (Jameson 1984: see, for example, 55–58, 87). We see that the nature of culture depends on the nature of the society which produces it.

The relation of literature in particular with material social processes has been studied by Lucien Goldmann (1971). Goldmann distinguishes between the comprehension and the explanation of what he calls a *"structure significative"* (signifying structure or, in semiotic terms, a text). The description of the internal structure of a text leads to its *comprehension*, while the description of the larger structure englobing it leads to its *explanation*. For Goldmann, "*Comprendre un phénomène c'est décrire sa structure et dégager sa signification. Expliquer un phénomène, c'est expliquer sa genèse à partir d'une fonctionnalité . . .*" [To understand a phenomenon is to describe its structure and reveal its signification. To explain a phenomenon is to explain its genesis on the basis of its functionality], that is, its function within a wider context. Goldmann gives as example Pascal's *Pensées*, which can be inscribed as a partial structure within the larger structure of the Jansenist movement (21). This is the first step towards a social semiotics.

Goldmann then takes a second step. The insertion of a text within its larger cultural framework does not cover the full procedure of explanation, because "[. . .] *un dialecticien ne peut pas faire de l'histoire des idées en dehors de l'histoire de la société* [. . .] *c'est la catégorie de la structure significative qu'on ne comprend que par l'insertion dans une structure plus vaste et dans l'ensemble de l'histoire*" [A dialectician cannot do history of ideas outside a history of society [. . .] it is the category of the signifying structure that can only be understood through its insertion into a larger structure and the whole of history] (1971: 162).

This anchoring of the semiotic domain in material society was formulated more than forty years earlier by Medvedev and Bakhtin. They point out that ideology, by which they mean philosophical views, beliefs, etc., as the social consciousness of a collectivity (cf. the cultural/semiotic component of Figure 48), is always embodied in a "semiotic material", such as words, actions, manners, clothing, organisation of people and things, and this process leads to products (our component of manifestation), among them works of art and scientific works, as well as religious symbols and rites. The "object-signs" in which ideology is embodied constitute the "ideological environment" of humans, i.e., manifested culture.

Medvedev and Bakhtin state that ideology is the domain of signification and signification is realised in social communication; different forms of signification are produced by different forms of social intercourse (cf. Bourdieu's *habitus*). These forms mediate between the determining socio-economic reality (the socio-economic component of Figure 48) and different ideologies. The ideological environment is determined by a collectivity's economic existence, but this is not, for Bakhtin and Medvedev, a passive determination, since simultaneously each ideological field exerts a return influence on socio-economic reality. The same idea lies behind their views on literature, when they specify – contrary to vulgar materialist reflection theory – that literature reflects only the ideological environment, "which itself is only the *refracted reflection* of real [i.e., socio-economic] existence" (Medvedev and Bakhtin 1978: 7–15, 18, our emphasis; see also Sebeok 1994, 1: Baxtin Circle).

To conclude, when sociology enters into the perspective of semiotics, it widens this perspective. We do not mean to imply, in the orthodox Marxist line, that reference to the extra-semiotic delivers some absolute objective knowledge escaping cultural determination. We simply argue that there is a legitimate non-semiotic viewpoint on society, the viewpoint of the social sciences. The articulation of the semiotic with this viewpoint is the articulation of two different forms of constructed knowledge, and views such as those discussed in the framework of Model 14 and in this chapter remind us that semiotic analysis cannot easily turn its back on the perspective of the social sciences without impoverishing its own analysis. Semioticians need to understand that there is a radical difference between the two terms "cultural" and "social" that they currently use interchangeably, considering them implicitly as identical.

3 Social semiotics as a legitimate field of semiotics

Today's (post-)Greimasian semiotics shows a tendency to move away from immanent analysis towards extra-textual factors, without violating the limits of the semiotic domain, but with a shift to a relevance of a superior level. From a certain point of view, they do so for good reasons, because, without compliance with the law of relevance (in the traditional or the extended sense), semiotics cannot be constituted as a scientific field. However, this defence mechanism must not obscure the fact that traditional semiotic fields have frequently had recourse to the social as an explanatory factor. It is simply impossible for a literary historian, for example, to do an analysis of a historical text without a profound knowledge of the semiotic universe of the society where the text was produced, which presupposes research in cultural history. But cultural history is not a self-explanatory reality, since it is inextricably involved with the more general dynamics of society as studied by economic and social history. A medievalist, for instance, is in no position to understand medieval culture without knowledge of the feudal system, the economic activities sustaining it and the ensuing social relations. This is the domain the literary scholar has to assimilate in order to analyse any text produced by a society other than our own. If the need for such an understanding is obvious in the case of historical analysis, it is no less necessary for the study of more recent societies: the presuppositions for the analysis of contemporary texts are in no way different epistemologically from those required for the analysis of historical texts.

The limitations of immanent analysis are also obvious in the understanding of the addresser and addressee of a text. Greimas and Courtés (1979: Énonciation) define enunciation (the production of discourse) by using the concept of the "instance of enunciation", the implied speaker. Courtés (1991: 245–246) leaves to the (other) human sciences the search for the external origin of a text, a task he considers as parallel to his own. However, this task cannot be simply parallel, because as he himself states, these other approaches aim at explaining the composition and characteristics of a text, which is just as much a task for a (social) semiotics. This is also true for the reception of the text. Literary theory attempts to bypass actual readers in favour of the concept of the implied reader, an abstract construct defined through specific signs in a text and thus internal to it. But the actual audience of a text consists of readers from different social strata, different genders, different age groups, and their readings of a text are far from uniform. Manifestly, the semiotic study of these different readings cannot be accomplished without an articulation with their sociological references: actual readers and their readings are a subject of study for social semiotics.

It seems to us that, for semiotics to be able to answer some of its own theoretical questions, it must necessarily go beyond its present limits, but the tradition of the field acts as an obstacle. The insistence on maintaining the law of relevance at all costs implies the explanation with semiotic instruments of a heterogeneous domain and unwarranted extrapolations. Semiotics is an autonomous field, certainly, but it must not end up in epistemological isolation.

Greimas and Courtés reject "interdisciplinary" sociosemiotics because they see it as the combination of two heterogeneous fields. But why not replace this phrasing with epistemological *articulation*? We believe that it is possible to bypass the contradiction of the Paris School with a superordinate theory articulating the semiotic with the sociological. This second possibility is not in competition with semiotics and is not intended to replace mainstream immanent, textual semiotics as the centre of gravity of the field, but to extend and complete it. There is no completely autonomous epistemological object in the social sciences; their objects are linked through relations of nesting, hierarchy and articulation. The articulation of a lower level (in this case, of semiotics) with a higher level (the sociological) allows what Goldmann calls "explanation" in addition to "comprehension", and leads to a political economy of semiotic texts.[125]

Such an articulation bypasses Greimas and Courtés's fear of the subjugation of semiotics to the social sciences, because the concept of determination adopted here is not the Stalinist notion of determination as reflection, but a relative determination, setting limits and exerting pressures, and allowing for the relative autonomy and internal dynamics of semiotic systems, as well as their return influence on the socio-economic component.

---

[125] Not to be confused with the similar term used by Baudrillard (1972).

Such an articulation reveals a strong link between semiotic and social processes. There is a striking similarity between the model of the fundamental communication circuit (production of a message – circulation (sending) of the message – reception / consumption of the message) and the model of political economy, of fundamental importance in society, concerning the circulation of commodities and capital, according to which there is a circulation process before production, a production process, and a second circulation process during which the produced commodities reach their destination and enter into the consumption sphere. Both models can be subsumed under a general circulation model, showing that there are deep structural similarities between the life cycles of all products of society, whether they are material or semiotic, commodities or non-commodities (Lagopoulos 1996: 589–590).

Articulations of semiotics with a higher-level domain have been attempted, but instead of turning to the social sciences, they have generally succumbed to the positivist temptation to anchor themselves in the positive sciences, the "real" sciences supposedly offering an "objective" foundation. The typical example is Lévi-Strauss. The "human universals" of Lévi-Strauss, for the study of which he considers that the so-called primitive societies offer the ideal ground, emerge from the unconscious (his symbolic function), which imposes a logic in the form of an innate and unconscious universal algebraic matrix producing structural laws which govern all semiotic systems (Lévi-Strauss 1958: 40–41, 224–225 and 1955: 469–470). It is thus possible for him to regress from the "I" of an individual or a culture to the higher-level "us-matrix" of humanity and finally to an "us" belonging to biology and nature. This continuous and overambitious regression, which also aims to cover animal psychology, ends for Lévi-Strauss with the integration of life within its physico-chemical origins (Lévi-Strauss 1962: 326–328, 347).

We find the same ambition in the work of Lotman. Lotman considers that the foundation of communicative processes can be found in what he considers as an invariant (structural) principle that makes them similar to each other. This principle is the pair symmetry–asymmetry, following from the breaking-up of a form by a symmetrical element. According to Lotman, the simplest form of this pair is mirror symmetry, because the two parts of the mirror are in one sense similar, but they are still related as right and left and in that sense different. This is "enantiomorphism", which combines structural similarity and structural difference, and is the foundation of meaning and dialogue (Lotman 2005: 219–220).

Lotman then takes the radical step of considering that mirror symmetry reflects the bilateral, right–left asymmetry of the brain. He considers that this is the foundation of the mechanism of thought and "one of the basic structural principles of the internal organisation of meaning-making constructions" (Lotman and

Uspenskij 2013: thesis 3.0). This idea leads him to an organicist attempt at synthesis of cultural studies with the positive sciences based on the ambitious premise that the right–left pair is a basic universal structure, presiding over a range of phenomena from the genetic–molecular level to the general structure of the universe to semiotic systems (Lotman and Uspenskij 2013: thesis 1.2).

Recently, there has been a movement towards a biological explanation of semiotics on the part of cognitive semiotics, which attempts to relate semiotic systems to the cognitive processes of the brain by having recourse to neuroscience. While this enterprise is of course legitimate if we are interested in the biological origins of semiosis, it does not provide a foundation for an understanding of culture and risks leading to premature generalisations from biology to culture. Biology may offer knowledge of the biological processes taking place in the biological *brain*, which are more or less common to the human species. They are not without interest, since they establish the framework within which semiosis takes place, but they are not in themselves relevant to semiotics. Any biological explanation of the semiotic is unable to account for the cultural *mind*, that is, the structuring of the semiotic systems in their cultural relativity. Extrapolation from the brain to the mind ends up in an unfortunate search for biologically determined cultural universals,[126] a search which violates cultural relativity.

The above approaches attempt to explain meaning through biology precisely because they lack the concept of society (which is the first place to look when the concept of society is introduced into the equation). It is not the first time that such explanations have been proposed. The human ecology of the Chicago School of sociology, in its "classical" formulation in the 1920s and 1930s, attempted to explain the spatial distribution of social phenomena through animal and plant ecology. (Theodorson 1961: 3). Its founding concepts were "competition", complemented by "competitive cooperation", on the basis of which it built a set of socio-spatial processes that were supposed to explain the organisation and characteristics of the American metropolis. Such an approach amounts to social Darwinism, the biological determinism of society.[127] This biological interpretation of society was severely criticised, and before WWII had already been abandoned by the school, which subsequently turned to the study of society as such.

---

126 Not to be confused with metalinguistic universals.
127 According to one of the founders of classical human ecology, Robert E. Park, competition and competitive cooperation lead in all societies to the constitution of the pre- or sub-social "biotic" level of society, and the latter is the central object of human ecology. The fundamental idea is that social structure can be explained by biology, though the school recognises that society also has a "cultural superstructure" (Park 1961; Theodorson 1961: 3–4).

The biological approaches in semiotics adopt a biological perspective but an individualistic paradigm, looking for the foundations of culture not in the collectivity, in social intercourse, but in the individual. Such approaches are positivist, reductionist, society-insensitive and a-political. They are a-political in the sense that they are blind to the material socio-historical determination of semiosis. To see semiosis as socially determined is, on the other hand, deeply political, because the a-historical naturalisation of society ends up being an apology for the *status quo*.

We can imagine a counter-argument to our proposal on the articulation of semiotics with the social sciences on the basis that this articulation is not the business of semiotics but of the social sciences. But an articulation is a junction with two directions, one from above to below, the other in the opposite direction, and social semiotics has a leg on each side. There is no doubt that the social sciences are in a position to contribute to this articulation, but they will do so from their own point of view and with their own methodologies. On the other hand, semiotics has its own point of view and a highly developed methodology oriented toward finer analysis, in which the social sciences are only marginally interested. The sociological problematics of the semiotician is not asymptotic with that of the social sciences, but it is definitely different.

It is somewhat awkward to be arguing this position today, when we already have the legacy of Saussure's external linguistics and the precedent of sociolinguistics. It is even embarrassing to give the impression of presenting something iconoclastic for semiotics, when this issue has been settled by Hjelmslev three-quarters of a century ago with his definition of the *metasemiotic of connotative semiotics*. In this metasemiotic, writes Hjelmslev, "the largest parts of specifically sociological linguistics and Saussurean external linguistics will find their place in reinterpreted form. To this metasemiotic belongs the task of analyzing various – geographical and historical, political and social, sacral, psychological – content-purports" and "Many special sciences, in the first place, presumably, sociology, ethnology and psychology, must be thought of as making their contribution here" (1961: 125). This is, for Hjelmslev, the higher order of metasemiologies, in line with his simplicity principle.

Hjelmslev here is faithfully following Saussure, who repeatedly insisted that language is a *social* phenomenon. The social collectivity is "*dès l'origine le veritable endroit de développement où tend dès sa naissance un système de signes*" [from the beginning a veritable nursery towards which a system of signs tends already from birth] (Saussure 2002: 289–290). Thus, "*la langue est un produit des forces sociales*" [*langue* is a product of social forces] (Saussure 1971: 108).

Saussure's conception of language as a product of social forces is apparent, first, in his discussion of how language changes. The social grounding of *langue* (in the form of *communauté, masse parlante, fait social, masse sociale, forces sociales*) means that time (in the form of tradition) and society act on *langue* as a stabilising factor, explaining its immutability (Saussure 1971: 104, 107, 108, 112–113). But simultaneously, time is a factor of mutability for the language system, since it allows the social use of language (*parole*) to effect changes in *langue*. These two apparently contradictory aspects of time lead Saussure to formulate both the continuation and alteration of the sign in time as a principle of general semiology. The passage of time is the factor that shows the working of social forces on language (Saussure 1971: 108, 111, 112). As Saussure states "*le temps permettra aux forces sociales s'exerçant sur elle [langue] de développer leurs effets*" (time will allow the social forces acting upon it [*langue*] to have their full effects" (Saussure 1971: 113).

However, the social nature of language, for Saussure, goes far beyond the dynamics of language change. The quotations above refer to social forces as an external environment influencing the language system. But Saussure takes a final step, stating that its "*nature sociale est un de ses caractères internes*" [its social nature is one of its internal characteristics] (Saussure 1971: 112). For the "*phénomène sémiologique*", the semiological phenomenon, "*la collectivité sociale et ses lois est un de ses éléments internes et non externes*" [the social collectivity and its regularities are one of its *internal*, not *external*, elements] (Saussure 2002: 290). The laws of the social collectivity are *internalised* into *langue* and into all semiotic systems.

Saussure's understanding of language thus unexpectedly converges with a Marxist understanding of culture: culture is produced by material social regularities and the latter are reshaped within the former. This is what we mean by articulation of a lower-level with a higher-level epistemological object (chapter 3: 2) and by articulation of the semiotic with the social sciences (section 2 above). It is of course unlikely that our understanding of the socio-economic component would coincide with Saussure's conception of the "*forces sociales*", but we are undoubtedly referring to the same kind of phenomenon: the semiotic systems are the result of a social process of production, though (to recall Althusser and Balibar) they are relatively autonomous; in Saussurean terms, they obey the imperative of value, that is, whatever influence comes from the "*forces sociales*" is filtered through the regularities of the semiotic system.

It is thus with a certain confidence that we propose that Saussurean semiotics requires a threefold approach: immanent semiotic analysis, semiotics in the strict sense, which remains the nuclear object of semiotics; sociosemiotic analysis and related approaches, extending to the broader domain of communication and situation; and, when appropriate, social semiotic analysis, or otherwise Hjelmslev's metasemiotic of connotative semiotics, articulating semiotics with the material processes of society.

References

Ablali, Driss. 2003. *La sémiotique du texte: Du discontinu au continu*. Paris: L'Harmattan.
Acta Sanctorum, vol 31. 1868. Paris & Rome : Victor Palmé. https:/archive.org/details/actasanctorum31unse.
Althusser, Louis & Étienne Balibar. 1968. *Lire le Capital*, vol. 1. Paris: Maspero.
Anderson, Myrdene, John Deely, Martin Krampen, Joseph Ransdell, Thomas A. Sebeok & Thure von Uexküll. 1984. A semiotic perspective on the sciences: Steps toward a new paradigm. *Semiotica* 51 (1/2). 7–47.
Apostolopoulou, Athina. 2005. I engrafí tou ypokeiménou ston (ana)kataskevasméno chóro [The inscription of the subject in (re)constructed space]. Thessaloniki: Aristotle University of Thessaloniki seminar paper.
Bakhtin, Mikhail. 1989. Discourse in life and discourse in art (concerning sociological poetics). In Robert C. Davis & Ronald Schleifer (eds.) *Contemporary literary criticism: Literary to cultural studies*, 391–410. New York, NY: Longman.
Barthes, Roland. 1957. *Mythologies*. Paris: Seuil.
Barthes, Roland. 1964a. Éléments de sémiologie. *Communications* 4, 91–135. English trans. Annette Lavers & Colin Smith, *Elements of semiology*. New York, NY: Hill & Wang, 1967.
Barthes, Roland. 1964b. Rhétorique de l'image. *Communications* 4. 40–51.
Barthes, Roland. 1970. *S/Z*. Paris: Seuil.
Barthes, Roland. 1988a. The death of the author. In David Lodge (ed.) *Modern criticism and theory: A reader*, 167–172. London & New York, NY: Longman.
Barthes, Roland. 1988b. Textual analysis: Poe's "Valdemar". In David Lodge (ed.) *Modern criticism and theory: A reader*, 172–195. London & New York, NY: Longman.
Baudrillard, Jean. 1972. *Pour une critique de l'économie politique du signe*. Paris: Gallimard.
Baudrillard, Jean. 1981. *Simulacres et simulation*. Paris: Galilée.
Baudrillard, Jean. 1992. The ecstasy of communication. In Charles Jencks (ed.) *The post-modern reader*, 151–157. London: Academy & New York, NY: St. Martin's Press.
Bernstein, Basil. 1971. *Class, codes and control*, vol. 1. *Theoretical studies towards a sociology of language*. London & Boston, MA: Routledge & Kegan Paul.
Biglari, Amir. 2017. La sémiotique des passions: Hier, aujourd'hui, demain. *Semiotica* 2017 (219). 201–217.
Boklund-Lagopoulou, Karin. 1984. *The life of Saint Alexius*: Structure and function of a medieval popular narrative. *Semiotica* 49 (3/4). 243–281.
Borroff, Marie. 1967. *Sir Gawain and the green knight: A new verse translation*. New York: W. W. Norton.
Bourdieu, Pierre. 1971. Le marché des biens symboliques. *L'Année Sociologique* (3ème série) 22. 49–126.
Bourdieu, Pierre. 1977. The economics of linguistic exchange. *Social Science Information* 16 (6). 645–668.
Bourdieu, Pierre. 1980. *Le sens pratique*. Paris: Minuit.
Brandt, Per Aage. 2003. Toward a cognitive semiotics. *Recherches en Communication* 19. 1–15.
Brandt, Per Aage. 2017. D'où vient le sens? Remarques sur la sémio-phénoménologie de Greimas. *Semiotica* 2017 (219). 75–91.
Bruno, V.J. 1977. *Form and color in Greek painting*. New York, NY: Norton.
Castells, Manuel. 1972. *La question urbaine*. Paris: Maspero.

Child, Lee. 2011 [1999]. *Tripwire*. London: Bantam.
Chomsky, Noam. 1964. *Current issues in linguistic theory*. The Hague & Paris: Mouton.
Chomsky, Noam. 1971 [1957]. *Syntactic structures*. The Hague & Paris: Mouton.
Cobley, Paul. 2016. *Cultural implications of biosemiotics*. Dordrecht: Springer.
Couégnas, Nicolas & Aurore Famy. 2017. La part sémiotique de l'anthropologie des modernes. *Semiotica* 2017 (219). 435–454.
Courtés, Joseph. 1991. *Analyse sémiotique du discours: De l'énoncé á l'énonciation*. Paris: Hachette.
Daylight, Douglas. 2012. The difference between semiotics and semiology. *Gramma: Journal of Theory and Criticism* 20. 37–50.
Deely, John. 2001. *Four ages of understanding: The first postmodern survey of philosophy from ancient times to the turn of the twenty-first century*. Toronto, etc.: University of Toronto Press.
Derrida, Jacques. 1967a. *L'écriture et la différence*. Paris: Seuil. English trans. Alan Bass, *Writing and difference*. Chicago, IL: University of Chicago Press, 1978.
Derrida, Jacques. 1967b. *De la grammatologie*, Paris: Minuit. English trans. Gayatri Chakravorty Spivak, *Of grammatology*. Baltimore, MD & London: Johns Hopkins University Press, 1976.
Derrida, Jacques. 1972a. *Marges de la philosophie*. Paris: Minuit. English trans. Alan Bass, *Margins of Philosophy*. Chicago, IL: University of Chicago Press, 1982.
Derrida, Jacques. 1972b. *Positions*. Paris: Minuit. English trans. Alan Bass, *Positions* (London: Anthole Press, 1981).
Ducrot, Oswald & Jean-Marie Schaeffer. 1995. *Nouveau dictionnaire encyclopédique des sciences du langage*. Paris: Seuil.
Durkheim, Émile & Marcel Mauss. 1903. De quelques formes primitives de classification: Contribution á l'étude des représentations collectives. *L'Année Sociologique*, sixième année 1901–1902. 1–72.
Eco, Umberto. 1972 [1968]. *La structure absente: Introduction à la recherche sémiotique*. U. Esposito-Torrigiani (trans). France: Mercure de France.
Eco, Umberto. 1976. *A theory of semiotics*. Bloomington, IN & London: Indiana University Press.
Eco, Umberto. 1984 [1979]. The *role of the reader: Explorations in the semiotics of the text*. Bloomington, IN: Indiana University Press.
Eco, Umberto. 1986 [1984]. *Semiotics and the philosophy of language*. Bloomington, IN: Indiana University Press.
Eco, Umberto. 2000 [1997]. *Kant and the platypus: Essays on language and cognition*. Alastair McEwen (trans.). London: Vintage.
Evans, Gary W. 1980. Environmental cognition. *Psychological Bulletin* 88 (2). 259–287.
Fontanille, Jacques. 1999. *Sémiotique et littérature: Essais de méthode*. Paris: Presses Universitaires de France.
Fontanille, Jacques. 2017. Les voies (voix) de l'affect. *Actes Sémiotiques* 120. 1–24.
Fontanille, Jacques & Nicolas Couégnas. 2018. *Terre de sens: Essai d'anthroposémiotique*. Limoges: Pulim.
Fontanille, Jacques & Didier Tsala-Effa. 2017. Pour une sémiotique pilotée par la méthodologie. *Punctum* 3 (2). 92–110.
Foucault, Michel. 1966. *Les mots et les choses*. Paris: Gallimard.
Frank, Manfred. 1989 [1984]. *Qu'est-que le néo-structuralisme?* France: Cerf.

Gay, Pierre & Agnes Rosenstiehl. 1989. *Cris d'Europe*. Paris: Seuil.
Godelier, Maurice. 1978. La part idéelle du réel: Essai sur l'idéologique. *L'Homme* 18. 155–188.
Goldmann, Lucien. 1971. *La création culturelle dans la société moderne*. Paris: Denoël-Gonthier.
Gottdiener, Mark, Karin Boklund-Lagopoulou & Alexandros Ph. Lagopoulos (eds.). 2003. *Semiotics*, 4 vols. London, Thousand Oaks & New Delhi: Sage.
Greimas, Algirdas Julien. 1966. *Sémantique structurale: Recherche de méthode*. Paris: Larousse. English trans. Daniele McDowell, Alan Velie & Ronald Schleifer (trans.), Ronald Schleifer (intro.), *Structural semantics: An attempt at a method*. Lincoln, NE & London: University of Nebraska Press, 1983.
Greimas, Algirdas Julien. 1970. *Du sens: Essaies sémiotiques*. Paris: Seuil.
Greimas, Algirdas Julien. 1976. *Sémiotique et sciences sociales*. Paris: Seuil.
Greimas, Algirdas Julien 1983. *Du sens II*. Paris: Seuil.
Greimas, Algirdas Julien & Joseph Courtés. 1979. *Sémiotique: Dictionnaire raisonné de la théorie du langage*. Paris: Hachette. English trans. Larry Christ, Daniel Patte, James Lee, Edward McMahon II, Gary Phillips & Michael Rengstorf, *Semiotics and language: An analytical dictionary*, Bloomington, IN: Indiana University Press, 1982.
Greimas, Algirdas Julien & Joseph Courtés. 1986. *Sémiotique: Dictionnaire raisonné de la théorie du langage*, vol. 2. Paris: Hachette.
Greimas, Algirdas Julien & Jacques Fontanille. 1991. *Sémiotique des passions: Des états des choses aux états d'âme*. Paris: Seuil. English trans. Paul Perron & Frank Collins, *The Semiotics of passions: From states of affairs to states of feelings*. Minneapolis, MN: University of Minnesota Press, 1993.
Guiraud, Pierre. 1971. *La sémiologie*. Paris: Presses Universitaires de France.
Hall, Edward T. 1982 [1966]. *The hidden dimension*. New York, NY: Anchor Books.
Halliday, M. A. K. 1978. *Language as social semiotic: The social interpretation of language and meaning*. London: Edward Arnold.
Harvey, David. 1989. *The condition of postmodernity: An enquiry into the origins of cultural change*. Oxford: Blackwell.
Hassan, Ihab. 1987. *The postmodern turn: Essays in postmodern theory and culture*. Columbus, OH: Ohio State University Press.
Hénault, Anne. 1983. *Narratologie, sémiotique générale*. Paris: Presses Universitaires de France.
Hénault, Anne. 1992. *Histoire de la sémiotique*. Paris: Presses Universitaires de France.
Hénault, Anne. 1993 [1979]. *Les enjeux de la sémiotique*, 2nd edn. Paris: Presses Universitaires de France.
Hénault, Anne. 1994. *Le pouvoir comme passion*. Paris: Presses Universitaires de France.
Hesiod. 2007. *Theogony, Works and days, Testimonia* (Loeb Classical Library 57). Glenn W. Most (ed. & trans.). Cambridge, MA: Harvard University Press.
Hjelmslev, Louis. 1961 [1943]. *Prolegomena to a theory of language*. F. J. Whitfield (trans). Madison & Milwaukee, WI & London: University of Wisconsin Press.
Hjelmslev, Louis. 1971. *Essais linguistiques*. Paris: Minuit.
Hymes, Dell. 1974. *Foundations in sociolinguistics: An ethnographic approach*. Philadelphia, PA: University of Pennsylvania Press.
Iser, Wolfgang. 1972. The reading process: A phenomenological approach. *New Literary History* 3 (2). 279–299.
Jakobson, Roman. 1963. *Essais de linguistique générale*. Nicolas Ruwet (trans.). Paris: Minuit.

Jameson, Fredrik. 1984. Postmodernism, or the cultural logic of late capitalism, *New Left Review* 146. 53–92.
Japanese tea ceremony. N.d. *Wikipedia*. https://en.wikipedia.org/wiki/Japanese_tea_ceremony. (accessed 10 April, 2019).
Jencks, Charles. 1991 [1977]. *The language of post-modern architecture*, 6th edn. New York, NY: Rizzoli.
Jenkins, Henry. 2006. *Convergence culture: Where old and new media collide*. New York, NY & London: New York University Press.
Johansen, Jørgen D. 1998. Hjelmslev and glossematics. In Roland Posner, Klaus Robering & Thomas A. Sebeok (eds.) *Semiotik/semiotics: A handbook on the sign-theoretic foundations of nature and culture*, vol. 2, 2272–2289. Berlin & New York, NY: de Gruyter.
Joseph, John E. 2012. *Saussure*. Oxford: Oxford University Press.
Kaklamanidou, Despoina. 2005. *Afígisi kai estíasi stis* Epikíndynes schéseis *tou Choderlos de Laclos kai tis tésseris kinimatografikés metaforés tou mythistorímatos* [Narrative and focus in *Dangerous liaisons* by Choderlos de Laclos and the four cinematic adaptations of the novel]. Thessaloniki: Aristotle University of Thessaloniki dissertation.
Karagiannis, Konstantinos. 2019. Analysi tis tainías *Mávros pánthiras* [Analysis of the film *Black panther*]. Thessaloniki: Aristotle University of Thessaloniki seminar paper.
Kerbrat-Orecchioni, Catherine. 1977. *La connotation*. Lyon: Presses Universitaires de Lyon.
Kharbouch, Ahmed. 2017. De Greimas à Jean-Claude Coquet: Le discours et son sujet. *Actes Sémiotiques* 120. 1–21.
Koestler, Arthur. 1960 [1959]. *Les somnambules: Essai sur l'histoire des conceptions de l'univers*. Georges Fradier (trans.). Paris: Calmann-Lévy.
Kristeva, Julia. 1978 [1969]. *Σημειωτική: Recherches pour une sémanalyse (Extraits)*. Paris: Seuil.
Kristiansen, Gitte & René Dirven. 2008. Cognitive sociolinguistics: Rationale, methods and scope. In Gitte Kristiansen & René Dirven (eds.) *Cognitive sociolinguistics: Language variation, cultural models, social systems*, 1–17. Berlin: de Gruyter.
Kull, Kalevi, Terrence Deacon, Claus Emmeche, Jesper Hoffmeyer & Frederik Stjernfelt. 2009. Theses on Biosemiotics: Prolegomena to a theoretical biology. *Biological Theory* 4 (2). 167–173.
Labov, William. 1972. The study of language in its social context. In Pier Paolo Giglioli (ed.) *Language and social context*, 283–307. London: Penguin Books.
Lagopoulos, Alexandros Ph. 1995. *Urbanisme et sémiotique, dans les sociétés préindustrielles*. Paris: Anthropos.
Lagopoulos, Alexandros Ph. 1996. Social space: An articulation of the material and the semiotic. *S: European Journal for Semiotic Studies* 8 (4). 579–596.
Lagopoulos, Alexandros Ph. 2004. *Epistimologíes tou noímatos, domismós kai simeiotikí* [Epistemologies of meaning, structuralism and semiotics]. Thessaloniki: Paratiritis.
Lagopoulos, Alexandros Ph. 2009. The semiotics of the Vitruvian city. *Semiotica* 175 (1/4): 193–251.
Lagopoulos, Alexandros Ph. 2012a. Saussure and Derrida: The semiotics of limitlessness. *The American Journal of Semiotics* 28 (3/ 4),. 231–255.
Lagopoulos, Alexandros Ph. 2012b. *O symvolismós tou chórou tis archaías Elládas* [The symbolism of space in ancient Greece]. Athens: Academy of Athens.
Lagopoulos, Alexandros Ph. & Karin Boklund-Lagopoulou. 1992. *Meaning and geography: The social conception of the region in northern Greece*. Berlin: Mouton de Gruyter.

Lagopoulos, Alexandros Ph. & Karin Boklund-Lagopoulou. 2014. Semiotics, culture and space. *Sign Systems Studies* 42 (4): 435–486.
Lagopoulos, Alexandros Ph. & Maria-Georgia Lily Stylianoudi. 2004. Classification, metaphor and power: Built space in Ethiopia. *Koht ja Paik (Place and Location)* IV: 11–56.
Landowski, Eric. 2017. Interactions (socio)sémiotiques. *Actes Sémiotiques* 120. 1–40.
Leach, Edmund. 1976. *Culture and communication: The logic by which symbols are connected.* Cambridge: Cambridge University Press.
Ledrut, Raymond. 1986. Speech and the silence of the city. In Mark Gottdiener & Alexandros Ph. Lagopoulos (eds.) *The city and the sign: An introduction to urban semiotics*, 114–134. New York, NY: Columbia University Press.
Lefebvre, Henri. 1974. *La production de l'espace*. Paris: Anthropos.
Lévi-Strauss, Claude. 1967 [1949]. *Les structures élémentaires de la parenté*, 2nd edn. Paris: Mouton & Co and Maison des Sciences de l'Homme.
Lévi-Strauss, Claude. 1955. *Tristes tropiques*. Paris: Plon.
Lévi-Strauss, Claude. 1958. *Anthropologie structurale*. Paris: Plon. English trans. Claire Jacobson & Brooke Grundfest Schoepf, *Structural Anthropology*. New York, NY: Basic Books, 1963.
Lévi-Strauss, Claude. 1962. *La pensée sauvage*. Paris: Plon.
Lotman, Juri M. 1975. On the metalanguage of a typological description of culture. *Semiotica* 14 (2). 97–123.
Lotman, Yuri M. 1990. *Universe of the mind: A semiotic theory of culture*. London & New York, NY: Tauris.
Lotman, Juri M. 2005. On the semiosphere. *Sign Systems Studies* 33 (1). 205–229.
Lotman, Juri M. & Boris A. Uspenskij. 2013. Heterogeneity and homogeneity of cultures: Postscriptum to the collective theses. In Silvi Salupere, Peeter Torop & Kalevi Kull (eds.) *Beginnings of the semiotics of culture*, 129–132. Tartu: University of Tartu Press.
Lukács, György. 1971 [1923]). *History and class consciousness*. Cambridge, MA: MIT Press.
Lyons, John. 1968. *Introduction to theoretical linguistics*. Cambridge: Cambridge University Press.
Lyotard, Jean F. 1979. *La condition postmoderne: Rapport sur le savoir*. Paris: Minuit.
Manazi, Athanasia. 2019. Afigimatikí análysi tis tainías *Kódikas Da Vinci* [Narrative analysis of the film *The Da Vinci code*]. Thessaloniki: Aristotle University of Thessaloniki seminar paper.
Martinet, André. 1970. *Éléments de linguistique générale*. Paris: Armand Colin.
Mayr, Andrea. 2008. Introduction: Power, discourse and institutions. In Andrea Mayr (ed.) *Language and power: An introduction to institutional discourse*, 1–25. London & New York, NY: Continuum.
McGroarty, Mary E. 2010. Language and ideologies. In Nancy H. Hornberger & Sandra Lee McKay (eds.) *Sociolinguistics and language education*, 3–39. Bristol, New York, NY & Ontario, Canada: Multilingual Matters.
McLuhan, Marshall & Quentin Fiore. 1967. *The medium is the message: An inventory of effects.* New York, NY: Bantam.
Medvedev, Pavel N. & Mikhail M. Bakhtin. 1978 [1928]. *The formal method in literary scholarship: A critical introduction to sociological poetics*, Albert J. Wehrle (trans). Baltimore, MD & London: The Johns Hopkins University Press.
Mesthrie, Rajend. 2009. Clearing the ground: Basic issues, concepts and approaches, In Rajend Mesthrie, Joan Swann, Ana Deumert & William L. Leap (eds.) *Introducing sociolinguistics*, 2nd ed., 1–41. Edinburgh: Edinburgh University Press.

Meyerhoff, Miriam. 2006. *Introducing sociolinguistics*. Abingdon: Routledge.
Middleton, John. 1973. Some categories of dual classification among the Lugbara of Uganda. In Rodney Needham (ed.) *Right and left: Essays on dual symbolic classification*, 369–390. Chicago, IL & London: The University of Chicago Press.
Moles, Abraham A. & Claude Zeltmann. 1973. La communication: L'environnement culturel de l'homme. In Abraham André Moles & Claude Zeltmann (eds.) *La communication et les mass media*, 120–157. Verviers: Gérard et Co.
Moretti, Franco. 1998 [1997]. *Atlas of the European novel, 1800–1900*. London & New York, NY: Verso.
Morris, Charles. 1971. *Writings on the general theory of signs*. The Hague & Paris: Mouton.
Mullins, Laurie J. 2010 [1985]. *Management and organisational behaviour*. 9th edn. Harlow, etc.: Prentice Hall & Financial Times.
Nikolaou, Mariana. 2007. Epanaliptikótita, neanikótita kai álles isotopíes [Repetition, youth and other isotopies] (in Greek). Thessaloniki: Aristotle University of Thessaloniki seminar paper.
Ogden, C. K. & I. A. Richards. 1985 [1923]. *The meaning of meaning: A study of the influence of language upon thought and of the science of symbolism*. London, Boston, MA, & Henley: Ark.
Osgood, Charles E. 1952. The nature and measurement of meaning. *Psychological Bulletin* 49 (3). 197–237.
Osgood, Charles E., George J. Suci & Percy H. Tannenbaum. 1975 [1957]. *The measurement of meaning*, 9th edn. Urbana & Chicago, IL, & London: University of Illinois Press.
Pape, Helmut. 1998. Peirce and his followers. In Roland Posner, Klaus Robering & Thomas A. Sebeok (eds.) *Semiotik/Semiotics: A Handbook of the sign-theoretic foundations of nature and culture*, vol. 2, 2016–2040. Berlin & New York, NY: de Gruyter.
Park, Robert Ezra. 1961. Human ecology. In George A. Theodorson (ed.) *Studies in Human Ecology*, 22–29. Evanston & New York: Harper and Row.
Peirce, Charles S. 1931–1935. *Collected papers of Charles Sanders Peirce*, 6 vols. Charles Hartshorne & Paul Weiss (eds.). Cambridge, MA, & London: The Belknap Press.
Petitot, Jean. 1990. Semiotics and cognitive science: The morphological turn. *The Semiotic Review of Books* 1 (1). 2–4.
Petitot, Jean. 2017. Mémoires et parcours sémiotiques du côté de Greimas. *Actes Sémiotiques*. 1–34.
Petridis, Sotiris. 2019. A case for joint brand management in film and television promotion. Thessaloniki: Aristotle University of Thessaloniki post-doctoral thesis.
Phillips, Louise & Marianne W. Jørgensen. 2002. *Discourse analysis as theory and method*. London, Thousand Oaks & New Delhi: Sage.
Pontosidou, Aikaterini. 2007. I póli kai i taftótita: Synéntefxi gia ti simiotikí tis Thessaloníkis [City and identity: An interview on the semiotics of Thessaloniki]. Thessaloniki: Aristotle University of Thessaloniki seminar paper.
Posner, Roland, Klaus Robering & Thomas A. Sebeok (eds.) 1998. *Semiotik/semiotics: A handbook on the sign-theoretic foundations of nature and culture*, 4 vols. Berlin & New York, NY: de Gruyter.
Propp, Vladimir. 1968 [1928]. *Morphology of the folktale*, 2nd revised ed., Laurence Scott (trans). Austin, TX: University of Texas Press.
Rastier, François. 2009. *Sémantique interprétative*. Paris: Presses Universitaires de France.
Rastier, François. 2017. De la sémiotique structurale à la sémiotique des cultures. *Actes Sémiotiques* 120. 1–23.

Rigopoulou, Chrysoula. 2007. Thessaloniki, Lefkós Pýrgos i PAOK? Simeiotikí análysi tou chórou: O astikós chóros os politismikó proïón [Thessaloniki, White Tower or PAOK? Semiotic analysis of space: Space as a cultural product]. Thessaloniki: Aristotle University of Thessaloniki seminar paper.

Rossi-Landi, Ferruccio. 1983. *Language as work and trade: A semiotic homology for linguistics and economics*. South Hadley, MA: Bergin & Garvey.

Saussure, Ferdinand de. 1971 [1916]. *Cours de linguistique générale*. Charles Bally & Albert Sechehaye (eds.). Critical edn. Tullio de Mauro. Paris: Payot, 1979. English trans. & ed. Roy Harris, *Course in General Linguistics*. London: Duckworth, 1983.

Saussure, Ferdinard de. 2002. *Écrits de linguistique générale*, Simon Bouquet & Rudolf Engler (eds.), in collaboration with Antoinette Weil. Paris: Gallimard.

Sayers, Dorothy L. 1936. *Gaudy night*. London: Gollancz.

Sebeok, Thomas A. 1988. In what sense is language a "primary modeling system"? In Henri Broms & Rebecca Kaufmann (eds.) *Semiotics of culture* (Proceedings of the 25th symposium of the Tartu–Moscow School of semiotics, Imatra, Finland, 27–29 July, 1987), 67–80. Helsinki: Arator.

Sebeok, Thomas A. 1997. Global semiotics. In Irmengard Raugh & Gerald F. Carr (eds.) *Semiotics around the world: Synthesis in diversity* (Proceedings of the 5th congress of the International Association for Semiotic Studies, Berkeley, 1994), vol. 1, 105–130. Berlin & New York, NY: Mouton de Gruyter.

Sebeok, Thomas A. (ed). 1994 [1986]. *Encyclopedic dictionary of semiotics*, 2 vols. Berlin & New York, NY: Mouton de Gruyter.

Sonesson, Göran. 2017. Greimasean phenomenology and beyond: From isotopy to time consciousness. *Semiotica* 219. 93–113.

Steiner, Peter (ed.). 1982. *The Prague School: Selected writings, 1929–1946*. Austin, TX: University of Chicago Press.

Theodorson, George A. 1961. Introduction. In George A. Theodorson (ed.) *Studies in human ecology*, 3–7. Evanston & New York: Harper and Row.

Thornborrow, Joanna & Jennifer Coates. 2005. The sociolinguistics of narrative: Identity, performance, culture. In Joanna Thornborrow & Jennifer Coates (eds.) *The sociolinguistics of narrative*, 1–16. Amsterdam & Philadelphia, PA: Benjamins.

Troubetzkoy, N. S. 1964 [1939]. *Principes de phonologie*. Paris: Klincksieck.

Uspenskij, B.A., V. V. Ivanov, V. N. Toporov, A. M. Pjatigorskij & J. M. Lotman 1973. Theses on the semiotic study of cultures (as applied to Slavic texts). In Jan van der Eng & Mojmir Grygar (eds.) *Structure of texts and semiotics of culture*, 1–28. The Hague: Mouton.

Vitruvius. 1983 [1931]. *De architectura*, vol. 1 (Loeb Classical Library). Frank Granger (trans). Cambridge, MA: Harvard University Press & London: William Heinemann.

Vitruvius. 1985 [1934]. *De architectura*, vol. 2 (Loeb Classical Library). Frank Granger (trans). Cambridge, MA: Harvard University Press & London: William Heinemann.

Vološinov, Valentin N. 1977 [1929]. *Le marxisme et la philosophie du langage: Essai d'application de la méthode sociologique en linguistique*. Paris: Minuit.

Williams, Raymond. 1977. *Marxism and literature*. Oxford: Oxford University Press.

Wimsatt W. K. Jr. & M. C. Beardsley. 1946. The intentional fallacy. *The Sewanee Review* 54 (3). 468–488.

Winner, Thomas G. 1998. Prague functionalism. In Roland Posner, Klaus Robering & Thomas A. Sebeok (eds.) *Semiotik/semiotics: A handbook on the sign-theoretic foundations of nature and culture*, vol. 2, 2248–2255. Berlin & New York, NY: de Gruyter.

Yeats, William Butler. 1956. *Autobiographies*. London: MacMillan.

Index

Ablali, Driss 239, 242, 246, 246, n. 94, 247
acoustic image 31, 54–55, 255–256
Acta sanctorum 123
actant 88, 105–106, 108–109, 115–116, 125–126, 173, 201, 229, 232, 236–237, 241, 244, 246, n. 94, 248, 256, 260, 305–306, 311
– proto-actant 238, 244
actor 108, 115–116, 118, 120–122, 125, 173, 184, 198–202, 237, 241, 248, 256, 260, 295, 315
actorialisation 115–117, 121, 236
actualising 114, 236, 238
addressee 109, n. 43, 254, 255, n. 97, 257, 260–261, 264, 266, 273–274, 304, 331 and *passim*
addresser 109, n. 43, 254, 255, n. 97, 256–261, 263, 266, 273–274, 331 and *passim*
advertising 15, 279, 279, n. 103, 280, 281, n. 105, 295, 299, 329
aesthetic 9, 101, 136–137, 187, 193, 237, 261, 266, 271, 275, 278–280, 284, 308–309, 329
affect 15, 99, 101, 114, 235–240, 245–246, 248–249
alliteration 138, 162, 277
Althusser, Louis 323–324, 327, 336
ambiguity 131, 177, 287–288
analogy 64, 143, 145, 145, n. 59
Anderson, Myrdene 19
anthropology V, 3, 14, 28, 51, n. 18, 54, 57, 66, 88, 185, 189, 190, n. 71, 191, 241, 243–244, 269
Apostolopoulou, Athina 217–218
appropriation 265, 268
arbitrariness 32–33, 39–40, 62
architecture 3, 15, 261, 279–281, 297
art 3–4, 9, 11, 28–29, 70, 160, 261, 263, 266, 268, 278, 289, 295, 309–310, 318–319, 326, 329–330
articulation 6, 10, 30, 33, 45, 53, 74, 74, n. 29, 85, 87, 122, 143, 152, 242, 246, 249, 316–317, 322, 327, 331–333, 335–336 and *passim*
– linguistics 45
– phoneme 43
aspectualisation 117, 239
assertion 98, 100
attribution 268–269
audiovisual 267, 329
axiological 93, 99, 101, 114, 235–237, 268
axis of simultaneity 25, 49
axis of succession 25–26, 49

Bakhtin, Mikhail M. 10–11, 263, 266–267, 285, 287–288, 317, 330
Balibar, Etienne 323–324, 327, 336
Balzac, Honoré de 196
Barthes, Roland V, 12, 14–15, 17–18, 26, 31, 40–41, 49, 73–74, 88, n. 35, 196–197, 267, 286, 288, 303–304
Baudrillard, Jean 18, 272–273, 332, n. 125
Beardsley, Monroe C. 264, n. 100
behaviour 21–22, 241–242, 263, 307–308
behavioural geography 241, n. 91, 309
Bernstein, Basil 85–86, 307
Biglari, Amir 244, n. 93
binary 44, 46, 97, 133–134, 138, 149, 167, 184, n. 70, 185, 188, 214, 227, 229–230, 236
biology 13, 15, 20–21, 249, 333, 334, n. 127, 335
Blanché, Robert 100, n. 39
body 187, 238–239, 246, 246, n. 94, 247, 248, 273, 284–285
Boklund-Lagopoulou, Karin 13, 123, 140, 197, 203
Borroff, Marie 137
Bourdieu, Pierre 305, 317–319, 321, 328, 330
Brahms, Johannes 293
Brandt, Per Aage 15–17
Bruno, V. J. 70

canonical
– model 244, 270

– schema 104–105, 109–111, 113, 269–270, 273
– theory 235, 246, 248, 270
capitalism 19, 244, 247, 266–267, 327–329
Castells, Manuel 324, 324, n. 121, 325
channel 209, n. 83, 258, 260, 270–273, 275, 277, 299, 303–304, 315 and *passim*
Chaplin, Charlie 292, 292, n. 109
Child, Lee 4–5
Chomsky, Noam 82–83, 88–89, 94–96, 305–306
cinema 3, 15, 22, 29, 45, 122, 144, 267, 286, 289, 291, 295–300
circulation 59, 306, 318, 329, 333
circumstance 84, 162, 264, 300, 302–304
circus 326
citation 289, 291, 291, n. 108, 294
classeme 131–132, 134 and *passim*
classification system 88, n. 35, 184–190
Coates, Jennifer 86
Cobley, Paul V, 21, 253
code 29, 133, 147, 150, 153, 196, 271, 303
– Barthes 196
– Bernstein 85–86
– dominant 186–188, 227
– Eco 271, 274, 301–304, 306
– Jakobson 273, 277
– partial 133
– transmission 271, 329
coding 29, 113, 303
– extra- 302
– over- 302
– under- 302
cognitive 15–17, 20, 60–62, 62, n. 23, 106, 125, 246, 248, 278, n. 102, 307–309, 317, 327, n. 124, 334
coherence 82, 131, 132, n. 51, 141, 143, n. 58, 162, 210
cohesion 82, 161–162, 162, n. 62
colour 69–72, 77–78, 299
– four-colour school 70
communication 3, 5–6, 11–12, 83, 87, 109, n. 43, 133, 184, 245, n. 94, 253, 254, 254, n. 96, 255, n. 97, 256, 258–259, 265, 268, 273, 303, 309, 318–319, 336 and *passim*

– circuit 10, 31–32, 55, 110, 253–254, 256–259, 261–264, 269, 275, 300, 304–305, 308, 310, 313, 317, 322, 333
communicative event 86
commutation 48
competence 106, 108, 111–112, 240, 260, 270, 305–306
– Chomsky 96, 305
– cultural 5, 305–307, 317–318
– linguistic 305, 318
– modal 105–106, 108, 110, 126, 236
– pragmatic 307–308
complementarity 98–100, 143, 175
congruence 162
connotation 44, 72, 73, 74, n. 29, 75, 76, n. 31, 77–81, 132–133
connotator 74
consciousness 17, 31, 54, 255, 327
– collective 25, 305
– possible 305–306
– practical 328
– social 11, 306, 330
consumption
– material 333
– semiotic 86, 253–254, 263–264, 319, 325, 333
context 46, 48, 77–78, 130–132, 273, 282–285, 287–289, 291, 296–298, 300, 301, 301, n. 114, 302–305, 308
– of situation 83–84, 282
– social 84–86
continuity 28, 238–239, 245, 246, n. 94, 253
contract 110, 112, 125–128, 269
contradiction 97, 97, n. 38, 99–101, 103, 143, 174, 183
contrariety 97, 97, n. 38, 99–103, 107, 109, 117, 143–144, 174–175, 183, 185, 187, 230–231
conventionality 32–38, 49, 51–52, 68
Coogler, Ryan 159
cooking 28
Coppola, Francis Ford 293
Coquet, Jean-Claude 245–246, n. 94
corpus 83, 96, n. 37, 139–140, 197, 202–203, 206, n. 80, 208, 210, 213, 217, 241, 242, n. 92, 244, 268, 287, 295–297

Costa, Lúcio 79–81, n. 33
Couégnas, Nicolas 242, n. 92, 243–244, 244, n. 93, 269–270
Courtés, Joseph VI, 5, 15–16, 19, 26, 29, 31, 39–40, 44–46, 66, 72–73, 75–76, 83, 87, n. 34, 87, 88, 88, n. 35, 95–97, 97, n. 38, 99, 100, 100, n. 39, 101, 104, 105, 106, n. 42, 107–109, 109, n. 43, 110, 112–113, 115–118, 120–122, 130, n. 48, 131, 133, 135, 138, 140, 142–144, 151, 183–185, 189, 230, 235, 236, n. 88, 239, 241, n. 91, 253, 255, n. 97, 260, 267–268, 278–279, 282, 286, 288, 305, 307–308, 321–323, 331–332
cross-tabulation 197
cultural
– competence 5, 305–307, 317–318
– field 318
– materialism 327
– network 319, 321
– sciences 7
– studies V, 7, 21, 138, 334
– theory 6, 20
– unit 68–69, 302, 304
culture 3, 5–6, 10, 13, 19, 22, 62, n. 23, 328–330, 334–336 and *passim*

Daylight, Douglas 22
Deacon, Terrence 31, 340
Debord, Guy-Ernest 18
deconstruction 18–19, 51, 93, 287
Deely, John 21, 62, n. 23
defamiliarisation 9
Deleuze, Giles 302
denotation 72–73, 75–76, 79, 132, 135, 193, 259, 261, 264–265, 274, 284–285, 297, 301, 304
Derrida, Jacques 18, 21, 51–53, 53, n. 20, 75–76, 286–288
determination 58, 96, n. 37, 318, 324, 327–328, 330, 332, 335
diachronic 26–28, 259–261, 309
diachronic linguistics 26
dialogical 265, 266, 287
dialogue 198, 209, 222, 267, 287, 312–313, 333

differance 287
differential 48–52, 287
Dirven, René 86
discontinuity 238–239, 245
discourse 77, 83, 86–87, 93, 288
– figurative 120, 173
– level of 95, 130, 149, 163, 165, 173, 186, 235, 276
– order of 86
discourse analysis 82, 86
– critical 86, 93
discursive
– event 83
– formation 83
– linguistics 83
– practice 86
– process 41, 83
– structure 29, 66
discursivisation 115, 118
dispossession 268
distinctive features 43–44, 46–48, 56
dramatis personae (Propp) 94
dress 3–5, 11, 309–310, 326
Ducrot, Oswald 27
Durkheim, Émile 185
dynamic 15–16, 27, 49, 58, 82, 98, 133, 139, 160, 239, 244, 245, 245, n. 94, 263, 296, 304, 318, 322, 326
dynamics 249, 313, 327, 336
– of communication 254
– of speech 253
– of semiotic systems 332
– social 10, 30, 306, 317, 331
dysphoria 99, 101, 103, 115, 149, 235, 238

Eco, Umberto V, 3, 5–6, 15, 16, 16, n. 2, 19, 21, 29, 41, 45–46, 60, 60, n. 22, 61, 62, 62, 62, n. 23, 63, 63, n. 24, 64, 66–69, 72, 132–133, 143, 143, n. 58, 260–261, 264–265, 267–268, 271, 274–275, 279, 279, n. 103, 280, 281, 281, n. 105, 299, 301–304, 306–308
Eichenbaum, Boris M. 9
Emmeche, Claus 340
Empedocles 70
enunciatee 255, n. 97, 287

enunciation 83, 104, 115, 160, 233, n. 87, 241, 243, 245, n. 94, 255, n. 97, 321–322, 331
enunciator 115, 117, 255, n. 97, 287
épistémè 77, 184–185, 273, 326
epistemology 6, 12, 15, 19–21, 28, 30, 32, 37–38, 63, 77, 87–88, 93, 118, 122, 184, 191–192, 239, 241, 244–249, 269, 306–307, 316, 323–324, 331–332, 336
esthesic 245
ethnography of speaking 83
euphoria 99, 101, 103, 115, 149, 235, 238
evaluation 27, 57, 133, 139, 145, 149–150, 152, 213–214, 224–226
Evans, Gary W. 197
exchange 110, 244, 253, 268–269, 283, 310
extra-textual 29, 246, n. 94, 282, 285, 288–289, 296, 298, 300, 331

Fairclough, Norman 86, 307
Famy, Aurore 244, n. 93
feeling 57, 136, 208, 226, 228, 239, 247, 328
figuration 120–121
figurativisation 118, 120–122, 163–164, 173, 186, 237
figure 120, 175
Fiore, Quentin 272
Firstness 16, 60–161
Fodor, Jerry A. 132, 301
Fontanille, Jacques 15, 83, 147, 160, 161, 162, 162, n. 62, 163, 187, 237–242, 242, n. 92, 243, 244, 244, n. 93, 246–249, 269–270, 328
form
– of the content 53 and *passim*
– of the expression 53 and *passim*
– Barthes 74
– Eco 61–62
– Fontanille 241–244
– Hjelmslev 53–55, 58–59, 242
– Saussure 33, 53, 59, 61, 238, 270
formalism 245
forms of living 242–243, 321, 328
Foucault, Michel 18, 77, 83, 184–185, 273, 326
Frank, Manfred 17–18
Frankfurt School 18

frequency 192, 196, 218, 220 and *passim*
– absolute 192, 200
– relative 192, 195–196, 200, 217, 219–220, 229, 233
function *passim*
– conative 274, 279–280, 307
– expressive 274, 280
– Jakobson 273–274, 278–280, 298, 305, 307
– metalinguistic 277, 279–280, 289
– phatic 275, 277, 279–280, 292
– poetic 12, 278–280
– Propp 11, 94–95, 109, 111–113
– referential 274, 279–280
– relation-function 104–105, 114
– sociolinguistics 84–85
– symbolic 333
functionalist 12, 87
functions of semiotic systems 281–282, 298

Gay, Pierre 37, n. 11
Geertz, Clifford 241
generative grammar 82, 94–95
generative trajectory 16, 29, 83, 95–97, 100, n. 39, 101, 108, 114–115, 118, 119, n. 46, 122–123, 125, 143, n. 58, 229, 232, 235–238, 249, 269
generativity 96, n. 37
genre 10, 19, 31, 59, 87, n. 34, 113, 184, 278, 288, 296–298
gesture 11, 299
gift 269, 310
glossematics 12, 33, 58
Godelier, Maurice 281, 281, n. 104, 327
Goldmann, Lucien 305–306, 329–330, 332
Gottdiener, Mark 6
graph
– basic 156–157, 233
– final 157–158, 194, 198, 233
Greimas, Algirdas Julien V–VI5, 11–12, 14–16, 19, 25, n. 4, 26, 29, 31, 39–40, 44–47, 66, 72–73, 75–76, 83, 87, 87, n. 34, 88, 88, n. 35, 89, 93–95, 96, 96, n. 37, 97, 99, 100, 100, n. 39, 101, 104, 105, 106, 106, n. 42, 107–109, 109, n. 43, 110–113, 115–118, 120–122, 130, 130, n. 48, 131–135, 138–140, 142–144, 149,

151, 162, n. 62, 182–185, 189, 192, 230, 235, 236, n. 88, 237–240, 241, n. 91, 246, 249, 253, 255, n. 97, 256–257, 260, 267–269, 278–279, 282, 286, 288, 305, 307–308, 321–323, 328, 331–332
ground, Peirce 60–61
Groupe de Recherche Sémio-linguistique VI, 14, *See* also Paris School
Guattari, Félix 302
Guiraud, Pierre 274–275, 299

habitus 318, 327, n. 124, 330
Hall, Edward T. 299
Halliday, M. A. K. 84–85, 307
Harris, Roy VI
Harvey, David 328–329
Hassan, Ihab 19
Heidegger, Martin 237, n. 89
Helper 109, 111–113, 116 and *passim*
Hénault, Anne 94, 109, 122, 126, 131, 249
Hesiod 189
Hjelmslev, Louis V, 12, 14, 15, n. 1, 25, n. 4, 29, 33, 39–40, 53–59, 60, n. 21, 61, 67–70, 72–76, 78, 134, 137, 209, 237–238, 241–242, 277, 335–336
Hoffmeyer, Jesper 340
homology 143, 144, 145, n. 59, 159
Howard, Ron 159
Hughes, John 294
Husserl, Edmund 14, 16
Hymes, Dell 83–85, 274, 278, 307

icon 64–67
iconic 39, 271, 274
iconisation 120–121
iconism, primary 16, 60–61
idealism 3, 18–20, 38, 62, 247–248, 323, 323, n. 120
ideological 11, 88, 247, 256–257, 305–306, 316, 324–326, 330
ideology 5, 10–11, 74, 77, 88, 88, n. 35, 138, 140, 184–185, 187–189, 197, 222–223, 228, 231, 233, 247–248, 265–266, 272, 279, 325, 327, n. 124, 328, 330
idiolect 184, 322
image

– mental 54
– visual 66, 271, 274
immanence 19
immanent analysis 12, 29, 242–243, 303, 331–332, 336
implication 98, 102
index 21, 61, 64, 64–65, n. 25, 65–67
indicator 99
information theory 109, n. 43, 254, n. 96, 271, 273
intention 123, 253, 256, 258–259, 261–266, 327, n. 124
interpretant 60–61, 64–65, 69, 75, n. 30, 302
intertextuality 59, 285–289, 291–292, 294, n. 112, 296–298, 300, 321, 323
– citational 289, 291, 293
– free 289
– transformational 291–296
interview 197, 202, 215, 217, 242, n. 92
intonation 136–137
Iser, Wolfgang 282, 303
isomorphism 73, 143–144, 159 and *passim*
isotopy 81, 88, 130–131, 133, 143, n. 58, 247 and *passim*
– agglomerate 161–162, 187, 213, 215
– bi- 143
– complex 143, 177–180
– composite 133, 147–150, 152–153, 155, 157, 166
– dominant 153, 157–158, 194–195, 217, 221, 233
– family 161–162
– pluri- 142, 193
– series 161–162
Ivanov, Vjačeslav V. 12, 343

Jakobson, Roman 9–13, 21, 41, 83, 93, 109, n. 43, 138, 216, 255, 255, n. 97 261, 273–275, 277–279, 298, 303, 307
Jameson, Fredric 329
Jencks, Charles 76, 297
Jenkins, Henry 299–300
Johansen, Jørgen D. 12
Jørgensen, Marianne W. 86
Joseph, John E. 25–26, 32, n. 7, 39, 39, n. 13
junction 104, 114, 118, 236, 245, 335

– conjunction 104
– disjunction 104

Kaklamanidou, Despoina 198, 199, 199, n. 75, 200
Kant, Immanuel 59
Karagiannis, Konstantinos 159
Karcevskij, Sergei J. 9, 11
Katz, Jerrold J. 132, 301
Kepler, Johannes 77
Kerbrat-Orecchioni, Catherine 74, n. 29, 76, 76, n. 31
Kharbouch, Ahmed 245, n. 94, 246, n. 94, 247–248
kinesic 299
kinship, atom of 145
Klein, Felix 100, n. 39
Koestler, Arthur 77
Krampen, Martin 337
Kristeva, Julia 10, 18, 286–288, 297
Kristiansen, Gitte 86
Kull, Kalevi V, 20

labour, semiotic 263–265, 278, 282, 286
Labov, William 85–86, 307
Lacan, Jacques 18
Laclos, Pierre Choderlos de 198, 295
Lagopoulos, Alexandros Ph. 9, 13, 53, n. 20, 140, 187–188, 197, 203, 253, 259, 265, 285, 333
Landowski, Eric 15, 244–246, 249
language, natural 8, 45, 58–59, 69, 73, 95, 98, 104, 114, 123, 256, 262, 264, 266, 278–279, 298–299
languages 29, n. 6
language system 25–26, 28–33, 37–40, 40, n. 14, 41, 48–51, 63, 74, 81–83, 85, 88, 93, 96, 96, n. 36, 99, 115, 130, 133, 136, 140–141, 160, 253–254, 302–303, 316, 336 *See* also *langue*
langue 32, 33, 36, 37, 38, 39, 40, 45, 49, 56, 57, 59, 60, 97, 105, 109, 255, 280, 309, 326, 341 and *passim*. *See* also language system
Leach, Edmund 257, 260, 263, 269, 317
Ledrut, Raymond 258, n. 98, 259

Lefebvre, Henri 325
legitimation 188, 281, 282, 319
Leone, Sergio 292
level *passim*
– Hjelmslev 54–55, 57–59, 61, 241–242
– of social appreciation 54–55, 57–58
– physical 54–59
– physiological 55
– socio-biological 54–58
Lévi-Strauss, Claude 13–14, 28, 51, n. 18, 88, 93, 145, 184, n. 70, 185, 244, 253, 257, 261, 267, 269, 286, 296, 333
lexeme 46 and *passim*
linearity 38–39, 95, 131
Linguistic Circle of Copenhagen 12
Linguistic Circle of Moscow 9
linguistic community 29, 33
linguistics *passim*. *See* also sociolinguistics
– diachronic 26–27
– external 26, 30, 316, 335
– of speech 26, 88
– structural 30, 63, 246
– synchronic 25–26, 49
– text linguistics 141
– translinguistics 288
literature 3–4, 9–10, 13, 25, 74, 77, 87, n. 34, 283, 286, 296, 299, 326, 329–330
– popular 10
localisation
– spatial 117–118
– temporal 117
logical hexagon 99–100, n. 39
Lotman, Juri M. 12–13, 119–120, 333–334
Lukács, Györgi 305
Lyons, John 44
Lyotard, Jean F. 18

Malinowski, Bronislav 275
Manazi, Athanasia 159
manipulation 110, 112
Martinet, André 44–45
Marx, Karl 88, 269
Marxism 10–11, 14, 18, 86–87, 246, 305–307, 316–318, 323–324, 327, 331, 336
material vehicle 3, 31, 33, 54

Mathesius, Vilém 11
matrix 154, 155, 155, n. 64, 156, 158, n. 65 and *passim*
Mauss, Marcel 185, 269
Mayr, Andrea 86
McGroarty, Mary E. 86
McLuhan, Marshall 272–273
media V, 81, 83, 86, 88, 272, 295–296, 300, 303, 326
– inter- 296
– trans- 59, 293, 300
Medvedev, Pavel N. 10–11, 330
mental image 241, n. 91
mental map 216, n. 84, 309
Merleau-Ponty, Maurice 14
message 254, n. 96, 273–275, 277–278, 298 and *passim*
Mesthrie, Rajend 87
metalanguage 72, 74–77, 98, 209, 277, 318
metalinguistic 16, 43–44, 46, 57, 59, 74, 77, 101, 103, 122, 133, 138, 153, 184–186, 189–190, 216, 277, 283
metalinguistic universals 334, n. 126
metaphor 41, 74, 141 and *passim*
– Jakobson 41 and *passim*
metasemiotic 74, 335–336, *See* also metalanguage
metonymy 163, 294
– Jakobson 41
metre 136–138, 138, n. 55, 162
Meyerhoff, Miriam 86
micro-universe 101, 133
Middleton, John 185, 188
Mnouchkine, Ariane 265
modal 106
– apparatus 240–241
– competence 105, 108, 126
– dimension 307
– pre-modal 238
modalisation
– affective 237
– meta- 238
modality 105, 107–109, 111, 115, 115, n. 45, 120, 127, 230, 237–238, 240, 244, 246, 256
Moles, Abraham A. 260, 270
monologue 257, 259

Moore, Charles 297
Moretti, Franco 112, n. 44, 119, 119, n. 46
morpheme 44–46, 96, n. 37, 132, n. 51 and *passim*
Morricone, Ennio 293, 295
Morris, Charles W. 8, 27, n. 5, 307
motivated 34
Mukařovský, Jan 11
Mullins, Laurie J. 313–314
multimedia 267, 293, 298
music 3, 13, 122, 135, 292–293, 295–297, 299–301
myth 119, 147, 149, 188–189, 261, 272, 286, 296
mythology 28, 326

narrative *passim*
– grammar 95, 322
– model V, 268
– programme 104–106, 110, 113, 117, 119–120, 236
– schema 109–111, 113, 269, 273
– semantics 95, 114–115, 118, 120, 186
– syntax 95, 104, 108, 115, 229
– theory VI, 6, 95, 229, 235, 270, 310
– trajectory 106, 110–111, 113, 118–119
narratology VI, 11, 89, 93, 159, 198, *See* also narrative theory
negation 97, 97, n. 38, 100
Nikolaou, Mariana 217–220, 222
noise 271, 304, 306
nomenclature 37, 37, n. 12, 38, 50, 63–65, 68

object
– dynamical 61
– immediate 61–62
– material 268
– Peirce 60–61, 63–64
– use 263, 267–268, 281
Object 104, 109–110, 113–114, 118–120, 173, 236, 238, 268–269, 313 and *passim*
– anti-Object 113, 126–127
object-sign 11, 330
Ogden, Charles K. 65–67
onomastics 120–121, 276
onomatological 38

onomatopoeia 35, 36, 37, n. 11
Opponent 109–113, 116, 174 and *passim*
opposition 44, 46, 47, n. 17, 49, 51, 69, 76,
    97–101, 103, 142, 146, 151–152, 157,
    172–173, 184, 188–189, 245
– privative 97
order of appearance 196, 198, 217, 233
Osgood, Charles E. 209

painting 3, 13, 29, 59, 70, 243, 270–271,
    289, 309–311, 319, 326
Pape, Helmut 64
paradigm 40–41, 42, 130, 140–141
paradigmatic 39–42, 49, 63, 72–73, 88, 101,
    103, 106, 115, 130–131, 184, 236, 243,
    286, 291
Paris School 14–15, 235, 238, 246, 321, 332
Park, Robert E. 334, n. 127
parole 26, 29, n. 6, 54, 83–84, 89, 104, 254,
    277, 281, 322, 336
participation 265–267, 269, 311
passional 244, n. 93, 247, 249
Peirce, Charles Sanders 8, 15, n. 1, 16,
    19–22, 59–61, 62, n. 23, 63–67, 69, 75,
    n. 30, 76
performance 105–106, 111–112,
    269–270, 310
Petitot, Jean 15–16, 97, n. 38
Petridis, Sotiris 267, 329
pheme 43, 46, 135
phemic category 44, 138
phenomenology 14, 16, 59, 239, 241,
    246–247, 249
Phillips, Louise 86
phoneme 42–46, 48, 135–137, 162
phonetics 44, 56
phonology 9, 11, 13, 43–44, 135
physiological 44, 55–56, 58, 255,
    270, 272
Piaget, Jean 100, n. 39
Piette, Albert 241
pitch 136, 136, n. 54
Pjatigorskij, Alexander M. 343
plane

– Hjelmslev 53–55, 59, 75, 143
– of content 53–54, 73–74, 134–135, 143,
    238, 277
– of expression 53–54, 59, 61, 73–74, 135,
    137, 143, 162, 238, 243, 277, 303
Poe, Edgar Allan 275, 277
poetic language 9, 287–288
poetry 9, 119, 135–137, 179, 196, n. 74, 202,
    216, 264, n. 100, 266, 278, 280, 288,
    297, 299
political 324–326, 335 and *passim*
political economy 305, 318, 325, n. 122,
    332–333
Polygnotus 70
polysemy 142
Pontosidou, Aikaterini 218, 223
Posner, Roland 6
Postal, Paul M. 132, 301
postmodernism 6, 18–19, 21, 272, 297,
    328–329
potentialising 115, n. 45
power
– communicational 282, 306–307, 319
– political 188, 328
– relationships 86–87, 188, 282, 307, 318
– strategies 318–319
– symbolic 188, 281–282, 318
practice
– cultural 17, 253
– discursive 86
– pragmatic 308, 311
– signifying 263, 299, 307–309, 311, 318,
    321, 326
– social 86, 328
– symbolic 313, 319
pragmatics 244, 307–309, 311
– symbolic 313
Prague Linguistic Circle 11
precapitalist 88, n. 35, 144, 147, 185–186,
    189–190, 258–259
production
– aesthetic 266, 329
– cultural 241, 267, 317, 328–329
– linguistic 43–44, 86, 318

– material 263, 308, 318, 324–326, 328, 333
– semiotic 33, 61, 79–80, 95, 114–115,
    122, 253, 258–259, 264–266, 271, 286,
    288, 304, 322–323, 325, 327, 331,
    333, 336
– symbolic 318
programming
– spatial 117–118
– temporal 117–118
Prokofiev, Sergei 295
Propp, Vladimir 11, 88, 94–95, 108–112, 112,
    n. 44, 116, 119
proprioceptivity 235–239
prosodic 75, 135, 162, 299
Proust, Marcel 247–248
proxemics 244, 299, 312–313
psychic 55, 255–256
psychoanalysis 6, 14, 18, 29, 262
psychology 3, 22, 322, 335
– animal 333
purport 53–54, 57, 68–69,
    241–242, 335

qualitative 6, 16, 153, 158, 165, 191, 193–197,
    202, 211, 222–223, 227, 229, 232, 232,
    n. 87, 233, 254, n. 96
quantitative 6, 153, 155, n. 64, 165, 190,
    n. 71, 191–196, 201, n. 76, 202, 233, n.
    87, 216, 222–223, 227, 229, 232–234,
    254, n. 96

Ransdell, Joseph 337
Rastier, François 96, n. 37, 98, 100, n. 39,
    130, n. 48, 132, n. 51, 140–141, 145,
    n. 59, 146, n. 60, 153, 154, 154, n. 63,
    192, 192, n. 72, 232, n. 87, 233, n. 87,
    247
realising 115, 238
reception theory 10
Recipient 109, 109, n. 43, 110, 112, 236, 241,
    n. 91, 255, n. 97, 269, 313 and *passim*
– final 126, 257
recurrence 130, 140–141, 150
referent 37, 63, 65–68, 97, n. 38, 121,
    272–274, 280, 327
referential 233, n. 87

register 84–85, 184, 202
relation 144
– binary 97
– elementary logical 99, 103, 143
– of complementarity 98, 100
– of contradiction 97, 99
– of contrariety 97, 144
– of presupposition 97–98
relevance 28–30, 65, 67, 153, n. 62,
    247–249, 316–317, 321–323, 326,
    331–332
religion 28
renunciation 268–269
representamen 60–64
representation, Peirce 20, 22, 60, 63, 67
Revised Model, Eco 132, 301
rhetoric 41, 74, 136, 138, 162, 249, 271, 275,
    279–280
rhyme 137, 162, 276–278
rhythm 136–138, 176–177, 275–277,
    292–293
Richards, Ivor A. 65–67
Rigopoulou, Chrysoula 217
Robering, Klaus 6, 342
Rosenstiehl, Agnes 37, n. 11
Rossi-Landi, Ferruccio 305
Russian Formalists 9–14, 93, 296

sanction 111–112, 270
Santana 293
Saussure, Ferdinand de V, VI, 68–9, 12, 14,
    22, 25, 25, n. 4, 26–29, 29, n. 6, 30, 31,
    32, 32, n. 7, 33–35, 37, 37, n. 12, 38–40,
    40, n. 14, 41–43, 43, n. 15, 44–46,
    49–52, 52, n. 19, 53–55, 58–60, 60, n.
    21, 61–67, 72, 75, 77, n. 31, 81–83, 89,
    93, 95–96, 96, n. 36, 99, 130, 137, 238,
    253–256, 259–263, 265, 267, 270, 273,
    287, 291, n. 108, 302–303, 305, 316,
    319, 322, 335–336
Sayers, Dorothy L. 121
Schaeffer, Jean-Marie 27
schema 16, 99, 237
– canonical 104–105, 113, 269–270
– narrative 109–111, 113, 269, 273
Scorsese, Martin 294

sculpture 270–271
Sebeok, Thomas A. 6, 8–9, 19–21, 64,
    281, n. 104, 330
Secondness 60–62
semantic differential 209
semantic *passim*
– axis 97–98, 147, 165
– category 46–47, 98–99, 101, 103, 109, 131,
    133–134, 138–143, 146–151, 153, 157,
    160, 174, 184–185, 187, 189–190, 208,
    230–231 and *passim*
– field 40, 47, 49, 101, 141
– marker 46, 132, 301
– model 301
– richness 192, 214, 218
– zone 68–70, 72
semantics 27, n. 5, 46 and *passim*
– discursive 96, 116, 118–119, 122, 186,
    236–237
– fundamental 95, 101, 106, 114, 118, 173,
    184, 186, 230–231, 235–236, 238
– narrative 95, 114–115, 118, 120, 127, 163,
    173, 186
– semio-narrative 236
semantisation 261, 263–264, 267–268,
    300–301, 303
seme 46–47, 134 and *passim*
– contextual 130, 132, 283
– nuclear 130–132, 134, 143, 283
sememe 46–47 and *passim*
semic
– nucleus 134
– system 46
– trajectory 131
– units 134
semiology V, 8, 14, 75–76, 336
– metasemiology 56
semio-narrative 96, 114, 235–236, 238
semiosic 21, 62, 66
semiosis 3, 15–16, 20, 33, 38, 54, 58,
    60–62, 62, n. 23, 63, 67, 96, n. 37, 239,
    242, 254, n. 96, 258, 301, 334–335
– presemiosis 63
– primary 62–63
– spontaneous 59, 209
– unlimited 60–61

semiosphere 13, 119–120
semiotic square 97–99, 99, n. 39, 100, 101,
    106–107, 109, 112, 114, 143, 153,
    173–175, 182–184, 229–232, 234, 236
semiotic *passim*
– connotative 73
– extra-semiotic 3, 19, 29, 54, 65–66, 85,
    248, 250, 264, 281, 308, 311, 316, 321,
    323, 331
– non-semiotic 3, 67, 331
– Peirce 8, 59–60, 64
– presemiotic 60
semiotics 3 and *passim*
– anthroposemiotics 20, 243
– biosemiotics 15, 20–21
– biplanar 16, 73, 75
– cognitive 15–16, 246, 334
– connotative 75–76, 335–336
– denotative 56, 73–75
– gestural 35, 75
– global 20
– metalinguistic 75
– metasemiotics 75
– monoplanar 45, 75
– non-scientific 45, 75, 209
– object-semiotics 5
– pluriplanar 75
– protosemiotics 60
– scientific 45, 75, 325
– semi-symbolic 75
– social 6, 10, 26, 30, 85, 250, 253, 317–318,
    330, 332, 335–336
– sociosemiotics 6, 10, 87–88, 184,
    244–245, 253, 304, 317–318, 321–322,
    332, 336
– spontaneous cultural 57, 75, 189, 209,
    323, 325
– visual 14–15, 22, 66, 312
– zoosemiotics 19–21
semiotics of
– culture 10, 66
– food 312
– passions 15, 17, 115, n. 45, 236–238, 238,
    n. 90, 240, 244, n. 93, 244–247, 249,
    253, 269
– the natural world 16, 66, 73, 120

sender 115, 254, , 254, n. 96, 255, n. 97, 298, 304 and *passim*
Sender 109, n. 43, 109–112, 201, 244, 255, 269 and *passim*
– anti-Sender 109
– final 112, 257
Shannon, Claude E. 254, n. 96
Shklovsky, Viktor B. 9
sign *passim*
– feeling-sign 65
– Ogden & Richards 65
– Peirce 59–61, 63–64, 66
– Saussure 31–35, 38
significance
– Barthes 286, 288
– statistical 197
signification 3, 5, 10–11, 19, 22, 29, 44–46, 48–50, 52 and *passim*
signified 26, 31–35, 37–38
signifier 26, 31–38
simulacrum 272
situation 16, 57, 59, 83–85, 132, 241, 244–245, 248, 250, 282, 300–301, 303–304, 307–308, 311, 313, 313, n. 118, 317, 336 and *passim*
– macro- 250, 300, 317
– micro- 133, 248–249, 300, 317
social 250
– class 86, 202, 317, 321, 323, 328
– division of labour 85, 326
– field 318
– forces 335–336
– formation 325, 329
– group 184, 191, 266, 301, 305–306, 317, 323
– processes 323, 329, 333, 336
– sciences 7–8, 14, 20, 30, 138, 191, 245, 247, 321–324, 331–333, 335–336
– structure 6, 85, 188, 318, 327
– system 22, 85, 87
social Darwinism 334
Society for the Study of Poetic Language 9
socio-economic 11, 86, 243, 247, 316, 325–328, 330, 332, 336
sociolect 184, 189–190, 322–323

sociolinguistics 17, n. 3, 57, 63, 82–88, 93, 307, 317, 335
sociology V, 3, 18, 22, 28, 184, 191, 245, 305–306, 322, 331, 334–335
Sonesson, Göran 246
space 11, 22, 25, 54, 56, 58, 79, 119, 140, 186, 188, 197, 202–203, 208, 222, 225, 227–228, 233, 258–259, 263–265, 280, 324–325
spatialisation 115, 117, 119, 119, n. 46, 121, 165, 236
speech 3, 28, 30, 40, n. 14, 41, 63, 81, 83–84, 93, 115, 160, 261, 281, n. 104, 307 and *passim*
– act 83–84, 115
– circuit 31, 39
– circumstances 84
– community 84
– event 84–85
– living 160
– situation 83–85
Stanislavski, Constantin 274
statistical analysis 197
Steiner, Peter 11, 27
stereotypes 308–309
Stjernfelt, Frederik 340
Stoics 67
stratum 53, 55, 57–58, 245, n. 94, 246, n. 94, *See* also Plane
structuralism 12–14, 17–19, 52, 93–94, 239, 245, 245, n. 94, 286
– neo-structuralism 17–18
– poststructuralism 6, 17–19, 21
structure 5, 12–13, 16, 28, 37–38, 52, 63, 73, 84, 94, 237, 245, 254, 328 and *passim*
– actorial 116
– axiological 88, 101
– contractual 110
– deep 16–17, 82, 85, 88, 95, 115, 187
– discursive 95, 106, 115, 165
– economic 324
– elementary axiological 236
– elementary syntactic 236
– elementary 99, 133–134, 145
– EPA 208, n. 82

– modal 105
– narrative 86, 94, 110–111, 163, 173, 182, 237, 239, 270
– of exchange 269
– paradigmatic 103, 106
– polemical 110
– pragmatic 311
– semantic 16, 163, 169, 182, 232, 286
– semio-narrative 96
– signifying 329–330
– superstructure 324
– surface 82, 85, 88
– syntactic 16, 165, 232, 286
– syntagmatic 103, 106, 236
– triadic 59–60, 63, 67
– virtual 115
style 4, 86, 264, 288, 296–298
Stylianoudi, Maria-Georgia Lily 188
Subject 104, 108–111, 113–114, 119–120, 173, 236–238, 244, 250, 268–269, 313 and *passim*
– anti-Subject 109
– tensive 238
subject of enunciation 255, n. 97, 256
substance
– body as 4–5, 33–34, 52–53, 239, 270
– Eco 62
– Fontanille 241–244, 247, 249
– Greimas 238
– Hjelmslev 53–55, 57–59, 61, 238, 241–242
– of content 53–55, 57–59
– of expression 53–56, 58–59, 122, 267–268, 270–271, 298, 327
– ontological 270–271, 299
– phonic 33, 55, 69
– Saussure 33, 53–54, 59, 61
Suci, George J. 209, 342
suprasegmental 271, 274, 277, 299
symbol
– Greimas 75
– Hjelmslev 74
– Ogden & Richards 65–66
– Peirce 64–67
– Saussure 34–35, 72
symbolic capital 305–307
symbolic field 318–319
synchronic 26–28, 30, 32, 259–261

syntactics 27, n. 5, 46
syntagm 39–42, 45, 81, 88, 104
syntagmatic 39, 39, n. 13, 40–42, 44–45, 49, 55, 63, 88, 103, 105–106, 115, 117–118, 122, 130–131, 212, 214, 236, 243, 282, 295
syntax 39, n. 13
– deep narrative 236
– discursive 96, 104, 115–116, 118, 121–122, 236, 239
– fundamental 95, 97, 103, 106, 236
– intermediate narrative 236
– narrative 103–104, 106
– semio-narrative 236
– surface narrative 236
system 6, 27, 42, 50–51, 68, 104, 245 and *passim*
– accompanying 298–299
– axiological 237, 326
– Barthes 74
– Chomsky 82
– communication 268
– complex semiotic 298–299
– cultural 3, 8, 10, 15, 59, 72
– Derrida 52, 287
– economic 253, 329
– kinship 28, 253
– linguistic 253, 287
– of exchange 110
– of signification 5
– of speech 84
– primary modelling 13
– proprioceptive 236
– Saussure 31–32, 38–39, 42, 49–51, 63, 69, 118, 335
– secondary modelling 13
– semantic 149
– semiotic 3, 5, 13, 73 and *passim*
– signification 247
– simple semiotic 298
– use 267, 281
systems theory 246

Tannenbaum, Percy H. 209, 342
Tartu–Moscow School 12, 93, 321
Tchaikovsky, Pyotr Ilyich 292, 292, n. 109
tea ceremony 311, 313

television 260, 267, 270, 272–273, 295, 297, 300–301, 309, 311, n. 117, 329
temporalisation 115, 117, 119, 121, 165, 236
tensile 235
tensive 235, 238, 240–241, 245
tertiary 149
Tesnière, Lucien 93
test 110–113, 119, 126, 269 and *passim*
– decisive 111–112, 127
– glorifying 111–112, 128
– qualifying 111–112, 126–128
text 13, 83 and *passim*
– pseudo- 258
– recipient 286–289, 291–297
– source 286, 289, 291–295, 298
– target 282–285
textualisation 122
theatre 265, 274, 296, 298, 326
thematisation 116, 118–121, 163, 165, 170, 173, 173, n. 69, 174, 237
theme 11, 41, 116, 118–120, 128, 163, 173–174, 186, 232, 282, 291–293, 295, 297
Theodorson, George A. 334, 334, n. 127
Thirdness 60–61
Thom, René 16
Thornborrow, Joanna 86
thymic 99
Tomashevsky, Boris V. 9
Toporov, Vladimir N. 343
transfer 253, 267–269
transmedia storytelling 299–300
triadic 59–60, 63, 65, 67, 114, 139, 185
Troubetzkoy, Nikolai S. 9, 11, 13, 43–45, 48
Tsala-Effa, Didier 241–244, 247–248, 328

Uexküll, Jakob von 19, 21, 62, n. 23
Uexküll, Thure von 337
Uldall, Hans Jørgen 12
Umwelt 20, 62, n. 23
universals 15, 62–63, 103, 138, 185, 230, 333–334
unmotivated 32
Uspenskij, Boris A. 12–13, 334
utterance 104, 255, n. 97
– descriptive 105

– modal 105–107
– of doing 104–107, 117, 236
– of state 104–108, 114, 117, 236

Valerii, Tonino 292
value 253
– cultural 265, 268, 319
– descriptive 114
– Eco 69
– exchange 268, 310, 319, n. 119
– Greimas 88, 101, 106, 114–115, 118–120, 146–147, 173, 184, 186, 232, 238, 244, 269
– modal 114
– Saussure 32, 38, 49–52, 59, 64, 287, 302, 336
– statistics 201
– symbolic 319
– system 86
– truth 100, n. 39
– use 319, n. 119
veridical 235–236
Vernadsky, Vladimir I. 13
virtualising 114, 238
visual 4, 66, 86, 274, 289, 293, 296, 299, 312–313
Vitruvius 248, 283, 283, n. 106, 284–285
Vološinov, Valentin N. 10, 263
voluntarism 248

Wagner, Richard 293, 293, n. 110
weight 192, 194, 196, 200–201, 205, n. 79, 223, n. 85, 233
– absolute 192
– relative 146
Williams, Raymond 296, 327–328
Wimsatt, William K. 264, n. 100
Winner, Thomas G. 12
worldview 88, 138, 185, 228, 273, 306, 326, 328

Yeats, William Butler 137, 176, 183, 196

Zeltmann, Claude 260, 270

www.ingramcontent.com/pod-product-compliance
Lightning Source LLC
Chambersburg PA
CBHW030519230426
43665CB00010B/678